Library of
Davidson College

SUPPLYING THE TROOPS

Supplying the Troops

General Somervell and American Logistics in W W II

John Kennedy Ohl

▥ Northern Illinois University Press • DeKalb • 1994

©1994 by Northern Illinois University Press
Published by the Northern Illinois University Press,
DeKalb, Illinois 60115
Manufactured in the United States using acid-free paper ∞
Design by Julia Fauci

Library of Congress Cataloging-in-Publication Data

Ohl, John Kennedy, 1942–
    Supplying the troops : General Somervell and
American logistics in WWII / John Kennedy Ohl.
       p.   cm.
    Includes bibliographical references and index.
    ISBN 0-87580-185-4
    1. World War, 1939–1945—Logistics—United
States. 2. Somervell, Brehon Burke, 1892–1955.
3. United States. Army—History—World War,
1939–1945. I. Title.
D810.L64O36 1994
355.4'11'092—dc20   93-39869
                                              CIP

For my parents, Henry and Martha Ohl

CONTENTS

Acknowledgments   ix

       Introduction   3
1   Soldier and Manager   9
2   A One-Man Show   25
3   Construction Division   38
4   Organizing for War   55
5   Industrial Mobilization   72
6   Shipping   98
7   The Allied Supply Orbit   127
8   War Department Battles   143
9   Canol   161
10   Logistics and Strategy, 1942–1943   181
11   Logistics and Strategy, 1943   205
12   Logistics and Strategy, 1944–1945   225
13   Industrial Manager   252

Appendix: Maps and Charts   261
Glossary: Acronyms, Code Names, Major Figures   269
Notes   277
Bibliography   305
Index   321

ACKNOWLEDGMENTS

I am indebted to a number of people and institutions for their assistance in the preparation of this book. Many archivists and librarians were most gracious in guiding me through their collections and arranging for the copying of documents and other materials. I would like to single out the staff of the Mesa Community College library for special thanks for its diligence in fulfilling my countless requests for interlibrary loan items. I have also benefited from the advice and encouragement of my fellow historians, and I was fortunate to have had Daniel R. Beaver, Robert W. Coakley, Richard M. Leighton, Robert R. Nathan, Forrest C. Pogue, and the anonymous readers for the Northern Illinois University Press read part or all of the manuscript and offer many sound suggestions for revisions. Any errors, faulty judgments, or other shortcomings that remain are my responsibility. Moreover, I am grateful to Mrs. Mary Brenza, Mr. and Mrs. John Griswold, and Mr. and Mrs. E. Macdonald Matter, as well as several of General Somervell's associates at Koppers Company, for their willingness to visit with me or answer mail or telephone inquiries.

There are other debts as well. The United States Army Military History Institute at Carlisle Barracks, Pennsylvania, provided needed financial assistance in the early stages of this project. A. H. Vandeventer and Robert Farwell did outstanding work with the maps and charts. The staff of Northern Illinois University Press, particularly my editors, were skillful and efficient in polishing my prose and moving the manuscript through to its final form.

Last, but not least, I must give heartfelt thanks to my family. My parents, both deceased and to whom this book is dedicated, provided encouragement and support over the years that made it possible for me to pursue, as a teacher and as a writer, my love of history. Equally important, my wife, Maria, and our children, Alison, Justin, and Jocelyn, were a great source of love and understanding while I was absorbed in research and writing, more than I can ever adequately express.

SUPPLYING THE TROOPS

INTRODUCTION

LOGISTICS IS THE BRANCH OF MILITARY SCIENCE THAT, IN ITS broadest sense, focuses on the economics of warfare. Although the term came into general American military use only in the twentieth century, logistics has been of primary concern to military leaders as long as there have been wars. In earliest times it was a relatively humdrum activity that involved little more than armies living off the land, but in the twentieth century, as nations engaged in greater and greater struggles, logistics became a big business. It came to encompass the following: (1) supply, the design, procurement, and distribution of military materiel; (2) transportation, the movement of materiel to the fighting forces; (3) the construction and management of fixed and temporary installations; and (4) personnel services, the furnishing of services, such as hospitalization and personnel administration.

During World War II, the United States mounted a logistical operation of unprecedented magnitude and complexity that was of central importance to its war effort. Through effective managerial systems that included both soldiers and civilians, the nation successfully organized its armaments production and supply links with the fighting fronts so that its forces had plentiful weapons to help them defeat the German-Italian-Japanese Axis.[1]

Among those who contributed to the success of the American logistical operation, none was more important than Brehon Burke Somervell. An army engineer with considerable achievements before the war, Somervell, as chief of the army's construction program, helped prepare the nation for war in the year before Pearl Harbor by building training camps and munitions plants and by convincing President Franklin D. Roosevelt to erect the Pentagon. Then, as head of the army Services of Supply, later known as the Army Service Forces, he was responsible for the supply and administration of the army within the United States and the support of troops overseas. Finally, Somervell was the principal logistical advisor and troubleshooter for War Department Chief of Staff General George C. Marshall. In effect, Somervell was the army's principal logistician.

My purpose in this book is to examine Somervell's work as a wartime logistician. I contend that he played a significant role in the American logistical operation and, by describing and analyzing his activities, I will highlight the vital place of logistics in the American war effort. However, I have not limited my focus to Somervell's wartime years. I also look at his prewar career because it was marked by experiences and accomplishments, both in and out of uniform, that prepared him for his wartime responsibilities. Moreover, I look at his postwar career in business, where he utilized the skills he had perfected in the army to become a successful industrial manager.

My focus on the role of one person supports my view that individual leaders do make a difference in a large endeavor. In recent years, many social scientists have insisted that leaders of governmental programs and agencies have only a limited effect and that the nature of organizations themselves, along with the established patterns of bureaucratic routine and institutionalized processes, are almost always determinative. Others, however, argue that individuals can shape organizational direction through the definition of new goals, the motivation of staffs, and effective management.[2]

Somervell reflects this pattern of leadership, what some call entrepreneurial leadership. He was an instrument, not a maker, of high policy, and he was not a deep thinker. But, he had ideas on logistics, and he fought for those ideas with vigor and conviction. Distinguished by ambition, energy, and managerial brilliance, Somervell was a formidable figure who reveled in big tasks and was "enough of an S.O.B." to get them done.[3] Through force of personality, shrewd accumulation of power, and sheer ability, he carved out a dominating role for himself in the procurement, supply, and movement of materiel forces. Thus, he became a powerful influence in America's conduct of the war.

Themes

In examining Somervell's World War II years, five themes are explored. The first arises out of the long-standing desire for and resistance to centralized control of the War Department supply organization.

The army supply organization at the beginning of the twentieth century consisted of a series of semiautonomous bureaus, each responsible for specific items, such as ordnance supplies and quartermaster supplies. While theoretically under the supervision of the secretary of war, the bureaus were virtually independent agencies, operating separate systems for purchase, finance, storage, and distribution.

Military reformers, who desired to impose a rational order on, as well as to regulate from the top down, previously unregulated activities, established the War Department General Staff in 1903. The General Staff was, among many things, to supervise the supply bureaus. However, its effectiveness was hampered by disputes with the bureau chiefs and their congressional allies, and when the United States entered World War I in April 1917, it had yet to solidify its position in the army.

In April 1918, Chief of Staff General Peyton C. March, who was determined to exercise executive control over War Department operations, created, under Major General George W. Goethals, the Purchase, Storage and Traffic Division in the General Staff to oversee the bureaus. Later that year, Goethals was granted executive authority over the bureaus, and despite the vehement opposition of their chiefs, he created a consolidated service of supply in the General Staff. These steps represented a radical departure from the traditional War Department organization and accepted General Staff theory that the General Staff should plan and direct the army but not operate it.

Following the war, the National Defense Act of 1920 essentially restored the old bureau system. Thus, on the eve of American entry into World War II, there was no direct command authority over the bureaus and no machinery for the close coordination of the entire logistical level below the secretary of war himself. According to the prevailing procedures, the War Department Assistant Chief of Staff, G-4, developed the army's shopping list and sent it to the under secretary of war, who then sent it to the appropriate supply bureaus for procurement. Under his direction, they placed the orders, followed production, and made inspections. When supplies were ready for delivery, G-4 supervised their distribution.

In early 1942, Chief of Staff Marshall reorganized the War Department to substitute the vertical pattern of military command in place of the established pattern of bureaucratic coordination. Thus, a new command structure was created between the General Staff and the combat arms and the supply and administrative services, making the supply bureaus part of a unified command.

A participant in the Marshall reorganization, Somervell was a strong believer in the necessity for a unified logistical command, and during the war, he struggled to bring about a new logistical edifice based on complete unity of command and functional lines of operation. He encountered strong resistance from bureau chiefs and others who still favored the traditional pattern, and in the end, they defeated his efforts to bring about permanent centralized control over the bureaus. Nevertheless, his efforts anticipated by twenty years the kind of functional organization that one day would be adopted as part of a new effort to bring greater efficiency and order to the American military through centralized authority.[4]

A second theme concerned with Somervell's World War II years centers on the relationship between military and civilian mobilization agencies. Prior to World War I, no mechanism existed to bind together industrial and military institutions, but as the United States mobilized in 1917, it was apparent that the ballooning supply requirements of modern war could be met only by the systematic integration of the military and industrial sectors. As a result, in the summer of 1917, President Woodrow Wilson created the War Industries Board to oversee this integration. The War Industries Board was staffed by businessmen on the assumption that industrial mobilization was a business proposition.

Fearful the businessmen of the War Industries Board were attempting to usurp legitimate military authority, the army supply bureaus did not regularly consult them on the magnitude of their requirements or utilize them to locate sources of supply. Eventually, with the war effort floundering, the General Staff and the civilian mobilizers formed an alliance, and in 1918, they reined in the independent-minded bureaus and forged a workable integration of the military and industrial sectors. However, with the war's end, the War Industries Board disbanded before a standard doctrine for integrating the two could be finalized.[5]

During the interwar period, the Army Industrial College served as a forum for businessmen and soldiers to consider the multifarious problems involved in industrial mobilization. However, neither viewed the other primarily as a partner in a common endeavor, and competition, as much as cooperation, was the underlying motif of the interchange as they contemplated future war. For their part, most army officers now accepted the need for a civilian agency to supervise industrial mobilization. But, in their view, the responsibility for supplying the army was still primarily a military one, and thus, most of the authority in operations should remain in military hands.[6] As war approached, President Roosevelt began creating civilian agencies to mobilize the economy to meet wartime demands, and within weeks after Pearl Harbor, the administrative structure for an integrated industrial mobilization reached an advanced state with the creation of the War Production Board.

It was within this setting that Somervell operated as the army's buyer. While accepting the existence of the War Production Board, he believed that the army knew best about its requirements and how to satisfy those requirements. He further believed that he could use the civilian mobilizers as he saw fit. These civilians, however, argued that the army should procure its supplies within the requirements and production guidelines laid down by them. Neither side totally triumphed, but by the war's end, the army and the War Production Board had arrived at an accommodation concerning industrial mobilization that left the army largely in control of those aspects it considered of greatest importance.

A similar struggle between the army and a civilian mobilization agency took place in regard to shipping. In early 1942, Roosevelt established the War Shipping Administration, whose responsibility was to allocate shipping assigned to it among competing claimants. Somervell had misgivings about entrusting such a significant aspect of the army's logistics to an outside agency and clashed with it on a number of occasions, but in the end, a basis for cooperation was established so that missions were accomplished.

A third theme concerns the crucial relationship between strategy and logistics. Logistics greatly influences and is influenced by strategy, and while there were certain obvious strategic moves or choices for the Allies in World War II, more often than not the high-level strategic decisions were based on logistical considerations and were themselves essentially logistical decisions. Only at the level of planning for specific operations were logistical plans based on strategic decision making.

Since Somervell was responsible for supplying and transporting the army, he was deeply concerned with the strategic conduct of the war. Ideally, he would have at hand strategic plans sufficiently explicit and approved far enough in advance to provide a clear guide for production programs. In fact, the shifting fortunes of war, shipping uncertainties, and the continuing debate over priorities between various strategies and theaters of war made it virtually impossible to arrive at firm, long-range logistical plans. Hence, for much of the war, production was based on building an arsenal of materiel that would be available to implement future strategic plans, and shipping allocations were often based on what was currently available.

Frustrated by this situation, Somervell insisted that he should be advised of strategic plans as soon as possible in order to allow for logistical planning on the part of his organization. He also insisted logisticians should be responsible for interpreting and presenting logistical data to the strategic decision makers, as well as advising them on the logistical ramifications of proposed operations. Strategic planners, who believed logisticians should not share in the making of strategic decisions, resisted him. Logisticians, in their estimation, were nothing more than technical experts who submitted logistical data for strategic consideration and then carried out the decisions made by the high command. This was an issue that was never completely resolved one way or the other, although Somervell, because of his personality and position in the War Department hierarchy, was often a participant in the formulation of strategy.[7]

A fourth theme relates to the coalition aspect of the American war effort. Materiel aid, given through lend-lease, was at the heart of America's partnership with its wartime allies. Since much of this aid was military in character, procurement and delivery of supplies and equipment to Britain, the Soviet Union, China, and the Free French placed many demands upon Somervell. Emphasizing that American interests must take precedence, his approach to lend-lease was highly nationalistic, contributing to strains in America's relations with its allies. However, the strains were not so great that they prevented lend-lease from being an effective instrument of coalition warfare.

The fifth, and final, theme concerns the emergence of the military leader as a manager. Historically, victory in war required leaders who were heroic warriors. However, in the industrial age, victory also required leaders similar to those found in business, and by 1940, the United States Army had produced a number of officers capable of managing a logistical effort of extraordinary complexity. To the traditional soldierly adherence to duty, honor, and country, they brought the managerial virtues of efficiency, expertise, and organization. Through their ability to feed, clothe, arm, and transport troops on fronts around the globe, they contributed as much to the victory in World War II as battlefield commanders.[8]

Somervell epitomized this new type of military leader. Through a variety of assignments before 1940 and through attendance at the army's professional schools, he devised a managerial system that allowed him to know what his organization was doing and to act quickly to correct deficiencies. This system included such things as a control section operating out of his own office, a program for action projected as far into the future as possible, extensive use of statistics, a determination to cut red tape, strict accountability for subordinates, and an unrelenting drive for efficiency on the part of every member of his team. During the war, Somervell tried to impose his control over the supply bureaus with these tools. In the process, he earned the enmity of many bureau chiefs, but in the minds of many observers and his superiors, he brought greater effectiveness to army supply. After the war Somervell took his managerial system and expertise to business, seeking a new world to conquer as a captain of industry.[9]

Because he had strong opinions on many of the issues involved with logistics and because he had a craving for power and a readiness to use it to satisfy the army's requirements, Somervell feuded with many agencies, both inside and outside the army; the British; and congressional and administration members. While recognizing his ability, many of his opponents saw him as secretive, deceitful, arrogant, and power hungry and were certain that many of his actions hurt the war effort. Fighting him tooth and nail, they often prevented him from having his way. However, Somervell also had many admirers who praised his contributions to the Allied victory. No matter how one judges him, though, Somervell's activities during World War II illuminate much about the bureaucratic, strategic, logistics, coalition, and personal factors that shaped the transformation of America's industrial might into combat power on the battlefield.

1. SOLDIER AND MANAGER

BREHON BURKE SOMERVELL, NICKNAMED Bill by his parents, was the product of a well-established and socially prominent west Tennessee family. His paternal grandfather, Richard Bullock Somervell, was a wealthy planter and prestigious political figure, who was in the forefront of the Tennessee secessionist movement during the Civil War. Raised in the lap of luxury, Brehon's father, William Taylor Somervell, was educated at the University of Virginia and earned a medical degree from the University of Louisville. Mary S. Burke, fourteen years his junior and a member of an equally prominent Tennessee family, was educated at home by a tutor. For a number of years, she taught school in Dyersburg, Tennessee. Then she met William, also teaching in Dyersburg, and they were married in 1891.[1]

Shortly after their marriage the Somervells moved to Little Rock, Arkansas, where William practiced medicine. There on May 9, 1892, Brehon, their only child, was born. Growing up in what was then an essentially small town, Somervell enjoyed the typical boyish activities of that time. The dominant influence in his boyhood was his mother. A striking, elegant, and highly cultivated woman, Mary emphasized the importance of strong character, lofty goals, and the obligation to do one's best, imparting to Brehon the belief he was something special because of his ancestry and upbringing.[2] This belief gave him a certain arrogance that many people found annoying. Yet, it also gave him a supreme confidence that he exhibited throughout his life.

William's medical practice was never especially remunerative, and a progressively serious hearing difficulty prompted him to change professions. For a time he managed Arkansas College, but when his hearing worsened, the family moved to Washington, D.C., in 1906, where William and Mary opened Belcourt Seminary, a girls finishing school.[3]

For Brehon, the years in Washington meant immersion "in an atmosphere of tittering young girls, classical literature, and relentless application of the principles of good breeding." Perhaps in revolt against this stern, genteel upbringing, he was something of a show-off at Central High School, from which he graduated in 1909. Amplifying this side of his high school years, *The Brecky*, the school annual, dubbed Somervell "The Irrepressible One" and noted that he was "about the liveliest one we have come across lately and no one knows what he is going to do next."[4]

Years later Somervell could not recall anything in particular, from this period or earlier, that spurred him to consider a military career except that the bearing and commitment to service exhibited by the large number of army officers he had met while living in Washington had captivated him. "They looked perfect to me," he later stated.[5] Once Somervell made it clear he was serious about his choice, his parents persuaded Congressman Charles C. Reid of the Fifth District of Arkansas to appoint him to the United States Military Academy at West Point.[6]

At West Point, Somervell, a member of the 1914 class, had few peers in the classroom. Without much effort he was near the top of his class in each of the major areas of study, and by careful attention to detail, he minimized the skins, or demerits, he received for violations of regulations. Somervell also excelled in horsemanship, marksmanship, and swordsmanship, and during his last three years at the academy, he advanced in cadet rank from corporal to lieutenant. At the end of his first-class, or senior, year, he stood sixth in a class of 107, and the class yearbook, summarizing his qualities, remarked that he was "clear-cut . . . not only externally but internally." His final fitness report rated him "excellent as far as general abilities for an officer in the army."[7] On June 12, 1914, Somervell graduated from West Point and, like the other top graduates in his class, was commissioned a second lieutenant in the Corps of Engineers.

West Point affected Somervell in several ways. It provided him with the engineering skills around which he shaped his military career. It also enabled him to know by name every member of seven classes of graduates (1911–17) and establish close friendships which would have substantial value in later years.[8] But most important, Somervell learned what it meant to be a good soldier. He was highly motivated, was able to size up a situation quickly and act accordingly, respected the privileges and responsibilities of rank, and was loyal to superiors and subordinates alike, as well as dedicating his life to his country and taking pride in his profession.[9]

Before assuming duty with the Engineers, Somervell used his graduation leave in the summer of 1914 to travel to Europe. He was in Paris in August when World War I erupted, and for the next month, he helped expedite the return home of Americans anxious to escape the war.[10] In September 1914, Somervell was assigned to an engineer battalion stationed at Washington Barracks, District of Columbia. There he concentrated on the details of troop duty and studied courses through the Garrison Officers' School looking to the all-important promotion examinations. As a result of his high scores on the examination and an outstanding efficiency report, Somervell, not even a year out of West Point, was promoted to first lieutenant in February 1915.[11]

Somervell spent the summer and fall of 1915 in New England conducting various engineer surveys, and in December 1915, he was transferred to Fort Sam Houston, near San Antonio, Texas. After the Pershing Punitive Expedition entered Mexico in March 1916 in pursuit of Pancho Villa, Somervell for several weeks was depot manager at Columbus, New Mexico, the expedition's rear base. He then joined the expedition in Mexico, serving first on road construction work and later as a regimental supply officer.

During these first years as an officer, the elements of the Somervell style fully emerged. Standing 5 feet 9½ inches tall and weighing 154 pounds, Somervell was impressive in appearance. Wiry, although not especially athletic, he was extremely well groomed, with a close-cropped moustache as one of his trademarks.

Now that he was established in his military career, Somervell exhibited a driving ambition, fueled by the desire for promotion. No other profession is more competitive than officership, and those who refuse to push rarely get ahead. This push means hard work, long hours, and tough assignments, none of which discouraged Somervell. Rather, he thrived on them. He attacked every assignment as if it were the most important thing in the whole army. In fact, the assignment at hand was so important to Somervell that he often did whatever was necessary to finish it on schedule, even if it meant making his own rules. Somervell's disregard for red tape disturbed his superiors. But they also marveled at his ability to get hard things done quickly and well without close supervision.[12]

Somervell's aggressive manner was masked somewhat by the dual nature of his personality. "Dynamite in a Tiffany box" was how one industrialist described him during World War II. On the exterior, Somervell could be a man of great personal charm. Exceedingly urbane when he wanted to be, fully acquainted with the arts, and possessing an extensive knowledge of Biblical characters, he normally presented himself as "all lace and velvet and courtliness."

However, beneath this gentlemanly exterior, there lurked a short temper and an utter unwillingness to suffer fools gladly or tolerate mediocre performance.

When angered by dullness or mediocrity, Somervell readily lost his temper and exploded with a fiery outpouring of sarcasm or profanity in which he rarely repeated himself. Over the years soldiers, from privates to generals, who let him down would be subjected to his wrath, and the wise subordinate quickly learned, as engineer John Hardin remembered, that "you were going to pay a heavy penalty if you didn't give him what he wanted." Somervell, he added, would "chop people's heads off without giving them any explanation at all."[13]

Somervell's relations with his fellow officers were mixed. He forged many lasting friendships in his early years in the army and did not hesitate to make effective use of them when he needed assistance. Not all his fellow officers were drawn to Somervell, however. Many were repelled by his overwhelming aggressiveness and single-minded drive for promotion. For these officers, Somervell had disdain, and as he rose in rank, he could be spiteful and even vindictive toward them.

In September 1916, Somervell returned to Washington Barracks to attend the Engineer School. The course came to an abrupt end, however, in April 1917 when the United States declared war against Germany. In preparation for the creation of a large army, the War Department ordered Somervell and hundreds of other junior officers to appear before examination boards to determine their fitness for promotion. Somervell's board submitted a favorable report on him, and on May 15, 1917, he was promoted to captain.[14]

• • •

Soon after the United States entered World War I, the War Department created nine regiments of troops to build and maintain railway lines in France. On May 5, Somervell was named adjutant of one of these regiments, the 5th Reserve Regiment (later the 15th Engineers) and dispatched to its headquarters in Pittsburgh, Pennsylvania. Arriving there soon after, he supervised the training of the 1,150 officers and men of the 15th Engineers at a makeshift training camp just north of the city. Training was haphazard because of the press of time. Nevertheless, Somervell made the best of the situation, and years later many enlisted men fondly recalled his drive while whipping the regiment into shape.[15] By the middle of June 1917, the regiment was ready for overseas duty, and during the last weeks of June and the first week of July, it broke camp and proceeded to New York City for shipment to France.[16]

Following the regiment's arrival in France on July 25, Somervell, now a temporary major, assisted Colonel Edgar Jadwin, the regimental commander, in examining possible sites for a main intermediate storage depot between Brest and the ports on the Loire River and the front. He also selected sites for railroad yards and regulating stations and worked on various construction duties. In each of his projects, he grabbed everything available and drove the job through to completion, with little regard for the cost. His immediate superior, Lieutenant

Colonel Ernest Graves, was uneasy about his methods, but Somervell got his construction jobs done on time. For this reason, Graves summed up his performance in his fitness report by noting that "this is the best officer I ever saw, or hope to see."[17]

On April 5, 1918, Somervell was placed in charge of the construction work at Is-sur-Tille, the principal American Expeditionary Forces (AEF) advance depot and regulating station. Located within a short distance of all sections of the American front and on the controlling railroad lines, it was the neck of the bottle through which most of the supplies from the ports and base and intermediate depots had to pass to reach the fighting men. By the time Somervell assumed command, most of the initial project, known as the east depot, was finished and in operation. Yet much remained to be done, and Somervell was given the task of completing additional warehouses and tracks and expanding nearby Camp Williams so that it could accommodate more than double the 7,000 men it held when he arrived at Is-sur-Tille.

Over the next few months Somervell worked his men around the clock, and by the fall all tasks were completed except Camp Williams. In addition, Somervell oversaw the construction of the Poincon Gas Depot, seventeen miles to the north of Is-sur-Tille, and the Etain engine terminal.[18]

After sweating for more than a year over ammunition dumps, depots, and barracks, Somervell, recently promoted to the temporary rank of lieutenant colonel, was ready for a well-deserved leave. Rather than spend his time in Paris, he persuaded Graves to lend him his Cadillac sedan so that he could visit the front and see what the fighting was like. "I have yet to hear a hostile shot," he told Graves, and "I'm not going home with that on my record."

Leaving his construction assignment on October 24, Somervell decided first to visit some friends at the headquarters of the 89th Division, which was taking part in the Meuse-Argonne Offensive. Caught up in the bustle of the 89th's preparations for an upcoming attack, Somervell volunteered his services to the division's chief of staff, Colonel John C.H. Lee, a 1909 West Point graduate and a fellow engineer. Finding that he and Somervell worked well together, Lee asked him to remain with the 89th as a temporary replacement for the G-3, or operations officer, who had been captured by the Germans several days before. Somervell readily accepted, thus beginning a close friendship that would last for decades.[19]

The final push to the Meuse River began on November 1, and by November 5, the 89th was at the Meuse in the proximity of Pouilly. A reconnaissance early in the morning of November 5 indicated that all the bridges in this area had been demolished by the retreating Germans, but another one later that day indicated the bridge at Pouilly could be crossed.[20]

Lee and Somervell went forward to assess the situation, and, with the help of a sergeant, determined that men could apparently make their way across the bridge if they went single file. Lee then asked Somervell to conduct his own reconnaissance.

Just before midnight, Somervell and two scouts wormed their way across the bridge. Once on the far side of the river they encountered a detachment of Germans and in a brief flurry of shooting, drove them off. In all, Somervell and the two scouts had advanced more than 500 yards beyond the American outposts, a feat of "extraordinary heroism in action with the enemy" for which Somervell was awarded the Distinguished Service Cross, the nation's second highest decoration for bravery.[21]

Several days later Lee arranged to have Somervell permanently assigned to the 89th Division as G–3. For Lee, the transfer was "an answer to a prayer." Somervell, in his words, learned the job "with lightening-like rapidity" and quickly demonstrated that he was brilliant.[22]

After the Armistice, the 89th Division was assigned to the American occupation army in Germany. Once it settled into its occupation zone in the Rhineland, romance entered Somervell's life when he began to date Anna Purnell, a Y.M.C.A. volunteer who assisted the division entertainment officer in putting together soldier shows and the daughter of a Chicago businessman. She and Somervell felt most comfortable with each other, and in August 1919, they married. Ten months later the first of their three children, all daughters, was born.[23] Anna died in January 1942, and in March 1943, Somervell married Mrs. Louise Hampton Wartmann, a onetime student at Belcourt Seminary.

In May and June 1919, the 89th Division returned to the United States. However, Somervell remained in Germany as the staff supply officer, or G-4, of the American Third Army, which after the signing of the Versailles Treaty at the end of June, was designated American Forces in Germany (AFG) and placed under the command of Major General Henry T. Allen. Somervell worked on logistical concerns and helped escort important visitors from the United States inspecting Allen's command.[24]

While in Germany, Somervell established a close relationship with Walker D. Hines. A prominent New York corporate lawyer, Hines was vacationing in Europe in June 1920 when President Woodrow Wilson asked him to arbitrate problems affecting shipping on the rivers of central Europe. Needing help, Hines went to Allen, who quickly assigned Somervell to the project. During the remainder of the summer, Somervell was at Hines's side in making a survey and report on the navigation and regulation of shipping on the Rhine River. In the process, he greatly impressed Hines with his intelligence, judgment, and efficiency.[25]

Somervell's work with Hines brought his service in Europe to an end. Recently promoted to the permanent rank of major and now also recipient of the Distinguished Service Medal for his work as an engineer and as a staff officer, he returned to the United States in September 1920.

His three years with the AEF and AFG completed the making of Somervell the soldier. At West Point, he had acquired the book learning associated with officership, as well as the intangibles the American army officer corps prized. As a fledgling engineer officer, he had learned what it meant to command. In France and Germany, he had demonstrated the wide range of his abilities, from directing large-scale construction projects to performing an array of staff assignments. Few officers of comparable rank and age returned home with such an impressive record (Somervell was one of only nine officers who had been awarded both the Distinguished Service Cross and the Distinguished Service Medal), and already the word in the army was to "Watch Somervell."[26]

• • •

Somervell was twenty-eight years old when he returned to the United States. At the time, his career prospects looked bleak. The officer corps was double its pre-1917 strength because of the absorption of a large number of men who had held temporary commissions during the war, and the effect of this size was to limit severely the prospect for promotion for captains and majors. Thus, there were 1,700 majors like Somervell, waiting for 570 lieutenant colonels to vacate their positions. Since the National Defense Act of 1920 had decreed a single promotion list for the entire army in contrast to the prewar system of promotion by branch, seniority became the determining factor, forcing most officers to wait years for their next promotion.[27]

Despite the generally unsatisfactory circumstances in regard to promotion, Somervell was content with his military career. The sense of patriotism and duty he had acquired at West Point was now reinforced by his wartime service, and the army offered the best opportunity to continue to satisfy that patriotism. Moreover, Somervell was able to channel his drive and ambition into varied and stimulating assignments that kept him intellectually alive.

Somervell resumed his service in the peacetime army with a tour as assistant to the officer in charge of war plans, training, and intelligence in the Office of the Chief of Engineers in Washington. In 1922, his outstanding war record earned him the coveted assignment as a student at the Command and General Staff College at Fort Leavenworth, Kansas, which trained officers for staff work and command at the division and corps level. Only the best officers, each one handpicked by his superiors, were sent to Leavenworth. Students were thrust into direct competition in war games to see who had the initiative, energy, physical capacity, tact, judgment, common sense, temperament, and intelligence for staff work and command.

Leavenworth was a trying experience for many officers. However, Somervell found its competitive environment exhilarating and the course of study taxing but not especially difficult. Much of it centered on problem solving designed to duplicate the basic staff work at the division and corps level, and Somervell had already done this kind of work during the war. As a result, he ranked among the top fifteen in the competitive ranking of the 150 students who graduated in June 1923 and was designated an honors graduate. In the future, he could expect to be one of the first to be considered for the choicest assignments.[28]

Somervell was next assigned to the 1st New York Engineer District, headquartered in New York City, as assistant district engineer. In this post, he had little independent responsibility, and in March 1925, somewhat bored with the job, he secured leave to assist Walker Hines in another assignment in Europe.

Earlier that year, the League of Nations had asked Hines to make a special study of the navigation conditions on the Danube and Rhine Rivers. To a degree, this work was a continuation of what the two men had done in the summer of 1920, although now most of their attention was to be devoted to the Danube where international complications had prevented river traffic from returning to its prewar level.

Preceding Hines by two months, Somervell arrived in Europe in late March and spent the next months traveling down the Danube from Ratisbon, Germany, to Sulina, Rumania, where the river enters the Black Sea.[29] Along the way, he familiarized himself with the technical, commercial, and administrative problems affecting river traffic and conferred with governmental officials and representatives of commercial and shipping interests. In June, Hines joined Somervell, and for the rest of that month and most of the next, they traveled from Vienna to Sulina and back again, following up on the data Somervell had collected and putting together their report. Their report deftly dissected the problems affecting the Danube, but its influence was limited. As its authors acknowledged, satisfactory traffic on the waterway could not be achieved unless the riparian nations put aside narrow nationalistic differences, a development that was not forthcoming.[30]

In the summer of 1925, Somervell was posted to the Army War College at Washington Barracks. Reserved for only the best of the army's younger officers, it was the pinnacle of the army's postgraduate education system. Those chosen had already proven themselves, and it was assumed those in attendance would be generals if war came.[31] During the first half of the course, the students investigated the operations of the various staff sections and prepared individual and group research projects. Somervell's primary project was an examination of the use of Negro manpower in wartime. This was completed in cooperation with two other officers at the request of the school's commandant. The culmination of years of study by the school's faculty and student body, the report portrayed the Negro as inferior to whites as a technician or fighter and posited that Negroes, as was the practice, should be largely placed in segregated noncombat units to ensure military efficiency.[32]

The second half of the War College course focused on student war plans. Somervell's major paper was on possible future American wars and was hardly prescient. The only likely war he foresaw for the United States was one brought about by a possible surge of the Soviet Union into China, an eventuality he thought might cause the United States, Japan, and Britain to join together and oppose the Soviets.[33] The paper was indicative of Somervell's bent. Not an intellectual, he never showed any great interest in the larger questions of power and policy or developed any new ideas on strategy and warfare. His writings through the years were largely technical in nature, and his reputation would be based on his accomplishments as a manager.

Somervell's first independent command since his wartime service in France was as district engineer for the Washington, D.C., Engineer District. The post of district engineer was given only to the Engineers' most competent officers, for it was through the district engineer that the corps performed its highly politicized civil works, the corps' principal peacetime activity. A successful district engineer not only had to be an able engineer, he also had to be a good manager because he had to supervise the civilian employees in his office, administer a sizable budget, interact with officials at all levels of government, negotiate contracts and be familiar with appropriate laws, maintain a good public image for the corps and its projects, and deal with a spate of contractors and the sometimes obstreperous labor force that did the actual work. In Somervell's mind, there was no better assignment in that era, for it provided responsibilities far beyond those which an officer of his rank would have had in the strictly military side of the army. It was also the only meaningful way for an engineer to perfect his skills and to learn what it took to make a large organization a success.[34]

Taking office on August 16, 1926, Somervell held the post of district engineer in Washington for four years. He was responsible for the rivers and harbors projects in the district, which mostly involved the dredging of the Potomac River, as well as nearby streams and rivers, and several special projects, including a long-standing project to increase Washington's water supply through a host of improvements to the water system.[35]

In doing his work, Somervell gave ample evidence of his emerging managerial style. Captain Hugh Casey, assistant to the chief of rivers and harbors in the Office of the Chief of Engineers, recalled that Somervell would "keep driving and driving to get the maximum in the way of approach or authority or funds or whatever was required in order to prosecute that particular operation." Somervell also maintained very careful records of progress and performance, and when figures were not what he wanted them to be, he quickly identified the problems and made whatever changes were required. He was not one to get deeply involved in the details of a project, however. His way was to see that a competent organization was in place and then give it maximum authority and support in performing the engineering, design, and construction while he was the "live-wire" who drove the job through to completion.[36]

In his last year in Washington, Somervell was at the center of a controversy that pitted electric power interests against advocates for more parks and recreation areas for the District of Columbia. Several years previously, a predecessor of Somervell had prepared a plan for the development of electric power on the Potomac by means of two dams and power houses, one at Great Falls and the other at Chain Bridge. The Federal Power Commission rated the project "a national asset of incalculable value," and beginning in 1927, Somervell conducted an extensive field investigation of it and held public hearings. His report strongly endorsed the Potomac project on grounds of production of electric power, flood protection, improved river navigation, and better treatment of the Washington water supply. He postulated that it could be completed without sacrificing the long-recognized recreational and scenic value of the area.[37]

As Somervell's investigation of the power proposal was proceeding, the National Capital Park and Planning Commission became the locus of opposition. Charged by Congress with acquiring land for park development in Washington and recommending plans for the city's growth, the commission strongly condemned the power project on the grounds that it would flood out the Great Falls and forever destroy the scenic and recreational value of a major and unique feature of the nation's capital.[38]

Through the winter of 1929–30, the struggle over the Potomac raged unabated. It was a classic struggle between those who measure progress in terms of construction and commerce and those who want to preserve the pristine beauty of nature. The leading spokesmen for the power project were Elisha Hanson, attorney for the Potomac Power Company, and Somervell. It was just the type of project that excited Somervell. Ever since his management of construction projects in France, Somervell had seen himself as a builder, and the bigger the project, especially if it were grandiose in conception, the more it appealed to him.[39]

The controversy climaxed with the debate over the Cramton-Capper George Washington Memorial Parkway Bill. Passed by the House of Representatives in January 1930, it provided a mechanism for an extensive park system on both shores of the Potomac inside and outside the District of Columbia, as well as a parkway from Mt. Vernon to a point above Great Falls. As a sop to power interests, the bill also permitted Congress to authorize whatever navigation, flood control, or power projects it thought necessary. Notwithstanding this provision, Hanson and Somervell were convinced that if the upper Potomac were made available for parks there would be insurmountable obstacles to the development of the river for power. Consequently, they decided to persuade the Senate to alter the bill so that the power project could go forward.

The high point of their effort came on March 27, 1930, when Somervell testified before the Senate Committee on the District of Columbia. Appearing as an expert witness, Somervell, presenting a mass of data about the natural features of the Potomac, the flow of the river, and Washington's projected need for electric power, argued that it was possible to utilize the river for both power and parks development.[40]

Somervell's appearance was a virtuoso performance. It was Somervell at his best—informed, logical in his presentation, confident in the correctness of his position, determined to prevail. But it was all for naught.

In an effective rebuttal, the project's critics contended that Somervell's fear that park development would render future development of the river for others purposes impossible was overstated and questioned his view that power and parks were compatible. Given these arguments, the Senate committee approved the House bill, which later that spring was approved by the whole Senate and signed into law by President Herbert C. Hoover.[41] For Somervell, the outcome was a great disappointment. He had fought hard for the project and had lost, a bitter pill to swallow for one who was used to having things turn out his way.

Following the Engineers' practice of limiting the length of assignments for district engineers, Somervell was relieved of his post in Washington on September 1, 1930, and named assistant to the president of the Mississippi River Commission, a group of seven civilian and military engineers who were responsible for navigation and flood control on the Mississippi, as well as assistant to the chief of the Lower Mississippi Valley Division of the Corps of Engineers. In the spring of 1931, he was made assistant to the district engineer in the Memphis, Tennessee, district, and on June 19, 1931, he assumed the post of district engineer.[42]

Much of his energy was directed toward flood control, for in 1928, Congress had adopted a comprehensive program of flood control, proposed by Chief of Engineers Major General Jadwin, consisting of heightened and enlarged levees, floodways, and spillways. By the early 1930s, flood control work on the Mississippi, especially in the Memphis District, was being vigorously pushed by the river commission in line with Jadwin's prescription. Moreover, the district was engaged in an experimental cutoff project, which although not part of the Jadwin Plan, was inaugurated in 1931.[43]

By early 1933, Somervell was maneuvering to leave his Memphis post. The primary reason was his poor relationship with Brigadier General Harley B. Ferguson, president of the Mississippi River Commission. During Somervell's last year in Washington, Ferguson, as chief of the Atlantic Division, had been his immediate supervisor. Very early, the two had developed a strong dislike for each other. Ferguson believed that Somervell was too showy in his approach to his projects, too prone to attract unwanted controversy, and too ambitious. Somervell, meanwhile, resented a dressing down he had received from Ferguson during a run-in over Somervell's prominent role in the Potomac power controversy.

Their strained relationship worsened when the two paired up again in the Mississippi Valley. Somervell had long been known as a Jadwin man, while

Ferguson had long held well-developed professional differences with the now-deceased Jadwin over the efficacy of cutoffs in flood control, a program Ferguson championed. Somervell applied himself to the cutoff program, but he never disguised his hostility toward Ferguson, who responded in kind. By the end of 1932, the two were bitter enemies.[44] Using his connections, Somervell finally got away from Ferguson by securing a leave to work on another project with Walker Hines that took him out of the country for a year

• • •

In the 1930s, officials of the Turkish Republic were anxious to modernize their nation through economic planning, which required considerable data. Lacking the expertise to gather and analyze such data, the Turkish government engaged Walker Hines in early 1933 to conduct an economic survey of Turkey and submit conclusions to guide its planners.[45] Once he agreed to the Turkish proposal, Hines recruited Somervell to be the principal field representative at a salary of $1,000 a month. Somervell was to organize the survey in Turkey, make a personal inspection of the country and its economic activities, appraise the material collected, and formulate a comprehensive preliminary report.[46]

Somervell arrived in Ankara, Turkey, on May 15, promptly set up an office, and lined up Turkish interpreters and stenographers to supplement the staff he had brought with him. By late summer, the introductory work was completed, and Somervell launched the heart of the survey—a tour of practically the entire country, accompanied by O.F. Gardner, an agricultural expert, and two Turkish assistants. Slow-moving trains and ships made the tour seem endless, and at times, the primitive Turkish road network made the going for their car nearly impossible. But the hardships were worthwhile. After completing the tour, Somervell had seen as much of the country as any Turkish official had ever visited and possessed an encyclopedic firsthand knowledge of its geographical, social, and economic conditions.[47]

His tour of Turkey finished, Somervell in the fall of 1933 began work on the preliminary report. For three months, he worked without stop. Dictating to his secretaries for hours at a time, he turned out lengthy sections on population, mineral resources, fuel and power, water, industry, domestic commerce, prices, communications, private capital, finance, land tenure, the role of the government in Turkish economic life, foreign trade, health and education, labor, and legal complications.[48]

Somervell completed the preliminary report in January 1934. By this time, new personalities were joining the survey team. In late 1933, Hines recruited Professor Edward W. Kemmerer of Princeton University, an economist famous as the money doctor because of his financial advisory missions to many nations. Kemmerer was to review Somervell's draft and then travel to Turkey to assist in the development of a plan to implement the recommendations.[49]

Of more immediate importance, though, was the death of Hines. On his way to Turkey to join Somervell, he became ill and died in Italy in January. His place as director of the survey was taken by Goldthwaite Dorr, one of his law partners.

After Dorr arrived in Ankara, he and Somervell reviewed the report in light of the comments sent by Kemmerer. For the most part, Kemmerer's comments changed little, as Somervell proudly noted in a memorandum to Dorr: "So far practically no exceptions have been taken to the conclusions. On the basis of four hundred and fifty conclusions and recommendations, my batting average seems to be between 980 and 990 at the present time."[50]

Somervell and Hines had originally planned to have the final report completed before Somervell's leave expired in April 1934. However, Hines's death and the difficulties encountered in putting together the report pushed back the schedule, and by the middle of March, when Somervell left Turkey, the report was far from finished. A month later, Somervell arrived in New York City, and during the last two weeks of April, he had many meetings with Kemmerer to hash out points of confusion and to reconcile differing opinions.[51] By May 1, Somervell's work with the survey team was completed, and he was back on active duty with the Engineers in Washington.

The report, submitted to the Turkish government in July 1934, was seen by newspapers as a candid exposure of the deficiencies of the Turkish economy and as the essential guide for the government in its modernization program. For all practical purposes, however, the report had little impact and was soon forgotten. While thorough and competent, it included so many detailed recommendations that it was too easy to lose sight of its general principles. Equally important, the time was probably not right for any report to be effective considering that Turkey was still adjusting to the many revolutionary changes made by President Mustafa Kemal after Turkey's defeat in World War I. Years later, another expert who went to Turkey to make an economic report searched at length for a copy before unearthing an uncataloged one in the archives of the Finance Ministry.[52]

• • •

Somervell returned to the United States from Turkey without a specific assignment waiting for him. His eyes were set on the post of engineer commissioner for the District of Columbia, which was scheduled to be vacant in June 1934. It was a post of considerable influence since the occupant was one of the three members of the Board of Commissioners that administered the District's government, and by law, it had to be filled by an army engineer appointed by the president. Somervell quickly gained the endorsements of Chief of Engineers Major General Edward M. Markham and Secretary of War George Dern and arranged for other notables to submit supporting letters to President

Franklin D. Roosevelt.[53] But in the end, Roosevelt gave the post to Lieutenant Colonel Dan Sultan because in his opinion, Somervell had pushed too hard for the post, violating the unwritten rule that an officer was never to seek or turn down an assignment. Obviously this rule was honored more in theory than in practice, and few officers, especially if they were as ambitious as Somervell, were content to sit and wait for an assignment that they desired to come unassisted. But, Somervell's incessant campaigning for the post seemed excessive to Roosevelt, and after a member of the board of commissioners indicated that Somervell lacked the necessary tact for the board, Roosevelt concluded that Somervell was not the man for the engineer commissioner's job.[54]

For want of anything available, Somervell was attached to the Rivers and Harbors Section in the Office of the Chief of Engineers, where there was little for him to do at first. Quickly becoming restless, he encroached on the work of others in an early example of his penchant for empire building for which he would later be famous. Captain Lucius D. Clay, then serving in the section, remembered that Somervell "with his usual drive and energy . . . wanted to take . . . over" his work. Clay was not about "to let him do that," causing Somervell to complain to section chief Lieutenant Colonel Glen Edgerton, whom he had known since the days before World War I when Edgerton commanded a company in which Somervell was serving. Edgerton backed Clay, stating, in Clay's words, "that he understood why I wouldn't and that he wasn't going to have me do it, because he knew that the job was not one that Somervell would be content with—that he was just using it as a stepping stone to go somewhere else."[55]

Finally, in the late spring of 1935, Somervell left the section to work with the New Deal's National Emergency Council processing applications for federal work relief projects, a job he held through August 1935. In the meantime, he received his first promotion in fifteen years. Promotion had long been a sore point for army officers, and in 1935, Congress partially assuaged them by providing for the immediate promotion of half the officers below the rank of colonel. Somervell moved to lieutenant colonel, and like other promotion-starved officers, the effect on him was electric.[56]

In September 1935, Somervell was named district engineer for the Ocala, Florida, district, which was responsible for constructing a canal across north Florida from the Atlantic Ocean to the Gulf of Mexico. For centuries, many had talked about the desirability of a water route across Florida to make unnecessary the hazardous and lengthy passage through the Florida Straits, and in 1933 the Florida legislature created the National Gulf-Atlantic Ship Canal Association to push for a canal. Through the winter of 1933–34, it applied to several federal agencies for funds to initiate the project but was uniformly rejected on grounds of cost. However, the association was not deterred, and on its appeal, Roosevelt appointed the Interdepartmental Board of Review in 1934 to study the matter. It consisted of five engineers, including Somervell.[57]

The Interdepartmental Board conducted an intensive onsite inspection of potential routes, reviewed data prepared by previous investigations, and studied proposed methods of construction, costs, effect on ground water, and need for bridges and other appurtenant structures. In two reports, one submitted in July 1934 and the other in September 1934, the board recommended that the project be undertaken.[58] However, the reports brought no immediate action. Southern railroad interests feared a loss of revenue if the canal were built, and Florida fruit and produce growers said the canal would endanger their water supply by draining the underground reservoir and diffusing salt water through the limestone underlying much of the state. Faced with this opposition and not anxious to have to choose between various Florida interests, Roosevelt let the matter rest.

Then, at a news conference on August 30, 1935, Roosevelt mentioned that he would allocate $5 million in depression-fighting relief money for the canal. This amount was nowhere near the estimated $99 to $119 million (soon revised to $146 million) needed for the project, nor did it come from the normal congressional appropriation by which these types of projects were funded. But it was a start. The Emergency Relief Appropriations Act of 1935 had provided more than $4 billion for work relief, and Roosevelt was determined to get as many men as possible to work on meaningful projects before the winter. The canal project fit the bill.[59]

The Engineers had never looked upon the project with any great enthusiasm, regarding it as an interesting canal to dig and dredge but one that would probably not justify its cost. But, with Roosevelt now publicly endorsing it, Chief of Engineers Markham immediately created the Ocala Engineer District to conduct the project and chose Somervell to head it.

The choice of Somervell was obvious. Because of his work with the Interdepartmental Board, he knew as much about the project as any army engineer. He also had a reputation for making things happen quickly. With Somervell supervising the project, men would be hired and dirt would be excavated, enhancing the likelihood that Congress would officially authorize the project and fund its completion.

Two days after Roosevelt's announcement, Somervell was on the job. In scale the canal was one of the biggest projects ever undertaken by the Engineers. Stretching approximately 195 miles across Florida, it was to consist of a 90-mile artificial cut through the earth and rock of the spine of Florida, as well as the widening, deepening, and straightening of existing waterways. When finished the canal, four times longer than the Panama Canal and two times longer than the Suez Canal, would accommodate more than 90 percent of the seagoing vessels in service and be traversable in twenty-four hours.[60]

Somervell quickly showed that Markham knew his man. Work on the project began on September 6, and within three weeks, Somervell was awarding contracts, had more than 3,000 men on the job, and was lobbying Washington for an additional $20 million for the first year's work. Why the hurry some asked? Somervell curtly replied, "We've got to clean up the relief rolls, that's the hurry. The whole New Deal work program must be under way by November first and the Florida canal is one of the outstanding projects of the New Deal."[61]

By calling attention to the relief aspect of the canal and wrapping it in the New Deal cloak, Somervell was trying to distract attention from the controversy swirling around the project. Opponents claimed that the canal would cause sea brine to seep into the ground water that growers and towns depended upon to meet their needs, a charge that took on added weight when Secretary of the Interior and Public Works Administrator Harold Ickes condemned the project on environmental and economic grounds.[62]

Through the winter of 1935–36, controversy over the canal raged unabated. From both sides, there came an endless barrage of statement and counterstatement, statistics, and geological data. Roosevelt, concerned about the political consequences growing out of the opposition of southern Florida to the canal, decided not to allot any more relief funds to the project, thus placing its fate in the hands of Congress. Despite extensive lobbying by the canal's proponents, the opposition was too strong, and in June 1936 the Congress rejected any further funding.[63]

The canal would not die, however. Proponents lobbied Congress for the canal throughout the late 1930s, and on three occasions, Somervell testified at length before congressional committees looking into the project. By now an old hand in testifying before these committees, he was an impressive witness, displaying an encyclopedic knowledge of the engineering and economic aspects of the canal. Despite his efforts and those of others, the Congress in 1939 again turned down the canal, although the battle continued in varied forms long into the post-World War II period.[64]

By the time he was through with the Florida canal assignment, Somervell had emerged as a complete manager. He had initially demonstrated his managerial abilities in France with the various construction projects he supervised and in Germany as a staff officer. The assignments he received in the period 1920–36 enabled him to develop these abilities more fully. Through formal training at the army's postgraduate schools and through the projects he supervised as a district engineer, he had been schooled in almost every aspect of managing a large enterprise. At the same time, he had showed he put zip into everything with which he was associated. Thus, even as he closed down the canal project, officials in Washington already had him in mind for one of the most exasperating tasks facing the Roosevelt administration—management of the contentious Works Progress Administration (WPA) program in New York City.

2. A ONE-MAN SHOW

• • • • THE WPA WAS ESTABLISHED IN MAY 1935 TO provide emergency public employment for large numbers of the nation's unemployed. Headed by Harry L. Hopkins, a one-time social worker, it was divided into forty-nine programs, one for each of the forty-eight states and one for New York City, which, next to Pennsylvania, had the largest relief load in the nation. Under its first director, Hugh S. Johnson, the WPA program in New York City quickly moved from the planning stage to one of the largest single employers in the nation, with nearly 208,000 workers on the job after three months of high-geared hiring of the unemployed. This rapid growth spawned widespread inefficiency, and by the time of Johnson's departure in October 1935, the city's WPA desperately needed organizational refinements, the tightening up of practices, careful review of projects, and the assignment of workers to jobs to which they were best suited.[1]

Johnson's successor, Victor F. Ridder, worked diligently to bring efficiency to the WPA. However, in the spring of 1936, Washington's orders to lay off thousands of workers because of a shortage of funds engulfed him in controversy. Protesting the cutbacks, representatives of various jobless organizations picketed WPA headquarters almost daily and staged sit-down strikes. Ridder responded by blaming the trouble on Communists, refusing to see delegates from any group picketing his headquarters, and threatening to fire any WPA worker spotted in a protest. Believing Ridder had overreacted and was jeopardizing cooperation between the WPA and those dependent upon it,

Washington officials advised him to approve the right of WPA workers to picket local offices and recognize their unions as legitimate organizations. But, rather than follow Washington's advice, Ridder concluded he had lost the confidence of his superiors and submitted his resignation, effective August 1, 1936.[2]

Hopkins chose Somervell to replace Ridder. Somervell's selection was part of a larger pattern of bringing army engineers into the New Deal relief program. Finding competent engineers and politically savvy administrators to oversee WPA projects was difficult because of the low pay and the lack of job security. After a number of early projects were botched by poor engineering and plagued by politicians trying to get contracts and jobs for their friends, Hopkins turned to the Engineers for assistance. Since they had experience in managing large enterprises, possessed engineering skills, were free of partisan entanglements, and were familiar with the handling of public money, army engineers seemed ideal officials for the work relief program. The War Department agreed, particularly since the small size of the army meant that many officers lacked suitable assignments. Thus, the army stood to gain from WPA projects, which also included the construction of airports and the reconditioning of military installations and roads.

Putting aside his initial fear that soldiers would be unsympathetic toward the unemployed, Hopkins persuaded Chief of Engineers Markham to lend Colonel Francis "Pinky" Harrington to the WPA as chief engineer. Harrington, in turn, brought other army engineers into the WPA, where they dominated the engineering and construction divisions all over the country, even running major offices.[3]

Mayor Fiorello La Guardia of New York City had misgivings about Somervell's appointment. For one thing, he feared that as an army officer Somervell would evince little concern for the plight of the unemployed, especially given his Southern upbringing and the city's sizable black unemployed population. He also feared Somervell would expect to do everything his way and ride roughshod over city officials and anybody else who stood in his way. But after talking over his concerns with Hopkins and Somervell, La Guardia consented to the appointment, perhaps as much as anything out of relief that Washington was not imposing a Tammany Hall politician upon him.

When Somervell's appointment was announced in early July, skeptics said he would run afoul of the same problems that had plagued his predecessor and predicted his early departure. As it developed, he was on the job for more than four years, and during that time, he stamped his personality upon the New York City WPA, practically turning it into a one-man show.

• • •

In announcing Somervell's appointment as WPA administrator for New York City, Hopkins said, "I consider it to be the most difficult WPA job in the nation."[4] Indeed it was. As an article in the *New Yorker* put it:

No other WPA district is so congested, which means that building projects are more expensive and harder to plan. No other has such a mixture of races, creeds, and tongues. No other has so many unemployed whose particular lines of work are almost impossible to fit into WPA projects—everything from bus-drivers to taxidermists. In no other district are the unemployed so articulate about their demands. They are concentrated in a small area, so they can easily come together in great numbers and bring pressure on the WPA. New York is the basis of the various Left Wing parties which have done the most about organizing the unemployed. Finally, New York is a strong union town, whose workers are essential to any WPA program.[5]

For Somervell, the difficulties of running the city's WPA program became readily apparent as he coped with labor disputes and adjusted to ever changing employment quotas.

Somervell's most pressing task in the summer of 1936 was to improve WPA's relations with the left-wing groups of relief workers. These relations had been badly damaged by Ridder's anti-Communist crusade. Fortunately, the layoffs ordered by Washington the previous spring were already completed, and in several statements, Somervell announced that he planned "no slashing of the WPA rolls."

At the same time, he eschewed Ridder's Red-baiting stance and launched an offensive to make peace with labor. On August 4, he said he had no objection to the picketing of WPA headquarters, terming it "just another form of amusement" and would receive small delegations of protestors. He also declared that there was no Red Menace in the WPA: "I wouldn't know a Red if I saw one," he said, "and I wouldn't do anything about it if I did. We maintain the rule . . . of no discrimination because of political beliefs." Most importantly, in October 1936, Somervell affirmed the right of WPA workers to form any group they desired and collectively to present any matter affecting their employment. Somervell's announcements gratified both workers and the unions, and during the early fall of 1936, the city's WPA program enjoyed its first labor peace in months.[6]

In November the peace ended when Hopkins, citing a shortage of funds, ordered all WPA personnel cut by 20 percent. Complying with Washington's instructions, Somervell gave thousands of workers pink slips. In response, the work relief unions organized sit-down strikes and stoppages, and pickets continuously circled Somervell's headquarters.

The protests from the arts projects personnel were especially vehement because they doubted they would receive much assistance from Somervell in trying to either head off the cuts or, at least, to minimize such cuts. To them, Somervell was a heartless martinet who blindly followed orders no matter whom they hurt and who believed that all artists were "layouts who were trying to sponge on the state."[7]

For the most part, the arts personnel were correct, for early in his New York City tenure, Somervell gave them ample reason to believe he did not like or even understand the arts projects or the actors, writers, artists, and others they employed. When Henry G. Alsberg, head of the Federal Writers' Project, proudly showed Somervell the project's first publication, *Guide to North Little Rock: Industrial Center of Arkansas,* Somervell responded with contempt, saying "Who in the hell wants a guide to North Little Rock." "Don't you know it's the asshole of the world?" he added. In a similar vein, he angered writers by objecting to a translation of King Solomon's Song of Songs from Hebrew into Yiddish on the grounds they were the same language.[8]

Somervell dealt firmly with the wave of protests and demonstrations, threatening to fire all WPA workers who interfered with normal activities and calling on the police to evict those who occupied administrative offices. Anxious to avoid further turmoil, Hopkins advised Somervell to take no action against WPA strikers or sit-downers except for docking their pay and authorized him to reinstate persons already laid off if the city's Emergency Relief Bureau certified their eligibility for relief.[9]

Gradually, matters improved. On December 14, Somervell announced that 1,000 people who had been dropped from the projects would be reinstated as a result of the recertification of their relief status. The next day several unions pledged they would not stage any more sit-down strikes. As Christmas approached, Somervell announced that another 3,000 workers would be reinstated. Consequently, WPA employment in New York City at the end of the year was 193,833, only 8,000 fewer than when Somervell arrived the previous August, which was certainly not the mass hemorrhaging of the program many had feared.[10]

Even so, the disturbances had severely strained relations between Somervell and the arts projects, and in February 1937, Hopkins chose to end what *Variety* called the "contest between the army and the artists" by removing the New York City arts projects from Somervell's jurisdiction and turning them over to the national office.[11]

During the summer of 1937, Somervell faced further controversy over curtailments. In June, Congress appropriated $1.5 billion for 1937–38 relief projects, a figure which meant that 500,000 workers would have to be cut nationally from WPA rolls. Pursuant to instructions from Washington, Somervell announced massive layoffs, and by September, New York WPA employment numbered only 133,000, nearly a 70,000-worker reduction from when Somervell had arrived in New York City thirteen months previously.[12]

Somervell had no sooner completed the mass layoffs of 1937 than he was adding to the city's WPA employment. By the fall of 1937, a severe downturn in the economy was causing New York City's welfare rolls to climb at the rate of 5,000 a month, and in November, the city's unemployed exceeded 600,000 people. Alarmed by this mounting unemployment, Roosevelt accelerated the allocation of relief money to the WPA, enabling Somervell to hire 10,000 individuals off the relief rolls. In February 1938, Congress approved a $250 million deficiency appropriation to expand the WPA through June, adding one million people to the national rolls and 22,000 to Somervell's. Later that spring, it voted $1.425 billion to carry the WPA through the end of December 1938. This appropriation provided Somervell with enough funds to expand New York City's employment to 175,000 by the fall. Given these developments, Somervell's job had become much easier, for as he hired workers rather than fired them "his labor problems . . . diminished to minor complaints and skirmishes."[13]

Firing and hiring workers by the thousands according to the changing moods in Washington and handling the attendant labor disputes had not been easy for Somervell. At any one point, he did not know more than a few weeks ahead how much money would be available and how many people he could have on his payroll. Further, as the immediate supervisor of those who lost their jobs, he was the object of their ire, even though he was only carrying out his orders. Notwithstanding all the demonstrations and epithets hurled at him, Somervell, the good soldier, did not complain. Always carrying out his orders as efficiently as possible, he earned the gratitude of La Guardia, Hopkins, and Roosevelt by shielding them from agitation that would otherwise have been directed at them.

• • •

As time-consuming as firing and hiring workers and coping with labor disputes were to his first years as WPA administrator for New York City, Somervell found time and energy for what interested him most—"turning the New York City WPA into a smooth-running organization that would rival the efficiency of business corporations or the best-run federal department." In doing so he faced many obstacles. WPA's work force and budget were determined by Washington's inclinations, not the needs of the work to be done, and as a relief agency, it had to take on batches of unemployed workers and then plan projects that would effectively use their skills. Moreover, as a public works agency, the WPA had to perform work that did not compete with private industry or take on jobs normally done by local governmental agencies, and yet, it had to avoid make-work jobs that could lead to charges of boondoggling. Finally, it had to spend less than the desirable amount of money on machinery and equipment so that more funds were available for laborers. Somervell was not deterred by these obstacles, however, for he intended to give the taxpayers their money's worth.[14]

Somervell began with the administrator's office. He believed Ridder had tried to make too many decisions himself and had erred in centralizing too much of WPA's administration in his own hands, with seven sections responsible for housekeeping or management activities reporting directly to him. As a result, Ridder overworked himself and stifled the initiative of his subordinates.

Determined not to fall into the same trap, Somervell quickly abolished some of the sections in the administrator's office and consolidated others. Utilizing the army method of entrusting subordinates with the authority and responsibility for a job and then staying out of their way, his normal practice was to meet with his principal assistants and question them about the progress of various projects and decide future actions. While open to the ideas of others, Somervell was not one to engage in long discussions. Once he made up his mind about a course of action, he issued orders with the expectation that they would be carried out immediately and without question. If a subordinate encountered a specific problem affecting only his own operation, Somervell preferred him to make a decision himself, and then, Somervell would either back him or take responsibility for altering it if he did not approve the decision.[15]

Regarding the WPA primarily as a work program, Somervell moved early to improve the efficiency of its workers. In the case of supervisors, white-collar, and skilled blue-collar workers, he required that they demonstrate their qualifications either through oral and written examinations or performance tests before they were hired and that, thereafter, they receive satisfactory ratings to keep their jobs. He also threatened loafers with dismissal, fired those who had excessive absences, and weeded the rolls of those who were deemed ineligible for work relief on grounds of two-timing (holding a private job while working for the WPA) or were careermen (WPA workers who made no effort to find private employment, even if it would pay more money). These measures were accompanied by a number of different methods to inspire his workers "to higher and finer things," including a job-training program to make workers more useful to the WPA and ultimately more attractive to private companies.[16]

Before the WPA could be operating in a truly businesslike manner, all its separate undertakings had to be integrated into a comprehensive program. From the outset, Somervell pushed for such a program in the face of major obstacles. First, neither federal nor city officials showed any interest in a long-term master plan, because no one knew what the life-span of the WPA might be.

Second, Somervell did not know what his funds would be from one month to the next. Washington usually doled out funds thirty days at a time, and even then, Somervell did not always know for sure that he would receive the money he had been promised. In September 1936, for example, he was told that his allotment for October would be $17 million. Several days later, however, it was dropped to $10 million. Although additional funds were soon forthcoming, Somervell was exasperated by this cavalier approach to planning and complained to Aubrey Williams, Hopkins' deputy, that "I would like very much, for one month, to . . . get . . . started on a business basis."[17] Several months later, Hopkins solved this problem by announcing that Washington would inform state WPA directors of the minimum cash allotments they could expect from July 1 to December 1, 1937.

Somervell's third problem was in pinning down La Guardia to the city's specific contributions of materials, equipment, and labor. Until he received specific commitments from the mayor, his goal of a master plan that covered a period of six months to a year could not be fulfilled.

The matter of city contributions to the WPA had long been a source of friction. Initially, Washington financed the WPA almost entirely in recognition that state and local governments were caring for the unemployed not hired by the WPA. But Roosevelt wanted the sponsoring agencies to pay a significant part of project costs, and by the summer of 1936, he was pressing them to commit to specific donations over a designated period. La Guardia hit the ceiling when Somervell first told him that the WPA could not continue projects if the city did not put up more money.

Most cities acceded to Roosevelt's request and agreed to pay about 20 percent of the costs of their WPA projects, but La Guardia, saying that the city lacked money, stalled. When Somervell continued to press Roosevelt's request, La Guardia telephoned Williams and demanded Somervell's removal. "I am not going to let a two by four soldier come in and run New York," he complained. "Get this 'cracker' out of here." Williams pacified the mayor, and eventually, La Guardia agreed to provide $2.8 million for the purchase of materials to assist in WPA work through June, 1937, as well as $750,000 a month for the last half of 1937.[18]

On the basis of La Guardia's commitment, Somervell had his staff draft a rough outline of activities for the WPA for the latter part of 1937. But to a great degree, Somervell had won only a skirmish, for La Guardia was reluctant to discuss Somervell's request for a commitment from the city for 1938. In fact, the mayor even avoided meeting with Somervell for a time in the fall of 1937.

Angered by "this run around business," Somervell demanded that the city increase its contributions to the WPA from its present 6 percent to 20 percent of the total or have many of its project applications disapproved. La Guardia countered that the city could not pay more because its direct relief program was so costly.

But as before, La Guardia yielded. In December, he agreed to triple the city's commitment to the WPA, and in January 1938, he and Somervell agreed on specific figures. Under the projected program, the WPA would spend $180 million in 1938, 22 percent, or $39.5 million, of which would be supplied by the city. As a result of Somervell's prodding, therefore, the city's contribution to the WPA had gone from practically nothing in 1936 to close to $40 million in 1938.[19] The agreement with La Guardia enabled Somervell to put together a reasonably comprehensive package of WPA activities in 1938, and thereafter, he prepared a master plan each year based on expected WPA revenue.

By 1939, Somervell had gone far toward achieving the efficiency he sought in the city's WPA. Between 100,000 and 200,000 New Yorkers were employed in a reasonably efficient and useful manner that suited the needs of the workers and the city alike. Strict discipline and an emphasis on productivity marked the program, and although Somervell's single-minded drive for efficiency did not always endear him to his workers, few could deny that he had improved the city's WPA and enabled it to complete the most impressive list of projects of any WPA program in the nation.

• • •

Of the many WPA endeavors, Somervell felt most at home with the construction projects, which in 1938 accounted for 125,000 of the city's 175,000 WPA workers and approximately 60 percent of all construction work in New York City. These projects were closely related to his previous experience, and their worth and the progress toward their completion were easily measured when contrasted to the agency's other projects. They included construction of highways, bridges, sewers, buildings, athletic facilities, monuments, and especially important to Somervell, North Beach Airport, the most ambitious and expensive project undertaken by the WPA anywhere in the United States.[20]

North Beach Airport, renamed La Guardia in 1940, owed its inception to La Guardia, who persuaded Roosevelt and Hopkins to support its construction under WPA auspices. It was located at North Beach in Queens along the east shore of Flushing Bay, a largely unused marsh shelving off into muddy water. North Beach Airport was unquestionably La Guardia's project, but Somervell quickly took a proprietary interest in it when work began on it in September 1937. Large-scale in conception, the object of much public interest (often drawing crowds of more than 100,000 sightseers), consisting of many components, employing thousands of workers, and presenting many varied engineering and construction problems, North Beach was the type of project to excite Somervell. It challenged all his managerial skills and, if successfully completed, was sure to add luster to the WPA and his own record.[21]

Determined to meet the mayor's deadline for completion in the spring of 1939, in time for the opening of the World's Fair whose site was only a few miles from the airport, Somervell placed army engineers in charge of key aspects of the construction and had his work crews on the job around the clock. All felt Somervell's whip in his unceasing drive to finish the airport on schedule. William A. Delano, whose architectural firm assisted in the plans for the buildings and the landscape, recalled that everything was a rush job. Each time he asked Somervell when "he needed such and such a drawing," Somervell's "invariable reply was 'The day before yesterday.' "

Construction of North Beach required a degree of planning and administration far beyond any other project under Somervell's command. More than 60 percent of the 558-acre airport had to be reclaimed from the East River, a task accomplished by hauling 1.5 million cubic yards of fill—ashes, rubbish, iron bedsteads, stoves, and every kind of scrap imaginable—from the Department of Sanitation's dump at Riker's Island by means of a specially designed steel trestle with a floating draw to provide a truck way from the island. Because the manmade land was soft and subject to settling, all the hangars for landbased aircraft and the main terminal were perched on concrete piles driven between 35 and 125 feet into the ground. Four macadam runways, a steel-framed administration building, six large hangars, a complete seaplane facility, and a parking area for 5,000 automobiles were the main features.[22]

Somervell had hoped to meet La Guardia's spring 1939 deadline, but labor difficulties pushed the opening back to the fall. Little more than a week after the dedication in October, War Department Chief of Staff George Marshall visited the airport. A man who set high standards for himself and others, he came away with the opinion that Somervell had done a splendid job and, in a brief note to him, remarked, "I was much impressed." For Marshall, these were high words of praise, and undoubtedly, he now added Somervell's name to the list of promising young majors and lieutenant colonels whose services he intended to call upon for key assignments if the United States entered the war that had erupted in Europe a month earlier.[23]

• • •

During his years as head of New York City's WPA program, Somervell was never far from controversy. Some of this arose because of his readiness to speak his own mind. Most, however, was an outgrowth of the very nature of the program and the nation's political climate.

Infuriated by what they considered undue pressure from Roosevelt for additional funds for the WPA, economy-minded conservative congressmen persuaded the House of Representatives in March 1939 to authorize an investigation of the WPA by a subcommittee of the House Appropriations Committee, led by Clifton Woodrum, Democrat from Virginia. Beginning on April 17, the committee's hearings quickly turned into a witch hunt. WPA's enemies, including "disgruntled building contractors, ex-WPA employees who had been fired for various reasons, self-confessed former Communists, and lobbyists," were given free rein to hurl accusations against the agency, while its defenders were often cut short by committee members or never given the opportunity to testify at all. Somervell, who was most anxious to rebut the charges leveled against the New York City WPA, was not permitted to appear, although he was able to file a written statement with the committee attacking in detail the criticism of his program.[24]

Somervell's staunch defense of the New York City WPA defused the charges leveled against it. But the conservatives had their way. The Emergency Relief Act of 1939, approved on June 30, 1939, provided only $1,755,600,000 for the WPA and other relief agencies, a drastic reduction from the total spent the previous twelve months. Beyond the reduced appropriation, Congress prohibited the employment of any worker for more than eighteen months and required all WPA workers to be on the job for thirty hours a week. It also killed the Federal Theatre Project, claiming that it was absolutely dominated by Communists, and mandated that the art, music, writers', and history projects might continue only if local sponsors covered a portion of their expenses.

The ramifications of the new relief act for Somervell were staggering. At the beginning of 1939, the city's WPA quota of employees was 175,000. Beginning in April, Washington reduced it to 143,000 by the end of June. Then came the new relief act. Under it Somervell had to drop 75,000 workers in eight weeks, half of his work force, because Washington had tentatively reduced the New York City quota to 127,000 in August and 107,000 in September and because of the eighteen-month rule.

Protests against the cuts developed quickly, but Somervell forged ahead in compliance with his instructions. The first pink slips went out on July 17. Counting all those let go under the provisions of the Emergency Relief Act of 1939, the total number dismissed during 1939 was more than 100,000.[25]

The wholesale dismissals hampered Somervell's efficiency drive by costing the services of many experienced foremen and managers. These difficulties were compounded by labor strife. By requiring all employees to work thirty hours a week, Congress in effect lowered the hourly rate of building-trades union members well below the union scales paid by private contractors. Arguing that the government terms would undermine wages throughout the construction industry, the American Federation of Labor's Building and Construction Trades Council in New York City struck the WPA on July 5.

For weeks, the strike dominated the front pages of the city's newspapers. Equipment operators employed by vendors at North Beach Airport and other projects quit in a sympathetic gesture, as did truck drivers, and by the end of August, thirty construction sites were idle for want of workers. However, Somervell, fully supported by the Roosevelt administration, gave "the strikers no quarter." To break the strike, he declared he would fire anyone who stayed off the job for five consecutive days, threatened to have arrested anyone interfering with WPA work, filled gaps in WPA's skilled ranks with applicants from the city's home relief rolls, and shifted skilled nonunionists from job to job as they were needed. Unable to shut down the WPA, the strikers gave up the fight by October 1. It was a decisive victory for Somervell.[26]

Somervell's problems with layoffs and strikers were paralleled by renewed controversy over the arts projects. Under the 1939 relief act, the arts projects in

New York City were again placed under his direction, and before long, his distaste for them reemerged, especially in his handling of the art project. He had never had much regard for the quality of the artists' work, and he was now certain the project was a nest of Reds who were using government money to propagate the party line. In Somervell's opinion, Holger Cahill, the national administrator of the project, was an intellectual whose sympathies were with the Communist Party. As for Audrey MaMahon, the local administrator, Somervell was certain she either coddled Communists or was too naive politically to appreciate what was going on around her. Repeatedly he called her on the carpet and demanded to know the names of Communists on the project and insisted they be summarily dismissed. Her assertion that she was "not overly politically minded, and had no idea of the political tenets of . . . project members, was written off by him with angry belief as being the idiotic methods to be expected from a woman."[27]

Within weeks after taking control of the art project, Somervell dismissed 85 percent of its nearly 1,800 employees because of the eighteen-month rule, set the new employment ceiling at 1,000, and announced that, hereafter, supervisors would focus greater attention on individual works so that some measure of control could be achieved over the character of the work done by WPA artists. He further indicated that he intended to guard against any production whose main idea was social content.[28]

During the summer of 1940, Somervell personally took to reviewing the artwork. August Henkel, a fifty-nine-year-old artist who had been involved in leftist activities dating back to 1917 and who had failed to sign a loyalty oath, had just completed four canvases for the administration building at Brooklyn's Floyd Bennett Airport. Before the murals were officially approved by the Art Commission, the Art Project Mural Committee, and the city dock commissioner (the official sponsor), the director in the field charged they were Red Propaganda. He alleged that they contained a likeness of Joseph Stalin, the Wright Brothers in Russian-style costumes, a Russian plane with a red star, aviators who were heroes to American Communists, people who were "strangely un-American in expression and garb," and depictions of war promoting the Communist Party's anti-war activities.

Deciding that the charge was correct, Somervell ordered the murals to be fed to a potbellied stove and fired Henkel for not signing the loyalty oath. In a meeting with Somervell on the day he ordered the murals destroyed, an act they were not yet aware of, representatives of the United American Artists explained that most of the charges were sheer fabrication and the others debatable. Refusing to concede he had acted too hastily, Somervell stated that, although he knew little about art, he recognized propaganda when he saw it.

Taking the offensive, Somervell ordered a comprehensive investigation of all employees in the New York City art project in search of Communists. He also appointed an advisory committee of prominent artists to make "oral or written comments or criticism" that would be used in evaluating "the efficiency record of the artists." Not wanting to be a firing squad to rid the project of people deemed undesirable by Somervell, sixteen artists quit the committee after he refused to consider any constructive changes in the functioning of the committee. They further asked those who disagreed with Somervell to leave. Within days, Somervell replaced the sixteen with artists who, in his words, had "enough sense of civic duty to make certain that employment in the art project was limited to artists."[29]

Congress, meanwhile, passed the Emergency Relief Act of 1940. For Somervell, the provision barring Communists and Nazis from holding WPA jobs and requiring all relief personnel to sign a loyalty oath brought the most immediate repercussions. Convinced that Communists had been tolerated too long, he announced that all 101,000 WPA employees in New York City must sign loyalty oaths or lose their jobs. However, he was not content to leave the matter there. Estimating there were at least 1,000 Communists on the rolls, he declared he would not rely on affidavits alone in carrying out the law because of the well-known practice of Communists to deny their membership in the party and to use false names in enrollment with the WPA. Determined to uproot them, Somervell had the WPA payroll checked against the voter registration lists to turn up the names of Communists. He also asked federal, state, and local agencies to help him investigate the politics of his personnel and called upon responsible citizens to make available any information they had on subversive activities by relief workers. Somervell's purge drew a mixed response. The conservative press praised his actions, while liberals and labor unions branded them as un-American. Despite all the hullabaloo, Somervell's purge was, for all practical purposes, a wasted effort. By the end of 1940, only 365 people had been dismissed, and all but 46 were reinstated after review officers from Washington conducted hearings in which the accused were permitted to defend themselves.[30]

• • •

As the year 1940 progressed, Somervell increasingly looked forward to returning to the army. He had accomplished about all he could do in New York City, and he feared he might be overlooked for an attractive assignment if war came to the United States and if he were still a WPA administrator. In the summer, he went to Washington to see Brigadier General Richard C. Moore, an engineer who was serving as G-4 on the General Staff, and said he "would like to enter the preparedness picture." Then in October, Somervell approached Roosevelt, arguing that the WPA in New York City was functioning better than ever before and that he might better serve the nation on military duty. After reviewing Somervell's request with Marshall, Roosevelt agreed and authorized his transfer.[31]

On November 8, 1940, Somervell announced he would be leaving the WPA within days. The left-wing unions cheered the announcement, but most city officials, who had come to respect and appreciate his managerial abilities, regretted his departure. While often displaying a disregard for the positions and sensibilities of others and autocratic tendencies, he had given New York City more parks, firehouses, clinics, roads, sewers, and services for the dollars spent than it would have had otherwise, leaving the city more livable than when he arrived. La Guardia, commenting on the announcement of Somervell's departure, spoke for most city officials when he told reporters that "I understand Army officers must be called back into military service. But when it hits Colonel Somervell in my city then I say it hurts."[32]

Somervell's performance in New York City also won him high marks from his superiors in Washington. Hopkins had been most pleased with the way he had carried out his job and his ability to take the heat that came with a controversial post, and Roosevelt, Marshall, and the civilian heads of the army were also impressed. In their minds, Somervell had demonstrated he was one of the outstanding managers in public service.

3. CONSTRUCTION DIVISION

• • • • DURING THE LAST WEEKS OF NOVEMBER 1940, Somervell frantically searched for a choice assignment. Chief of Engineers Major General Julian L. Schley had already selected him to be executive officer of the new Engineer Training Center in the 7th Corps Area at a location yet to be designated. While it was a responsible position, it hardly carried the challenge and importance Somervell had in mind. Fortunately for Somervell, there was no need to assume the post until the location of the training center was determined, and so, for the time being, he was placed in the Office of the Inspector General of the army, headed by a longtime friend, Major General Virgil Peterson. Although Somervell did not know it at the time, this assignment came at the specific request of Secretary of War Henry L. Stimson, who wanted "to get a look at him without Somervell being aware of this" so as to judge if Somervell were the man to take charge of the floundering Construction Division.[1]

Part of the Quartermaster Corps, the Construction Division was charged with the construction of camps, munitions plants, hospitals, ports, and depots. Commanded by Brigadier General Charles D. Hartman and designed largely for peacetime maintenance of existing army posts, the Construction Division had not been up to the task of accommodating the hundreds of thousands of men who were inducted into the army as a result of its rapid expansion in 1940, which saw its authorized strength go from 174,000 to 1,400,000. The large size of individual camps, the great number of projects simultaneously under construction, the shortages of both materials and skilled labor, and Chief of Staff Marshall's unrealistic deadline to have the camps completed in ninety days strained Hartman's "woefully undermanned" organization to the limits. The inadequate buildings left over from World War I could not handle anything near the rush of men called into uniform, and an attempt to speed up the construction program led to spiraling costs. By November, public complaints were forcing the army to defend itself against charges of "incompetence, ineptitude, and stupidity" from the press and from Capitol Hill.[2]

As the construction program floundered, Benedict Crowell, a major participant in the mobilization for World War I, called for the Construction Division to be divorced from the Quartermaster Corps and reestablished as an independent corps under the direct control of a civilian. At the same time, officials in the War Department determined that Hartman's division needed better management. In particular, Michael J. Madigan, special assistant to Under Secretary of War Robert P. Patterson, was impatient with the Quartermaster systems of cost control, job planning, and progress reporting. When Hartman disregarded his advice, Madigan concluded that he was "a complete road block" to progress in the construction program and should be relieved.

Madigan, a New York City engineer, already had his eyes on Somervell to replace Hartman. He was certain that Somervell, whose work with the WPA he had admired, was the man to bring order to the construction program. In a November luncheon, Madigan told Somervell about the construction situation, and Somervell replied that he would love the job of running the program.

Madigan was now determined to replace Hartman with Somervell. According to his own account, he advised General Moore, now deputy chief of staff, that the army must do what he thought was necessary or he would state that it could not handle the construction job, adding impetus to Crowell's idea to turn construction over to a separate agency.

Actually, Madigan did not have to push hard. Stimson believed the construction "problem would only be solved by getting a man" with the drive "to invigorate the program and bring it to fruition" and already had Somervell in mind for the assignment. Harry Hopkins gave his enthusiastic backing, expressing "high praise" for Somervell's work with the WPA. And Colonel John P. Hogan, a reserve officer and head of the Construction Advisory Committee under the Army and Navy Munitions Board (ANMB), also backed Somervell. His firm had acted as a consulting engineer for the WPA in New York City, and he was telling everyone that Somervell's drive and managerial ability made him "a natural to replace Hartman."

During the last week of November and the first week of December, "things moved fast" in regard to Somervell. Working out of Peterson's office, Somervell conferred with various people familiar with Hartman's difficulties. Between

November 30 and December 4, he made a whirlwind visit to the Midwest to inspect construction projects and gather firsthand knowledge for use in making his own assessment of what should be done.

In the meantime, Quartermaster General Major General Edmund B. Gregory, averse to having Somervell as a subordinate out of concern about his aggressiveness, tried to save Hartman by establishing new procedures, shuffling personnel, and beseeching him to reorganize his operation. But Hartman was reluctant to make changes, prompting Gregory to decide to relieve him.

Before Gregory could relieve Hartman, higher-ups intervened. The civilians in the War Department were frightened by the criticism being leveled at the construction program and thought Somervell was the man to pull it through. The White House, which previously had been leaning towards Crowell's scheme, quickly changed course once it learned that the War Department wanted Somervell, and Harry Hopkins, Roosevelt's unofficial right-hand man throughout World War II, gave his endorsement. In early December, Marshall decided that Somervell should replace Hartman, and on December 11, Gregory went to Hartman's office and told him of the decision. Without replying, Hartman left by one door as Somervell came in the other. Several days later Stimson, after meeting Somervell for the first time, noted in his diary that Somervell "was like a breath of fresh air in the talk I had with him this morning." After introducing him to reporters, he wrote that "the sight of Somervell was enough to show . . . the Press that progress was being made."[3]

Somervell was in a much stronger position as chief of the Construction Division than Hartman had been. Gregory, who was not really interested in construction anyway and knew that higher-ups were looking for Somervell to get things done, gave him practically a blank check to run the division. Moreover, Somervell enjoyed the support of Stimson and Marshall and, through his connections with Hopkins, direct access to the White House. As two of Somervell's contemporaries recalled, "the back door to the White House was always open and he used it. Even when he didn't, it was widely known that it was there."[4]

From his years as a district engineer and WPA administrator, Somervell knew exactly what he wanted to do with the Construction Division. Very quickly, he reorganized it. The eleven branches of Hartman's organization were reduced to five, and two new sections—the Control Section, which prepared statistics and reports and coordinated the work of the various branches, and the Public Relations Section—were created and added to the office. Somervell moved just as quickly to decentralize the division's operations, for he was convinced Hartman had undermined his organization's efficiency by trying to do too much himself. By the end of December, he had established nine territorial construction zones, each headed by a constructing quartermaster who was responsible for the supervision and control of all construction projects in his zone and was specifically charged with relieving Somervell of any problem that could be handled locally.

Staffing the construction division was a vital concomitant to the streamlining of its organization. Above all else, Somervell wanted operators, go-getters, crack executives, and prominent consultants. Lacking confidence in Hartman's men, Somervell dismissed scores of them, leaving a residue of bitter feelings. To replace them, Somervell brought in a number of engineers who were close to him personally. Lieutenant Colonel Edmond Leavey and Major Clinton Robinson came from the New York City WPA to head Engineering and Control respectively, while an old friend, Lieutenant Colonel Wilhelm Styer, became Somervell's deputy and executive officer. From this point on, Somervell and Styer were inseparable, and during the next four years, the extremely capable Styer was an indispensable assistant to Somervell, seeing "that things functioned and were fully coordinated." Others were recruited from retired and reserve lists, and civilians were also brought in to fill various posts. Before long the roster of the division looked like a who's who in engineering and related professions.[5]

As a result of these actions, by early 1941, Somervell had an organization more to his liking. Much remained to be done to staff it fully and to have it running smoothly. But these concerns could wait, while he pushed ahead to accomplish what he had been brought to Washington to do—complete the construction program as soon as possible.

• • •

Somervell's immediate concern was the completion of more than sixty construction projects that were scheduled to be ready by April 1941. It was a stiff assignment, because it had to be accomplished in the face of severe materials shortages, changing requirements, and limited budgets, as well as at a time of year when bad weather normally compelled the suspension of work in many parts of the country. The most pressing problem was a shortage of funds. By the middle of December 1940, the deficit in the program was approaching $150 million, and the latest estimates of the division's projects indicated that approximately $337 million would be necessary to complete the projects. Somervell added $25 million for contingencies, placing the total at $362 million. On January 13, 1941, Somervell asked Budget Director Harold D. Smith for $535 million in constructions funds: a deficiency request of $362 million to complete the existing program, a maintenance and repair fund of $32.6 million, and a contingency fund of $140 million to purchase land and additional items for the camps. However, Smith, angered by Somervell's refusal to guarantee these funds would be sufficient, slashed the deficiency request to $338 million and the maintenance fund to $19,835,000 and completely eliminated the contingency request. In early February, Somervell attempted to get the War Department to push Smith for restoration of the contingency fund. But Stimson, Marshall, and Moore decided Somervell's proposal was politically unwise and resolved to defend the $338 million laid down by the budget director and ask for no contingency fund.[6]

When the House Subcommittee on Deficiency Appropriations began hearings on February 12 on the fourth supplemental defense appropriation bill for 1941, Somervell, who had just two weeks before been raised to the temporary rank of brigadier general, was the principal army witness on the construction program. Effectively presenting the army's case, he attributed the cost overrun to skyrocketing labor and materials charges, to changes in design, to a need for additional buildings, and to extensive work on utilities to complement the building program. He stated that $338,880,000 would complete the program under way. Impressed by Somervell's presentation, the committee approved his figure, although not before rejecting two pleas from him for $25 million for contingencies. A month later, after both the full House and Senate approved it, Roosevelt signed the measure into law.[7]

These funds eased Somervell's financial problem for the time being, and despite a plethora of problems, such as bad weather, materials and labor shortages, strikes, union restrictions and resistance to timesaving methods and machines, "belated and oft-changed" plans, and conflicts between the military and contractors, his division labored at breakneck speed to complete the camps by spring. As a result of these efforts, Marshall reported on April 22 that "we have gotten over the hump," and two days later, Somervell announced that "The new Army is housed."

Considering the difficulties, Somervell's success in getting the camps completed by spring 1941 fully satisfied Stimson's and Marshall's expectations when they had selected him to head the construction program. Granted the camps had cost about double the figure first given to Congress in the fall of 1940, and the induction of many National Guardsmen and draftees had to be delayed. Nevertheless, Somervell had driven the job through to completion in a reasonable time and shown Congress and the public that the army could handle its own construction. In this way, he headed off the creation of a civilian agency to take over the job.[8]

Besides building new camps, Somervell was also responsible for constructing and equipping new facilities to make and store munitions. By late December 1940, the War Department had allotted nearly $700 million for these facilities, and by early 1941, the so-called first-wave plants munitions program—thirty-four manufacturing facilities for the Ordnance Department and the Chemical Warfare Service—was making fairly steady progress.

Nevertheless, Somervell was concerned. Cost overruns were common, and the number of agencies involved in the munitions program had produced complications. Lacking enough experienced Quartermaster officers to supervise projects, Hartman had permitted the Ordnance Department to assume responsibility for construction at several key jobs. Some officers handled the construction job in a satisfactory manner, while others, as Somervell noted, attempted to command architects and engineers who knew more about construction than they. More importantly, these officers served two masters, Somervell and the Ordnance Department, and their branch loyalty usually proved the stronger of the two when they had to choose between enforcing Somervell's policies and preserving Ordnance Department prerogatives.

To remedy the problems, Somervell stressed simplicity, efficiency, and economy, and he instructed constructing quartermasters for munitions plants to consider the wishes of the Ordnance Department at all times but to keep in mind that they were subject only to his direction. As a result of these measures, Somervell was satisfied with the munitions program in early 1941. Except for one or two trouble spots, the plants launched in the summer and fall of 1940 were nearing completion, and new projects were progressing at an acceptable rate. Further, the planning for a second wave of munitions plants necessitated by Roosevelt's call for the nation to become the Arsenal of Democracy was underway. By the end of 1941, construction of the first-wave plants was practically finished. Although rounding out these plants and finishing the second wave remained to be accomplished, the munitions industry required for war was a reality.[9]

• • •

Despite the attention he devoted to completing the camps and first-wave munitions plants, Somervell never lost sight of the need to plan ahead. Changing world conditions were leading the United States to cement itself to Britain in that country's war against Germany, and Somervell was certain that the army would soon be increased far beyond the numbers for which he was presently building. Determined to avoid the chaos that accompanied the initial building program, he decided that planning for a second and larger building program should begin promptly.

Thus, in December 1940, Somervell persuaded Virgil Peterson to approach Marshall about the need for immediate long-range planning for another major building program. Marshall readily agreed with Somervell's thinking, and soon after, Somervell ordered Leavey to calculate housing requirements for another one million men. He also conferred with representatives of the National Defense Advisory Commission and the Office of Production Management (OPM) about the availability of materials, looked into the labor situation, and convinced the Congress to give him $15 million for engineering surveys.[10]

Through the spring, Somervell forged ahead with his advanced planning. New barracks and other buildings were designed, new site plans and layouts were devised, and a new estimating system was introduced to predict, with a high degree of accuracy, the cost of constructing a building anywhere in the nation. By May, the War Department was selecting sites for more than twenty-odd camps, leading Somervell to put architect-engineers to work laying out the detailed plans for their locations. Although Congress had not appropriated money for construction or even authorized the expansion of the army necessitating the erection of these camps, Somervell had achieved his planning objectives. If the need to house a large army became apparent, construction could be started with "maximum economy and minimum delay."[11]

At the same time, Somervell pressed ahead with plans for the second-wave program for munitions plants.[12] He was especially anxious about the requirement that he share construction with the Ordnance Department. As he saw it, the Ordnance Department's predilection for frequent design changes and its tendency to award contracts to firms chosen on the basis of their operating ability rather than on their experience in design, engineering, and construction had created unnecessary delays. The simplest solution in his mind was to entrust him alone with construction.

But the Ordnance Department would have none of this. Rejecting Somervell's criticism, Brigadier General Levin H. Campbell of the Ordnance Department's Industrial Service, Facilities Branch, asserted that the Ordnance Department could do the job better than Somervell and questioned his motives. In Campbell's eyes, Somervell was out to advance himself at the expense of the Ordnance Department, and Campbell was determined to resist.[13]

Somervell launched his offensive to play a larger role in the design of munitions plants and selection of contractors in March 1941. Initially rebuffed by Campbell in regard to design, he took his case to Under Secretary of War Patterson. Brushing aside Campbell's claim that the complex nature of munitions plants required the Ordnance Department to have complete control, Somervell said that there was nothing complicated about their construction and no reason why they should be handled differently from other construction projects. Patterson partially agreed with his argument and ruled in early April that the Construction Division would thereafter design all facilities except for the manufacturing buildings. But, in the matter of selecting contractors, he initially ruled against Somervell, giving the Ordnance Department the responsibility for choosing the prime contractor who would handle all work from designing a plant to operating it. Somervell would not admit defeat, however, and eventually Patterson gave him full responsibility for choosing architect-engineers and contractors. The Ordnance Department could approve plans and specifications, but it would have no authority over construction.[14]

While he was pushing ahead with the planning for new camps and munitions plants, Somervell was also strengthening his organization. His reorganization in December 1940 had brought many changes. However, Somervell never regarded these changes as final, and he was continually improving administrative procedures by eliminating duplication, shortening channels of communication, coupling responsibility with authority, and limiting the number of people any one individual supervised.

But, for Somervell, these matters took second place to personnel. What was left of Hartman's team after the December reorganization rapidly "faded from the scene." Demonstrating an outstanding knack for recruiting the talented, Somervell brought in new people almost daily. Many of the new faces were men Somervell knew from his years as a military engineer and as head of the WPA in New York City. For example, James P. Mitchell, a former WPA employee in New York City and a future secretary of labor, became head of the Labor Relations Section. And Lieutenant Colonel William E.R. Covell, a retired engineer and the top graduate in the West Point class of 1915, became Leavey's assistant.

By the fall of 1941, Somervell's planning was bearing fruit. He had selected new sites for camps, improved plans and procedures, and strengthened his organization. The Construction Division was now ready to meet any future demands for camps and plants.

• • •

When Somervell became head of the Construction Division, the military construction program was the target of unending criticism. The press generally gave the impression that it was being bungled by thickheaded construction officers, and congressmen and senators were bombarded with complaints about the selection of contractors, the quality of work, the amount of corruption, and other real or perceived ills. Somervell was anxious to minimize the effect of the criticism, and so unlike Hartman, who had angered congressmen by sometimes keeping them waiting in the halls of the Construction Division, Somervell was never too busy to see legislators. Ranking members of key committees even received invitations to Somervell's home to talk over pending legislation related to the construction program.[15]

Despite these efforts, the construction program still underwent intensive scrutiny from Congress. Previous wars had produced full-scale congressional probes, and in early 1941, the House and Senate launched formal inquiries into the defense program, with military construction as their initial target.

The House Military Affairs Committee opened its investigation of the army's preparations in February. Somervell testified at length about the construction program. But there was little about his testimony or that of the other army witnesses that made headlines, and this investigation turned up little. As a result, a special subcommittee headed by R. Ewing Thomason, Democrat from Texas, undertook a more systematic look into military construction.

Through the late spring and summer, this subcommittee took testimony in closed session, sent out questionnaires, and visited construction sites. Somervell cooperated closely with the subcommittee to ensure a favorable report and, according to one insider, even dangled the possibility of a commission before its chief counsel to facilitate this result. While not a whitewash, the final report, much of it written by Somervell's liaison officer with the subcommittee, praised the Construction Division for a "magnificent and unparalleled job" in housing the army.[16]

The House probe was soon overshadowed by that of a special Senate committee headed by Harry S. Truman, Democrat from Missouri, which was created in March 1941 to look into the entire defense effort and which began with the construction program. The committee opened its hearings on April 18, 1941, and over the next several weeks, it took testimony from top defense officials and a host of actors in the construction drama. Initially, the senate committee looked into charges of cost overruns, dishonesty, and extravagance, focusing on profits, salaries, wages, equipment rental rates, and contracts. Later, it turned its attention to the army's mobilization plans.

Somervell testified at length on April 24 and 25. In the course of the questioning, he made the damaging statement that lack of planning by the army had increased the cost of the program by at least $100 million. Otherwise, he generally defended the army's program, emphasizing, in his words, that "the whole thing is speed, the speed in construction. That is what caused the increase in cost."[17]

Through June and July 1941, Somervell waited for the Truman Committee's report. From the outset, he expected it to be a "stinking" one, for he was certain Truman was a publicity-seeking politician seeking to punish him for refusing to award a contract to a St. Louis firm that Truman had recommended. He was not disappointed.

Released on August 14, the report was a scathing indictment of military ineptitude, shortsightedness, and extravagance. Charging the army with the needless waste of $100 million through bad planning, inexperience, speed, cost-plus-fixed-fee contracts, high materials and labor costs, and improper location of sites, the committee blasted armchair generals for errors in planning and the Construction Division for mistakes in estimates and slipshod administrative methods.[18]

The Senate committee's inquiry engendered bad blood between Somervell and Truman. Somervell came away certain that his original suspicions about Truman were correct and that the Missouri senator had unfairly stuck pins in the army to further his own career and could be counted upon to do the same again.

Truman, meanwhile, came away with a strong dislike for Somervell. Ever since World War I, when he had served with the National Guard, Truman had disapproved of Regular Army officers. In his opinion, they were absurd martinets and Somervell epitomized all that he despised in these officers. Moreover, Truman was not impressed with Somervell's statement during the course of the inquiry that "it's axiomatic that you can't save time and money at the same time," and he later told a journalist that Somervell "cared absolutely nothing about money."[19]

• • •

During the first half of 1941, the War Department was aiming for a mobilization force of four million men by spring 1942. Many new facilities had to be constructed to meet this goal, and armed with millions of dollars provided by Congress in regular and supplemental appropriations bills, Somervell rushed ahead with projects. The monthly value of work placed by the Construction Division shot up sharply. In June 1941, the division put in place nearly $90 million of construction work; in October, it put in place more than $150 million; and in November, it set a high point during Somervell's tenure of $175 million. By early December 1941, there were 375 completed projects and 320 still underway, with a total value of $1.8 billion.[20]

Of the projects started in 1941, the most notable was the Pentagon, "a monument to Somervell's dynamism" and "the ultimate symbol of America's armed might." As the defense program gained momentum, there was not enough office space in the Washington area to meet the government's burgeoning needs. The War Department alone had nearly 24,000 military and civilian employees scattered among seventeen buildings in the Washington, D.C. area. The conditions everywhere were cramped. The Public Buildings Association and many in Congress wanted to solve the office problem by consolidating agencies in temporary buildings constructed within the District of Columbia. Chief of Staff Marshall strongly favored consolidating the War Department offices, but he believed the proposed sites for the War Department facilities were inadequate because of overcrowding in the District. Thus, on June 11, while testifying before a House subcommittee, he proposed that the War Department utilize temporary buildings to be located at the former Governmental Experimental Farm in Arlington, Virginia, previously transferred by the Department of Agriculture to the War Department.

Hearing of Marshall's proposal, Somervell came forth with his own. His plan, however, was to maximize efficiency by placing the entire War Department under one roof. In early July, Somervell talked with Representative Woodrum about his scheme. When the Budget Bureau's request for $6.5 million for temporary buildings came before his subcommittee on appropriation on July 17, Woodrum suggested that the War Department work out an overall solution to its space problem. Woodrum's proposal was the go-ahead signal for Somervell, and by the end of the day he was busy on the project.[21]

That evening Somervell called Leavey; Lieutenant Colonel Leslie Groves, chief of his Operations Branch; George E. Bergstrom, a civilian who had headed the American Institute of Architects before joining Somervell's team; and a few others to his office and told them that he wanted a basic plan and architectural perspectives for an office building to house all the War Department on his desk by Monday morning, July 21. The only guidelines he offered were that the building, to be located on the Virginia side of the Potomac, on land drawn from the Gravely Point Airport and a proposed Quartermaster Corps depot nearby, was to be a modern four-story, air-conditioned structure with no elevators that was capable of housing 40,000 people and of being completed in a year.

Startled by Somervell's request, the men in the room promptly questioned his requirements. Paying little attention to their concerns, Somervell shut them up, saying "don't question . . . [the] requirements. That isn't your job. Your job is to get them [the plans and perspectives]."[22]

No sooner had they started than Somervell was making changes. Since the projected site was situated on the river bed and thus subject to flooding, Somervell, at the suggestion of Colonel Eugene Reybold, the War Department G-4, moved the location of the building to the sixty-seven acre experimental farm, which would situate it between the Arlington Memorial Bridge and Arlington National Cemetery.

At nine o'clock Monday morning the final plan was delivered to Somervell. Designed to fit its site, which was bounded by five roads, the building was to have five sides, hence the name Pentagon given it in early 1942. With floor space of more than five million square feet, twice that of the Empire State Building, it would be the world's largest office building. The estimated cost of construction was $33 million. That same day Marshall and Patterson approved the plan, and the next morning, Somervell presented it to Stimson, who was frankly skeptical of its grandiose size but gradually came around after Somervell convinced him that "it will solve not only our problem . . . it will also solve a lot of other problems, including the Navy and a lot of other people all around." Two days later, Stimson obtained Roosevelt's approval.[23]

Meanwhile, Somervell on July 22 took the plan to Woodrum's subcommittee. Armed with figures to demonstrate that the new building would save the War Department in rentals, relieve congestion in Washington, increase War Department efficiency, and make business between the public and the government more convenient, Somervell easily sold it to Woodrum and his colleagues. The next day, Wednesday, July 23, Somervell persuaded the House Committee on Public Buildings and Grounds to approve the project, and on July 24, the Appropriations Committee recommended that $35 million be appropriated for the project. On July 25, the full House gave its approval. By this time, Somervell had already chosen John McShain, Inc., of Philadelphia, Pennsylvania, which had built the Jefferson Memorial and National Airport, along with two Virginia firms, to erect the building. The contract, completed in August, set the cost at $29,551,400.[24]

In the interim, opposition to Somervell's plan emerged. During a House debate on July 24, some members questioned the scope and cost of the project, and July 25 editions of the Washington papers played up the War Department's "$35 million cubbyhole." By the next week, the clamor of protest was deafening. Many said that the project would cost twice the amount Somervell estimated, consume labor and materials already in short supply, increase existing traffic congestion over the Washington bridges, and be a white elephant after the war was over. Especially prominent among the protestors were two of Somervell's nemeses from the Potomac power controversy—Gilmore D. Clarke, chairman of the Commission on Fine Arts, and Frederic A. Delano, chairman of the National Capital Park and Planning Commission and an uncle of President Roosevelt.

Writing to the Senate Appropriations Committee, Clarke strongly objected to the location of the building, pointing out that it would encroach upon land that had been officially set aside for the future use of the National Cemetery and result "in the introduction of thirty-five acres of ugly, flat roofs into the very foreground of the most majestic view of the national capital." Mincing no words, he accused Somervell of creating what would turn out to be "a blot upon the landscape which can probably never be erased and which will be regretted for decades after this emergency is past history in the minds of future Americans." Delano also argued against the project and proposed that Somervell's building be located elsewhere and scaled down to accommodate only 20,000 people. With Budget Director Smith, an opponent of the building on grounds of cost, at his side, Delano took his concerns to Roosevelt on July 30 and persuaded him that the building should be reduced by half. They were unable, however, to persuade the president to change the location.[25]

Somervell was still convinced that the Arlington farm site was the most convenient for the building, and he would not budge, even when other locations were suggested. These alternatives included many in the District and the area earmarked for the Quartermaster depot, which was about three-quarters of a mile southeast of the Arlington farm. So, determined to have his own way, Somervell staunchly held out for the Arlington farm site. Appearing before a subcommittee of the Senate Appropriations Committee on August 8, he argued that a change of location would significantly add to the cost by delaying the start of construction and opined that there was nothing inappropriate in having Arlington National Cemetery overlook the home of the War Department. Following the hearing, Somervell had both Patterson and Bergstrom reinforce his arguments with written presentations to the committee.

Somervell was successful, sweeping "all before him" in the words of Secretary of the Interior Harold Ickes. After visiting both the Arlington farm and depot sites, the Senate subcommittee approved Somervell's choice, as did the Senate on August 14. Only the president's signature on the bill was needed for him to break ground. Anticipating no hitch with this formality, Somervell met with his staff on August 19 to review the plans. Waving a tentative directive in his hand, he announced he wanted 500,000 square feet of floor space available by March 1, 1942, and the entire building finished by September 1, 1942.[26]

Somervell's plans were quickly upset. While the Senate was considering Somervell's proposal, Roosevelt absented himself from the capital to confer with British Prime Minister Winston Churchill in a meeting off the coast of New Foundland. Upon his return, Clarke visited him to detail the Fine Arts Commission's objections to Somervell's plans, and in a news conference on August 19 the president indicated his opposition to Somervell's location and implied he might veto the defense appropriation bill providing for the building in order to prevent its construction in front of Arlington National Cemetery. The next day Roosevelt met with Somervell and John McCloy from Stimson's office and told them "to go back and restudy the plans and report as soon as possible." Somervell's retort that a change would cost money failed to move Roosevelt. Five days later, on August 25, the president signed the bill providing for Somervell's building, reserving for himself the right to select its location.[27]

On August 26, Roosevelt announced that the new War Department building would be located at the depot site and that he wanted it to be about half the size Somervell had originally contemplated. Three days later, he summoned Clarke, Somervell, and Budget Director Smith to the White House for a tour of the site and a general discussion of his thinking about the building. With Somervell, Clarke, and Roosevelt in the back seat of the car and Smith and Roosevelt's dog Fala in the front seat, they headed across the Potomac to inspect the site. As they rode in the car, Somervell aggressively restated his case for the Arlington farm site. Clarke recalled that

> as we drove on the General became more and more insistent that the Pentagon be located next to the driveway from the Arlington Memorial Bridge to the Arlington Cemetery. I could see that the President was getting increasingly annoyed by General Somervell's insistence about this, and when we got on the 14th St. bridge, the President leaned in front of me and said, "My dear General. I'm still the Commander-in-Chief of the Army!"

Realizing he had gone too far, Somervell "desisted and didn't pursue his argument any further." As they approached the depot site, Roosevelt had the car stop and, pointing, said "we're going to put the building over there, aren't we?" To emphasize that the matter was now closed, he said to Somervell, "Did you hear that, General? We're going to locate the War Department building over there."

Somervell agreed, but he was not ready to concede everything to Clarke. As they rode back to Washington, Roosevelt said to Somervell, "General, you're going to show the plans for this proposed building to the Commission on Fine Arts, are you not?" Somervell demurred, saying that, since the building was in Virginia rather than the District and hence outside the commission's jurisdiction, he had no intention of showing any plans to it. Infuriated by Somervell's petulance, Roosevelt sternly told him, "Well, General, you show the plans to the Commission on Fine Arts and, when they're approved by them, show them to me." Not wanting to alienate Roosevelt, Somervell agreed to this order.[28]

Certain Roosevelt would soon lose interest in the details of the project, Somervell decided to ignore the president's thoughts about the building. In the words of the army historians of the construction program, "pulling down a curtain of secrecy over the project, Somervell followed an independent course," making plans for a building about four-fifths of the size of the original planned for the Arlington farm site. Retaining its pentagonal shape despite the shift—the plans called for a four-story edifice of five concentric five-sided rings with radiating corridors. Altogether, there would be four million feet of floor space set in a 320-acre landscaped park. A six-acre inner court, ramps and escalators, a large shopping concourse on the first floor, a cab stand and bus lanes in the basement, parking lots for 8,000 cars, and an elaborate network of roads were some of the Pentagon's prominent features.

On October 10, Somervell and Lieutenant Colonel Clarence Renshaw, who was in charge of the actual construction, went to the White House to tell Roosevelt about what they had done. Walking "in as if he owned the place," Somervell presented Roosevelt with an accomplished fact. More than 1,000 men had been at work for nearly a month, part of the foundation had been poured, and forms for a section of the first story were ready. Roosevelt was taken back by Somervell's aggressiveness, but after Somervell predicted he could complete the building in fourteen months for a cost of about $33 million, the president fell into line.[29]

As construction proceeded, Somervell turned the details over to Renshaw and Bergstrom. By the end of May 1942, with more than 13,000 men working around the clock, one million square feet were ready for occupancy, and by early 1943, the Pentagon was complete—an imposing and handsome building capable of accommodating 40,000 workers and already too small to handle the mushrooming armed services bureaucracy.

However, with Somervell's emphasis on speed as well as the decision to add a fifth floor, costs quickly escalated to $63 million, which led to a rash of accusations of extravagance and bad management. To the critics, the Pentagon was "Somervell's Folly," for they could see little use for it after the war ended and the army shrank, in traditional manner, to "a small obsolescent force." Even Roosevelt had no idea what would eventually become of the building, and he half jokingly told the press that the army could use it as a warehouse to store the records that showed what it did during the war.[30] But, viewed from the perspective of the massive postwar military establishment that emerged with the Cold War, to many, the Pentagon became a wise investment and Somervell a man of vision.

• • •

When Somervell became chief of the Construction Division, responsibility for military construction was divided between his division, part of the Quartermaster Corps, and the Engineers, which had been assigned air corps construction to lessen the burden on Hartman's badly strained organization. Brought about by pressing circumstances, this arrangement, in the words of Patterson, was "neither logical nor . . . wholly satisfactory in practice." Contractors complained about having to deal with two different agencies, two sets of regulations, and two systems of bookkeeping, and many Quartermaster officers, who correctly believed that the Engineers coveted control of all military construction, only reluctantly cooperated with the other corps.

In the late spring and early summer of 1941, Michael Madigan looked into the problem. Already convinced that the Quartermaster Corps could not withstand the increased pressures that war would bring, he had all but made up his mind that construction should be transferred to the Engineers or placed in a separate corps. During his investigation Madigan conferred with many interested parties, although he did not consult anyone in the Quartermaster Corps except Somervell. He justified this approach on the belief that Somervell had already pushed Quartermaster General Gregory into the background in the construction program and that consulting anyone else would only spur Quartermaster opposition to his plans. Since Somervell was not a Quartermaster officer and had no loyalty to the corps, Madigan was confident he would be a valuable ally and asked him for his assistance.

Most receptive to Madigan's request, Somervell lent him several officers to help in his study and offered a steady stream of advice. However, Somervell did not inform Gregory of his own involvement in Madigan's investigation, causing some War Department insiders later to accuse him of disloyalty and looking to further his own ends at the expense of the Quartermaster Corps.[31]

Somervell's critics were essentially correct. Although one might explain his involvement with Madigan and failure to inform Gregory of it on the grounds that Marshall and Stimson had intended him to handle construction as he saw fit, Somervell let his ambition get the better of him. He aspired to succeed Schley as chief of engineers when the latter retired in October 1941, and going "all out to get" the post, he had good friend John Lee, himself a possible candidate for the post, speak to Stimson on his behalf. He also asked Madigan to get the post for him, quite possibly expecting that Madigan would use whatever influence he had because of the assistance with Madigan's investigation. Somervell was never one to forget a debt, and he was certain that neither did Madigan, a veteran of the rough-and-tough New York City political wars. As Somervell saw it, if the Construction Division were transferred to the Engineers, Madigan could make the argument that its current chief was the logical choice to head the combined construction organization as chief of engineers.

In August 1941, it appeared Somervell's hopes might be realized when Madigan recommended to Patterson that all military construction activities should be consolidated in the Engineers. Relying heavily on arguments and data provided by Somervell, he stated that the Engineers had a stronger organization and more expertise in construction than the Quartermaster Corps and, thus, was better able to handle all military construction. Marshall, Patterson, Stimson, and Roosevelt all agreed with Madigan's finding. In September, Congress took up a bill effecting the transfer of the Construction Division to the Engineers, and on December 1, 1941, it became law.

Contrary to his hopes, Somervell was not really in the running for the post of chief of engineers. Stimson declined to intervene, and Somervell overestimated Madigan's influence. More importantly, Somervell was too young to be chief. True, at the temporary rank of brigadier general, he stood fourteenth on the list of engineer officers, but, at the permanent rank of lieutenant colonel, he stood fifty-eighth. If that were not enough, he had not held an assignment with the Engineers since 1935, and his purloining of engineers for the Construction Division had irked many of the corps' top officers. Reflecting this attitude, Schley wrote the following comment on Somervell's efficiency rating in the summer of 1941: "Officially, the whereabouts of this man is unknown to me."

Deputy Chief of Staff Moore thought Eugene Reybold was "great" and lobbied hard for him with the three-man board charged with making the selection. Outside of Lee, no other candidate was seriously considered, and in August, Reybold received the coveted appointment. Somervell was "as mad as hell" when he was not named chief, and for the next month and a half, he hounded Madigan to get him a second star (rank of major general). But Madigan could do nothing, leaving Somervell "thoroughly discouraged."[32]

Once it was apparent he would not be named chief of engineers, Somervell became quite worried about his future since the consolidation would effectively eliminate his position as chief constructing quartermaster. As a result, he proposed that all military and civilian construction be placed in the hands of a deputy chief of engineers with the rank of major general, laying the foundation, he hoped, for his own appointment to that job.[33] But, as the weeks passed, it became obvious that there would be no place for Somervell in the new construction organization. Reybold decided that responsibility for construction would be vested in the head of the Corps of Engineers Construction Division, eliminating the need for a deputy chief along the lines Somervell envisioned. He also decided that Brigadier General Thomas M. Robins, an engineer with thirty-six years of experience who was highly respected by other engineers and had been highly praised for his direction of the air corps construction program, should be the division's head.

Even if Robins had not been available, Reybold would not have given the construction job to Somervell. He respected Somervell's accomplishments as chief of construction, labeling them as excellent. However, he also saw him as "quite a hustler," a "steamroller" who "didn't care who he hit" as he went about his job and furthering his career. With the example of Gregory before him, a man Somervell had treated with disdain, Reybold wanted nothing to do with Somervell in the construction program.[34]

Learning of Reybold's feelings through discussions with Moore, Marshall looked for another spot for Somervell in the War Department. At Patterson's suggestion, he decided his talents could best be utilized in the post of War Department G-4, which had not been permanently filled since Reybold's departure to become chief of engineers. Soon after, on November 25, Somervell left the Construction Division to assume his new post.

• • •

Somervell's sojourn at the Construction Division was a year of considerable accomplishment. Taking over the division at a time when the building of camps and munitions plants for the army had bogged down and fallen behind schedule, he expedited the lagging program with a typical Somervell sprint. The division's organization was streamlined, and construction of camps and munitions plants was accelerated, saving the army from anything worse that "a Dutch-uncle scolding" from Congress. Somervell, however, had his critics, mostly officers who disliked him personally or resented their treatment at his hands. While granting that he had demonstrated tremendous ability and was a great organizer, they contended that Somervell, always with an eye on his own career advancement, had been too ready to concentrate power in his own hands, run down opponents, crawl "up over the bodies of some very fine officers," disregard superiors, and seize credit for himself. However, these criticisms meant little, for Stimson, Patterson, and Marshall lauded him for speedily bringing the construction program "up to date and into order." In their view, Somervell's work as head of the Construction Division was "one of the outstanding jobs of the prewar defense era."[35]

4. ORGANIZING FOR WAR

• • • • AS WAR DEPARTMENT G-4, SOMERVELL WAS responsible for the preparation of basic supply plans and, along with the office of Under Secretary of War Patterson, the supervision of the supply services. It was not an assignment he had sought or one he wanted. If anything, he considered it a career reversal since it did not offer the high visibility and opportunities for accomplishments around which careers are made. Reflecting her husband's disappointment, Anna Somervell complained that "we are right back where we started from."[1]

That was hardly true, for the post was a vital cog in the military buildup, but as G-4, Somervell could easily be passed over when choice assignments became available, especially if Chief of Staff Marshall decided he could not be spared. In addition, Somervell did not relish the prospect of sharing authority and responsibility with the under secretary's office. It went against his managerial style and personality, and he doubted that he could be successful under this condition. Disappointed though he may have been about his new assignment, Somervell had little time to sulk. Two weeks after he became G-4, the Japanese attack on Pearl Harbor propelled the United States into World War II and his office into a vast surge of activity organizing the army supply effort.

• • •

During the first months of the war, Somervell plunged into the work required to develop the programs for mobilizing the munitions and shipping that would be necessary for ultimate victory. In 1941, the War Department had laid out the general contours of a mobilization program if the United States entered the war. Known as the Victory Program, it contemplated an army that, by June 1944, would number 8,759,658 troops and some 215 divisions. Of this total, 3.6 million were to be under arms, with 71 divisions organized, by the end of 1942. At the time of Pearl Harbor, the army had approximately 1.6 million men and 37 active divisions.

Several days after the attack, civilian production experts from the Supply Priorities and Allocation Board asked the War Department to translate the Victory Program into a complete statement of requirements so that it could plan for the army's share of the nation's total production. The board wanted the rates of monthly production of specific items considered essential for achieving the Victory Program, and it wanted these rates up to June 1942, December 1942, and September 1943. At a conference on December 14, Somervell, Moore, John McCloy from Stimson's office, and several others worked out a procedure for meeting this request. Two days later, the War Department advised the board that, by March 1942, it would attempt to provide an overall statement of its munitions requirements as of December 31, 1942, and December 31, 1943.

On December 27, 1941, the War Plans Division (WPD) of the General Staff laid down a revised troop estimate for the Victory Program, setting goals for long-range supply planning at 4,150,000 men to be mobilized by the end of 1942 and 10,380,000 by June 30, 1944. Shortly afterward, Somervell ordered the army supply bureaus to recompute their total requirements for equipment and munitions on the basis of these new troop estimates.

However, they had no sooner started their computations than Roosevelt came forth with his own "must" production program. Spurred by British officials to think big about the munitions needed to win the war and the vast potential of American industry to supply both American and allied needs, he announced on January 6, 1942, production goals that went far beyond the current ones. The numbers in Roosevelt's "must" program were staggering—from 28,600 planes in 1942 to 60,000 in 1942 and 125,000 in 1943; from 20,400 tanks in 1942 to 45,000 in 1942 and 75,000 in 1943; from 6,300 antiaircraft guns in 1942 to 20,000 in 1942 and 35,000 in 1943. He also called for six million deadweight tons of merchant shipping in 1942 and ten million in 1943. When asked about the industrial practicality of his figures, Roosevelt reportedly quipped: "Oh—the production people can do it if they really try."[2]

Three days before Roosevelt's announcement, Marshall gave Somervell the task of determining whether the "must" goals could be achieved within the context of a balanced military program that took into account all ancillary requirements that sprang from them. After all, the production of 185,000 planes over the next two years without adequate landing fields, hangars, operating supplies, maintenance facilities, and trained personnel at all levels served no military purpose and might even be a liability to the war effort. Comparing Roosevelt's goals with the quantities of corresponding items already incorporated in the army's developing procurement plans, Somervell optimistically advised Marshall on January 7 that "the accomplishment of the President's directive for 1942 can be accomplished by the production of a balanced equipment program." He was equally optimistic about 1943.[3]

Using Roosevelt's major-item goals as a starting point, army planners drew up a detailed procurement program known as the War Munitions Program. Dated February 11, 1942, it brought the estimated total of all war needs to $62.6 billion for 1942 and $110 billion for 1943.

Initially, civilian production experts were optimistic about the prospect of meeting Roosevelt's "must" goals. But once the Planning Committee of the War Production Board (WPB) looked closely at the War Munitions Program their views changed. Measuring the program against their estimate of the nation's economic capacity, the committee determined that the total war procurement objectives, when added to the needs of the civilian and industrial economies, could not be filled in a reasonable time. To go ahead with the war objectives that had been prescribed, the committee opined, would be wasteful and delay the delivery of many essential war goods. The planes and tanks that Roosevelt wanted could likely be built but not in conjunction with the multitude of ancillary items that needed to be procured on a similar scale. The result would be a piling up of partially finished goods. Convinced of the correctness of the committee's conclusions, Chairman Donald Nelson of the WPB informed Somervell on March 4 that Roosevelt's goals for 1942 should be adjusted "with a view to securing a better balance in the program as a whole."[4]

Somervell was not ready to write off Roosevelt's goals, for he had not gotten where he was by coming up with reasons why things could not be done. Unwilling to accept the Planning Committee's findings as final, he asked his staff on March 8 to reexamine the likelihood of filling Roosevelt's "must" program. He expected his staff's examination would reinforce his original judgment, for as he stated, "We cannot afford to state these goals can not be achieved, or to take any such attitude towards the instructions of the Commander in Chief." Several days later, however, his staff gave him bad news: Roosevelt's goals would not yield a balanced fighting force. The president's goal of 45,000 tanks in 1942 was 50 percent more than the army required, whereas his target for antitank guns amounted to only 30 percent of the army's expected need.

While shaken by his staff's report, Somervell still was not convinced Roosevelt's goals should be abandoned, but two weeks of further study, along with supporting reports from the ANMB and the joint U.S.-British tank committee, caused him to change his mind. At the end of March, therefore, he told Marshall,

Stimson, and Patterson that the goals had to be modified.

In conjunction with Nelson and Harry Hopkins, Marshall persuaded Roosevelt in April to alter his goals in line with a more balanced program. For example, Roosevelt authorized that his "must" goal of 45,000 tanks in 1942 be changed to 46,523 tracked vehicles (tanks, armored cars, and self-propelled artillery), of which only 24,700 were to be tanks.

However, Roosevelt was not ready to reject completely his earlier approach. In a directive to the Joint Chiefs of Staff (JCS) on May 4, he stated that a balanced program was not to be attained at the expense of his overall goals and that "maximum production of major items of military equipment must be obtained without delay." While Roosevelt's action gave the army a greater opportunity to procure for a strong offensive force with adequate amounts of various categories of arms and munitions, it left unresolved the whole matter of the war program's impact upon the economy and the war effort.[5]

Whatever the size and composition of the munitions program, the success of the American war effort ultimately depended upon the ability to deploy and support forces overseas. Through the expansion of troop-carrying capacity, both accomplished and projected, the army was putting together, in conjunction with the British, a lift of 500,000 men by May 1942.

However, cargo shipping was in limited supply, and determined to see that freighters would be available, Somervell in mid-January 1942 pushed the United States Maritime Commission, the agency responsible for the construction and management of the merchant marine, for a definite allocation of shipping to the army to support a substantial overseas deployment. At the time, the army had about 110 freighters under its control through such forms as ownership, charter, or allocation from the commission, and Somervell told Rear Admiral Emory S. Land of the Maritime Commission that this number of ships could not support enough troops overseas "to meet the military situation."[6]

Initially, Somervell eyed some of the 180 American ships used in the lend-lease program to make up the army shortage. Writing to Marshall in December 1941, he had warned that the Victory Program was incompatible with the Arsenal of Democracy theory, which held that the American effort would essentially be industrial while the allies provided the fighting forces. Shipping, he postulated, "might in time permit the fulfillment of one program, or parts of both, but not both." Later, he told Marshall that, if lend-lease were sharply curtained, especially to the Soviet Union, there might be enough available shipping to build up overseas forces to 1 million men by the end of 1942, depending upon whether or not the main effort came in the Far East or in the Atlantic. However, this curtailment was out of the question because Roosevelt was committed to expanding rather than contracting lend-lease.[7]

Given Roosevelt's priorities, Somervell was left with two options—ruthless economy in nonessential uses and further increases in the ship construction program. He quickly acted on both. In January and February 1942, he strongly urged the elimination of several commercial services and the reduction of others.

These, however, were stopgap measures. Only an enlarged construction program offered a meaningful solution to what was obviously an ever-growing shipping problem. The army expected to have several million troops ready for overseas service at the end of 1943. Yet, even with present building programs, there would be enough shipping to support only one million men. While further increases in 1942 were probably not possible, Somervell believed it was entirely possible for the present program to be expanded by 50 percent to fifteen million tons in 1943, enabling the army to raise overseas deployment to 2.26 million men. On this basis, he advised Marshall to tell Roosevelt that "an all-out effort in this field [ship construction] must precede an all-out military effort."[8]

Whether because of Somervell's proposal, which Marshall sent to the White House on February 18, or the views of others, Roosevelt on February 19 summoned Land to the White House and instructed him to build nine million tons of shipping in 1942 and fifteen million in 1943. Later that spring, the rising demands for steel caused Roosevelt to reduce the 1942 goal to eight million tons, although the total for 1942 and 1943 remained at twenty-four million tons.[9]

In the interim, steps were implemented to lessen the shipping problem by pooling shipping and bringing it under centralized control. Along this line, Somervell in December 1941 had proposed the creation of a Central Shipping Administration, headed by the chairman of the Maritime Commission and under the general supervision of a board consisting of himself, his navy counterpart, and a representative of the OPM. All American transoceanic merchant ships, except those already operated by the army and the navy, would be pooled under the direction of this new agency which would be guided by "the joint decisions of the Secretary of War and the Secretary of the Navy."[10]

During January 1942, Somervell's proposal served as the basis for discussion for a new shipping arrangement. The army and the navy soon agreed on a plan confirming Somervell's contention that shipping allocations should be in accordance with the joint decisions of the army and the navy. But Land opposed the plan because it would detract from his authority as head of the Maritime Commission. Hopkins also objected on the basis that lend-lease might not receive sufficient attention.

After considering these views, Roosevelt on February 7, 1942, created the War Shipping Administration (WSA). Modeled after the British Ministry of War Transport, it was headed by Land in the dual capacity of chairman of the Maritime Commission and war-shipping administrator. Land was responsible directly to the president with full authority to "control the operation, purchase, charter, requisition, and use of all ocean vessels" except those in the army and navy transport fleets, which were exempted at Somervell's insistence.

Somervell was far from pleased with the sweeping powers granted to Land. All along he had favored an arrangement that endowed "some agency . . . with absolute power over the allocation of shipping" but always one in which the armed services had the major voice. Roosevelt's action, however, placed control of shipping in the hands of someone responsible only to the president. In this case Somervell was certain military requirements would suffer.[11]

• • •

At the same time he was helping to develop the munitions and shipping programs, Somervell was involved in the reorganization of the army supply effort. Dissatisfied by the relationship between G-4 and the under secretary's office, he looked for ways to simplify the War Department supply organization, preferably by consolidating everything involving supply under a single command.

Somervell began on January 6, 1942, by asking Goldthwaite Dorr to study the War Department supply organization. A friend of Somervell since their work together on the Turkish economic survey, Dorr had served as assistant director of munitions during World War I and was well versed in the army's procurement organization and operations. Readily agreeing to Somervell's request, Dorr immediately brought together an informal committee, consisting mostly of civilians, to make the study. From his staff Somervell lent Dorr Clinton Robinson while Colonel Henry S. Aurand, defense aid director in the War Department and a vocal advocate of a unified supply system since 1940, served as a consultant.

Meeting on a hush-hush basis, Dorr's committee explored all dimensions of the supply problem. It concluded that the War Department supply organization could be made more effective by recreating the structure that had existed at the end of World War I. According to this scheme, all G-4 functions and the procurement functions of Patterson's office would be placed under one man in the General Staff, "who would report to the Under-Secretary on the business end of his job and to the Chief of Staff on the military."[12]

As the Dorr committee was making its study, Brigadier General Joseph. T. McNarney of the WPD was completing the plan for a radical reorganization of the War Department undertaken in secret on Marshall's order. Designed to centralize executive control in Marshall's office and decentralize operating responsibilities, McNarney's plan made the chief of staff a manager, similar to the top manager of a major corporation, thus giving him the time to devote to the larger issues of planning strategy, allocating resources, and directing global military operations. Instead of the numerous commands and agencies that presently had access to the chief of staff, three commands—one each for ground forces, air forces, and supply and services—would be substituted.

Somervell learned of Marshall's intention to reorganize the War Department when the chief of staff met with the chiefs of the General Staff divisions; the deputy chiefs of staff; representatives of the General Headquarters, which was running the army training program; and the Army Air Forces (AAF) to explain McNarney's plan to them. Marshall gave those present forty-eight hours to file comments and appointed an executive committee with McNarney as chairman to put the plan into effect.

Somervell promptly swung into action to have his input in the final plan. With McNarney's consent, he put together a proposal for a unified supply and services organization. All the supply bureaus were to be under its wing, as well as the other War Department bureaus, such as the Office of the Adjutant General and the Office of the Judge Advocate General, that did not logically fit into the other two commands that McNarney contemplated. Heading the organization would be an officer who in matters of procurement would be under the direction of the under secretary of war and, in military matters, the chief of staff.

In the second week of February, McNarney approved Somervell's proposal for the unified supply and services command to be part of the reorganized War Department. It was then presented to Patterson, who expressed concern that the interposition of a new command between himself and the supply bureaus would weaken the authority granted him by the National Defense Act of 1920. However, knowing Marshall wanted to have the reorganization wrapped up quickly, Patterson decided to go along with Somervell's proposal. By this time, Roosevelt and Stimson had endorsed the reorganization, and on February 28, under the authority of the War Powers Act of December 18, 1941, it was officially announced in Executive Order 9082. Two days later, a War Department circular detailed the operational plan for the new supply and services command, called the Services of Supply (SOS), even though it dealt with much more than supply.[13] In March 1943, the SOS was renamed the Army Service Forces (ASF) in fuller recognition of its functions. (For purposes of clarity ASF will be used in the narrative from this point onward.)

As G-4, Somervell was the logical choice to head the ASF, although at the time he started working on the projected organization, there was no hint from Marshall that he had Somervell in mind for the post. But, whatever Marshall's original thinking, Somervell certainly wanted the job. His limited service with troops in World War I and his essentially nonmilitary career in the interwar period effectively ruled him out of any significant field command. Therefore, if his role were to be a major one in the American war effort, it would have to be with logistics, and no assignment in this arena would be more important than head of the supply and services command.

Telling McNarney and others that he wanted to be chief of the ASF, Somervell threw himself into the planning for the new command and convinced Marshall and Stimson he was the man for the job. By February 18, they had made their wishes known to Somervell, and in the final stages of preparing for the new organization, Somervell knew he was shaping one that he would head.¹⁴

The executive order implementing Marshall's reorganization of the War Department took effect on March 9, 1942 (see Chart A). Directly beneath Marshall on the revised War Department organizational chart were three officers who gained new prominence: Lesley J. McNair, head of the Army Ground Forces (AGF), Henry Arnold of the Army Air Forces (AAF), and Somervell. With the exception of overseas commands and theaters, every unit and activity of the United States Army was now controlled by one of these men.

Also, on March 9, Somervell, who little more than a month before had been promoted to the temporary rank of major general, was elevated along with McNair and Arnold to the temporary rank of lieutenant general. For an officer several months short of his fiftieth birthday and with the permanent rank of lieutenant colonel, Somervell's new assignment and promotion were "eye catching," even when viewed against the rash of new assignments and promotions that accompanied the high-geared military buildup now underway.

• • •

As commanding general of the ASF, Somervell was in a somewhat peculiar position. He had not one but two masters: the under secretary of war and the chief of staff. This arrangement was fraught with potential trouble, for it violated the basic army doctrine of unity of command and presented Somervell with the temptation to play one master against the other. Despite the potential pitfalls, the arrangement proved workable, largely because of the satisfactory working relationships that developed between Somervell and both Patterson and Marshall.

A circuit court of appeals judge before coming to the War Department, "Judge" Patterson had served as an army officer in World War I and reportedly wore around his waist, as a reminder of those exciting days, the belt of a German soldier he had killed. Energetic, single-minded, and at times, stubborn, he approached his job "in the spirit of a man who knew what the Army had to have and what he had to do to get it."¹⁵ The emergence of Somervell, in many ways, threatened Patterson's position in the War Department, for much of the supervisory apparatus which previously enabled him to fulfill his responsibilities was now under Somervell's aegis. But, if Patterson lost an organization, he gained a manager of great ability and drive.

At first, relations between Patterson and Somervell were "somewhat trying." Lacking any sense of organization, Patterson preferred to get right in touch with the "guy who was handling a particular thing and . . . find out what he was doing about it." Although appreciating the need for flexibility in any operation, Somervell was a stickler for clearly defined procedures, and Patterson's "unorganization-mindedness" irritated him. Gradually, the two men arrived at a mutually agreeable arrangement in which Patterson could consult directly with the ASF staff divisions dealing with matters of greatest interest to him—requirements, procurement, and contract termination.[16]

As time passed, Patterson came to depend heavily upon Somervell. The general brought to the War Department an energy and a willingness to make decisions that were vital to procurement and the supply support of the army, qualities Patterson admired. Hence, he stood by Somervell, and those who tried to go around Somervell quickly learned that a direct appeal to Patterson in the event of a disagreement with Somervell availed them little. Recalling a conversation he had with Patterson over the unwavering support the under secretary gave to a controversial Somervell project, one War Department insider had the following to say:

> finally he [Patterson] said, "You remember the kind of people we found when we first came down? They were timid. Many of them were quite stupid. They were afraid of Congress, of being criticized, and afraid of making a mistake, and they were kind of do-nothings. Somervell is a brilliant, able, aggressive, forceful fellow. He's got guts." And he said, "I'm not going to see him smeared. Part of my job, as the civilian head of the department, is to protect our military leaders from this kind of attack."[17]

Generally, Patterson "was agreeable to allowing Somervell to run the show." But, if something developed that particularly interested him, Patterson did not hesitate to assert himself. As one of Patterson's aides recalled, "Patterson wasn't very reticent or holding back on the thing. He'd say anything he wanted to do. He was clearly in command of Somervell . . . when he'd want the thing done." Somervell, meanwhile, never tried to run over or ignore Patterson because he appreciated that an under secretary who was sympathetic to army needs was an asset in procurement operations. From the beginning, he invited Patterson to his twice-monthly staff conferences so that Patterson could keep abreast of what was happening and express his opinions on purchasing and production matters. And, in those areas of particular interest to Patterson, Somervell "was only too glad" to defer to his judgment.[18]

While the Somervell-Patterson relationship was important to the operation of the ASF, Somervell's relationship with Marshall was of prime importance. Somervell never doubted he owed his appointment to Marshall and that whoever headed the new supply creation was "General Marshall's man." In his mind, it was Marshall he had to satisfy with his performance at the ASF, or else he would be removed.[19]

Although he saw the chief of staff almost daily and lived in the quarters next to his at Fort Meyer, Virginia, Somervell's contact with Marshall was "direct but formal." Nevertheless, like Patterson, Marshall came to depend heavily upon Somervell. He wanted only one man reporting to him on supply matters, and he expected that man to make and execute decisions without bothering him. When Somervell emerged as the "uncompromising, ruthless expediter" he "needed for a nasty job," Marshall gave him virtually a free hand and unswerving support. On several occasions, Somervell's enemies attempted to have Marshall transfer him. However, Marshall never considered removing Somervell. To those who thought Somervell should be replaced by an officer "with a little less dynamic or less objectionable characteristics," Marshall remarked that "he had spent his whole life fighting under [these types of] generals, and that when he had a self-starter he wasn't going to change him."[20]

•••

Somervell's appointment as commanding general of the ASF provided him with a platform from which he could emerge as a key figure in the American war effort. He was now charged with control of supply and administration for the entire army in the United States and with control of supply to the overseas theaters.

Before Somervell could accomplish his assignment, however, he had to bring together the various elements of the ASF, a sprawling command that embraced three broad echelons of War Department offices and agencies (see Chart B). At the top was Somervell's headquarters, which included a wide array of agencies and personnel from G-4 and Patterson's office, as well as an ill-sorted collection of administrative and miscellaneous agencies that were assigned to Somervell for want of any other suitable place for them. The second echelon consisted of the supply arms and services—Ordnance, Engineers, Quartermaster, Transportation, Signal, Medical, Chemical Warfare—that were responsible for supplying and equipping the army and the administrative services. The final echelon consisted of eight corps areas plus the Military District of Washington, each responsible for a variety of administrative and housekeeping functions within a geographical area.

Somervell initially concentrated on his headquarters organization. Hurriedly, he linked the mobilization and production functions of Patterson's office with the requirements and distribution functions of G-4 into one operating agency and created staff divisions to supervise the supply and administrative services with the corps areas. In staffing his headquarters, Somervell filled many of the key posts with men who were already part of his circle, or at least, known to him. Wilhelm Styer, his deputy in the Construction Division, assumed the same post in the ASF, holding it until April 1945. Clinton Robinson became head of the Control Division, and Colonel Charles Gross, Somervell's good friend since their days as classmates at West Point, became head of the Transportation Division and later the Transportation Corps, which Somervell created out of the Quartermaster Corps in the summer of 1942.

Lucius Clay, an officer who possessed considerable political and administrative skills, was made assistant chief of staff for materiel in charge of supervising procurement. Somervell and Clay had crossed paths in 1934–35 when both were serving in the Office of the Chief of Engineers. Although the two had not established a close personal relationship, Somervell grew to appreciate Clay's abilities. Because he had great confidence in Clay, Somervell gave him "a very, very free hand." He might buzz Clay on the telephone as many as twenty times a day to check on some matter or another, but only rarely did he interfere with what the other was doing. When Somervell did, it was to give Clay the "needle."[21]

Colonel LeRoy Lutes, a coast artilleryman, was made assistant chief of staff for operations in charge of supervising overseas supply. Somervell had never met Lutes before the war and first learned of him from Aurand shortly after becoming G-4. Aurand had been in Louisiana in November 1941 for the army maneuvers and spent some time with Lutes, G-4 for the Third Army. Lutes came out of the maneuver with "quite a big reputation" in logistics, and when Aurand got back to Washington, he told Somervell about Lutes's book perfect setup.

Looking for someone with practical experience as G-4 of an army, Somervell, through Deputy Chief of Staff Moore, arranged in early January 1942 to have Lutes temporarily transferred to his office, where he looked over Somervell's plans. Impressed with Lutes's work, Somervell soon summoned him back to Washington on a permanent basis. When he arrived, Somervell tartly cracked, "Well—you finally got here," and told him to prepare a general plan under which all supply distribution operations from the United States to overseas areas could be supervised. Somervell's specific instructions were simple, "I hold you responsible for seeing that supplies and equipment reach the troops in the field throughout the world. Get things done—you will make mistakes—but get them done. I will not kick if 54% of the time you are right."

Two years older than Somervell, Lutes was instinctively drawn to him. In Lutes's words, "I knew I could work for him. He was the type I liked and respected—smart, dynamic, and practical." Somervell, in turn, was drawn to Lutes. Extremely dedicated, straightforward, hardworking, and willing to make decisions, Lutes was the type of officer he liked to have on his team. Next to Styer, Lutes was Somervell's most important advisor, and Somervell kept him until the end of the war despite several requests for his transfer to Europe.[22]

Unlike his first months with the Construction Division, Somervell did not launch a blitzkrieg of removals in his new command. It was not for want of trying, however, particularly in regard to the corps area commanders. Within days after becoming ASF commander, he urged Marshall to replace five of them with young men, who, he suggested, "will be on their way up, and should in general induce vigor and energy into the system." Marshall made some of the changes Somervell suggested, but it would be nearly two years before the majority of these area commanders were Somervell's selections.[23]

In the case of the supply bureau chiefs, Somervell had little freedom of action. Appointed by the president for specific terms, they often had close ties with key figures on Capitol Hill. Any move against one of them without the complete backing of Marshall and Stimson would arouse a storm of protest. Nevertheless, Somervell did what he could to have men in these posts to his liking.

Somervell's most significant personnel victory in his early months on the job occurred in May 1942 when he torpedoed Roosevelt's choice for chief of ordnance and engineered the appointment of a successor he desired. The previous month, the Senate had approved Roosevelt's selection of Major General James H. Burns to replaced the outgoing Major General Charles Wesson. Burns had an outstanding record as an ordnance officer and had been heavily involved with lend-lease, working closely with Harry Hopkins, but Somervell did not want him in the post, partly from his belief that Burns was "not a river burner" and partly from personal dislike. He also believed Burns, with his ties to Hopkins, would be prone to go over his head to the White House in the case of a dispute and, thus, would be difficult to handle.

Determined to be rid of Burns, Somervell devised an ingenious scheme to have the appointee remove himself from the post. He presented Burns with a list of ten Ordnance officers he wanted demoted on grounds of inefficiency. As Somervell expected, Burns balked, telling him he would run the Ordnance Department his way. Somervell retorted that it would be done his way or else. "What can you do about it," he snapped, "you've already been approved by the Senate." Some of Burns's friends told him to take the job and "do what he could to keep the country from going Nazi or Sommerville [sic]." However, Burns did not welcome fighting Somervell, for he knew that Marshall, Stimson, and Patterson believed that "Somervell must be backed up . . . in the interests of more efficient and speedy management."

Thus, as Somervell intended, Burns withdrew his nomination. Somervell then recommended that Levin Campbell be the new chief of ordnance, a choice his superiors readily accepted. Somervell had often been at odds with Campbell when he was director of construction, but he had great confidence in Campbell, and despite their differences, the two men had worked well together and become good friends.[24]

Once established in his new post, Somervell quickly asserted himself over the supply bureaus, insisting their chiefs report to the under secretary and the General Staff only through him and issuing a flurry of orders to them. Each was told to conform to organizational policies laid down by the Control Division and to submit all proposals for major organizational changes to it for approval.

None of this went down easily with the bureau chiefs. Already convinced that the inclusion of the bureaus in Somervell's supply net meant lowered prestige for them, they resented his claim that they had, in effect, been reduced to the status of Somervell advisors. Also, they feared that the designation of the bureaus as supply services meant their nonsupply functions would be overshadowed by the supply function.

In the case of the Signal Corps, Chief Signal Officer Major General Dawson Olmstead protested that his responsibilities would be restricted by Somervell's obvious intention, as indicated by the word supply, to see the corps primarily as an agency for procuring, distributing, and serving equipment. As soon as Olmstead saw Somervell's organizational chart for the ASF, he went to Moore and said that Somervell's setup was wrong for the Signal Corps and demanded "his day in court." Olmstead's protest availed him little. Somervell's superiors completely supported him, and Moore told Olmstead that "you won't have any day in court. This organization has been decided upon. Those are orders."[25]

Somervell moved more slowly in asserting himself over the corps areas, largely because he had no clear-cut concept of what role they should play. Before acting he had Robinson investigate the corps area situation and draw up "a consolidated and complete statement of the mission, duties, responsibility, and authority of the corps areas and their role in ASF." By early July, Robinson was finished with the assignment, and at the end of July, Somervell met with the commanding generals of the regional commands, now redesignated as service commands, in a conference in Chicago to spell out their new mission statement and the organizational pattern he wanted for each command. Except for functions relating to procurement, new construction, and the operation of depots, holding and reconsignment points, ports, and staging areas, he entrusted the service commands with the performance of the various housekeeping functions of the army in the continental United States. In this way, he freed the AAF, the AGF, and the bureaus to concentrate on their most important chores: training and supplying the army.[26]

Drawing upon his experience as an army engineer, a WPA administrator, and head of the Construction Division, Somervell began the war with a rather complete management philosophy that he implemented in running the ASF. As he explained in 1944:

> Successful management depends on five factors. The first factor is a precise understanding of the job to be done. The second is qualified and capable men in key positions. The third is a workable organization properly adapted to the job to be done. The fourth is a simple, direct system for carrying on the activities involved in the job. The fifth is a positive method of checking on results. Given any three of these five, a business or an agency can probably function with fair success. Four of them operating together will result in much better than average efficiency. However, it requires all five to create the best management obtainable.[27]

The most distinctive feature of Somervell's management philosophy was the pivotal role he assigned to a control division within his own headquarters. When Somervell took over army logistics in March 1942, control, which essentially entailed the systematic measurement of an organization's success and ongoing studies to improve its structure and procedures, was a relatively underdeveloped, if not entirely new, technique of management. Somervell, though, had begun to develop his own concept of control while serving as an engineer, as well as with the WPA and the Construction Division. As he explained to his service commanders in July 1942:

> This idea of handling the thing came to me a number of years ago, and I tried it in an organization where we had a lot of people who weren't too well instructed in executive duties or in handling a big organization, the type of organization where you could not by your own personal contact with the people impress your own ideas on them of how things ought to work. Gradually this idea evolved. We found in discussing it with people on the outside that there were not very many who had this same concept of what a control section is for . . . But there are a few people who have made a study of the conduct of big organizations, who have come to the conclusion that you have to have some kind of organism like this if you are going to put things over, something that is always on the job and always following through.

The business world had already developed some of the control techniques Somervell had in mind, and he readily admitted his debt to the business world for his ideas and reminded his subordinates that they could learn much from industrial managers. Yet, while noting his debt to private business for the theory of control, Somervell appreciated that business had never attempted to operate on such a large scale as the ASF and emphasized that the established techniques of control would have to be modified to the specific problems of an army fighting a global war. Again in his words:

> You can get some help from industry, men who can help you a lot, a good many of them, but you will have to train these people yourself, because what is regarded as a perfectly huge industry, in private industry, may employ eight or ten thousand people. That is a huge industry on the outside, enormous. If you had a concern, and could pay out of your pocket every month eight or ten thousand people, you would think you were quite a fellow, too. So when you get to comparing the problems that you have in private industry with the problems we have, they are on an entirely different scale, and things that are applicable there do not help you too much here. So you will have to train your own control people, but management experience will help. You will have to get your own philosophy worked into your control section, and unless you do that it will not give you the service which it can give you; but if you will get the right kind of an outfit, why, it will be invaluable.[28]

In the spring of 1942, Robinson put together a control division in Somervell's headquarters, mostly made up of former civilian management experts. By the summer, they had refined the concept of control to its basics—the discovery and correction of deficiencies in the organization and procedures and the continuous analysis of progress—and over the next months Robinson shaped his division to reflect these duties.[29]

This most important branch developed statistical methods for Somervell and his staff to utilize in reviewing ASF's operations. The utilization of statistics as a management tool had a checkered history. Large corporations had made extensive use of statistics in planning production and marketing operations, and their uses had been studied widely in universities. But, in public agencies, statistics had been underutilized. Most collected statistics to give the public some idea of their accomplishments and to justify their programs at budget hearings. However, these agencies' use of statistics to direct programs did not meet wartime needs. They emphasized cost and efficiency, and in wartime, these factors usually take second place to the need for speedy or even immediate output.[30]

Somervell's view of statistics was not necessarily new when Robinson's staff began to put it into practice, but it had often been obscured by popular notions of the complexity and meaninglessness of statistics and the tendency of statisticians to become preoccupied with the statistics themselves at the expense of the purpose for which they were to be used. Somervell and Robinson, in contrast, utilized an elaborate system of statistics as a "vital and meaningful" tool of management. As Robinson told the service commanders:

> What General Somervell wants to know is—not how well we are doing, but where we are falling down. Wherever our report shows we are not keeping up with the schedule, that is redlined so that the General looks at the thing and there it stands out and hits him in the face. Right there is where we are not doing so well, and he makes that the subject of personal interviews with the Supply and Service Chiefs responsible for that deficiency.

Collecting statistics covering all ASF functions that were susceptible to quantification, Robinson each month presented Somervell with a progress report, in itself a milestone on the road to modern information systems. An analysis summarizing the report and calling attention to specific problems indicated by the data, especially results that did not measure up to goals, accompanied the report. Somervell would then carefully review the report and use it as the basis for a staff conference each month.[31]

As part of Somervell's office, the Control Division had considerable clout. When it spoke, it spoke for Somervell, and consequently, Somervell gave Robinson his fullest support when disputes arose with the supply and administrative arms. This support was essential to the effectiveness of the division, for control aroused considerable opposition in many quarters. As Robinson commented, "it looked like we were the official SOB. The word got around that we were snoopers, and hatchet men, a sort of FBI for the Commanding General."

This view was not surprising. A body that existed to enhance Somervell's critical faculties was not going to be highly regarded by those who were criticized, and Robinson added to this inherent problem by acting as if he were in too big a hurry and by trying to impose systems that, in the opinion of many, did not adequately take into account the differences between industry and the army. Somervell tried to sell his concept of control with the argument that the division would not assume any operating functions or serve as a "super Gestapo" that cut off heads. But most supply and service officers continued to regard his efficiency experts as a horde of uninformed, meddlesome busybodies.[32]

Despite opposition to the Control Division, Robinson's operation introduced many noteworthy management improvements. Largely because of its efforts, the number of people working for Somervell declined as the war progressed even as the volume of work steadily climbed. And, the Monthly Progress Report enabled the general to keep close tabs on the supply effort. Similar management techniques were utilized in the AAF headquarters and other wartime agencies. But of all his contemporaries, Somervell probably made the most use of an institutionalized effort to achieve improved administrative performance, and his promotion of the concept of management improvement was one of his most significant wartime contributions.[33]

While he was welding together his new command, Somervell was also developing the fundamental mechanism by which he would attempt to meet the army's requirements—the Army Supply Program (ASP). As he was working on the requirements for the Victory Program and Roosevelt's "must" goals in early 1942, Somervell had determined that the existing statements of the army's supply requirements were inadequate. Formulated by a number of agencies within the War Department in conjunction with the civilian production agencies, they were short-range projections, tied to specific appropriations, and, by indicating only terminal and not immediate objectives, did not schedule requirements. In addition, they were generally limited to equipment rather than to such vital categories of supply as construction materials, fuel, and spare parts and omitted army-type materiel procured for the navy and lend-lease programs. Somervell's goal was to have the army produce a single, comprehensive program that stated all the requirements for which the army was responsible for the next two to three calendar years. It would serve as a directive to the procuring agencies, a basis for planning, and a vehicle for defending appropriations before Congress.

Somervell spelled out his thinking in a ten-page memorandum, addressed to

Deputy Chief of Staff Moore in January. In vigorous terms and great detail, he outlined the need for a consolidated supply program and emphasized that the military and economic situation must be "the impulse behind the entire Army Supply Program from the formulation of the program through allocation of facilities and raw materials, the placing of orders, production, and delivery."

Unwilling to wait for approval of his recommendation, Somervell forged ahead with the initial preparation of the program. However, little could be accomplished at the outset. At the time, Allied political and military leaders had produced only a concept of a general strategy, and until they developed specific courses of action to carry out this strategy, Somervell lacked the requisite basis for concrete programs of requirements, production schedules, and priorities. For this reason, the War Munitions Program was hardly what he had in mind since it set forth only ultimate objectives.[34]

Once he was named head of the ASF, Somervell made the development of the ASP a top priority. In a matter of days, his people were working out what eventually became "a complete but systematic organization and procedure for determining and presenting" army requirements. Somervell initially leaned toward theater plans as the avenue for determining requirements, and in the spring of 1942, he had his planners look into the requirements of hypothetical operations so that he could have bills of particulars ready if they were authorized. But, as the work progressed, it became apparent that no one could accurately predict ahead of time what operations the army would actually be undertaking and that the overall troop basis offered the only durable system on which to build a system of requirements.[35] On this basis, work on the ASP went ahead, and by September 1942, the first full edition was completed. Revised semiannually, the ASP brought "an unprecedented measure of common sense and rational Planning" to the complex business of buying huge quantities of a host of separate items in the middle of a global war.[36]

5. INDUSTRIAL MOBILIZATION

• • • • IN HIS FIRST YEAR AS HEAD OF THE ASF, Somervell's principal concern was the output of war supplies. This, in turn, centered on the army's relationship with the WPB. Created by Roosevelt on January 16, 1942, and headed by Donald Nelson, a one-time executive with Sears, Roebuck and Company, the WPB had wide powers to direct the "war procurement and production program." However, much about the role of the WPB in industrial mobilization was unclear when Somervell became head of the ASF, especially in regard to the military. Specific lines of authority between the two agencies had to be drawn, and a basis for harmonious cooperation had to be established. Eventually, a workable relationship was put in place, but only after "infighting, machinations, confrontations, and explosions" between soldiers and civilians.[1]

• • •

From Somervell's perspective, the most important area of concern in early 1942 about the relationship between the army and the WPB was the uncertainty over the responsibility for procurement of war supplies. Some members of the WPB suggested Roosevelt's order creating the board had vested it with responsibility for procurement, while Somervell insisted that statute and practice placed responsibility in the hands of the army procurement services.

Behind these positions were two sets of fears. On the one hand, individuals in the WPB believed that the civilian agency must exercise this responsibility to keep the army from hindering overall war production by running hog wild in placing orders. In their view, the army should submit its shopping list to the WPB so that all war-related needs were properly taken into account as the government entered the market on a massive scale. On the other hand, Somervell believed responsibility for military procurement must rest with the army, citing the long-standing dictum that he who controls strategy must also control supply. If the WPB had responsibility for procurement, in effect Nelson would be a commander-in-chief who could determine what kind of war was to be fought.[2]

Hoping to head off a clash between the WPB and the army, Somervell had Dorr's group work out an agreement with Nelson's assistants, approved by Nelson and Patterson on March 12, 1942. Under it, the WPB would supervise the general planning and scheduling of production, while the army did the actual procuring, including the determination of its own requirements, awarding of contracts, scheduling of deliveries, and inspection of finished products. Somervell was pleased with the agreement and subsequently asserted that all difficulties between the army and the WPB could be settled by its terms. However, many in the WPB were disappointed because in their opinion, the agreement compelled the WPB to carry out its functions indirectly, especially through the control of raw materials and the scheduling of production, rather than through the seemingly more effective means of direct supervision.

Because of the head-on collision that followed, the Nelson-Patterson agreement became a matter of considerable controversy. In his history of Somervell's command, John Millett posits that, since Roosevelt did not specifically invest Nelson with procurement responsibility, he meant for him to have only general authority over industrial mobilization and not responsibility for actual procurement. Nelson's biographer essentially agrees. Many WPB personnel and historians, in contrast, argue that Nelson either had the power to take over purchasing and the letting of contracts or that he could have had such authority if he wished.

Whether Nelson had the power to control procurement or could have had it is problematical. The fact is that he readily agreed that the army should control procurement. Writing in his memoir, Nelson stated that he considered the possibility of transferring military procurement to the WPB but "decided against such action in the interest of more rapid production." In other words, it was more important to concentrate on the swift conversion of industry to war production and the improvement of production figures than to wage a prolonged jurisdictional dispute with the army. Also, Nelson reasoned the army already had capable purchasing agents, and to replace them with civilians or to transfer them to the WPB would have led to confusion and disrupted established patterns of budgetary negotiations with Congress.

Even if these practical considerations had not existed, Nelson was not disposed by personality to assert himself by taking over control of procurement.

The subject of speculation by nearly every writer on the politics of wartime Washington, Nelson possessed a clear conception of the total effort that industrial mobilization would entail and fully understood the interrelationship between military production and the industrial economy. But, he was essentially uninterested in matters not directly related to broad policy and preferred to hear and weigh all options before acting. Pleasant, patient, and conciliatory, he preferred to persuade rather than to dictate, and he thought that differences could be resolved if one let time lapse. Thus, Nelson tended to vacillate and avoid conflict, leading him in March 1942 to seek the most expedient delineation of procurement responsibilities with the army.[3]

The Nelson-Patterson agreement looked good on paper. However, trouble soon developed. Part of the problem was the contrasting personalities of Nelson and Somervell. Nelson's vacillation and inattention to administrative detail infuriated Somervell, whose strengths were decisiveness and the mastery of organizational structures. At the same time, Somervell's brusqueness and determination to have his own way clashed with Nelson's strengths of persuasion and general affability. Although it is too much to say that the discord between the army and the WPB was simply Somervell versus Nelson, the interaction of the two quite different personalities made the clashes more bloody than they otherwise would have been.[4]

More important to the emerging discord between Somervell and the WPB were their different approaches to mobilization. Operating on the premise that his responsibility was to build up a massive pool of military materiel as quickly as possible, Somervell flooded the industrial sector with war orders with apparently little regard for the feasibility of military requirements; priorities and other controls; the scheduling and coordination of production; or the naval, maritime, and lend-lease programs. Many in the WPB criticized his approach, arguing that it made no sense to place orders for massive increases in armaments without coordinating the different programs or fully considering how the economy was to be organized to meet them. While appreciating the army's desire to meet its requirements, the WPB critics believed Somervell's approach clogged the lines of production, worked against maximum total war output, and delayed actual deliveries of goods. The best way for the army to meet its requirements, they contended, was for it to work with the WPB in establishing realistic goals and effective controls and carefully scheduling production.[5]

If these factors were not enough to heighten tensions between Somervell and the WPB, some in the WPB suspected Somervell was driven by an appetite for power and ultimately intended to make the military the dominant voice in the economy, either by transforming the WPB into an arm of the military or by rendering it meaningless. The flap in May 1942 over the development of machinery for handling raw materials was especially important in fostering WPB suspicions about Somervell. Believing Nelson was not moving forcefully enough in this regard, he proposed that raw materials should be allocated by a WPB committee system, whose decisions would be subject to appeal to a special board under the Combined Chiefs of Staff (CCS), the agency responsible for developing Anglo-American strategy. Nelson rejected Somervell's proposal out of hand, seeing it as an attempt to give the military complete control of the WPB and the economy. While recognizing that the existing machinery for allocating raw materials was inadequate, he told Somervell that "the battle of production is the primary responsibility of the chairman of the WPB in much the same sense that military battles are the primary responsibility of the military chiefs." The solution to the problems in industrial mobilization, he concluded, was not to place the economy under the CCS, as Somervell seemed to say, but through "close and continuous" relations between the CCS and the WPB.[6]

The claim that Somervell was trying to expand the army's authority over the economy at the expense of the WPB was widely publicized at the time and later worked its way into many histories and other accounts. According to this view, the issue was simple: Who was to control the economy? A power-hungry general who had no sense of the national interest, or civilians who understood the needs of both the military and the total economy?

However, this response is too simplistic. Somervell accepted civilian control of the economy and never wished to take over the economy in the sense that soldiers would make the actual decisions governing it. Rather, he believed the WPB should do a better job seeing that the army's requirements were met and, thus, was attempting to shove it in the direction he thought it should go.

But, to deny that Somervell deliberately plotted to be the nation's economic general is not to absolve him completely of the charge, for his approach to mobilization seemed to substantiate the charge. His relentless drive, single-mindedness, arrogance, bureaucratic adroitness, appetite for power, and even delight in tackling tough jobs inevitably encouraged many to think he was plotting an economic coup d'etat. His perception of the role of the civilian mobilization agency reinforced such suspicions. He saw Nelson as an errand boy, whose primary job was to see that army requirements were satisfied, and thus, he pushed for more efficient management in the WPB and a stronger voice for the military in the field of production. Jealously guarding the army's prerogatives, Somervell refused to accept the WPB as a superior agency and aggressively asserted military claims to scarce raw materials. Somervell may not have wanted a stranglehold on the economy. However, he had no intention of permitting the WPB and its claims to a national interest stand in his way.[7]

The May skirmish brought no change in the relationship between the army and the WPB. Roosevelt backed Nelson, and Somervell quickly dropped his proposal. But it created a breach between Nelson and his supporters and Somervell that never closed. The former were now certain that their suspicions about Somervell were correct. Vice President Henry A. Wallace, for example, noted in his diary that Somervell was trying to move into a position of dominating power in the civilian economy, while Harold Ickes branded him a "possible man on horseback." In their certainty, Nelson and his supporters steeled themselves to resist Somervell's power plays. And just as certain in his own belief that Nelson and the WPB were moving at a snail's pace, Somervell pressed military claims with all the considerable force he could bring to bear.[8]

• • •

The growing conflict between soldiers and civilians over industrial mobilization exploded into a number of overlapping battles in the summer and fall of 1942. One centered on the impact of the war program upon overall production and came to be called the Feasibility Dispute. The instigator of the dispute was the WPB's Planning Committee, chaired by Robert R. Nathan, a New Deal economist who had been educated at the University of Pennsylvania and was noted for his intelligence as well as "initiative, enthusiasm and aggressiveness in causes with which he was concerned." Aiding Nathan were Simon Kuznets, an expert on national income analysis and Nathan's old teacher at Pennsylvania, and Stacy May, director of the WPB's Office of Progress Reports. The committee was convinced it could determine the productive capacity of the economy, measured by dollar-value estimates, by analyzing the supply of labor, raw materials, and industrial facilities. It also believed that productive capacity should play a major role in the setting of military requirements.[9]

From the outset, Somervell opposed the Planning Committee's emphasis on the industrial feasibility of military requirements. He was convinced that there was not sufficient data by which to measure productive capacity at this early date of the war and, therefore, that it was folly to base production programs on dubious measurements of its capacity until the manifold problems of industrial conversion to war production had been ironed out. Other factors also played a role in Somervell's thinking. He believed in the efficacy of incentive goals as a determinant of the nation's productive capacity, operating on the assumption that one could not truly determine this capacity until demands were placed upon production.

Moreover, Somervell disliked the Planning Committee's approach to feasibility. Before the president had presented his "must" goals in January 1942, the civilian mobilizers had been pushing the army to adopt greatly increased production goals. Then, when the army came forth with its War Munitions Program, the same people suddenly decided the goals were too high and asked for a decrease, all this without waiting to see if these goals could be met. The change in the WPB's tune irritated Somervell, and he decided to pay no heed to it. He was expected to ensure an adequate flow of supplies to the American army, and he preferred to be optimistic about the possibility of rapidly increasing the rates of production rather than cutting schedules that were still in the planning stage.[10]

During the summer of 1942 the feasibility of the military program became a burning issue. Military production had soared in the first half of the year. However, monthly advances were uneven, and after midyear, alarming slowdowns developed in major programs. Civilian production experts looked at these developments with growing concern and suggested that overambitious production goals were throwing schedules out of line and causing maldistribution of raw materials and components. Assuming the point position on this issue, the Planning Committee had Kuznets analyze the nation's production potential from various angles: materials, facilities, and manpower. Finishing his analysis in August, Kuznets concluded that the existing objectives for the 1942 war program would fall $15 billion short of expectations (a relatively accurate prediction since it actually fell $16 billion short) and that the 1943 objectives, which were estimated at $92.9 billion, were even less attainable.

Since the military had not put forth a realistic war program, Kuznets proposed that a supreme war production council, composed of military and civilian representatives, be established to fuse strategic and production considerations in determining war needs. In his words,

> Unless such a body is established; unless a program can be formulated by a joint consideration of all its parts and in terms of the joint bearing of strategic, economic, and political considerations; unless this body operates continuously both to revise the program and to check its detailed information by the separate agencies, we are in grave danger of reducing materially the contribution that the productive system of this country can make to the war effort. We shall be threatened by continuous imbalance in output and by failure to obtain . . . the base flow of munitions which we are capable of producing.[11]

Nelson showed no interest in Kuznets's proposal because he knew the military would resist with all its force. He also believed there was no need for such a board if the army could be persuaded to bring its requirements in line with the nation's industrial capacity.

But, while Nelson displayed no interest in the proposed board, he did not specifically reject it. Nelson was convinced Kuznets's feasibility study was correct. However, his problem was how to use it to get the army to reduce its requirements. Apparently, he believed Kuznets's proposal for a war production council, one he expected Somervell would find unsatisfactory, would prompt the army to reduce its requirements and accept his own approach to correlating strategy and production. But he did not want to place his own prestige on the line by endorsing the proposal for a fear that a defeat would undermine his standing.

Consequently, in a display of bureaucratic subtlety that he had not previously evidenced, Nelson placed the onus for Kuznets's findings on the Planning Committee by transmitting them to the War and Navy Departments and to Harry

Hopkins as an impersonal note signed by Nathan rather than as a regular WPB document. Thus, the findings were presented as the conclusions of an economist far below the organizational level of Somervell and the other officers who would read them. In other words, Nelson did not have to assume responsibility for them.[12]

Neither Hopkins nor the Navy Department even acknowledged Nathan's letter or its accompanying documents. However, Somervell, who received them late on September 12, immediately responded in a blistering, hastily written reply that was dispatched to Nathan that night. He vigorously denied that "the variations between Mr. Kuznets's 'probabilities' and production goals," which Kuznets placed at 10 to 20 percent, were of such magnitude "percentage wise to justify a wholesale change in goals" and asserted that any problems in war production could be worked out through proper scheduling of orders. He saved his most pungent words for Kuznets's proposed war production council. "To me," Somervell wrote, "this is an inchoate mass of words. . . . I should much prefer to trust to proper decisions from The President, Mr. Nelson, and military personnel knowing something of production, than to his board of 'economists and statisticians.' " In words often quoted, he summed up his reaction to Kuznets's findings in a mocking manner by stating that "I am not impressed with either the character or basis of the judgments expressed in the reports and recommend they be carefully hidden from the eyes of thoughtful men."[13]

The fury of Somervell's response stemmed from two factors. First, the previous spring, he had scoffed at attempts to summarize the nation's production capacity at this stage of the war in the belief that the possibility of errors was too high to justify cuts. To Somervell, it was tiresome for the Planning Committee to broach the subject again, especially when it came from Kuznets, a man in Somervell's opinion who was "too academic and impractical to help us very much on the problem which he attacked." Nothing in these findings warranted any change in Somervell's position. The problems in war production were the result of inefficiency and lack of drive upon the part of the WPB, not the size of the war program. Even if the goals should prove to be excessive, Somervell was not prepared to admit they should be cut, for he was convinced that "if he gave in . . . you would immediately get a demand to give in further."[14]

Somervell's real anger, however, arose from the second factor, Kuznets's proposal for a war production council, which Somervell called a "grand super super board," to coordinate strategy and production. It would place civilians with social or political concerns on a board dealing with strategy, an appalling notion to the general. At the very least, it seemed that "representatives of the Joint Chiefs would have to meet with back room party bosses or with long-haired social visionaries." At the worst, it seemed that radicals were trying "to displace the Joint Chiefs of Staff in the conduct of the war."

Going beyond Somervell's perceptions, he and the Planning Committee were in effect opposite sides of the same coin. Each recognized that production and strategy were related. However, Somervell believed soldiers, as the ones who made strategy, should have a greater say over production, while the Planning Committee believed civilians, as the ones who best knew economic policy, "should have more to do with setting strategy."[15]

Nathan was taken back by Somervell's reply. He had not expected a reply so quickly, let alone one marked with such fury. His immediate thought was to keep it to himself so as not to arouse Kuznets, who he knew would be furious at Somervell's language and would want to dash off a response to the general. Such a response, he felt, would fuel a prolonged vitriolic exchange between Somervell and the Planning Committee that might not settle anything.

However, Kuznets soon learned of Somervell's blast and was not prepared to let Somervell treat him like some military underling. Securing Nathan's permission to draft the committee's response, he prepared a note, sent under Nathan's name, that began by telling Somervell that "in view of the gravity of the problem discussed in these Documents [the Kuznets studies], I hesitate to take your memorandum seriously." Kuznets went on to scold Somervell for "an ostrich-like attitude" in regard to feasibility and to label Somervell's judgment that the studies should "be carefully hidden from the eyes of thoughtful men" as a "non-sequitur."[16]

Underlying Kuznets's attack against Somervell was the Planning Committee's disgust with the general. To the committee, Somervell not only failed to comprehend the feasibility problem, he made no effort to understand it when it was presented to him. Thus, in his stubbornness, he was hurting the war effort by irresponsibly saddling the economy with excessive demands. If that were not enough, they were certain Somervell became irrational at times and misstated facts and distorted the truth, as well as misrepresented their positions on the relationship between the military and the WPB, out of a desire to build up his own power. In sum, they saw Somervell as a vicious, power-hungry conniver whose ultimate goal was to knife Nelson in the back.[17]

The September exchange prompted Nelson and Nathan to decide that the entire feasibility issue should be thrashed out before the WPB in a face-to-face discussion between Nathan and Somervell. Seeking support, Nathan presented his views to Leon Henderson of the Office of Price Administration and to Hopkins.

At the same time, Somervell marshaled his forces for the showdown. Patterson and Vice Admiral S. M. Robinson of the navy, both of whom regularly attended WPB meetings, agreed to support him on feasibility. In the final analysis, though, Somervell was less concerned about the economic aspects of the dispute, which he believed could be worked out, than he was about the proposal for a strategy-production board. To defeat this proposal, Somervell secured Marshall's signature on a letter to Nelson, undoubtedly written by Somervell, stating that effective and elaborate machinery has been established for the guidance of the strategic efforts of the combined armed forces. I do not believe that a joint committee consisting of an economist, a politician, and person familiar with strategy but not with production, could be an effective means of controlling the war effort.

To strengthen Somervell's hand in dealing with the WPB, Marshall designated Somervell as the "representative of the War Department for the presentation of strategy to the War Production Board."[18]

Nelson set aside the October 6 meeting of the WPB for a thorough discussion of the feasibility question, and as the day approached, tensions grew in anticipation of what everyone knew would be a sharp encounter. At the outset of the meeting, Nathan reviewed Kuznets's feasibility study and called for the creation of "an administrative mechanism to combine strategy and production." There followed an assertion by Somervell that the 1942 war program would probably fall 10 percent short of completion by the end of the year, not the 19 percent Kuznets estimated, and that this shortage could be alleviated by more effective control over the distribution of raw materials. He added that dollar figures could not be relied upon to measure national productive capacity, that the WPB should be focusing its attention on increasing supply rather than reducing demand, that the work involved in the recomputations necessary to reduce the program or change the schedules was not worth the doubtful benefits to be derived, and that adherence to the military's schedules would result only in late completion of objectives. In response to Nathan's call for a strategy-production board, Somervell said, "We already have the Combined Chiefs, the Joint Chiefs, the Combined Production and Resources Board, the Munitions Board, the Army and Navy Munitions Board, and the War Production Board. What good would be a board composed of an economist, a politician, and a soldier who does not know production?"

Somervell's refusal to make any major concessions to the Planning Committee's findings caused the civilians at the meeting to lash out at the war program and at him personally. Henry Wallace remarked that the war program would require a cut resulting in civilian expenditures 40 percent below that of the depression year of 1932. Behind his comment was the conviction that the civilian economy was being asked to sacrifice while the war program was "larded with fat."

After several others questioned the military program, Leon Henderson, a blustery New Dealer with a reputation as a fighter, commented that it seemed most unlikely that the nation could support a war program in 1943 of more than $90 billion. He further stated, "Maybe if we can't wage a war on 90 billions, we ought to get rid of our present Joint Chiefs, and find some who can." Henderson did not stop there, even though his statement was received in dead silence. Turning to Somervell, he then said that he was disgusted with Somervell's obstinacy, overbearing manner, and ignorance of production matters and scored him for always padding army requirements. It was "the most violent personal attack ever heard" in a WPB meeting, and Somervell, who was not used to being spoken to in this manner, chose to remain silent. When W. L. Batt, a WPB vice chairman, attempted to play the role of peacemaker by pointing out that Somervell was not responsible for strategy, Henderson, in reference to the letter Somervell had from Marshall, scornfully asked: "Ain't he got a letter?"[19]

After Henderson's tirade, the meeting came to a quick end without any resolution of the dispute. During the following days, Nathan's group recommended that the WPB in its next meeting agree on the size of the revision needed to make the war program feasible. The group estimated, even assuming adequate scheduling, that the 1943 program should not exceed $75 billion. Wanting to lessen the likely military opposition to this proposal, they also suggested that this goal could be met by extending the delivery date for parts of the program until some time in June 1944. Conspicuously missing from the thinking of Nathan's group was the proposal for a strategy-production board. Somervell remained unalterably opposed to it, and in the absence of any formal encouragement from Nelson, they dropped it.

Within the War Department, meanwhile, there was a rethinking of positions. Although Patterson had insisted at the meeting that the war program should be met as the JCS requested, he came away convinced that adjustments in the program would have to be made. The important point to him was that the determination of war requirements remain in the hands of soldiers, although not the exact size of the requirements, a point he believed most members of the WPB were willing to concede. In a memorandum on October 7, Patterson told Somervell that

> the WPB position, that production objectives ought not to be far in front of estimated maximum production, is believed to be sound as a general rule. Otherwise our scheduling of production cannot represent reality, and it is generally agreed that without realistic scheduling we will continue to suffer from maldistribution of materials, thus cutting down the actual output of finished weapons.

He went on to state that the JCS, acting within the framework of strategic considerations, should reduce the war program.[20]

Over several days, Patterson and Somervell discussed the dispute at length, with Patterson continually emphasizing he wanted it settled amicably. Knowing Patterson had made up his mind, Somervell was receptive to his views. All along his major concern had been to scotch the notion of a strategy-production board, and while refusing to admit his approach to mobilization might have fouled up production as the Planning Committee claimed, he viewed adjustments in the war program as secondary, especially since the army would be revising downward goals that had not been reached anyway.[21]

The October 13 meeting of the WPB was much different than the previous one. Nelson and Henderson again questioned the war goals, with Henderson even suggesting that the rest of the supply program might have to be cut by 50 percent if Roosevelt's "must" goals remained intact. It was this fact—that the "must" goals directed by Roosevelt and the program submitted by the JCS, when taken together, were unattainable within the established time frame—that brought the soldiers and civilians at the meeting together. To the amazement of the WPB officials, Somervell conceded that the total program could not be completed within the time allowed and suggested that Nelson should inform the JCS of this fact. The JCS would, in turn, be responsible for determining the necessary action "to bring the over-all program within the limits of production feasibility." In effect, Nelson would fix the maximum size of the war program for 1943, and the JCS would decide, after consultation with Roosevelt, whether the 1943 goals should be reduced or extended for some items into 1944. This proposal was immediately accepted by all present, ending the Feasibility Dispute.[22]

WPB officials quickly claimed victory. In their eyes, cutting the war program was the overriding objective. By putting forth unrealistic goals, Somervell had overloaded American factories with war orders. Now, after months of intransigence, he had come around to their view. Further, Somervell's proposal spared the WPB the distasteful necessity of again challenging Roosevelt's "must" goals. That job now lay with the JCS.

But, if Somervell retreated on the feasibility of the war program, he could also claim victory. There would be no "grand super super board." Reinforcing this victory, Admiral William Leahy, Roosevelt's personal representative on the JCS, informed Nelson that, "for the purpose of integrating strategy and production," the JCS had appointed officers from the army and navy to keep Nelson advised regarding "the requirements from production and personnel necessary to implement strategic plans." Along these lines, Somervell presented the WPB with a resume of the strategic situation as it affected production problems at its October 20 meeting.[23]

Meanwhile, Nelson went ahead with the course of action Somervell had proposed in the WPB's October 13 meeting. On October 19, he wrote to the JCS that only $75 billion of the 1943 objective of $98 billion—$92.9 billion scheduled for 1943 and $5 billion left unfinished from 1942—could be achieved. Some $23 billion would have to be eliminated or postponed. When the JCS received Nelson's memorandum, they reduced their 1943 objectives from $92.9 billion to $80.15 billion, with the 1942 deficit items either dropped entirely or included in the revised 1943 program. The new war program exceeded the Planning Committee's estimate of a feasible 1943 program by $5 billion. However, shortly afterward, Nathan judged the program "within the realm of possible achievement."[24]

• • •

At the same time that Somervell and the WPB were feuding over feasible requirements, they were also battling over the control of raw materials and the scheduling of production. Like the Feasibility Dispute, these conflicts laid bare the divisions between soldiers and civilians and engendered bitter recriminations.

During 1942, control of the distribution of raw materials was the number-one problem of production management. The WPB started the year with a hodgepodge of materials distribution controls that it inherited from the OPM, the agency it replaced. However, as military orders skyrocketed in the spring, the demand for raw materials outraced the supply. In response to the mounting crisis, a number of Nelson's assistants urged him to make the Production Requirements Plan (PRP), one of the WPB's major control devices, mandatory for all American industry. Applicable on a voluntary basis almost exclusively to the production of nonmilitary items, the PRP gave each manufacturer who elected to be governed by it "a preference-rated authorization to obtain a balanced supply of the materials he needed for his production during a three-month period, if that production was deemed by WPB to be essential to the war effort." With universal PRP coverage, Nelson's assistants argued, the WPB could compile total materials requests from all industry for a quarter in advance and then make allocations to all on a plant-by-plant basis. Through this mechanism, the total allocation would be kept in line with available supplies.

Somervell strongly opposed making the PRP mandatory. Under it, the WPB would rely on requirements statements from thousands of industrial establishments rather than a relative handful of procurement agencies in allocating raw materials, a task he considered beyond its capabilities and also one that would yield requirements statements that did not always conform with the needs of the military. Even more disturbing, the PRP broke the link between procuring officer and contractor. The procuring officer might let a contract and agree with the manufacturer upon delivery schedules, but since the contractor had to rely on the WPB for raw materials, he might receive different instructions from it, resulting in confusion and needless delay. Expressing his objections to the PRP on a number of occasions in the spring of 1942, Somervell called for a system under which the WPB would "tell us how much steel, and copper, and aluminum we may have, and we will then divide it in balanced proportions among our supply programs and inform our contractors what they can have and what they should plan to produce."[25]

Somervell's objections meant little. Nelson was determined to move forward with the PRP out of fear that the WPB would be swallowed by the army if he did not act. Earlier in the year, Nelson had granted the ANMB the power to issue priorities on military goods, and in May, Roosevelt had added to the stature of the ANMB by making its concurrence mandatory in the assignment of priorities and the allocation of facilities to achieve his "must" goals. If that were not enough, Somervell, who wanted to give the military "a big shot in the arm" by lifting "the military programs well out in front of all other production," convinced the ANMB to propose that its concurrence be mandatory for all ratings, whether for military or civilian items. If approved, this action would give the ANMB veto power over the WPB. Seeing the ANMB proposal as another effort by Somervell to take over the economy, Nelson concluded he must assert civilian authority by opposing the ANMB proposal and, at least for the time being, making the PRP mandatory.[26]

After extensive negotiations with ANMB officials, Nelson in a conciliatory gesture accepted the ANMB proposal in June, although not before having it watered down and not before asserting that he did not consider it binding. In the meantime, he announced that the PRP would become mandatory effective July 1, 1942.

As Somervell had predicted, the PRP quickly floundered. The administrative burden it presented overwhelmed the WPB. Contractors overstated their requirements to complete past orders or to better their position to get future ones, and procuring officers found their ability to direct their programs in regard to plans, production schedules, and related matters significantly impaired.

Nelson's effort to assert civilian authority did not end with the adoption of the PRP. In August, he let it be known that, because of shortages of critical raw materials, he was returning to the WPB the priority power he had given to the ANMB. Observers saw Nelson's action as a curb on Somervell's power, but this view was too myopic. Not wanting to alienate Somervell totally, Nelson in September attempted to placate him for the ANMB's loss of priority power by appointing Ferdinand Eberstadt, ANMB chairman, as WPB vice chairman on program determination.

A Wall Street financier, Eberstadt had been a forceful advocate of Somervell's position on military requirements, causing Nelson's supporters to brand him a tool or front for the general. Autocratic and a lone wolf by nature, Eberstadt was never General Somervell's man, and Somervell never saw him as such. Yet, like Somervell, he believed Nelson's approach to raw materials was wrongheaded. Thus, when he went to the WPB, he insisted that he should have extensive authority to reorganize the materials-allocation program around a plan eventually known as the Controlled Materials Plan (CMP), the army's preferred means for controlling raw materials.[27]

Originally known as the warrant plan and largely drawn from British experience along with several proposals that had been circulating around Washington, the CMP designated scarce raw materials—initially copper, steel, and aluminum—as controlled materials. Under it, government agencies would submit their requests for these raw materials to the WPB. On the basis of an analysis of supply and demand, the WPB would make allocations to the agencies in the form of a warrant, or check, to draw upon materials supply. The agencies would, in turn, make allocations by passing a warrant drawn upon their allocation along to their contractors, who then passed the warrant to their subcontractors for placement of orders with raw materials suppliers.

Encouraged by Eberstadt, the army began to give serious consideration to the CMP, and by the summer of 1942, Somervell had endorsed it in the belief that it would work better than the PRP and would provide the military with greater control over its own materials. Many in the WPB were apprehensive about the CMP. In their eyes, it would place too much power in the hands of the military and permit materials to be controlled by giant corporations to the detriment of small business. But, by September, with the defects in the PRP obvious for everyone to see and with Nathan's Planning Committee endorsing the CMP, Nelson agreed to bring Eberstadt into the WPB with authority to implement the new plan. On November 2, the WPB officially announced CMP's adoption, which would become fully effective on July 1, 1943.[28]

Somervell was convinced that the CMP by itself would solve the production problem. Nelson, however, believed that the problem had a dimension beyond the channeling of scarce materials to manufacturers, namely proper scheduling of production. Too often, supply officers had placed contracts for specific military items without coordinating the flow of materials needed to complete them. As a result, scheduled production of component parts was often not coordinated with their need. For instance, valves for ships might be produced months before they were needed, while at the same time, production of more immediately needed items lagged for want of steel that had been used to produce the valves. Scarce raw materials were not being used, in other words, for the proper goods at the proper time. If the CMP were to work, this bottleneck had to be eliminated.[29]

To deal with the scheduling problem, Nelson in September 1942 established the Production Executive Committee (PEC) under the chairmanship of Charles E. Wilson of the General Electric Corporation and charged it with developing a method for perfecting production schedules. Besides Wilson, the committee consisted primarily of Eberstadt and the top procurement officers of the armed services and the Maritime Commission.

Beyond the obvious desire to eliminate a production obstacle, Nelson had something else in mind when he brought Wilson into the WPB. Many interpreted his decisions to appoint Eberstadt to the WPB and adopt the CMP as a victory for Somervell. By appointing Wilson, who had reputation as a crackerjack production man and who was thought to be sympathetic to the civilian outlook, Nelson was attempting to balance Eberstadt. Where Eberstadt might permit the military to do as it pleased, Wilson could be relied upon to assert

WPB control over the production process. Commenting on this aspect of Wilson's appointment, unidentified WPB officials said "the broad powers given Wilson meant the recapture by the WPB of full control of any phases of the war production effort which may still remain in the hands of the armed forces."[30]

Somervell soon learned what this meant. In early November, Stacy May declared in the WPB's October Monthly Progress Report that recent deliveries of munitions were disappointing and that the flattening out of the trend line in production was the result of faulty production scheduling. Influenced by May's analysis, Wilson concluded that the WPB would have to assume full authority to schedule war production, which entailed recapturing some of the production authority Nelson had delegated to the services the previous March. Emphasizing that the military procurement programs must be consistent, balanced, and integrated, Wilson proposed at a PEC meeting on November 11 that a director general of production scheduling be appointed to serve as chairman of a PEC subcommittee on scheduling. Made up of representatives from the procurement agencies, the subcommittee would establish criteria for scheduling by the agencies, review their schedules for feasibility, and "insure proper balance of the schedules in relation to end items, complementary items and components." Final authority in the subcommittee would rest with the chairman who would be responsible solely to Wilson. In effect, Wilson's proposal would require the services to win his advance approval for their production schedules.[31]

The minutes of the meeting indicate that the PEC agreed to Wilson's proposal. But, in fact, only the navy and Maritime Commission representatives were receptive. Somervell had not attended the meeting, Lucius Clay having gone in his place, and as soon as the general learned of Wilson's proposal, he exploded. In a letter to Wilson dated November 16 and endorsed by other service representatives, Somervell blasted the proposal as "impossible of execution" and "in direct contravention" of the Nelson-Patterson agreement. Accusing Wilson of trying to usurp military prerogatives, Somervell stated that the proposal would enable civilians "to dictate whether we made cannons, tanks, airplanes, battleships, or other war material." Such powers, he affirmed, must rest with the services, for "the decision as to the priority in the manufacture of war material is closely related to strategy and tactics and must be made by Joint Chiefs of Staff."[32]

Wilson's proposal and Somervell's response were the opening salvoes in another round of the conflict over production control. Nelson immediately lined up behind Wilson, and on November 21, he sent Patterson copies of two administrative orders that he was prepared to issue implementing Wilson's proposal. Patterson showed the draft orders to Somervell, who told him they represented an abrogation of the Nelson-Patterson agreement and a direct challenge to military prerogatives that must be countered. That same day, Somervell and Clay prepared three papers criticizing the orders, sending them to Hopkins and Henry Stimson. In them, they argued that the orders ran counter to the agreement, would usurp the powers of the JCS, and would interfere with the smooth flow of materials. Calling the Nelson-Patterson agreement "logical and workable," they recommended that Nelson be given "explicit instructions" not to issue any orders contravening it.[33]

Somervell also attacked on another front. Fed up with Nelson, he went to see Leahy on November 24 and protested that Nelson was trying to take control of all war materials away from the services. Nelson, he stated, should be fired at once and replaced by Bernard Baruch, the famous World War I mobilizer who was thought to be more supportive of the military than Nelson.

Somervell got nowhere with Leahy. The admiral was convinced that the WPB was "doing a good job, considering the difficulties it faced" and distrusted Somervell's motives. Writing in his memoir, he says,

> I have the impression that Somervell was trying to expand his own operations radically—with the best of intentions. Two groups were mixing into war production—the Army and the WPB—and that was the trouble. It was duty of the Joint Chiefs to make war plans and there was an appropriate agency charged with procuring the things necessary to implement the war plans. I could see no merit in Somervell's recommendation.[34]

At this point, Roosevelt, who already had heard Somervell's position from Hopkins, invited Nelson to the White House to hear the WPB's side. After Nelson explained why "proper, orderly scheduling" of components was necessary, Roosevelt offered to help. Nelson, however, declined Roosevelt's offer, telling him that "I'll fight this through myself. All I ask of you is, don't help the other fellow." Roosevelt agreed to Nelson's request, but he also acted to end the dispute by calling Nelson, Stimson, and Secretary of the Navy Frank Knox together and instructing them to come to an agreement soon.

Taking the initiative, Nelson on November 26 sent two letters to Stimson and also visited him, beginning three days of negotiations that resulted in an agreement between Nelson and the service secretaries on the functions of the PEC. The agreement was a compromise which essentially left the balance between the WPB and the services intact. As one historian summarizes it, "the military services would say what they wanted and when, but the Production Executive Committee would review and balance their requirements and say how much of what they wanted could be obtained at any particular time."[35]

Somervell did not participate in the negotiations, for Nelson preferred to deal directly with Stimson, who he anticipated would be more accommodating than Somervell. In this way, the nasty personality clashes that had marked previous negotiations were avoided. Nevertheless, Somervell followed them and forcefully defended the army's scheduling and forecasting practices before the WPB in meetings on November 27 and December 1. His defense of the army's scheduling practices did not affect the outcome of the negotiations between Nelson and Stimson, but it clearly showed that nothing Wilson or Nelson had said had changed Somervell's mind about the army's practices and suggested that, if Roosevelt and Stimson had not entered the picture, there probably would not have been an agreement at all.

• • •

The fierce struggle between soldiers and civilians over industrial mobilization was closely followed by liberals in the Congress. Even before the United States entered the war, they felt that many of the dislocations that accompanied mobilization were attributable to carelessness and indifference on the part of the military procurement agencies. In 1942, their criticism of the military mounted, spurred by the failure to reach production objectives, the development of strained relations between the army and the WPB, and increasing complaints from small business that it had been left out of the procurement process.

During the fall, congressional liberals took the offensive against the army. Several committees issued reports endorsing the creation of a super civilian agency to assume the procurement functions of the military, and legislation to achieve this end was introduced in the House of Representatives by John H. Tolan, Democrat from California, and in the Senate by Claude Pepper, Democrat from Florida, and Harley M. Kilgore, Democrat from West Virginia. Pepper explained the purpose of the Tolan-Pepper-Kilgore bill in an article, "To Smash the Final Bottleneck," in the November *New Republic*. He argued that "the steady insistence of the military upon doing the job itself" had not worked. What was needed, he asserted, was the complete turning over of responsibility for production to an agency manned by "production men from industry" and headed by a director responsible to the president. In this way, the army could be "required to present its requirements in terms of a fully developed strategical program" and the drifting which characterized production could be ended.[36]

Pepper's article infuriated Somervell, and in a lengthy letter to the senator, he spelled out his opposition to any changes in military procurement. Declaring that logistics and strategy were inseparable, Somervell argued that the army could fulfill its wartime mission only if it had "complete responsibility and authority in a single chain of command" for the design, procurement, and distribution of weapons. To remove procurement powers from the military would break the chain, making it virtually impossible to determine which agency should be held accountable for production delays. Further, to remove procurement from the military would threaten military strategy because the military could not be held responsible for fighting a war if it did not have the authority to guarantee that it was adequately supplied. While admitting there were some specific failures, most of which he placed at the feet of the WPB, Somervell said that the army had compiled a magnificent production record and accused the senator of impugning the integrity and competence of the Regular Army.[37]

The congressional drive for a super agency sparked renewed attention to the question of whether or not the army was attempting to gain control of the economy. Critics of the military argued that "for months the Army had been 'edging in' on the control of production" through outright assignment by Roosevelt, the placement of army representatives in strategic policy-making positions, and Nelson's willingness to compromise in earlier controversies and to permit the army to assume functions that properly lay with the WPB.

The military strenuously denied it was trying to take over the economy in a debate that continued through the spring of 1943. The gist of the army's defense was that it had "no thought that the military departments should control the economy," that it was absurd even to suggest military domination since the top officials in the War Department were civilians, that what the army wanted was supplies, not control, that many civilians in the mobilization agencies agreed with the army's position in the various debates, and that the disputes between soldiers and civilians were just episodes in traditional bureaucratic wrangling with personality overtones. All the army wanted, it reiterated, was the right it already had by law of supervising the production of its own weapons, as well as more centralized authority and efficient management in the civilian agencies responsible for mobilizing industrial America. While there was validity to these arguments, as long as Somervell was the driving force in the War Department, the army's critics remained unconvinced and resisted his perceived militaristic influence.[38]

Despite the calls for a super agency, Roosevelt never considered combining central economic controls and military procurement in one agency. Always one who preferred to avoid confrontations with major power groups, he knew that ripping procurement from the military would antagonize it and its backers in Congress and could possibly lead to unnecessary disruptions in the war effort.

Yet, he was tiring of the constant brawling between Somervell and Nelson. He was also disenchanted with Nelson's leadership of the WPB. As a result, in May 1943, he created the Office of War Mobilization (OWM) in the executive office of the president under the direction of James Byrnes, a Southern conservative in whom he had the greatest confidence. The OWM did not absorb the operating functions of the WPB or disturb the existing responsibilities of the military procurement agencies. Rather, it was a sort of a top mediator with decision-making authority, a court of last resort where Roosevelt's personal representative could adjudicate disputes between soldiers and civilians.[39]

Somervell was pleased by Roosevelt's action. Since it left the military in control of its procurement, he considered it a presidential vote of confidence on his position and, indeed, of the army's production performance. Further, the creation of the OWM was a not-too-subtle vote of presidential nonconfidence in

Nelson, for it clearly made Byrnes Roosevelt's man for war mobilization matters. For this reason, Somervell looked confidently toward the future. In his earlier position as director of economic stabilization, Byrnes had shown his affinity for the army's position, and Somervell expected that, in the future, the OWM head could be counted upon to protect the military production program from his enemies in the WPB.

• • •

A new struggle between soldiers and civilians broke out in the second half of 1943 and lasted through 1944. The issue in this instance was industrial reconversion. Nelson and his supporters in the WPB, as well as their allies in Congress, labor unions, and small business, pushed for early reconversion of idle firms to peacetime production in order to create as many jobs as possible in the civilian economy before the war's end and thus ensure full postwar employment. They also hoped that early reconversion would enable small firms, which were struggling to survive since the bulk of government contracts were going to big manufacturers, to get a head start in peacetime production while large firms were still busy filling military orders. Such a move might eliminate the prewar dominance of some consumer industries by big business.

However, Somervell and other officials in the War and Navy Departments were opposed to any reconversion before the war's end in the belief that reconversion, or even talk of it, would interfere with the war effort. They were supported by powerful financial and industrial interests who distrusted labor, were generally unsympathetic to small business, did not want to see small business gain any competitive advantage, and argued that widespread wartime shortages of civilian goods would create an enormous postwar demand no matter when reconversion was instituted.

Planning for reconversion began even before the United States entered the war as virtually all agencies looked into the most appropriate methods for terminating war contracts, and by early 1943, the Congress, the WPB, and others were seriously examining the issue. At this point, some concluded that the reconversion issue should move from study to action. Italy had surrendered, the Soviet Union had taken the offensive, things were looking up in the Pacific, and the AAF was blasting Germany with bombs, leading commentators to speculate that Germany might be defeated by bombs alone. These propitious signs were accompanied by indications that the annual rate of munitions production could not only be cut in 1944 but perhaps, even sliced by more than half in 1945.

Against this backdrop, spokesmen for small business and labor called for action on reconversion. They were afraid that as prime contracts declined, big firms would terminate the subcontracts which had kept many small firms alive during the war. Unless the WPB quickly implemented a reconversion program, smaller firms would have to shut down, leaving pockets of unemployment.[40]

Faced with these pressures, Nelson concluded that he had to act because doing nothing would hinder the war effort and severely damage the nation during the transition to peace. In his opinion, many companies were holding inventories below efficient operating levels, and others were reluctant to take on new war contracts for fear that early contract cancellations would leave them with bloated inventories. He also believed that failure to ensure that factories kept their doors open in the face of military cutbacks would cause many women and older workers to drift out of the labor market and thus, not be available in the event of an increase in munitions requirements. These workers might even hesitate to take war-related jobs in the first place out of concern that they would soon be out of work. A reconversion program that did not hinder military production, he reasoned, would convince both producers and workers to give their all for the war effort because they would know the government would not permit factories and workers to be idle in the face of military cutbacks. By "chinking in" civilian production as war production declined, particularly where surpluses of manpower, facilities, and materials appeared likely, the economy's ability to produce war goods would be maintained, the economy would be going at full speed as the war ended, and postwar reconversion problems would largely be eliminated.[41]

Nelson was also moved to act by the need to shore up his own position in the WPB. Following a jurisdictional fight between Eberstadt and Wilson in early 1943, one Eberstadt lost along with his WPB post, Wilson had emerged as the WPB's top operating man. Through 1943, Wilson's power grew steadily. As the day-to-day boss of the WPB, he soon earned the instinctive loyalty of many of the dollar-a-year businessmen staffing the WPB. Equally important, the PEC extended its authority to cover most of the major responsibilities of the WPB. Outside of a major reorganization of the WPB, which was out of the question since Nelson had obviously lost standing with the White House, Nelson believed, by the fall of 1943, that he must assert himself on some issue or become an insignificant factor in his own organization. Reconversion became that issue.[42]

At the November 30, 1943, WPB meeting, Nelson announced he would authorize production of additional civilian goods as long as military production was not jeopardized. Somervell, however, thought it was too early to talk about reconversion. To his way of thinking, Nelson was in no position to predict the army's future needs. There was no assurance that the Russians could continue to tie down some two hundred German divisions on the Eastern Front, and if these divisions were freed to move to the West, American munitions requirements would undoubtedly skyrocket. To expand civilian production, even if it did not hurt current military needs, would undermine the ability of American industry to meet future contingencies by creating a peace psychology and an accompanying letdown in the military production effort. Thinking Nelson's gradual reconversion program would be interpreted as a sign the war would soon be over, Somervell feared that workers would refuse to take war jobs and that businessmen would refuse to take war contracts. The sense of urgency that he felt was necessary to the war effort would be lost, and with elections approaching in 1944, he was afraid the WPB would be unable, or unwilling, to resist the pressure for further expansion of civilian production, causing reconversion to snowball out of control. Somervell knew that failure to undertake reconversion before the war's end could create pockets of unemployment, but he considered that a minor problem. If some workers were idled by military cutbacks, these hardships would be insignificant when compared to those of the men in uniform, and in any case, such idleness would only be temporary because these workers would have no other choice but to seek employment in areas and industries where they were needed for war work.[43]

As long as reconversion would not take effect until the war's end and as long as it was given no publicity, Somervell had been willing to tolerate planning for its implementation. Nelson's November 30 recommendation, however, was unacceptable, not only because it would have negative psychological results but because it would leave the timing and character of reconversion in the hands of Nelson. However, since reconversion had considerable public support, Somervell decided not to oppose Nelson outright. Instead, he believed the evils that reconversion entailed could be mitigated if its operation were in suitable hands. Therefore, Somervell had Clay prepare a plan that would place control of reconversion in the hands of the PEC. Since this committee mostly consisted of top-ranking service representatives and WPB vice chairmen who had been responsible executives in peacetime, while having no representatives of agencies concerned with civilian production or small business and labor, Somervell was certain the PEC would handle reconversion the way he saw fit.[44]

This strategy also had the advantage of utilizing Wilson as an ally. Whereas Wilson and Somervell had feuded over scheduling in 1942, by the spring of 1943, they were warming to each other. Wilson believed he had been brought to Washington to speed war production, not to fight with the military, and as he worked with the services on a day-to-day basis, he began to see many things through their eyes. Convinced he could succeed only if he had the confidence of the military, Wilson set out to placate Somervell. Among other things, he eliminated the Planning Committee, which had antagonized Somervell in the Feasibility Dispute. Somervell, meanwhile, grew to like Wilson. Where Nelson, who always seemed to be arguing with the military, took forever to make up his mind and then often decided in favor of competing programs, Wilson usually gave "a yes-or-no answer without a delay" and more often than not in Somervell's favor. Simply put, Somervell saw Wilson as the type of man who should be running the WPB.[45]

Following Somervell's instructions, Clay had one of his assistants, J. A.

Panuch, draw up a recommendation to have the PEC form a subcommittee to develop reconversion policies. As Somervell had expected, Wilson endorsed the Panuch Plan. Immersed in the job of securing maximum war production, the PEC chairman tended to agree with Somervell that it was too early to take major steps toward reconversion. In addition, he and his closest advisors, reflecting the views of large manufacturers who wanted to protect prewar competitive patterns, questioned the wisdom of early reconversion out of concern that it would penalize major corporations by giving small firms that had no war contracts the opportunity to jump into civilian production before them. Wilson hoped that, if the PEC were responsible for reconversion, the committee could implement it in such a way as to protect the war effort and the interests of big business during the transition from war to peace.

With the support of the PEC, Wilson agreed at the end of December 1943 to issue a directive putting Panuch's plan into effect, subject to Nelson's approval. However, Nelson would not approve the plan since, in his opinion, it would give the military too much power to determine the reconversion policies.[46]

At the same time that Somervell had Clay trying to bring reconversion under the control of the PEC, he pressed Patterson to have Nelson's November 30 decision reversed. When Nelson asked for specific action on reconversion in line with the November 30 decision, Patterson objected on the grounds that "at a time when major military developments are pending, any action that might be interpreted as a relaxation on the home front would have a particularly unfortunate effect upon the morale of the fighting forces." He was joined by Under Secretary of the Navy James Forrestal, Paul McNutt of the War Manpower Commission (WMC), and many members of the WPB. Faced with this opposition, Nelson retreated, and in early 1944, he announced that there would not be any lifting of restrictions on civilian production "until the probable future course of the war makes it certain that a relaxation will not injure the war effort."

During the late winter and spring of 1944, the reconversion issue drifted with no apparent resolution in sight. In May, the stalemate ended when the navy gave a one-day notice that it was ceasing production of fighter planes at the Long Island, New York, plant of Brewster Corporation, throwing 20,000 surprised workers out of jobs in an area with a labor surplus. Spontaneously, 9,000 of the workers staged a sit-down strike to protest their treatment, and in the wake of public outcry, a new contract was rushed to the Brewster Corporation. The affair dramatically illustrated to the country what could happen nationwide if there were no advance preparations for the war's end and forced Nelson to take action.

Lacking any other quick solution, Nelson authorized the PEC to coordinate contract reductions with the understanding that it would not have overall control of reconversion. He also added civilian vice chairmen to the PEC in order to counterbalance the military's influence. More importantly, Nelson devised a reconversion program, which he announced on June 18 and planned to begin on July 1. Declaring that "restrictions which are not essential to war production and which hamper industry's preparations for the reconversion period need to be lifted at once," he presented a four-step program. The key part, later known as Priority Regulation 25, or spot authorization, called for the regional offices of the WPB to permit production of certain items on which WPB restrictions were lifted. This scheme was designed to wipe out small local pockets of unemployment without a genuine relaxation of the controls over materials, manpower, or production.[47]

A week after he presented the program to the public, Nelson was hospitalized for pneumonia. In his absence, Wilson, at Somervell's request, agreed to delay implementing Nelson's program until a special WPB meeting, which he convened on July 4, could review civilian and military production requirements. At the meeting, the services repeated their arguments against reconversion, asserting that a serious slippage in war production was impairing "the ability of our soldiers to pour it on in full measure to the Germans and the Japs." Ultimately, the WPB agreed not to take any action until Nelson returned, giving the services the opportunity to take their case to Byrnes, now head of the Office of War Mobilization and Reconversion (OWMR), who forced Nelson to institute his program gradually, with spot authorization to go into effect on August 15.[48]

During July and August, Washington was rife with controversy as the contending forces fought, in private and in public, for control of reconversion. Somervell played a prominent role by orchestrating an extensive propaganda campaign to convince the public that any reconversion steps outside of long-term planning would harm the war effort and cost lives. He personally delivered the biggest blow on August 1 in a press conference in which he described shortages in 320 vital categories and implied that reconversion was killing American soldiers.[49]

Nelson did not try to complete with Somervell for headlines, but when he returned to his WPB post on July 26, he complained to Byrnes about the army's exaggerated public releases and argued that, where production problems existed, they could be attributed to the War Department's downward revisions in the ASP earlier in 1944 or to unrealistic schedules.

Rather than silence Somervell or question his arguments, however, Byrnes gave him an important victory. Since the middle of July, the general had been pressing the army's case against reconversion with Byrnes, and feeling there was greater merit in the army's argument that a manpower shortage was hurting the production program, Byrnes decided in early August that the WMC must certify the availability of labor for renewed civilian production before it could be authorized under PR-25. Because the WMC generally agreed with Somervell's position, the decision effectively crippled Nelson's program.

Not content to savor his victory, Somervell continued his campaign in hopes of having Nelson's reconversion program completely revoked. Thus, on August 10, he told the Management-Labor Committee of the WMC that shortages in supplies, bombs, trucks, and other materiel had interfered with battle plans and that closer and more effective manpower control under Byrnes's recent decree was essential if the fighting men were going to have the guns and ammunition necessary for victory. "We'll have to make up what we've lost and more to meet the overseas demands," he stated. "We can't debate these things for a long time." Soon afterwards, Byrnes gave force to Somervell's warning by ordering drastic civilian employment ceilings in a move to mobilize 200,000 additional war workers for increased production of the items critically needed.[50]

Dissatisfied with the fracas over reconversion and anxious to eliminate a potentially damaging issue in the upcoming election, Roosevelt decided to send Nelson to China on a temporary special mission. In all probability, he intended to slip Wilson into his place as chairman of the WPB, but this scheme went awry when the press interpreted Nelson's exile as a repudiation of his reconversion policies, producing an outpouring of protests from Nelson's supporters. Realizing the protests ruled him out as Nelson's replacement, Wilson resigned on August 24. That same day, Roosevelt appointed Julius A. Krug, a former WPB official who had been serving in the navy, as Nelson's acting replacement. Krug had previously battled the military over increased production of civilian goods, and his appointment satisfied small businessmen, labor leaders, and other supporters of Nelson's policies. After returning from China at the end of September 1944, Nelson formally resigned from the WPB, and Krug was then named chairman.

With Krug as chairman of the WPB, the conflict over reconversion lost much of its nasty, personal character.[51] By and large, the new situation reflected Krug's appreciation of the circumstances surrounding his appointment. Experienced and conscientious, he knew that he must not weaken the president's reelection prospects by engaging in public controversy with the military. He also knew that, if controversy arose, he, like Nelson, would lose. Nevertheless, Krug did not roll over and play dead. He expressed general support of Nelson's program and pushed for the development of a reconversion program to take effect as soon as Germany surrendered, plans to provide needed civilians items, and the streamlining of PR-25.

Meanwhile, as requirements for artillery and small arms ammunition, trucks, tires, and communications wire shot up quickly because of heavy fighting in Europe, Somervell pressed Krug to suspend spot authorizations, only a handful of which had gone into effect, in areas with labor shortages. The general argued that they were attracting labor from essential industries. To determine the extent of production lags and the role of labor shortages in causing them, Krug appointed Hiland G. Batcheller, chief of operations for the WPB, to study the production problem. Batcheller's study, completed in November, reported that 40 percent of the production programs were behind schedule. Of these, only 22 percent could be traced to labor shortages. The rest could be attributed to sharp increases in requirements, new models or design changes, and facilities shortages. In other words, as much as 78 percent of the shortages were the result of the military's activities. Even where labor shortages were a factor, Batcheller attributed them to low pay, poor transportation, and inadequate housing and community facilities, not psychological causes growing out of the reconversion program.[52]

Somervell rejected Batcheller's conclusions, and after Krug refused his demand that spot authorization be suspended in key areas for at least 90 days, the military appealed to Byrnes for relief. Byrnes deferred action, but he warned the public on November 16 that he would stop all reconversion activities if manpower shortages were not soon remedied. Byrnes's action did not satisfy Somervell because he wanted reconversion stopped immediately. To achieve this goal, he launched a new propaganda campaign, and beginning on November 20, he gave a series of speeches emphasizing that munitions shortages were adversely affecting the conduct of the war and that "we are short 100,000 workers in plants producing essential materials for the Army supply forces alone."

Advocates of reconversion fought a desperate rearguard action against Somervell, disputing his "factual assertions and interpretations at every point." However, it was a losing fight, for it was too difficult to argue for increases in civilian production when men were dying overseas. Recognizing the weakness of his position, Krug capitulated. On November 23, in a memorandum of agreement with the army, the WPB agreed not to lift any further restrictions on civilian production for the time being and to expand civilian production in the future only after full consideration of any military objections. A week later, on December 1, the army, navy, WPB, and WMC, in a declaration largely drafted by Somervell, suspended spot authorization for 90 days in 103 areas where manpower shortages were critical or where war production was behind schedule. For all practical purposes, Nelson's reconversion program was dead for the time being.[53]

Despite Krug's surrender, Somervell kept on the offensive to ensure that there was no slackening in military production, telling audiences in speeches in early December that American troops were short of supplies because thousands of workers were abandoning war production for nonessential industries and because manufacturers were turning to peacetime production. Praising Somervell for "some commendable plain speaking," the *New York Times* editorialized that the nation should follow his lead and go all out for war production. The National Association of Manufacturers was also impressed, and largely as a result of his speeches, it abandoned all discussion of reconversion problems.

Thereafter, in rapid success, the final nails were driven into the coffin of reconversion. On December 11, Clay joined Byrnes's staff as deputy director of the OWMR, giving it more of a military tint and demonstrating to all observers that Byrnes's office intended to take a more active role in policy making. On December 16, the Germans opened the Battle of the Bulge, creating the sense of urgency Somervell had been trying to bring about since the previous summer. Using the crisis atmosphere spawned by the battle, Byrnes on January 1, 1945, in a report to Roosevelt and Congress bearing Clay's imprint, stated that the reconversion steps taken in 1944 were premature and incompatible with the conduct of the war and that further steps would be delayed until V-E Day.[54]

Not until March 1945 did the WPB again openly discuss reconversion, and not until April 27 did it resume spot authorization. Somervell now made no objection since victory in Europe was only days away. Even so the JCS, prompted by Somervell, argued for a voice in determining civilian requirements during reconversion. Byrnes, who had regularly sided with the military previously, was reluctant to go this far. However, by his not reviewing the military's requirements, the effect was essentially the same since the civilian requirements could be met only after the military services had satisfied their own. As a result, military procurement declined only 10 percent immediately after V-E Day, May 8, and then rapidly through the summer as the war with Japan came to a quick end in August. By the end of 1945, almost all controls had been removed and industrialists were reconverting their plants to civilian production as quickly as possible.[55]

6. SHIPPING

• • • • DURING 1942–43, THE CENTRAL QUESTION concerning the feasibility of any American operation was the availability of shipping. The United States could raise a large army and produce a vast number of supplies, but sufficient shipping was not available to deliver them to all the critical theaters. There were three solutions to this problem: curb ship sinkings, build new ships, and make more efficient use of available shipping. The first two solutions were outside of Somervell's areas of responsibility. In the case of the third, though, he was a major figure.

The effort to make more efficient use of available shipping had been assigned to the WSA. However, Somervell was unhappy with the sweeping powers granted the agency, for he thought they would hinder the military's efforts to meets its own needs. Therefore, he attempted to chip away at the WSA's authority and to assert military prerogatives whenever possible.

Lewis Douglas, the principal figure in the WSA, steadfastly resisted Somervell. A former congressman from Arizona, director of the budget, college president, and insurance company president, as well as a close friend of Roosevelt, Douglas combined managerial skill with "an informed world outlook and diplomatic talent to untangle" confusion. In February 1942, concerned about organizational problems in the WSA, Roosevelt had appointed Douglas as chief advisor to Admiral Land, the agency head, and in May 1942, after questions arose about Land's administrative abilities, the president named Douglas deputy WSA administrator with the understanding that Douglas was, in effect, to head the WSA, while Land concentrated on the ship-building program. Roosevelt assured Douglas that there would be no interference from Land and promised that when conflicts arose with other agencies "I will never fail to back you up."

Douglas's appointment to the WSA greatly disturbed Somervell. The former's close relationship with Roosevelt, as well as a similarly close relationship with Harry Hopkins, ensured that, if a dispute arose between Somervell and the shipping authorities, Douglas had inestimable clout with the White House. In addition, Douglas had a reputation as an Anglophile, and Somervell feared that he would be too prone to adopt a pro-British point of view if the WSA had to choose between American army requirements and British needs in allocating shipping. Despite Douglas's clout, Somervell was determined not to let this happen.[1]

• • •

Trouble between Somervell and Douglas developed early as both men sought to clarify the relationship between their respective agencies. Two issues predominated in the jockeying between the two. One concerned the control of loading and unloading cargo vessels allocated to the army. Previous to the creation of the WSA, the army had controlled the loading and unloading of its own ships, and Somervell, committed to military control of all aspects of the army's supply line, intended to continue this practice. But, soon after he was on the job, Douglas determined that the army was congesting ports by keeping ships tied up too long and, further, was wasting valuable cargo space by letting many of its ships sail without being fully loaded.

To remedy these problems, Douglas put forth a plan calling for greater collaboration between the WSA, the Office of Defense Transportation, the British Ministry of War Transport, and the army in the handling of military and nonmilitary cargoes. While apprehensive that Douglas's proposal might interfere with his ability to speed supplies to overseas forces, Somervell reluctantly accepted it in principle. But as it developed, Douglas's proposal had no practical effect.[2]

The other shipping issue concerned the method of allocating shipping. When Roosevelt created the WSA, both the army and the navy had assumed that their allocations would be made on a long-range basis, usually a minimum of six months. According to their assumption, the movement of vessels during the time they were allocated to the services would be controlled by them.

Douglas took a different position. Maintaining that the shortage of shipping tonnage was too great to permit any system that did not guarantee maximum constant employment of all vessels, he stressed that there must be a single pool from which all requirements—military and nonmilitary—were satisfied. Under Douglas's thinking, allocations of ships to any agency should be made by the

WSA on the basis of a single voyage, and ships would rotate from one claimant to another to secure the greatest number of sailing days for them. For the WSA to allocate a large block of tonnage to one claimant for an extended period of time would only mean less tonnage available for all.

Both services objected to Douglas's position because it significantly restricted their supply procedures by compelling them to calculate in terms of single voyages. The navy soon relented and agreed to Douglas's pooling principle, but Somervell was not ready to concede to Douglas and continued to argue for long-term allocations.[3]

Through the spring of 1942, Somervell and Douglas sparred over these issues. Finally, in early June, their differences came to a head. Hearing reports from Robert Patterson that the WSA intended to take over piers that had been leased by the army, Somervell blasted Douglas for trying to usurp the proper functions of the army and called for a meeting to iron out their differences. On June 11, Somervell and Douglas met over lunch, and on June 13, they signed a memorandum spelling out a modus operandi between their agencies. It represented a concession by Douglas on the port issue and Somervell on the pooling issue. Under the agreement, all cargo vessels assigned to the army were to be loaded and unloaded by the army, but they were to be assigned only for the outward lap of a single voyage and then revert to WSA control after they were unloaded. Both Somervell and Douglas qualified their concessions, however. The army was to depend on the WSA for additional terminal facilities and labor, while theater commanders could hold freighters at their designation "as the military necessity demands."[4]

The Somervell-Douglas treaty seemingly cleared the air between the army and the WSA, but in reality, neither side was truly satisfied. Douglas looked to have complete authority over cargo space by remodeling the WSA along the lines of the British Ministry of War Transport, which combined control of civilian and military shipping under a single civilian agency. In fact, he had negotiated the agreement with Somervell only to prevent ASF-WSA differences from becoming a legislative matter.

Meanwhile, Somervell was dissatisfied because ultimate control over the allocation of shipping remained in Douglas's hands. Convinced the army should have complete control over its shipping so that strategy and logistics could be coordinated, he regarded the agreement only as a stopgap measure.[5]

Not surprisingly, considering these attitudes, the agreement soon broke down. Energetically searching for economies in ship employment, Douglas in early August reported to Roosevelt and Churchill that military and nonmilitary cargoes should be freely mixed so that shipping space might be utilized to the maximum. Accordingly, in a "Dear Bill" letter to Somervell on October 9, 1942, Douglas cited evidence of inefficiency in the army's ship operations and called for the army to coordinate its loading operations with those of the WSA and British agencies in the United States. Under the plan he set forth, all army cargo except that scheduled to be sent on ships under permanent army control and those involved in combat operations would be pooled with other export cargo in a bank distributed among all American ports. Sailings would be scheduled and cargo space loaded with a view toward maximizing utilization of space, arranging short routes, and ensuring efficient unloading at the destination points. Departure ports would be assigned on the basis of destination points, and most voyages would have multiple destinations. Coordination for the program would be in the hands of a group drawn from the principal agencies concerned with shipping and under WSA chairmanship.[6]

Douglas's letter infuriated Somervell. While it proposed nothing more than informal interagency cooperation to bring about economical use of shipping, he saw it as the forerunner of future plans to place management and planning of all overseas cargo movements in a centralized agency under civilian control. To Somervell, the demands of military supply called for the right item to be at the right place at the right time and, thus, were not easily reconciled with the demands of the economy. For this reason, he was insistent that the army must control its own shipping if it were to meet its mission. Also, Douglas had suggested that as a natural corollary to cargo pooling "vessels should load their entire cargo at one berth and under the same continuous supervision." In Somervell's mind, this suggestion sounded like a subterfuge to cancel army control of its own loadings, which he considered a sacrosanct feature of the June modus operandi with Douglas.[7]

Matters were made more difficult by the timing of Douglas's plan. It arrived only days after the Feasibility Dispute had reached its climax, and it, along with the drive by the WPB to place limits on the army production program, persuaded Somervell that civilians were assaulting him on two fronts so as to strip from the army decisions that were "military in character" and "must rest with the military authority." To Somervell's way of thinking, the establishment of a group under WSA chairmanship to coordinate loading would further undermine legitimate military authority to the detriment of the war effort and, thus, had to be scotched.

In the background, Somervell saw something even more sinister at work. For some time, he had believed that the British were out "to destroy him" in order to have a greater voice in the American production and shipping programs. In this way, they could keep the American army small and "get a lot of equipment from this country" and enhance their own postwar position. He also believed that Douglas was pro-British and too ready to favor what Somervell regarded as inflated British shipping requirements. By proposing to pool all military and civilian cargo through a group chaired by the WSA, Douglas, in Somervell's opinion, was aiding his antagonists.[8]

A squabble over responsibility for consignment of lend-lease material further fueled the Somervell–Douglas dispute. Somervell wanted all cargo, military and civilian, consigned to commanding officers in the theaters of operations. Douglas strongly opposed Somervell's scheme in the belief that it would place undue hardship on the British. In a telephone conversation with Douglas on October 19, Somervell vented his anger over Douglas's refusal to endorse his plan. He said that "the army knew better than our allies where Lend-Lease materials . . . could best serve American interests, and that under . . . [his plan] British filching of cargo, which . . . [had been] outrageous in the past, could be avoided."

Douglas replied that, under Somervell's system "Lend-Lease material could be consigned to the commanding general in a theater of operations, and directed by him at any time at all from its original destination in the Lend-Lease country to wherever else the commanding general felt like sending it," leaving the British uncertain about what cargo they would actually receive. To Douglas, this was wrong because there were political considerations in some of the lend-lease countries that had to be taken into account. He added, "if we expected to have responsible allies, we had to treat them as responsible people and grant them at the least the courtesy of letting them know what they might expect in the way of war material to prosecute their war efforts." Restating that it was necessary for the army "to have the power to direct" cargo at any time, Somervell accused Douglas of "championing the British" and said that he "apparently could not agree" with Douglas "because he, Somervell, was 'on the American side.' "

Somervell's accusation deeply distressed Douglas. No doubt there was truth in Somervell's references to Douglas's pro-British stance. His presidency of McGill University in Canada and his long-standing appreciation of English culture inclined him to relate to the difficulties that Britain was facing, which was not necessarily a defect in light of existing circumstances. But, while a ready listener to British concerns and an advocate of fair treatment, Douglas never regarded himself "as an easy mark" for the British. Somervell's comments seemed to him as unfair and untruthful and only served to confirm in his mind what others had told him: Somervell was "unscrupulous, grasping and dangerous."[9]

On the same day as the telephone conversation, Somervell also responded to Douglas's new shipping plan in an "offhand, almost flippant reply," remarking that the best efforts had failed to discover any advantage that might be gained from it. Somervell called Douglas's conclusions non sequiturs, reminded the latter that commercial standards of stowage did not apply to emergency shipments of combat loadings (Douglas's proposals exempted these loadings), alleged that the British were wasteful in ship operations, suggested that the shipping savings projected by Douglas would be a small business, and objected to forming any more committees. Then, in a sudden turnabout, he invited Douglas to lunch to discuss their differences.[10]

Douglas was not deterred by Somervell's broadside. Several days before his telephone clash with Somervell, he had asked John McCloy, his brother-in-law, to mediate the dispute over consignment. After consulting with McCloy, Somervell agreed to his mediation, although at the time he did not know that Douglas and McCloy were brothers-in-law. On October 23, McCloy met with Douglas, Lucius Clay, and Sir Arthur Salter of the British Merchant Shipping Mission to hammer out a settlement. Speaking for Somervell, Clay insisted the army should be the consignee for all lend-lease cargo, but after hearing both sides of the argument, McCloy in principle supported the WSA as consignee. Later, Clay and Douglas worked out an arrangement under which the loading and shipment of lend-lease supplies would be the responsibility of the WSA. However, if the supplies were consigned to American commanders abroad for distribution within a theater, they would be moved under army control.[11]

On October 27, Somervell and Douglas met for lunch to discuss their differences. Considering their strongly held opinions and the harsh words they had exchanged, the meeting was "both anticlimatic and inconclusive." Both men agreed with great conviviality that it was silly for them to be canterkerous with each other and that they should refrain from writing nasty letters and "get together and fight the war." Somervell even hinted that the real source of their friction was their chief subordinates: Gross in the Transportation Corps and Captain Granville Conway, the WSA official at the port of New York. Conway, Somervell said, wanted "more and more authority," while Gross was predisposed to reject anything from the WSA simply because it came from the WSA.

Douglas politely rejected Somervell's thesis. He explained that he had originated the proposal on loading, not Conway, and that he knew Gross was only reflecting Somervell's thinking in his remarks about the WSA's pro-British positions in the ASF-WSA disputes. As for the consignment dispute, Somervell, knowing that McCloy had sided with Douglas against him, told Douglas, "I give in completely; we'll do what you want us to do.'" In the matter of combining cargo, Somervell and Douglas agreed to proceed very slowly and only to the degree that it proved practicable.[12]

The luncheon conference ended the latest imbroglio between Somervell and Douglas, but neither man was truly reconciled toward the other, and in early December, they were again "at each other's throats." On the grounds that army officials in England had complained that commercially loaded cargoes could not be sufficiently identified for "intelligent inland distribution" in the United Kingdom, Gross terminated the policy of combined loading in New York and decreed that army materiel would thereafter be loaded exclusively at army ports.

Appalled by the action, Douglas took his case to Hopkins. Combined loading had yielded economies in shipping during November, he pointed out, adding that Gross's unilateral decision could only produce "an unconscionable extravagance in the use of shipping." He further noted that "I am about at the end of my rope" in trying to secure Somervell's assistance in the economy program through persuasion and warned that he would not yield on this issue. Hopkins was sympathetic to Douglas's position, telling him that "these fellows will not be persuaded" and advising him to seek the support of Roosevelt.

On December 18, Douglas visited Roosevelt, armed with a directive formally addressed to Admiral Land that reaffirmed the authority of the WSA under its February 1942 charter to control the "operations, including loading" of all merchant ships except those allocated for special task and assault forces and those that could "truly be classified as fleet auxiliaries." This meant that the vessels which handled regular movements of military cargo to the theaters would be loaded at commercial piers under the auspices of the WSA.

Roosevelt approved of the thrust of the directive since Douglas advised him it merely told the services to do what Roosevelt had already told them to do, but he wondered if it were wise to issue the directive without consultation with the services. Douglas objected to this step, arguing that it would produce only violent discord with Somervell. Civilian authority had to be reaffirmed, and that could best be accomplished by issuing the directive without negotiating with the man who up to this time had "refused to obey" the authority already vested in the WSA and wanted "to take civilian functions over." Roosevelt agreed, but he added that "if this doesn't work you will catch hell."[13]

Roosevelt's comment proved correct. Enraged by Douglas's directive, Somervell persuaded Henry Stimson to ask Land not to put it into effect until the army had studied it. He also prepared a memorandum to Roosevelt, for Admiral Leahy's signature, protesting the directive. Since the JCS had "the full responsibility for active operations overseas," Somervell said, "[they] must therefore have the necessary authority, including full control of the flow of their supplies."[14]

The loading dispute was thrashed out at a meeting on December 28 in Leahy's office in the White House. Those present included Douglas, Land, Admiral Leahy, Chief of Staff Marshall, Chief of Naval Operations Admiral Ernest J. King, General Arnold, and Somervell. In an effort to defuse the conflict, Douglas asserted that the December 18 directive did not go beyond the WSA's charter of February 1942, which exempted the services' transport fleet from WSA control, and that the WSA had no desire to take over the actual loading functions of the army and navy transport services. Instead, the agency simply wanted to participate with the services in the overall planning of military cargo movements to make certain all merchant shipping and cargo movements of a nontactical character were brought under a single coordinated program.

None of the military and naval leaders was appeased by Douglas's explanations, and each expressed his anger over Douglas's failure to consult the JCS before going to the White House. They were also bothered by the discrepancy between what the directive stated and what Douglas now said he construed it to mean.

Somervell was especially biting in his comments. At one point, after indicating he had helped write the February 1942 charter, he charged that Douglas was stretching it when he extended the word operations to include the loading of military cargo. Somervell said that it would be detrimental to have a civilian agency exercising control over loading because it "would always have uppermost in its mind the full utilization of all available cargo space whereas for military purposes this ideal has to be sacrificed at times in order to have cargoes meet the needs of troops in theaters of operations in the most expeditious manner." At another point, Somervell implied that the WSA was trying to protect commercial interests at the expense of the war effort and demanded to know why, if the directive did not go beyond the February 1942 charter as Douglas stated, it should not be rescinded immediately: "go to the President and have him rescind the Directive; then we'll sit down."

Not fazed by Somervell's demand, Douglas bluntly said, "No, we'll let the Directive stand." Shortly after this exchange, Leahy ended the meeting with the recommendation that the representatives of the services and the WSA meet again "with the view to interpreting" the December 18 directive "to the satisfaction of all concerned."[15]

Over the next two weeks, the air gradually cleared. For one thing, Douglas persuaded Leahy and Marshall that an effort should be made to carry out the WSA's economy program. Moreover, on December 31, Douglas and Leahy agreed to a WSA proposal that protected combat and strategic loadings, allowed for civilian cargo on military loadings, and permitted the presence of service advisors when the WSA was loading military cargo. Somervell bridled at the very thought of WSA collaboration with the army on vessels for use by the army and, through Leahy, sent a protest to the White House, but it had no impact.

Through contact with Hopkins, Director of the Budget Smith, and White House assistants, Douglas effectively presented his position to Roosevelt. Equally important, the willingness of Leahy and Marshall to accept the December 31 compromise made a deep impression upon Roosevelt, who let it be known that he stood behind Douglas and expected the WSA and the services to sit down together every day "for the next three weeks" and reach an understanding for loading operations.[16]

During the next weeks, army and WSA representatives reached an agreement on operating principles. Under it, the army and the WSA were to work out, on a continuous basis, "a consolidated loading program embracing all cargo moving to identical destinations," subject to modification in the case of compelling military needs. The army still disagreed with the December 18 directive, but since it remained on the books despite Somervell's heated opposition, the ASF-WSA fight over loading was a victory for Douglas.

In some ways, the victory was "more form than substance." As a result of Douglas's statement that he had no desire to encroach upon the accustomed operations of the army transport service, the power of the WSA to supervise the loading of military cargoes was largely theoretical, and the pooling Douglas had called for still depended upon the cooperation of military officials. Generally, this cooperation was forthcoming. Obviously influenced by the thought that Douglas might invoke the provisions of the December 18 directive if the army did not cooperate and knowing Roosevelt would support the WSA deputy administrator, Somervell essentially collaborated with the WSA to make efficient use of cargo space. After January 1943, most ships left port fully loaded, which had been Douglas's goal in the first place.[17]

• • •

In the first half of 1943 Somervell and Douglas were once more enmeshed in a shipping controversy, this one centering around the British import crisis. The very existence of the industries and people of Britain depended on an uninterrupted flow of imports, which in the prewar years had averaged over 50 million tons a year. But under the press of wartime shipping shortages, British imports declined drastically. In 1940, they dropped to 42 million tons; in 1941, to 31 million tons; and in 1942, to a dangerously low level of 23 million tons. By the end of 1942, the British were eating into their stocks, which had fallen precariously close to a level that the War Cabinet regarded as irreducible. In sum, the British war economy was approaching the point of collapse.

During the summer and fall of 1942, American and British officials on both sides of the Atlantic grew increasingly concerned about the situation, and in October, the United States decided to allocate to the British "an appropriate portion of the net gain in the merchant tonnage" being produced in American shipyards. As welcome as the American decision was, the hard-pressed British, faced with the prospect of closing factories because of a shortage of raw materials, wanted specific assurances from the United States about the amount of shipping that would be made available to the British import program. Thus, when Sir Oliver Lyttelton, British minister of production, came to Washington in November 1942 to negotiate an understanding on several war-related matters, he was under instructions to obtain a definite commitment on shipping.

In meetings with Roosevelt and Hopkins, Lyttelton asked the United States to guarantee enough shipping in 1943 to bring British imports up to 27 million tons. After consulting with his civilian advisors, Roosevelt in a formal letter to Churchill on November 30 agreed to the request. Since the British estimated their own capacity for 1943 at 20 million tons, Roosevelt was committing American shipping (on loan rather than transfer of flag) to carrying seven million tons of imports to the United Kingdom, a requirement that would mean turning over to the British and, thereafter, leaving in continuous service to them "an average of nearly 300,000 tons each month of carrying capacity." Roosevelt qualified his commitment by warning that contingencies might delay the transfers in the first months of 1943. However, he assured Churchill that there would be no diversion of American shipping from the import program without his personal approval.

For some unexplained reason, perhaps because he considered it strictly a civil matter, Roosevelt did not inform military and naval authorities of his discussions with Lyttelton on the import program or his commitment to provide shipping for it. The JCS finally learned of the commitment in late December when a copy of Roosevelt's letter was shown to them "very unofficially and confidentially" by British representatives in Washington so that the chiefs might be aware of its potential impact upon their own plans. Only in early January 1943 did the WSA and British officials sit down and attempt to interpret commitments and implications, and only on January 18, did Land formally acknowledge the existence of the letter and present a tentative schedule, prepared by Douglas, of tonnage shipments through May 1943.[18]

Against this backdrop, American and British political and military leaders convened in Casablanca, Morocco, in January 1943 to plan their combined strategy for 1943. Because Roosevelt wanted the American delegation kept small, Somervell was its sole logistical expert, and curiously, the WSA was not represented at all even though the availability of shipping would have a decisive impact upon strategic planning. As a result, Somervell, who was predisposed to favor military interests over civilian interests in the allocation of shipping and was inadequately informed about the November 30 letter, was the only American present who could claim any familiarity with the shipping situation and was, therefore, given principal responsibility for handling shipping questions. Since Roosevelt regarded the British import program as a civil matter, it was not formally discussed except for affirming that maintenance of Britain's war economy was one of the first charges upon the Allied war effort. Nevertheless, consideration of the program played an important role in the conference's deliberations, especially in regard to BOLERO, a troop buildup in the United Kingdom for an invasion of France, and helped create results that were nearly disastrous.[19]

Anxious to resume the BOLERO buildup, which had been delayed by operations in North Africa, Marshall indicated that the flow of troops and supplies to the United Kingdom must be drastically increased in anticipation of a landing on the French coast, possibly in the fall of 1943 and certainly in the spring of 1944. Consequently, the CCS asked Somervell to draw up a schedule showing how many American troops could be deployed to the United Kingdom and supported there by the end of 1943. He was assisted by Lord Frederick Leathers, head of the British Ministry of War Transport. Crucial to Somervell's calculations was the amount of shipping that could be made available for

BOLERO, which in turn depended to a significant degree on Roosevelt's specific commitment to the British import program in his November 30 letter.

About this commitment, Somervell apparently had two misconceptions. First, he seemed to regard the American commitment as one aimed at replacing Britain's net shipping losses rather than meeting its marginal needs. Depending on the course of ship losses in 1943, the difference between the two "could mean much or little." Second, Somervell interpreted the phrase "nearly 300,000 tons each month" as an implied ceiling on the amount to be turned over to the British import program and as a single-voyage rather than a cumulative allocation of shipping to the British. On the basis of this interpretation, Somervell concluded that, with only eleven months remaining in the year, this would necessitate the carriage of at most 2.5 million to 3 million tons of British imports in American bottoms in 1943, not the 7 million tons the British expected. In addition, Somervell expected that figure to be too high, for he was optimistic, on the basis of a current downward trend in losses to German submarines, that the total required to be carried in American bottoms might be far less.[20]

Leathers, who was fully aware of Roosevelt's commitment, did not correct Somervell on the British understanding of the president's letter. In fact, all the discussions between Somervell and Leathers at the conference had an unreal character to them. At the beginning of the conference, Roosevelt, with the fight between Somervell and Douglas over loading fresh in his mind, had asked Leathers for help "in explaining to our Service Departments the utility and necessity of W.S.A.," a rather surprising request since Roosevelt had failed to bring a WSA representative to the conference. Leathers complied with Roosevelt's request, but his efforts were in vain because Somervell stated that he did not appreciate a lecture from a British official on the importance of civilian authority.

From that point on, the two men talked rather than communicated. When they discussed shipping for ANAKIM, a proposed operation to recapture Burma, Somervell came away with the impression that the British would provide all that was needed, while Leathers came away with the impression that the matter had not even been seriously discussed, let alone decided. Their lack of communication was more apparent when they discussed the import program and BOLERO. Leathers assumed that Somervell was fully versed in Roosevelt's letter and became confused and then frustrated by Somervell's apparent ignorance of its details. Rather than recognize that Somervell had a different interpretation, Leathers concluded that the American was engaging in trickery in order to "whittle down or ignore the President's commitment of 27 million tons for the Import Program" so there would be more shipping available for BOLERO.[21]

When their discussions threatened to break down, Leathers decided to be as accommodating as possible. Under Somervell's relentless pushing, he tentatively agreed to contribute 1.6 million tons of cargo shipping to BOLERO. However,

Leathers heavily qualified this commitment to protect the British import program and Britain's major operational needs. Specifically, his commitment to BOLERO was based upon Britain having a surplus of shipping over and above her needs. This was a wholly unrealistic condition since, under Roosevelt's letter, Britain was to receive only enough American shipping to fill the marginal requirements that her own shipping could not fill. In other words, there could be no surplus for the British to give back to the Americans. Further, Leathers emphasized that the figure of 1.6 million tons was a rapid estimate subject to check. Somervell, Leathers later proclaimed, "fully understood and repeatedly acknowledged his understanding."[22]

If Somervell fully understood what Leathers was saying, he did not evince it in drawing up his projected troop deployment schedule (CCS 172) for 1943. On the basis that the British would provide considerable assistance in shipping, Somervell laid out a schedule which, among other things, called for the transport of close to one million American troops to Britain by the end of 1943. This figure was derived from his estimate of the maximum capacity of cargo shipping that would be available in the first half of the year and of troop shipping in the second half, when 734,000 troops were to be sent, and assumed that British ports could handle an inflow of cargo at the rate of 150 ships per month. When the CCS discussed Somervell's schedule on January 23, Marshall supported his figures, prompting the chiefs to accept the schedule as the basis for detailed planning with the warning from Churchill that the British commitment should be considered minimal.[23]

The officials left Casablanca operating on assumptions very far apart. The British assumed that they would receive enough shipping from the United States in 1943 to carry more than seven million tons of their domestic imports and, in fact, were soon to ask for enough shipping to carry 7.6 million tons. Somervell and American military leaders, meanwhile, thought that the British would need only about one-third of that amount and would turn back to the United States a significant part of the shipping lent to them to carry military cargoes for BOLERO. The gap between the two assumptions was roughly six million tons of cargo capacity, or nearly one-fourth of the entire cargo tonnage the United States was planning to ship overseas to American army forces through the end of 1943. The gap was a ticking bombshell, and it was only a matter of time until it exploded and threatened to upset completely most of the strategic decisions made at Casablanca.[24]

An awareness that something might be amiss "came in stages and almost by accident." The first inkling came when Somervell had a meeting with Douglas on February 19, the day after the general had arrived back in Washington from a three-week trip through North Africa, the Middle East, Iran, and India. Somervell's purpose in meeting with Douglas was to arrange a special convey to carry supplies to North Africa to speed up the rearming of the French. In the course of their discussion, Douglas informed Somervell that "this was a demand that could not be met" unless ships were taken from other services, most probably the British import program. He added that, under the existing arrangement, this could be done only with Roosevelt's consent. Either out of ignorance or irritation at Douglas's refusal to accede to his demand, Somervell asked "What arrangement?" Thereupon, Douglas reminded Somervell of Roosevelt's November 30 letter, prompting Somervell to state that it had been superseded by his agreement with Leathers at Casablanca and to give Douglas a copy of CCS 172. Unaware of its provisions, Douglas decided it was better not to argue with Somervell until he investigated the details of the Casablanca agreement and promised to do his best to find some ships for the North African convoy.[25]

Over the next several days, Douglas learned of the British interpretation of what had taken place at Casablanca through a conversation with Sir Arthur Salter, Leathers's representative in Washington, and through an exchange of wires with Averell Harriman, the American lend-lease representative in London. At the same time, he consulted Hopkins about Somervell's request, telling Roosevelt's advisor that it probably could be met only by withdrawing ships from the import program. Since this action would require Roosevelt to invoke the escape clause in his November 30 letter, a step both men knew Roosevelt was loathe to do because it would necessitate extended consultations between the White House and London, Douglas decided to do what he could on his own to meet Somervell's demand while trying to protect the import program. Through a variety of means, he was able to release nineteen vessels for North Africa without damaging the import program, satisfying both Somervell and the British. But, his miracle only postponed full exposure of the Casablanca misunderstanding to a time when it threatened to become worse because of an alarming lag in the flow of British imports.[26]

Whether Somervell suspected that something might be wrong with his assumptions on shipping as a result of his meeting with Douglas is not clear. If he did, he did not operate on that basis over the next several days. On February 27, suspecting the British might not provide enough shipping for BOLERO, he instructed Gross to press Douglas to see that the British made good their commitment to BOLERO assistance. Two days later, Gross asked Douglas if he were aware of the agreement Somervell had made with Leathers. Douglas acknowledged that Somervell had given him a copy of CCS 172, but he added that the "arrangement seemed . . . to be inconsistent with the pressure placed upon us to allocate American controlled ships to UK service." He further added that Harriman had cabled him that "inasmuch as the import program had disintegrated so seriously and was not being met, the premise on which any suggestion of aid to us had rested was invalid, and that we could expect no assistance." Several days later, Douglas reexplained the British position to Somervell. Nevertheless, Somervell still did not fully comprehend the extent of the gap, for he continued to assume the British would need only 2.4 to 3 million tons of shipping for the import program.

Just how wrong Somervell was soon became apparent. For some unexplained reason, Gross suddenly realized his chief and the British had different understandings about the Casablanca agreement. On March 10, he alerted Somervell to this reality in a hastily scribbled note:

> Lord Leathers made his promise to you with U.S. help to the extent of lifting 7,000,000 tons in mind. You accepted it with that help reduced to 30 sailings a month in mind, or about 2,400,000 tons lift. The whole matter of U.S. help in the U.K. import program must come out in open for decision by CCS.

Gross's realization that Somervell's assumption about the Casablanca arrangement was wrong was driven home two days later when the British presented to the CCS their estimated shipping requirements to carry out their share of the Casablanca strategic program, laying bare for all to see the time bomb that had been ticking since Casablanca.[27]

The British had begun to work on a detailed schedule of their shipping requirements to carry out their share of the Casablanca strategy in February, and in early March, they sent Foreign Secretary Anthony Eden to Washington with word that Britain would require American shipping aid beyond the allocation already made to its 1943 needs. The starting point for the British presentation of their shipping requirements was their insistence that the import program of 27 million tons for 1943 must be carried out since maintenance of Britain's domestic war economy had always been recognized by Allied leaders as essential to the war effort. This meant, based on their most recent calculations of available shipping, that up to nine million tons would have to be carried in American bottoms. The British also stated that they needed additional American shipping assistance for British programs in the Indian Ocean, Africa, and Australia and would not be able to provide any shipping for BOLERO. Without aid, the British said they would have to limit their operations in the Mediterranean and their contribution to Russian convoys and, for all practical purposes, put their war effort in Burma on hold.[28]

The British schedule was presented to the CCS on March 12. As soon as he read it, Marshall had Gross calculate the likely effects of the British demand upon the American part of the Casablanca strategy. His findings were sobering. Somervell had estimated that 1.4 million American troops might be deployed overseas in 1943, but if the United States met all British demands, the deployment would be reduced to 800,000 troops. More importantly, since the British most needed the shipping in the first half of the year, meeting their demands would mean that the movement of American troops overseas would virtually cease until the second half of the year. "It would seem apparent," Gross concluded, "that the conflict between the rapidly increasing demand for U.S. shipping aid to the British and the fulfillment of 1943 Casablanca operational programs must be resolved by a reduction in that aid or a downward revision of the program with its implications on the size of the Army during 1943."[29]

Seeing the Casablanca strategic program possibly "going up in smoke," American military and naval leaders reacted with great vehemence to the British proposal. In the meeting of the CCS on March 12, they took the position that the irreducible minimum of British imports was not a question to be determined unilaterally by the British. Instead, it should be balanced against other demands.

Somervell was clearly of the mind to challenge the whole notion that the import program was sacrosanct, but before he could tackle it, Roosevelt asked Hopkins to dig into the matter, giving Somervell little to do until Hopkins completed his work. On March 20, Hopkins met with Gross and Clay and told them that he wanted Somervell to prepare the American viewpoint on the military's needs. He even suggested the outlines of that viewpoint by telling the two generals he would inform Roosevelt that the army would be unable to carry out its planned operations unless ships were taken from the run to North Russia and the British import program.[30]

Somervell immediately went to work on the project, and on March 22, he completed a plan that reaffirmed the JCS's thinking. Under it, both American and British military operations were to receive full support. This was to be accomplished by devoting enough American shipping to move only about 3.9 million tons of imports to Britain during 1943 (most of it in the second half of the year), or 5.4 million tons if ANAKIM were eliminated, and by cutting all "aid to Russia by the North Atlantic route without enlarging that not scheduled by the other routes."

Just as he completed the plan, Somervell received hints that Roosevelt, in light of a recent high-level decision to suspend temporarily North Russia convoys on the grounds of the submarine threat, favored a quid pro quo for Stalin. Thereupon, the general drew up a new plan that dealt more harshly with British imports and more leniently with Soviet aid shipments. It raised the number of Persian Gulf sailings during the second half of 1943, at least in part, by reducing the allotment of American shipping for the British import program to 2.3 million tons during the last nine months of 1943, with another 1.7 million tons to be sandwiched in with army cargoes to the United Kingdom. Combined with the shipments during the first three months of the year, this plan would have the United States carry 4.8 million tons of imports to Britain for the entire year. Justifying his cuts in the import program on the grounds of military necessity, Somervell insisted that the allocation of shipping he laid out was the "minimum which will insure a reasonable chance of success." The JCS agreed with Somervell's plan, and during the last days of March and early April, they discussed the best way to submit it to the president.[31]

By this time, Somervell had already lost the battle. Convinced that the British import program was vital to the Allied war effort, Douglas was anxious to find a way for Roosevelt to fulfill his original commitment to Churchill. He also had just come through a bitter struggle with Somervell over the control of ship loading and was predisposed to interpret Somervell's questioning of the import program as a challenge to WSA's control over allocation of American shipping. Talking with Hopkins on March 19, he complained that "Somervell and Gross were up to their old tricks, in a different fashion this time, trying to make the CCS the allocator of shipping." During the last week of March, Douglas convinced Hopkins that Roosevelt had already made a firm commitment to support the British import program at the rate of seven million tons "and that we had to look at the matter in that light." Equally important, he also convinced Hopkins that Somervell was unwilling to concede 7 million tons as a valid point of departure in discussions with the British. Thus, there was nothing to be gained by bringing the ASF head into the negotiations.[32]

Actually, Hopkins needed little convincing. He knew the importance of the commitment to the maintenance of the alliance, a top priority of Roosevelt, and for this reason, like Douglas, he was resolved to keep shipping in civilian hands.

The climax of the British import crisis occurred in a White House meeting on March 29 when Roosevelt met with Eden, Hopkins, and Douglas to discuss the import program. No military representatives were present. For the most part, Douglas held the floor. Prompted by Hopkins, he emphasized that the import program must be sustained and that, despite Somervell's warning, it could be done without crippling the Casablanca decisions. The army, he charged, had always overstated its requirements to cover every possible contingency, and its current requirements were probably overstated as well. If shipping were carefully budgeted, he continued, both military and civilian programs could be carried out beyond midyear, making the problem essentially a short-term one lasting through the second quarter of 1943. While conceding the situation was "very, very tight" for April, Douglas was confident that it could be handled if military needs were discounted somewhat. In fact, he opined it would be possible not only to accelerate the British import program but also to meet other British requests.

Douglas had not even completed his presentation when Roosevelt asked, "And you can do all these things and meet the UK import program?" When Douglas replied that WSA planning indicated this was the case, Roosevelt abruptly announced, "Well, we can consider the import program settled." Turning to Eden, he added, "You can tell the Prime Minister . . . that we will, for the reasons that have been enumerated here today and for many other reasons, make good our commitment."[33]

Roosevelt's decision to support the import program at the figure the British requested was a serious rebuff to Somervell, comparable in significance to that in the Feasibility Dispute. In both cases, Somervell had argued that the military viewpoint must be given first priority and that civilian agencies should defer to the military's judgment on war production and the distribution of American merchant tonnage, and in both cases, he lost.

Somervell did not take this latest rebuff without complaint. When Douglas met with him and Gross to discuss the April shipments for ANAKIM, Somervell, in referring to the import program, grumbled that the British "were getting off very light" and continued to insist "that during the month of May if the military movements were to be carried out they would make severe inroads on their import program." He added that the current rate of imports—16 million tons a year—was sufficient for Britain to remain a productive ally for the United States. Refusing to engage in an argument with Somervell, Douglas retorted that "the President had made the arrangement, that it would be a pity if the President, within one week of discussing the matter with Eden, were to call Churchill and to modify the arrangement he had made." Somervell, he noted in his diary, "seemed to agree to this for this month." But his agreement was only for the moment.

Several days later, Somervell complained directly to Roosevelt that the shipping allocations he had approved on March 29, contrary to Douglas' claims, would not provide enough shipping to carry out American military operations and proposed that Roosevelt adopt the shipping schedule the ASF had put forth on March 25 to Hopkins. However, Roosevelt "held to his course."[34]

Somervell was still not ready to give up the fight, for the TRIDENT Conference, held in Washington in May, gave him a new opportunity to curtail the American allocation for the British import program. In contrast to the situation at Casablanca, however, Roosevelt made sure that civilian shipping experts were intimately involved, providing Douglas the opportunity to protect the import problem from Somervell's assault.

In preparation for the conference, British and WSA officials calculated that there would be a total deficit of 336 sailings for the last half of 1943 (155 British and 181 American), which represented less than 5 percent of total requirements. Douglas did not consider this deficit as unduly formidable, and on the eve of the conference, he and Salter agreed that with careful economies it might "well prove to be manageable."

Somervell took a different position. Still smarting from Roosevelt's decision to support British shipping needs no matter what the cost to American military operations, he wanted to have the allocation for British imports designated as a residual legatee separate from other requirements and have the combined deficit charged against the import program. Douglas and Hopkins overruled him at a preconference meeting, but he was not deterred and renewed his effort once the conference was underway.³⁵

During the first stages of the conference, British and American officials reviewed their individual and combined resources while waiting for the CCS to draw up their strategic plans. Finally, on May 22, ten days after the conference opened, the CCS handed their plans over to the shipping people with the charge to evaluate their feasibility in light of available shipping. The American officials met first, with Somervell challenging the British import allocations and Douglas charging that army requirements were inflated beyond reason. Then, the Americans were joined by Leathers and several other British officials.

Like Douglas, the British questioned the army's requirements, while Somervell made numerous references to the unnecessary requirements of the import program. In response to his references, the British stated their intention to bring their "shipping position into equilibrium" by eliminating 155 sailings from less urgent theaters (most notably India since one of the decisions of the conference had been to postpone ANAKIM), as well as the import program, and suggested that Somervell "might do some shrinking" as well. Douglas, meanwhile, proposed that the shipping problem might be solved "by advancing the volume of U.K. import program into the summer months of 1943 when the U.S. Army program was at its lowest tide," thus making it possible to use the winter months for a larger number of ships carrying military cargo.

After a break, during which Gross had reduced the American deficit for 1943 from 181 to 135 sailings, Somervell was prompted to suggest the British pick up half of the American deficit. The British categorically refused, and after much heated argument with Leathers and Douglas, Somervell reluctantly conceded that the army could accomplish more shrinkage.

On May 23, Somervell presented their findings to the JCS and joined with Douglas in pronouncing the 1943 shipping deficit on the American side, estimated at less than 4 percent of projected requirements, as a manageable one. Later that day, Leathers presented the findings to the CCS. The key, as both Somervell and Leathers emphasized in their presentations, was the solution proffered by Douglas, namely, to meet both strategic requirements and the British import program by reorganizing sailings and port capacity to increase imports in the summer months and facilitate the movement of military cargo in the winter months. The CCS expressed their pleasure with the shipping verdict, ending the import program crisis.³⁶

Similar to the Somervell-Douglas fight over loading, the controversy over the British import program crisis was a victory for Douglas. Douglas's stance was something of a gamble in the spring of 1943, particularly given the high shipping losses to submarines in February and March 1943. It was a gamble Somervell resisted since American military operations stood to be cut if it were lost. However, a dramatic decline in losses to German submarines after March, a steady climb in the construction of new ships, more careful planning to eliminate wasteful scheduling and loading practices, and a reduction in army requirements, which as Douglas correctly asserted, Somervell had overstated, significantly increased the availability of shipping space. From a low point of 4.5 million tons in the first three months of 1943, the import program reached nearly 12 million tons by the end of June, a figure that seemed totally out of reach the previous March. At the same time, the TRIDENT calculations demonstrated that the import program could be satisfied without significant impact upon the military's strategic plans.

Somervell and his shipping experts were still skeptical that the trend in available shipping would continue to climb. However, the worst was behind them. When the Allied leaders met again in Quebec, Canada, in August 1943, the shipping deficits that Somervell had predicted had disappeared.[37]

• • •

Following the British import program controversy, relations between Somervell and the WSA improved. The major questions regarding the shipping situation had been resolved, largely in favor of the WSA because of the strong support Roosevelt had given to Douglas and because of Douglas's ability to fight off Somervell's attempts to assert military control over shipping. Somervell could now even find some good in the work of Douglas. At the Quebec Conference, Douglas took the side of the American military in a dispute over the availability of British troop transports and pressured Leathers to make concessions to the American position. Impressed by Douglas's performance, Somervell afterward patted him on the back with the accolade "Great job, Lew."[38]

In June 1914 Brehon B. Somervell graduated from West Point and was commissioned a second lieutenant in the Corps of Engineers. Over the next two decades, he served as an engineer and staff officer in France during WWI, attended the army's postgraduate professional schools, and directed numerous civil works projects. Courtesy of Mrs. Mary Brenza.

(above) Somervell headed the Works Progress Administration program in New York City from 1936 to 1940, where he earned the praise of Mayor Fiorello La Guardia, as well as that of his superiors in Washington, for his effective management of this controversial work relief program. Courtesy of Mrs. E. Macdonald Matter.

(left) As head of the army's Construction Division from 1940 to 1941, Somervell was frequently called to testify before Congress. He is seen here testifying before the Truman Committee, where relations often became quite strained because Chairman Senator Harry S. Truman and several other members believed Somervell was too ready to lavish large sums of money on extravagant projects. National Archives.

Taking over the Construction Division at a time when the building of training camps and munitions plants had fallen behind schedule, Somervell streamlined the division's organization and accelerated the construction of camps and plants. One of his many inspections of camp facilities took him to Camp Gordon, Georgia, in October 1941. National Archives.

(above) The War Department High Command in 1942: (front row, left to right) Lieutenant General Henry H. Arnold, General George C. Marshall, Lieutenant General Lesley J. McNair, and (back row) Lieutenant Generals Joseph T. McNarney and Somervell. In the reorganization that year, Somervell, as head of the Army Service Forces, took responsibility for the supply and administration of the army within the United States and the support of troops overseas. National Archives.

(right) At the Casablanca Conference in January 1943, Somervell drew up a shipping schedule for the projected 1943 troop deployment. The American delegation included (front row, left to right) General George C. Marshall, President Franklin D. Roosevelt, Admiral Ernest J. King, and (back row) Harry Hopkins, Lieutenant Generals Henry H. Arnold and Somervell, and Averell Harriman. National Archives.

In his first year as head of the Army Service Forces, Somervell's primary concern was the output of war supplies. Striving for high production, he often feuded with the civilian leadership of the War Production Board. Here he inspects production in Detroit, Michigan, in 1942. National Archives.

Allied commanders conferred in New Delhi in February 1943 to determine what forces and supplies were needed for proposed operations in India, China, and Burma. Pictured here are (left to right) Field Marshal Sir Archibald P. Wavell, Lieutenant Generals Joseph W. Stilwell, Henry H. Arnold, and Somervell, and Field Marshal Sir John Dill. National Archives.

Somervell worked closely with Major General Raymond A. Wheeler, commander of the Services of Supply in the China–Burma–India Theater in 1943. During the last two years of the war, Somervell maintained intense interest in this theater and pushed for the completion of the Ledo Road to carry supplies to China. National Archives.

In September 1943 Somervell visited the Solomon Islands as part of an extensive tour of supply operations in the Pacific Ocean Area, the Southwest Pacific Area, the China-Burma-India Theater, and the Persian Gulf Service Command. National Archives.

On an inspection tour of the Persian Gulf Service Command in October 1943, Somervell evaluated the operation of a supply line to the Soviet Union through this region. Here he is tugging on his moustache, a familiar trait when he was agitated. Major Generals Donald H. Connolly and Lucius D. Clay are sitting to Somervell's left. U.S. Army Military History Institute.

Investigating complaints about the flow of supplies to the European Theater of Operations, Somervell met with Lieutenant General Jacob Devers and General Dwight D. Eisenhower in France in January 1945. National Archives.

Lieutenant Generals Somervell (right front seat) and John C. H. Lee (the driver) inspected port operations at Antwerp, Belgium, in January 1945. Lee, the principal supply man in the European Theater of Operations and Somervell's close friend for many years, was often the object of criticism by other commanders. National Archives.

As president of Koppers from 1946 to 1955, Somervell instituted an aggressive program of expansion and used management practices he had developed in the army to turn around the company's fortunes. The monthly progress reports he studied consisted of detailed data on every division of the company. U.S. Army Military History Institute.

7. THE ALLIED SUPPLY ORBIT

● ● ● ● ESSENTIAL TO AMERICAN SUPPLY OPERAtions during World War II was the ability to make war materiel available to the nations fighting the Axis powers. This ability centered around lend-lease, which was initially launched in 1941 in hopes that American supplies would enable Britain and other nations to defeat the Axis without the United States having to enter the war. After Pearl Harbor, lend-lease was transformed into an instrument of coalition warfare. Somervell played a major role in its implementation. Beginning in 1942, Somervell procured military supplies for lend-lease as part of the ASP. Moreover, he influenced policy through exercise of his operational responsibilities. While always sensitive to American interests, Somervell fully appreciated the importance of lend-lease in the Allied war effort, and throughout the war, he exerted himself to see that America's allies received the war goods they required.

● ● ●

The machinery for administering wartime lend-lease to Britain was laid down at the ARCADIA Conference held in Washington in December 1941 and January 1942. Agreeing on the necessity for logistical coordination, American and British leaders decided that "the entire munitions resources of Great Britain and the United States will be deemed to be in a common pool," from which assignments would be made according to strategic necessities. To effect the assignments, they created the Munitions Assignments Board,

Washington, (MAB) and London (LMAB), both of which operated under the aegis of the CCS. Thereafter, the two allies fashioned a cooperative munitions effort unparalleled in the history of warfare, with collaboration and consultation at every phase of the planning and operation of the Anglo-American supply mechanism. By the war's end, the British Empire had received about one-fourth of its munitions through American lend-lease, and in this respect, lend-lease fulfilled its purpose—winning the war against the Axis.

Despite its successful role in the war effort, lend-lease was not without problems. The British and the Americans might agree on the principle of pooling, but they were not in agreement on what such pooling meant in practice. The British sought to give a literal interpretation to the common pool principle. Already well on the way to mobilizing the maximum fighting force from their available manpower and relying heavily on American and Canadian production for supplies and equipment, they felt they should have a voice both in the distribution of American munitions and the planning of American production programs. In this way, they could ensure their needs were met even as their war effort was overshadowed by America's might.

The American military, meanwhile, saw the common pool as little more than a figure of speech. Lacking any real need for British war goods, it had little interest in British production plans and saw pooling as a means by which British needs could be met from American production after the needs of the American army had been satisfied.[1]

Somervell was in the thick of the conflict over pooling. Highly nationalistic and determined not to be taken in by anyone, he was suspicious of the British. He believed that, if given the opportunity, they would use the combined boards to build up British forces at the expense of the American army so that they could have "more influence at the peace table."

Of more immediate importance, Somervell feared a generous lend-lease program would take crucial supplies away from the American army and prevent it from fighting effectively if the British collapsed and it had to fight alone. To his way of thinking, the American army had to "prepare to do this job ourselves." Consequently, Somervell took the position that the needs of the American army must take precedence in the allocation of American production and that the British should have no voice in the shaping of American military requirements and production.[2]

Motivated by these ideas and his inclination to expand his own domain, Somervell early acted to change the handling of lend-lease in the War Department. The administrative locus of lend-lease was the Office of the Defense Aid Director, headed by Henry Aurand. Initially an independent agency for all practical purposes, Aurand's office directed the procurement, transfer, and shipment of lend-lease military supplies. The independent status of Aurand's office disturbed Somervell's sense of organization, and in December 1941, only days after becoming G-4, he was complaining that "it was an entirely separate and uncoordinated outfit without any knowledge of, or interest in, the supply problem as a whole."

Equally important, Somervell lacked confidence in Aurand, whom he had known and disliked since their cadet days at West Point. Tall and handsome, Aurand was an able officer with a flair for political maneuvering. He also was the most vocal advocate in the War Department of pooling arrangements and of British proposals for the allocation of materiel. In these respects, he did not sit well with Somervell, who "did not rate allied-mindedness high on his list of qualities that he admired in an officer." Moreover, Somervell regarded Aurand as an unreliable prima dona "who sought personal aggrandizement" through his position as defense aid director.[3]

Upon becoming head of the ASF, Somervell quickly brought Aurand under his control. Without consulting the latter, he moved Aurand's office into the ASF, in effect reducing the prestige and importance of Aurand, and changed its name to the International Division. Accustomed to operating at a higher level, Aurand protested the subordination of his office to the ASF, arguing that it must have independent status within the War Department in order to avoid giving the impression to the British that lend-lease was not important to the American war effort. Infuriated by Aurand's stance, Somervell dismissed his argument as special pleading and told him to "get back to work and come off being so Goddamned British."

In the summer, Aurand left the International Division. His place was taken by Lucius Clay, who remained as director of materiel, thus placing the division some two steps lower in the echelons of the War Department than it had been under Aurand.[4]

Under Somervell's direction, the management of War Department lend-lease was now marked by "a more national outlook, aimed at preventing foreign raids on the U.S. supply pool." Emphasizing that lend-lease must not unduly interfere with the buildup of the American army, he consolidated long-range lend-lease requirements into the ASP and sought to keep them within reasonable bounds by establishing a rigid review of them.

The new situation was readily felt in the procurement of items not used by the American army. These included components for British-type weapons and vehicles and other materiel peculiar to the British army. While essential to the British, procurement of these items was a nuisance to Somervell, who believed his job was to plan a procurement program to take full advantage of American mass production methods. Since production of these items threatened to absorb materials and facilities out of proportion to their actual volume, he resisted extensive procurement of them, forcing the British to fight continually to keep these items from being completely submerged by the American program.[5]

At the same time that Somervell was tightening his grip over the War

Department's lend-lease operation, the British were pressing for a combined organization to coordinate and adjust the entire production of the United States and the British Empire, both military and civil, in accordance with global strategy and global supplies of industrial facilities, raw materials, labor, and shipping. Through such an organization, in the words of two British historians, they could then

> secure for themselves a greater influence upon the planning of AMERICAN munitions procurement; or more specifically to ensure that their particular, non-common requirements should be considered from a standpoint broader and more rational than that of the fulfillment or non-fulfillment of sacrosanct American programmes.

On the recommendation of Oliver Lyttelton, British minister of production, Church proposed that a board be created to combine the production programs of the United States and Britain into a single, integrated program adjusted to the requirements of the war. Harry Hopkins, who wanted to strengthen the WPB vis-a-vis the army and save the British from interference from the American military, persuaded Roosevelt to agree to the board. Known as the Combined Production and Resources Board (CPRB) and established in June 1942, it was chaired by Donald Nelson and Lyttelton and charged with assuring the continuous adjustment of the combined American and British programs in light of changing military requirements. Aurand became secretary and ultimately de facto executive of the board.[6]

The CPRB proved a disappointment to the British. In July, it asked the CCS to direct the services to furnish it with arms and munitions requirements necessary by the end of 1942 and by the end of 1943, setting a deadline of September 1, 1942, for this information. Little came of this request.

Led by Somervell, American officers saw it as just "another [British] method of needling the U.S. for material" and undermined it by feuding with the British over the basis for determining requirements. The British favored calculations of requirements in terms of specific numbers and types of troops in specific theaters of war, a scheme Americans thought would give an advantage to the British since their troops were already engaged in many theaters and those theaters would naturally tend to get higher priorities. The Americans, in contrast, favored calculations solely in terms of the overall size and type of military forces to be armed, a scheme the British thought would give the War Department a blank check to set out the requirements of whatever army it proposed to raise. The CPRB deadline already past, the army proposed that each nation furnish the board with its existing requirements program, the British program based on theater deployment and the American based on the size of the American army. The CPRB refused to accept this approach, and in late September, it called upon the CCS to meet the original request. Churchill added his weight to the board's request on October 4 with a letter to Roosevelt suggesting that American requirements should be adjusted by the CPRB on the basis of the CCS's strategic plans.

Wanting nothing to do with a review of their specific requirements by the CPRB, the JCS advised Roosevelt to reject Churchill's suggestion. Hopkins, whose commitment to the CPRB was never particularly strong in the first place because of a preference for personal and ad hoc arrangements over institutionalized structures, supported them. Hence, in a reply written by Somervell, Roosevelt politely rebuffed Churchill. While agreeing it was desirable to scrutinize production programs, this task should be handled by the MAB and the CCS. As for the CPRB, it should refrain from "questioning specific requirements items" and restrict itself to an analysis of the total American and British requirements to determine if the realities of production made it necessary to revise them.

Roosevelt's message ended any possibility of the close collaboration between the CPRB and the CCS that the British desired. In the absence of meaningful cooperation from the American military, the board was unable to draw up a combined production program, causing it gradually to decline in importance.

There was now no question that production requirements on American industry would be handled as American problems by American agencies. When the Americans drew up a definitive munitions program for 1943 after the resolution of the Feasibility Dispute, they insisted on formulating it on a unilateral basis and did not permit the British to participate. In other words, the British would not dictate the American production program.[7]

As it was, Somervell had effectively neutralized the CPRB by this time anyway. Aurand had been on the job as its de facto executive only a matter of days before he was angering Somervell with what Somervell perceived as his pro-British attitude. In August, when Aurand recommended to the CPRB that 15,000 tons of armor-piercing shot steel be transferred to Britain from American allocations, Somervell decided he had to go. Although having no authority to fire Aurand, Somervell got rid of him by the simple expedient of offering him command of the Sixth Service Command and promising him a promotion to major general. Aurand knew he was being kicked upstairs, for the new post gave him rank but no influence. However, wanting to have his own command and unwilling to face continual battles with Somervell, he accepted the transfer. With Aurand, the most fervent believer in lend-lease in the War Department, now gone, any possibility of the CPRB emerging as a powerful body had been dealt a crippling blow.[8]

The British were not much more successful in their efforts to have a major voice in the distribution of American munitions. In the spring of 1942, they had secured MAB acceptance of the principle of strategic necessity as the criterion for assignments. Even though this criterion did not prevent the Americans from equipping their own army, they did not like this approach. Not only did it favor the British because their troops were already in action in several theaters and thus had higher priority, it could cause excessive quantities of supplies to gravitate to relatively inactive theaters, such as India, simply because of the mere existence of a theater command. Instead, the Americans wanted assignments based on a realistic appraisal of production capacity, with that capacity to be shared to meet basic needs.[9]

By the fall of 1942, the British approach was hamstrung. The MAB had never been able to make firm assignments for more than a month in advance because of uncertain production schedules and competing bids for strategic priority, and in the absence of specific assurances from the United States about the scope of future aid, the British could not proceed with their own plans. To remedy the situation as well as negotiate an understanding with the Americans on a range of matters affecting the common war effort, Lyttelton, accompanied by Lieutenant General Sir Ronald M. Weeks, deputy chief of the Imperial General Staff, and Sir William Rootes of the Ministry of Production, came to Washington in November. In discussions with Somervell, Lyttelton pointed out that Britain had reached the limits of its resources and needed a firm commitment from the United States on future aid.

Somervell was impressed with Lyttelton's presentation, and like the British, he was just as anxious to have a firm understanding to make certain the ASP was an effective instrument for mobilizing American industry. As a result, the discussions between Somervell and Weeks concerning ground equipment generally went smoothly. They fixed the quantities of specific production on a range of items which the United States would provide Britain in 1943 and agreed that, if these targets could not be met, supplies would be made proportionately available.

The only major bone of contention involved tanks. In March 1942, British and American tank experts had agreed on a production program based on Roosevelt's goal of 45,000 tanks in 1942 and 75,000 in 1943. In July, the MAB attempted to convert these figures into assignment schedules. Very quickly, its efforts crumbled as a lack of priorities and other factors forced production cutbacks. When the British mission arrived in Washington in November, Somervell told Weeks that Roosevelt's 1943 goal had to be reduced to 35,000 tanks and self-propelled vehicles, with the British assignment set at 10,000 tanks. Weeks immediately protested that the British needed a minimum of 14,000 tanks with 12,000 as the absolute rock-bottom figure they could consider. He demanded the production goal be set at 40,000 tanks and vehicles and he further hinted that he would have Lyttelton take up the matter with higher authorities if Somervell did not yield. Angered by Weeks's position, Somervell replied that the latter was asking the impossible, pointing out that, from their own production and American production, the British were asking for twice the number of tanks required by the American army. Through Hopkins, Somervell tried to persuade Roosevelt to support his position. But, Roosevelt declined to intervene, and in their formal agreement, Somervell and Weeks stated their respective positions and stipulated that the situation should be reviewed on April 1, 1943, with a view to determining whether the goal of 40,000 tanks and vehicles could be met. Meanwhile, the British were assigned ten tanks to nine for the Americans out of American production. Before long, a reduction in Soviet requirements enabled Somervell to accept the British figure of 12,000 tanks for 1943 without any change in production plans.[10]

The effect of the Weeks-Somervell agreement was to base combined assignments of ground equipment to the British, at least for 1943, on the ASP rather than on strategic or operational needs. This approach contravened the theory on which the MAB had been operating, and it prevented the agreement from assuming the status of a protocol by stipulating that it should continue to make assignments in keeping with the strategic directives of the CCS. But, this principle had only a very general application, for both the British and Somervell were generally pleased with the agreement. For the British, it established the basis for planning that they had sought in sending the Lyttelton mission to Washington. Somervell, meanwhile, was satisfied with the agreement because it largely reduced British lend-lease to a regular schedule tied to the ASP. Now he was in a better position to ensure that the American military requirements program remained in American hands.[11]

After 1942, Somervell increasingly moved to make military lend-lease more an instrument for national policy than a mechanism for pooling resources. Congressmen and senators were suspicious that the British were using lend-lease for purposes not always directly related to winning the war, including using locomotives and rolling stock for civilian purposes and other materiel to speed reconversion of their industry to peacetime production. Sensitive to congressional concerns, Somervell demanded that the British justify their lend-lease requirements in operational terms. He also came up with his own interpretation of the common pool as a corollary to the Weeks-Somervell agreement. Known as the residual theory, it was based on the assumption that each country had primary responsibility to produce all the munitions it required and that each had first call on its own industrial capacity. The common pool should apply only to residual or marginal requirements the United States and Britain had the right to place on each other.

The British never accepted Somervell's interpretation, for it threatened to cut off or severely reduce American allocations at any time the Americans deemed it in their own interest. Even so, the residual theory steadily found expression in the American approach to assignments.[12]

The opposition of Somervell to the British interpretation of common pooling did not preclude generous assignments of American materiel to the British. In fact, the opposite was true. For all his suspicions of unjustified British demands, dislike for being taken in, and determination to see that nothing interfered with the arming of American forces, Somervell was receptive to British requests for aid if he were convinced of their immediate need and if the British asked for it rather than demanded it. Writing about this side of Somervell, Lieutenant General Walter Venning, director general of the British Ministry of Supply Mission in Washington, noted that Somervell "would give me the shirt off his back if he was satisfied that I needed the shirt." All that he demanded was full and convincing justification of British requests.[13]

During 1943 and the first half of 1944, there were few major policy issues dividing the Americans and the British regarding lend-lease, but in the second half of 1944, the two were at odds over an American move to restrict the flow of aid to Britain. Determined that American needs would be given top priority, many Americans argued that in the period between the defeat of Germany and the defeat of Japan, which the Americans called Period I of lend-lease, and the British, Stage II, the common pool would no longer apply. All belligerents would support their own war effort against Japan to the fullest extent possible, and lend-lease would be limited to quantities absolutely essential to meet the marginal requirements of forces actively engaged in the war against Japan. There would be no aid for the British civilian economy or any military aid that would enable the British to convert their war production to civilian production.

These views found strong support in the AAF and the navy, both of which felt that curtailment of lend-lease to Britain would effectively restrict its participation in the final drive against Japan to token forces and, thus, enable American forces to claim the lion's share of credit for the victory. As a result, in April 1944, the JCS's Joint Logistics Committee (JLC) drew up a broad set of guidelines embodying this nationalistic approach to govern military lend-lease during Stage II.[14] In May, the JCS and Roosevelt approved the basic thrust of the JLC's guidelines. Known as the corollary principle, it said that "Lend-Lease munitions will be limited to materials not available to nations concerned and which can be profitably employed against Japan in accordance with agreed strategy."

Somervell, in full agreement with the JLC's thinking, moved quickly to implement the new policy. On May 18, he asked Lieutenant General George N. Macready of the British Ministry of Supply Mission in Washington to supply the figures for British requirements for the first year of Stage II, which he assumed would begin on October 1, 1944. "The requirements so stated," he emphasized, "should be for the support of British forces which would be used in the war against Japan." In late July, Venning presented Somervell with figures, but they were "based on assessment of our entire needs during Stage II and not confined to operations in any particular theater of war." Through this method, he told Somervell, the British could reduce military production in such a way as to make "some approach to a level of existence which could be regarded as even tolerable in a civilized economy." Since Venning's figures were at odds with his request, Somervell refused to accept them and had the International Division make its own calculations of British requirements for the war against Japan. There the matter remained until the eve of the second Quebec Conference, code named OCTAGON, held in September 1944.[15]

In the meantime, the British went ahead with their own planning for Stage II on the assumption that civilian lend-lease would continue as during the two-front war and that military supplies would also be sent in generous amounts. Only in this way could they get the civilian economy back on its feet and, at the same time, meaningfully participate in the war against Japan and fulfill such commitments as the occupation of Germany and the maintenance of order in the Middle East.

During the summer of 1944, the British tried to convince American officials of the gravity of their problems. They stated they would not be able to handle postwar loans, even at very low interest rates, and required an extension of lend-lease during Stage II to provide part of their import needs and to facilitate the recovery of their export trade. Unfortunately, they presented the details of their plight only to a narrow segment of the American government, which did not include the armed services, out of concern that hostile elements would use their financial and economic difficulties to exact concessions contrary to British interests. Also, even those who were informed believed that the British were exaggerating the situation and could not possibly imagine that Britain with its vast empire would not be able to service loans, i.e., that Britain was broke.[16]

Outside of military needs, Washington was of mixed mind about the British plight. Many congressmen and senators, worried about the unprecedented cost of the war, regarded lend-lease strictly as an instrument of war, not a program for postwar recovery for allies. In their opinion, any aid not absolutely necessary to the defeat of Japan should be on a "strictly business basis." Others were more willing to help the British. Secretary of the Treasury Henry Morgenthau, Jr. was most sympathetic to the British, arguing that it was in America's political and economic interests that Britain should have a strong economy. He was probably influenced by a desire to gain British endorsement through generous aid of his punitive postwar plans for deindustrializing Germany. Secretary of State Cordell Hull likewise favored reasonable aid to Britain during Stage II, provided the British agreed to his long-sought goal of ending the discriminatory trade practices in their imperial preference system of tariffs. Roosevelt, while receptive to the advice of the Treasury and State Departments, was wary of firmly committing himself to Stage II aid in light of congressional sentiment and the upcoming presidential election. All he would do was agree to discuss the problem with Churchill at Quebec and issue a strong public statement that lend-lease should be continued until the defeat of Japan.[17]

Unmoved by Roosevelt's pronouncement and anxious to head off the advocates of generous Stage II aid, Somervell on the eve of OCTAGON argued in a memorandum to the JCS for an extremely tight policy for lend-lease. Lend-lease after the defeat of Germany, he stated, should be confined to supplies actually needed for fighting Japan. All civilian lend-lease should be stopped and Britain "thrown upon its own resources"; lend-lease items then in Britain's possession should be handed back on demand. In partial compensation for the remaining balance, he believed that the United States should obtain the following from Britain: "any extension that may be needed" of the rights the United States had acquired to bases in the British West Indies in the early stages of the war; "rights of similar kind in any part of the world under British control"; "assurance of full commercial rights for the U.S. and its nationals throughout the British Empire"; assurance of no discrimination against American purchases of raw materials, "such as petroleum, metals and rubber," which had been produced under "British control or auspices"; and repayment of the remaining debit balance on the lend-lease account.[18]

Somervell's vision of a postwar world, dominated by American bases and with its markets and raw materials readily available to the United States, showed his belief that the U.S. should flex its muscles for its own benefit. A similar vision was held by many of his uniformed compatriots, especially in regard to the Far East. However, when Admiral Leahy informed Hopkins of Somervell's proposal, the two agreed that the JCS should not endorse it because of Roosevelt's pronouncement. Moreover, having learned that Somervell had told the Transportation Corps to draw up orders halting lend-lease shipments to Britain as soon as Germany was defeated, Roosevelt informed Chief of Staff Marshall there was to be no unilateral action on lend-lease and that he intended to give instructions "relative to the Lend-Lease policy of this government at an early date." By this action, the president rendered his earlier approval of the corollary principle "a dead letter."[19]

At OCTAGON, Roosevelt, in response to Churchill's personal plea and probably in response to British acceptance of the Morgenthau Plan, agreed to the essentials of the British Stage II program in military and nonmilitary supplies. A special Anglo-American committee, headed by Morgenthau, was created to translate these guidelines into detailed plans. Roosevelt's somewhat breezy promise to Churchill aroused a hornet's nest in Washington. Somervell, Leahy, Stimson, Hull, and Secretary of the Navy James Forrestal all made it clear that they thought the president had made a mistake.

Still, the Anglo-American negotiations, which began in Washington in October 1944, went reasonably well, at least in regard to military lend-lease. Serving on a special subcommittee considering naval, air, and army ground requirements, Somervell proposed that the basis of negotiations should be the quantity of military supplies Britain actually required for operations against Japan. Nothing came of his proposal. Morgenthau ruled that it "too rigid to fall within the general understanding" reached at Quebec and said that all reasonable British requests must be considered. On this basis, the military subcommittee settled on a military lend-lease program for the first year of Stage II valued at $2.8 billion, one considerably below the $3.7 billion the British had asked for but, nevertheless, one they could accept.[20]

As it developed, the Stage II agreement meant little. Spurred by the German offensive in the Ardennes in December 1944, the JCS concentrated all available American resources they could on American forces and gave scant attention to British requests. In March 1945, Congress specifically prohibited aid for "post-war relief, post-war rehabilitation, and post-war reconstruction" except under specific conditions. And, on V-E Day, the army repossessed those shipments awaiting transport to Britain for use in the war against Germany.

Against this backdrop, General Arnold of the AAF asked the JCS on May 11, 1945, to reaffirm the May 1944 principles. Interestingly, Somervell, long the nemesis of the British, was a voice for moderation. Foreseeing that it would be practically impossible for the United States to cut off all support for the British occupation forces in Germany since they had previously depended on American support, he had the JLC modify Arnold's recommendation to permit use of military lend-lease for occupation forces and "exceptional military programs." As it was, Somervell's proposal was minimal since it pertained only to the period when financial arrangements other than lend-lease were adopted. Even so, Leahy objected on the grounds that Somervell's proposal violated the latest extension of the Lend-Lease Act, and so, it was not adopted. Two months later, President Harry S. Truman limited shipments of military lend-lease to the essential requirements for the war against Japan, in effect killing the Stage II program.[21]

Throughout his involvement with lend-lease for Britain, Somervell was consistently guided by his perception of the army's and America's interests. Concerned primarily with the army's needs during 1942–43, he felt his job was to see that British requirements did not hinder the buildup of the American army. Later, he felt his job was to drive a hard bargain for the United States and to minimize the prospect of Britain using lend-lease for postwar purposes. That these approaches were sometimes shortsighted and did not take into full account the tremendous burden Britain was bearing either did not occur to him or were not of sufficient import to justify a more generous and coalition-minded policy.

• • •

The American aid program for the Soviet Union began in the fall of 1941 when the United States agreed in the First Protocol to provide $1 billion of lend-lease aid to the Russians by June 30, 1942. The Second Protocol was negotiated in 1942 to cover the period July 1, 1942, to June 30, 1943, and the Third and Fourth Protocols covered similar annual periods in 1943–44 and 1944–45. These protocols were at the heart of the American relationship with the Soviet Union during the war, and Roosevelt, as part of his policy to keep the Soviet Union in the war and cement good relations with the Russians for the postwar period, insisted that the United States would make every effort to abide by the protocols.

Given the high priority Roosevelt placed on lend-lease to the Soviet Union, furnishing the supplies was not a major problem. However, delivering them was another matter. The northern route across the Atlantic Ocean and around the coast of Norway to Archangel and Murmansk in the Soviet Union was vulnerable to attacks by German submarines and aircraft and was difficult in winter. The route across the Pacific to Vladivostok and then across the Trans-Siberian railroad to European Russia was too close to Japan and of little use because of the limited capacity of the railroad. The Baltic and Black Sea routes were closed to Allied shipping because of German control of most of Europe. That left the southern route via the Persian Gulf as the only route relatively free of enemy influence, but its usefulness was severely restricted by the underdeveloped character of Iranian ports and the minimal capacity of the Iranian State Railway, which amounted to 6,000 tons of supplies a month in 1941 or the equivalent of a single ship load.

During August 1941, the British and Russians occupied Iran with an eye toward using it as a route for delivering supplies to the Soviet Union, but in the succeeding months, little was done to develop the country's facilities. The British lacked the resources for this development, and the Russians insisted on the use of the northern route because it promised quicker delivery of supplies. However, in late April 1942, submarine sinkings on the northern route led the Soviet Union to ask that all sorts of military equipment in the largest quantities available be sent via the southern route. Over the next several months, lend-lease, WSA, and ASF officials made plans to send twenty ships a month to Iran if the Iranian ports could handle them. But Colonel Don G. Shingler, recently appointed head of the Iranian Mission, advised that the ports could not handle the 120,000 tons of cargo until October 1942, and even then, inland clearance would be limited to 78,000 tons monthly.

Despite the limited capacity of the Persian Gulf route, Churchill and Roosevelt settled upon it as the logical way to send many of the supplies prescribed by the Second Protocol after the British completely suspended shipments by the northern route in July because of losses. If the protocol were to be carried out, the Persian Gulf route would have to handle 200,000 tons monthly, and it was obvious only the United States had the resources to expand Iranian capacity to handle this volume of cargo. On August 27, following studies and consultations between American and British officials in Cairo, Egypt, Churchill formally recommended that the United States assume responsibility for the Iranian State Railway and the Iranian ports, as well as operate a truck fleet in Iran to supplement that of the United Kingdom Commercial Company. Three days later, Roosevelt turned over Churchill's proposal to Marshall with a request that he have a plan drawn up showing how to accomplish this proposal.[22]

Marshall assigned the task to Somervell, who in turn referred it to LeRoy Lutes with instructions that the plan must be so detailed that Roosevelt's approval would set it completely in motion. This plan would also serve as a model for others. "This is the first opportunity that the SOS [ASF] has had to turn in a report of this kind," Somervell stated, "and I wish it to be the best we can do." Lutes's staff did exactly as Somervell required, and Somervell himself dictated the conclusions and final recommendations. The plan was completed on September 3 and sent to Marshall the next day.

Running nineteen typewritten pages with ten enclosures, Somervell's plan provided for a self-contained American service command in the Persian Gulf to work on rail, port, and road operations. The plan did not specifically postulate a date by which the command would be able to handle 200,000 tons of supplies a month, although the assumption was that it lay somewhere between February and June 1943. The CCS approved Somervell's plan on September 22, and in early October, Roosevelt instructed Stimson to see that it was assigned sufficient priority and support "to insure its early and effective accomplishment."

Eventually, the Persian Gulf route provided a satisfactory route to the Soviet Union, but it did not develop as quickly as Somervell had hoped. Mistakes were made both in the planning and early operations, and increasing the rail capacity took time. The ideal solution in speeding up deliveries in the short run was to send an emergency trucking fleet. However, sufficient heavy trucks were not available, and Brigadier General Donald H. Connolly, the service command chief, did not favor the smaller cargo trucks Somervell had proposed as a substitute. Heavy trucks finally made their appearance in early 1943, although the trucking fleet Somervell had envisioned never really materialized. Other mistakes, particularly the faulty design of wharfs at Bandar Shahpur and Khorramshahr and insufficient attention given to dockside storage, likewise contributed to delays. Consequently, the Americans were not able to ship 200,000 tons a month to the Soviet Union through the Persian Gulf until September 1943, several months later than Somervell's plan had projected.[23]

While the development of the Iranian route was moving ahead, Second Protocol deliveries were falling behind schedule. The protocol called for the shipment of more than four million tons of supplies to the Soviet Union from July 1, 1942, to June 30, 1943. In September, the northern route was again opened, but in October and November, northern route convoys were canceled because of losses to German submarines and planes and because escort vessels were needed for TORCH, the North African invasion. Thus, Second Protocol shipments at the end of November totaled only 840,000 tons instead of the 1,608,000 tons scheduled. In December, the British resumed convoys on the northern route, and in January 1943, Roosevelt said Soviet aid shipments must be put back on schedule.[24]

The problem of shipping for the Second Protocol was a major point of discussion at the Casablanca Conference. Reluctant to risk heavy losses on the northern route, the British indicated the best they could do on it with the escorts available was one convoy of twenty-eight ships every forty-two days. On this account, Somervell presented the conferees a shipping schedule, based on the use of the northern route as well as the Persian Gulf and Pacific routes. His schedule showed that Second Protocol shipments could not be brought up to the schedule by June 30, 1943, but if the deficit were spread over the year, assuming the Third Protocol commitments would be the same as the second, Somervell was optimistic that with a total of 722 sailings in 1943 it could be eliminated. After considering a number of related factors, the CCS approved Somervell's shipping schedule for Soviet aid.[25]

Somervell quickly expedited shipments to the Soviet Union under the schedule. While still at the conference, he had Wilhelm Styer appoint a general officer to ride herd on the Second Protocol by looking out for Soviet items. After the conference, Somervell visited the Persian Gulf region for three days. There he inspected key facilities at Teheran, Basra, Khorramshahr, and other locations and talked with American, British, and Russian officers and officials. During his talks, he emphasized that the CCS considered aid to the Soviet Union of first priority and said that the Persian Gulf command must be ready to unload and transport to the Soviet Union twenty-six shiploads of cargo each month by June. Also, Somervell learned of three needs in the area: better food rations for native labor, more accountants to record the receipt of supplies consigned to the Russians, and military police battalions to control traffic and reduce the pilferage rate, which had been running at a 5 percent rate. Somervell pointed out that such a rate was equivalent to the loss of one ship out of twenty, a higher rate than losses to German submarines, and told his subordinates that it "cannot be tolerated." At his command, additional military police were sent to the Persian Gulf. However, their numbers were never adequate, and pilferage remained a major problem in the region until the war's end.[26]

Back in Washington, the WSA, which had not been represented at Casablanca and was responsible for allocating shipping for the Soviet aid program, questioned whether Somervell's schedule could be met because of congestion in the Persian Gulf and the slow turn around on the Pacific run. It estimated there could be only 309 sailings to the Soviet Union in the first half of 1943 instead of the 376 proposed by Somervell, which would require 411 sailings in the second half of the year to make up the deficit instead of Somervell's 346. The WSA was particularly concerned about the Persian Gulf, where the unloading of ships was running seriously behind schedule. Therefore, it cut back February 1943 sailings from the eighteen Somervell proposed to seven and insisted that the March sailings be limited to fourteen instead of twenty.[27]

Somervell was not impressed by the WSA's findings. Asked by Roosevelt to comment on them, he granted that the Persian Gulf route was not expanding rapidly enough to meet needs and that delays of ships in ports were excessive, but he argued that as more service troops arrived in the region by April 1943, along with more trucks and rolling stock, the command should be able to handle 219,000 tons of cargo by June. The Pacific route remained a problem, he added, largely because the Russians had not made enough ships available for the route and made frequent changes in the order in which they wanted supplies sent. There was little the United States could do about the ability or willingness of the Soviet Union to make additional shipping available for the Pacific route. However, Somervell confidently assured Roosevelt that the shipping schedule for the other routes that he had proposed at Casablanca could be maintained.[28]

Before long, Somervell's hopes for ship sailings for the Soviet Union were dashed. In March, losses to German submarines and planes on the northern route, as well as the need for additional shipping in the Mediterranean for operations there in the summer of 1943, forced the British to suspend sailings to Murmansk until autumn. Simultaneously, his optimism about the Persian Gulf proved unfounded. Despite his exhortations to Connolly for "an all-out effort . . . to unload and release ships," shipments to the Persian Gulf dropped far below his Casablanca schedule. The transfer of additional American ships to the Soviet Union for its use in the Pacific route made up for some of the slack but not enough for the cancellation of the northern shipments and the disappointing performance of the Persian Gulf route. Thus, the deficit for shipments to the Soviet Union by the end of the Second Protocol period was nearly one million tons, approximately 25 percent short of the commitment.[29]

The deficit in the Second Protocol shipments did not mean that Somervell's Casablanca proposal was unrealistic. After receiving unfavorable reports on the Persian Gulf command from the Transportation Corps and the WSA at the beginning of the summer of 1943, Somervell directed Connolly to investigate these criticisms and to make the necessary improvements. He also ordered Styer, then visiting India, to look into the situation at Khorramshahr on his way home and instructed Charles Gross to send an experienced officer to inspect port operations.

The reports of Styer and the Transportation officer indicated that the criticisms were exaggerated and that what defects had existed had been corrected. As Styer told Somervell, the Persian Gulf operations were "over the hump," and the ports were ready to handle the 200,000 tons of supplies a month Somervell had projected. The ports finally reached capacity in September, and at the same time, the overall monthly shipping loss rate was lower than expected, enabling the WSA to make more ships available for the Soviet aid program. Together these developments permitted the United States to bring shipments to the Soviet Union up to schedule by the end of 1943.[30] Thereafter, the Soviet aid program was of minor concern to Somervell.

8. WAR DEPARTMENT BATTLES

AS G-4 AND THEN AS HEAD OF THE ASF, Somervell put zip into the War Department's supply operations. In the process, he aroused a storm of controversy. Some was the natural outgrowth of the emergence of such a large, new organization as the ASF, as well as from the subsequent realignment of responsibility and authority, but much was a direct outgrowth of Somervell the man.

Still relatively young, he commanded many officers better known in army circles and holding higher permanent rank than his own, circumstances that stimulated much resentment. Moreover, Somervell approached his job in a manner that sparked fears he was attempting to build an empire at the expense of others. He placed fellow engineers in many key slots in the belief that they would be the best logisticians because of the managerial experience they had gained from civil works, leading officers in other supply arms to grumble that they were being overlooked. Somervell also proposed countless organizational changes, all of which seemed designed to expand his turf and whittle down other War Department offices.

Wary of Somervell's growing power, many initially believed they must play ball with him or suffer the consequences. However, as the war progressed, various organizations, such as the AAF, increasingly fought back and eventually kept him in check.[1]

• • •

The ASF's relations with the AAF were often strained. Somervell was convinced that the greatest efficiency and maximum combat power could be achieved if the ASF functioned as the supply and services agency for both ground and air elements. The AAF, in contrast, wanted its own supply operation. Anxious to limit any restrictions on the autonomy that the AAF had achieved in the Marshall reorganization and to move in the direction of a totally independent air force, AAF officers fought any action or suggestion by Somervell that its official status as a command did not confer complete control over every phase of its work.[2]

One major dispute dealt with procurement. The Marshall reorganization recognized Somervell's command as the principal procurement agency of the War Department, but it also recognized the considerable autonomy the AAF already possessed in its logistical operations and made the AAF responsible for the procurement of all equipment "peculiar to the Army Air Forces." Resolved to bring the greatest efficiency to military procurement, Somervell thought it desirable that the AAF follow the standard policies that he laid down for the supply bureaus and that AAF requirements, which constituted about one-third of the army's procurement funds, be included in the ASP. By the device of having his staff officers designated as representatives of Under Secretary Patterson when dealing with the AAF rather than as agents of the ASF, he accomplished a measure of uniformity in purchasing policies, contract negotiations and terminations, and labor and manpower policies. Although not totally satisfactory to his sense of order, Somervell accepted this approach, for Patterson staunchly supported him, and AAF people "learned . . . that what Somervell said would stick and that there was absolutely no hope in direct appeal to Judge Patterson's office in the event of disagreement."

However, Somervell was less successful with requirements. The AAF developed its own methods of estimating raw materials requirements and presented them independently to the WPB, and only after much wrangling, was Somervell able to include some AAF items in the ASP. Most were items, such as bombs, that were bought by the supply bureaus for the AAF. Items peculiar to the AAF were consolidated into a separate section of the ASP.[3]

The dispute over the management of AAF bases and the operation of services attached to them was more acrimonious than those over procurement. While air bases in the United States were under the jurisdiction of the AAF, Somervell was to provide services. The AAF, however, was not satisfied with this arrangement. Since the commanding officer of an air base was an AAF officer, it seemed inconsistent to the AAF that he should receive some of his instructions from a headquarters outside the AAF. During 1942 and 1943, the AAF chipped away at ASF's role, tending to develop its own system for the operation of such things as base hospitals.

Increasingly frustrated by the AAF's actions, Somervell in 1944 asked Marshall to settle the ongoing controversy through a clear-cut division of responsibility between the ASF and the AAF. Although irritated by the ASF-AAF conflict, Marshall was reluctant to impose a solution that involved "any substantial organizational changes at the present time." He already had his eyes set on the creation of a single department of national defense after the war's end, and to his way of thinking, "if we are ever to secure acceptance of the idea of a single department . . . we must first demonstrate within the Army a satisfactory relation of service agencies to the combat forces." He hoped to avoid publicity by settling the ASF-AAF issue at the lowest level possible, so he asked Somervell, General Arnold of the AAF, and Lieutenant General Ben Lear, head of the AGF after Lesley McNair's death in France in July 1944, to settle among themselves "the over-all question of service and supply functions and responsibilities and their relation to command."[4]

During November 1944, Somervell, Arnold, and Lear held a series of meetings to discuss the role of the ASF. Arnold insisted that, if the AAF were to carry out its mission of controlling the air, all "administrative, supply, and service functions related to maintenance of air superiority" must be integrated under his command. Somervell, with Lear's support, replied that a single supply and services organization could "promote the maximum combat effectiveness . . . of the Army as a whole as distinguished from that of an individual component."

Unable to reconcile their views, the participants dumped the decision back in Marshall's lap. After considering their views, Marshall chose to make "no major changes in present procedures and organization." The AAF retained control over all but a relatively few responsibilities performed at its air bases, while the ASF still exercised supervision over supply and service functions not essential to AAF's mission.[5]

The AAF's resistance to the ASF continued in 1945. While it did not significantly alter the existing arrangement, the AAF's resistance was of considerable concern to the ASF. Complaining that the AAF was undermining the stability of his organization, Somervell in a strong memorandum on August 6 asked the chief of staff to shore up his standing in the War Department by affirming that the ASF should have responsibility for all AAF supply and service activities. One week after the memorandum was sent, the war ended, and Somervell's proposal was not considered.[6]

• • •

In 1942, Somervell emerged as Chief of Staff Marshall's principal advisor on supply and administration. This status was informal in character and, as a disapproving McNair bluntly told Somervell in June 1943, largely "due to the force of your personality." However, his status in this regard was not total. Several General Staff agencies continued to be involved in supply and administrative matters, and eventually, Somervell's "passion for organizational tidiness and clear-cut command channels" prompted him to urge Marshall to make his status official.[7]

Somervell was especially concerned about the Operations Division (OPD), the central wartime command post of the General Staff. Created in March 1942, it was charged with "those functions of the War Department General Staff which relate to the formulation of plans and strategic direction of the military forces in the theater of war." Interpreting its charge broadly, the OPD emerged as the army's top management staff and claimed an interest and asserted a final jurisdiction in logistics.

By the summer of 1942, it had two branches involved in logistical matters. The Theater Group, the control center of the various theater commands, naturally concerned itself with their logistical needs, while the Logistics Group dealt with overall logistical problems, with particular emphasis upon balancing requirements and assets. In carrying out its tasks, the Logistics Group depended upon the ASF for detailed logistical data, but unlike the ASF, it was aware of the latest strategic plans. Thus, the OPD became the army's highest logistical planning and coordinating agency and the final word on logistical matters in strategic planning and decision making.

Somervell's concern about the OPD centered on the place of logisticians in strategic decision making. Although recognizing the importance of logistical factors, the strategic planners in the OPD were convinced that logistical support should be developed in subordination to strategy. In their opinion, war was so risky and unpredictable as to make an accurate computation of future logistical requirements unwise and probably futile. Therefore, they always sought to leave a broad margin for error in their plans so as to give themselves the necessary leeway to respond to any unforeseen contingency. Logisticians, while subject to consultation, had little role to play in the actual planning in this approach to the making of strategy. Overly concerned about firming up facts so they would have every gun, tank, and ship in place for an operation, the logisticians, in the strategic planners' view, had a "too narrow and inflexible" outlook to be beneficial in framing a bold strategy. In sum, the OPD took the position that the ASF should provide logistical advice in a technical, but not a policy-making, sense and that it should speak only when spoken to about logistical matters.

Somervell rejected this position. He argued that logisticians should be responsible for interpreting logistical data for the strategic decision makers, as well as being responsible for drawing up the logistical plans growing out of strategic decisions. Several factors affected his thinking. For one thing, the OPD's approach reduced him to a mere factotum in the making of strategy, a secondary role that went against his personal inclinations and that was like the one he had played as G-4 in the early days of the war.

The OPD's approach also implied a vast supply pool from which the strategic planners could draw supplies as the occasion required. Somervell, however, wanted production calculated reasonably well so as to meet specific strategic requirements. Any other approach, in his opinion, greatly enhanced the possibility of waste and complaints from civilian administrators about the unnecessary accumulation of large stores of military supplies, complaints that would be directed at him rather than at the strategic planners.

Finally, Somervell believed OPD's contention that logisticians should concern themselves only with seeing that ships and supplies were in place for a strategic deployment was wrong. As evidence, he pointed to the preparations for TORCH, the Allied invasion of French North Africa in November 1942. Strategic plans were made on short notice and without complete consultation with him, and the resulting ad hoc approach to preparing the expeditionary forces created vexing and unnecessary problems for logisticians and potentially threatened the success of the operation.[8]

Trouble between Somervell and the OPD on this issue emerged in the late summer of 1942. Disturbed by his outsider status in the TORCH decision, Somervell made a bid to have himself included in the top strategic planning level. Writing to Marshall, he proposed that the JCS create a standing committee composed of himself and Vice Admiral Frederick J. Horne, the senior naval supply officer, to which the JCS would refer all matters specifically touching on logistics. Somervell also proposed that the JCS and the CCS be given specialist advisors from the ASF on procurement, supply, transportation, and related logistical problems instead of relying on experts from the Joint Staff Planners (JPS) and the Combined Staff Planners (CPS), which were the principal planning agencies respectively for the JCS and the CCS and whose army representatives came from the OPD. Somervell told Marshall that the JPS and CPS experts were not competent to appraise logistical capabilities: "There is no one among the Staff planners who knows much about supply, and the views they express must therefore be those of others . . . or else their own opinions which are predicated neither on knowledge nor experience."[9]

Somervell's proposal, especially for a logistics committee, evoked a strong protest from the OPD. Major General Albert Wedemeyer, the army's representative on the JPS, conceded that logistical knowledge was essential to strategic planning, but he said that it was OPD's business to interpret and use as it saw fit the logistical data generated by the ASF. He advised Major General Thomas Handy, OPD head from 1942–1944, that "our planning must . . . be based on operations, and not on logistical factors alone. Otherwise we will have the tail wagging the dog." Using Wedemeyer's arguments, Handy told Marshall that the creation of a logistics committee that reported directly to the JCS would inevitably undermine the JPS, "since supply matters have a definite bearing on all subjects dealing with strategy." Marshall found Handy's position persuasive. Given Marshall's position, Somervell dropped the matter for the time being.[10]

In the spring of 1943, the feud between Somervell and the OPD resumed. At the instigation of Deputy Chief of Staff McNarney, a special JCS committee investigated the workings of the entire joint committee system, and at the end of March 1943, it recommended a spate of changes. From Somervell's perspective, the most important were the limitation of membership on the JPS to four members—an army planner from the OPD, an AAF planner, and two navy planners—and the creation of a three-man committee to be called the Joint Administrative Committee (JAdC). This committee was to take over from the JPS all matters "not primarily concerned with war plans" so that the JPS could concentrate on strategic plans. There would be no ASF membership on either the JPS or the JAdC, thus excluding the ASF from planning of a general strategic nature.

Learning of the committee's recommendations on March 25, Somervell saw them as an OPD plot to have its Logistics Group completely divorce him from strategic planning. In a letter of protest to Marshall, he branded the plan "as tragic evidence of the lack of understanding of its framers of logistics and shows a faulty concept of the elementary principles of sound administration." Emphasizing the vital character of logistics in the making of strategy, he continued, "if this war has shown anything, it has shown that our efforts to launch attacks on the enemy have in every case been governed by logistics—transportation and supply. When these factors have not been given due weight, confusion, delay, and disaster have come only too rapidly."

Somervell based his protest on what he considered the incompetence of the OPD to do justice to the logistical aspects of strategic planning and the need for a knowledgeable logistician on the JPS. He told Marshall that during 1942

> it became evident that the recommendations you are receiving from the Joint Planners were superficial, that they were based on a lack of knowledge of the problems in so far as the Army was concerned and used quantities of time for their preparation and consideration with a sound solution impossible as the premises on which they were based were incorrect. The production papers, the shipping papers, the aluminum papers and others of similar character are examples of this. . . . It was for this reason that I sought to be present to give you full information on logistics problems and to be represented on lower committees so that papers presented to the Joint Chiefs of Staff would be real staff papers and not so superficially treated as some have been. . . . Unless you are represented on the Planners by an able officer who KNOWS supply, its ramifications, requirements, adaptability, production, availability, etc. and our capabilities in transportation, and moreover by one who has intimate touch with all sources of information, you will be badly served, the Army will suffer, the war will suffer, and America will suffer.

Somervell concluded by asking Marshall to advocate the creation of a joint logistics committee with membership from the ASF, the navy, and the AAF in place of the JAdC.[11]

During April and early May 1943, the JCS studied and discussed at great length the disagreements within the army over the logistical aspects of the proposed reorganization. Somervell again presented his case for ASF membership on the JPS, and in a compromise arranged in mid-May, he gained some of his requests. An ASF representative replaced the proposed OPD one on the JAdC, the ASF retained or secured a place on all JCS committees concerned primarily with logistics, and Somervell was returned to the Joint Military Transportation Committee, from which he was to be dropped under the special committee's plan.

But these changes were only half a loaf for Somervell. The ASF did not acquire official representation on the JPS, and the JAdC, which did include an ASF representative and was later reconstituted as the JLC, in effect operated only as an advisory body for the JPS. Thus, to Somervell's disappointment, army logisticians remained outside the inner realm of strategic planning and decision making.[12]

Meanwhile, Somervell in April recommended that Marshall eliminate logistical planning completely from the General Staff by abolishing the Logistics Group, G-1 (the agency responsible for planning and coordinating personnel matters), and G-4. Their functions and authority would be transferred to the ASF or the AAF as deemed appropriate. Because his own organization carried out the detailed supply planning for the broad operational plans developed by the OPD, Somervell seriously doubted that G-4, for example, could play any meaningful role; if it were involved, it could do little except delay and confuse final decisions. In the instance of the Logistics Group, he insisted that it merely duplicated work his own people were doing. Arguing that his proposal was in line with the purposes behind the March 1942 reorganization, Somervell also said the OPD ought to absorb the functions of G-3, the Training Division of the General Staff, which would have left the General Staff only the OPD and G-2, the Intelligence Division. The effect of Somervell's proposals would have been to strip the General Staff of all its coordinating and supervisory roles in regard to supply and administration and confine it to strategic planning and the direction of military operations. Everything else in the War Department would be in Somervell's hands.[13]

Somervell's proposals hit the War Department "like a bombshell." Those relating to G-1 and G-4 were only requesting ratification for a condition that already existed since both had declined in importance because of a lack of staff and the emergence of the ASF, but that relating to the Logistics Group had serious implications for the OPD. Under Somervell's proposals, Marshall would have a second command post in the War Department, one, in addition to the OPD, to handle logistics. If that were not enough, Somervell would be the major staff advisor to the chief of staff and at the head of the operating logistics command. Ultimately, this concentration of power in his hands would have challenged, and probably surpassed, the authority of the OPD. Not surprisingly, the OPD saw in Somervell's proposals a plot by an ambitious empire builder to build up his own position to the detriment of the General Staff principle that had governed the army for decades.[14]

Marshall turned over Somervell's proposals to OPD head Handy for his reaction. In his response, Handy reaffirmed the General Staff concept and said that no changes were necessary because "the present organization is working fairly well." Marshall too believed the existing arrangement was working satisfactorily. In all probability, he regarded the issues raised by Somervell as theoretical, or perhaps even relatively unimportant, and he could see no pressing need for making any significant change. Somervell's proposals would not have made that much of a difference in Somervell's status, and Marshall was always more interested in the realities than in the formalities of individual position and authority or in the niceties of organizational structure. Therefore, he let Somervell's proposals die without comment.[15]

However, Somervell would not let these proposals die easily. Two months later, he repeated them in an enclosure attached to a memorandum dealing with the organization of service activities in overseas theaters. As before, the OPD strongly opposed them, calling upon the memory of the pre-1917 struggle between the bureaus and the General Staff to warn Marshall that such ideas might undermine the chief of staff's position in the postwar army.

Others joined the OPD in opposing Somervell. Brigadier General Raymond G. Moses, G-4, who previously had generally supported much of Somervell's program out of a long-standing friendship, now lashed out at him, writing that "I do not approve of doing away in a general way with the staff system taught to all of us before the war and in common use everywhere now." McNair also spoke out against Somervell. In a highly personal memorandum to Somervell, he charged that the supply and administrative commander Somervell proposed would break down "the functions of the over-all commander" and violate "the fundamental principle of unity of command."[16]

Faced with opposition from these quarters, Marshall again took no action on Somervell's proposals, yet they did not disappear without having some effect, albeit not what Somervell had intended. They had called attention to the fact that, except for the OPD, all the General Staff divisions had atrophied and that something must be done to strengthen them or else they would die. After considerable debate during the summer of 1943, McNarney increased G-4's formal functions and its staff so that G-4 was to review existing supply regulations, oversee the formulation of the ASP, and establish policy for and supervise a wide variety of other supply activities.

In the final analysis, not much changed. Major General Russell L. Maxwell, who became G-4 in September 1943, asserted G-4's right to review policies and procedures developed by Somervell's staff and to issue them as War Department directives. However, Somervell continued to initiate policies and procedures, and given his aggressive defense of his own turf, G-4 rarely overruled him. As a result, Somervell remained the supply staff and the supply command of the War Department through the end of the war.[17]

• • •

Like his relations with the AAF and the OPD, Somervell's relations with the technical services were often strained. The technical services were the army's supply bureaus. Before May 1943, they had been known as the supply arms and services and then as the supply services. Differing widely in organization and purpose, they had developed over the years more as a result of historical accident than of conscious planning and were marked by administrative independence and dual roles as staff agencies and operating commands. Each had control over its organization, procedures, personnel, training, supply, planning functions, and budget, and each possessed commodity and service functions, although in most cases, one element was subordinate to the other.

When the technical services expanded their operations to meet the demands of war, the differences between them and the combination of commodity and service functions created serious management problems. As a result, the March 1942 reorganization imposed centralized control over the technical services in the person of Somervell. Appalled by the organizational chaos inherent in the existing system, he was determined to rationalize their structure and operations along sound business principles. The technical services, possessing a long history of resisting external control over their structure and operations, were just as determined to resist.[18]

No technical service more resisted Somervell or his moves to shape its operations than the Ordnance Department. Before Somervell's appointment as head of the ASF, the Ordnance Department had experienced minimal supervision by Patterson's office, and this usually took the form of informal conferences between Patterson, Ordnance officers, General Staff officers, and representatives of the civilian production agencies in which the Ordnance officers dominated the discussion. Somervell ended these conferences and replaced them with impersonal supervision and reporting. Resolved to harness the Ordnance Department and demonstrate his new authority as head of the ASF, Somervell exercised closer supervision over it by having the Control Division review all proposals for major organizational changes in the department, regularly inspect bureau activities, and demand a steady flow of statistical reports.

Infuriated by Somervell's determination to look over their shoulders, Ordnance officers constantly complained about ASF interference in the details of their operations and ASF criticism of the department's organization. As stated by one Ordnance officer,

> Somervell had a large number of what we used to call parachute jumpers who

had nothing in the world to do except criticize. While most of them had little or no experience and less ability, I will concede that they did a top-notch job of criticizing. We used to often wish that their efforts were directed toward correcting the abuses of . . . [the ASF] rather than the Ordnance Department. Frankly, knowing the background of many . . . [ASF] men, none of their criticism could be taken seriously, and I recall at the time we certainly did not.[19]

The clash over a control division in the Ordnance Department epitomized Somervell's differences with the department. Shortly after becoming head of the ASF, Somervell ordered that a control division be formed in each supply bureau. His purpose was to have an investigative and fact-finding agency in each one to study organizational matters and to keep him informed about rates of progress.

Chief of Ordnance Wesson hit the ceiling when he learned of Somervell's plans. Interpreting the word control literally, he assumed the control division would actually exercise control over his department, and he told Somervell's representative that Ordnance did not need any such unit because he exercised full control over it himself. Wesson fought Somervell on this issue until his departure in the late spring of 1942. His successor, Levin Campbell, agreed to the creation of a control division in the Ordnance Department, but he never showed any enthusiasm for it. As a result, it never did anything more than the most routine statistical work and had little success in putting its recommendations into effect.[20]

Somervell tolerated Campbell's opposition to many of his management controls because Ordnance was getting the job done and because he respected Campbell's ability. In other cases, however, he was more than ready to move against those who crossed him. Such was the case with the chief of the Signal Corps, Dawson Olmstead.

Often out of his office, ill, or away on long trips, Olmstead was a gruff individual who was careless of personal relations and had failed to win many backers in the War Department following his appointment as chief signal officer in 1941. Olmstead first angered Somervell in the spring of 1942 by formally protesting the Signal Corps' placement under the ASF. Thereafter, relations between the two men steadily deteriorated, largely because of the difficulties the Signal Corps faced in satisfying its responsibility for procuring communications and electronics equipment on the one hand and operating army-wide communications on the other.

Somervell increasingly saw Olmstead as the communications problem, and by early 1943, his opinion of Olmstead sank to a low ebb. After visiting Caribbean areas in January, he wrote Wilhelm Styer that he had been shocked at communications conditions in Puerto Rico and Brazil "after all the song and dance I have received from Olmstead." Later, Somervell criticized the placement of a radio station in Eritrea in eastern Africa. "Our radio installations at Eritrea appear to be too far in the rear," he told Olmstead. "The same should be moved to the vicinity of Cairo at the earliest possible moment. I understand that you have refused to give your consent to this and I wonder why." With this comment Somervell, a busy administrator who tended to make snap judgments that were not always based on complete information, demonstrated he did not fully grasp the magnitude and complexity of the communications field. The Eritrea station was actually quite valuable because it occupied a strategic position on the equatorial belt of the Signal Corps radio stations that formed the army's round-the-world communications line.[21]

Once Somervell had decided Olmstead was the problem, the ASF head was unrelenting in his criticism. Writing to Olmstead in March 1943, he said,

> All of the reports which I have received on combined operations variously called amphibious operations, landing operations, indicate that the Army Signal Corps has fallen down during the operation. I want you to be sure to remember the Chief of Staff's admonition in regard to your responsibility for seeing that the equipment is provided and that the training is adequate for the job.

Apparently, when Somervell sent Olmstead this ominous memorandum, he had in mind the breakdown of the radios serving Major General George S. Patton's headquarters aboard the cruiser *Augusta* during the TORCH landings at Casablanca. He conspicuously choose to ignore the signal success at other points along the beaches.[22] Olmstead retorted that the signal difficulties could be resolved by removing the Signal Corps from under Somervell's umbrella and placing the chief signal officer directly under the chief of staff with direct access to the heads of the AGF, AAF, and ASF through signal officers in each command.

During May and June 1943, a special War Department board looked into the Signal Corps' problems, and in his testimony before the board, Somervell pulled no punches in identifying the source of the difficulty. Asked what might be done to improve army signals, Somervell said, "Get a new Signal Officer." Professing that the established organization could be made to work without changes, he declared that "I see no difficulties at all in the situation provided the Signal Corps is handled by a man with some imagination and get-up and go to him." When asked by a board member, "in other words, to get rid of the man you have there and get another man will solve the entire communications problem?," Somervell replied, "Yes." He added "Did you ever hear of Napoleon's remark that there weren't any poor regiments, there were just poor colonels?"

Few others accepted Somervell's judgment that Olmstead was the only problem, and in its final report, the board recommended drastic organizational changes, some in line with Olmstead's thinking. However, its views carried little weight against Somervell's opinion and McNarney's opposition to the transfer of any or all parts the Signal Corps to the General Staff.[23]

In early June, Somervell persuaded Marshall that the chief signal officer should be replaced. More willing than Somervell to credit Olmstead with accomplishments, Marshall was not convinced that Olmstead was the only problem in the Signal Corps, but he was swayed by Somervell's argument that Olmstead had lost the confidence of superiors and subordinates alike, making his position untenable. Thus, on June 11, Marshall informed Olmstead that he was to be relieved and replaced by Major General Harry C. Ingles, who had spent much of his career as an infantry officer and was one of Somervell's West Point classmates.

Marshall did accede to Olmstead's request that he remain temporarily on active duty, with Ingles as acting chief signal officer, to head a communications board that the State Department was establishing. Hence, the chief of staff did not present Olmstead with the letter of retirement that Somervell had prepared for him to sign. Somervell would not let the matter rest and wanting it to be clear to all that Olmstead had been fired, he confronted Olmstead that same day and got him to sign the retirement letter, thus ending the latter's service with the Signal Corps.[24]

The conflict between Somervell and the technical services climaxed in late summer 1943. From the beginning, Somervell had been dissatisfied with the ASF's organizational structure. Overlapping functions between his headquarters, the service commands, and the technical services abounded, leading to inefficiency and to very large operating staffs, especially in Washington. The wide variety of field units employed by the technical services and the great disparity in the workload carried by the service commands added to Somervell's dissatisfaction. Unwilling to tolerate what he regarded as an organizational jumble, Somervell felt the time was ripe in the summer of 1943 to rationalize the ASF. A year's operations under the existing structure had provided sufficient experience to warrant a change, and in May, he put the industrial management experts in the Control Division to work drawing up a new organization for the ASF.

Control's plan, finally prepared in August, called for the specialized, commodity type of organization represented by the technical services to be reorganized along functional lines. The technical services would be divested of their field commands, which would be transferred to the service commands, and otherwise combined with the staff of Somervell's headquarters into a single staff for procurement, supply, personnel, administration, fiscal, medical, utilities, transportation, and communications. In short, the technical services were to be abolished. As for the service commands, their number would be reduced to six (see Chart C).

Somervell knew such a far-reaching reshaping of the War Department would encounter strong opposition from the technical services and their allies in the army and Congress. Therefore, he hoped to keep it largely under wraps until he won the support of his superiors. Both Marshall and McNarney were receptive to his plan, for it promised to improve efficiency. Then, just before leaving in early September on a trip to the Pacific, India, and China, Somervell presented his plan to Stimson, who deferred judgment until learning of the reaction of Patterson, absent from the capital on a trip to the South Pacific.[25]

Patterson and Somervell crossed paths in Hawaii during the second week of September, providing Somervell an opportunity to present his plan in detail to the under secretary. While indicating an interest in some of Somervell's proposals, Patterson refused to assent to all of them. As Somervell reported to Marshall,

> He stated that he thought an extraordinary good job was being done and he hated to be a party to making a change at this time, when matters were moving so smoothly. I explained to him that although I also believed this to be the case, I felt we can do a better job with the reorganization and that it would have far reaching effects, extending to the next war. He seemed to be concerned about the sentimental side of the change, . . . and . . . he was afraid that if there were to be any suppression of the existing services we would lose an asset in the espirit in these services, which had been built up in the past hundred years. I explained the various steps which were to be taken, and indicated . . . that they could all be carried out without any dislocation of production or interference with our operations. As to the sentimental angle, I told him . . . that the clear-cut logic of the arrangement would dispose of these sentimental objections.[26]

Despite Patterson's reservations, Somervell was confident that he would prevail, for he assumed Marshall, who had already indicated his support, would make the final decision.

With Patterson opposed to part of the plan and Marshall favorably disposed toward all of it, Stimson stepped into the discussion. He conceded that Somervell's streamlining would probably bring greater efficiency, but he also remembered from his earlier tenure as secretary of war during the presidency of William Howard Taft that the technical services could create a violent furor whenever someone wanted to reform them. In that instance, Chief of Staff General Leonard Wood, "who was not unlike General Somervell in his temperament and other characteristics," aroused such a storm with his reform proposals that the allies of the bureaus in Congress made an effort to eliminate the chief of staff's office. Stimson knew that the technical services, jealous of their power, would resist Somervell with every weapon at hand and carry their case to Congress and the press, creating a tremendous uproar that would not serve the army well. Consequently, he questioned whether the improvement in efficiency would outweigh "its concomitant disadvantages in the creation of bad feeling." The technical services had been "slow and unimaginative" in the early days of the war in Stimson's opinion, but by the summer of 1943, he was satisfied with their work and saw no reason to create bitterness which could just as easily be avoided.

On September 22, Stimson explained his position to Marshall and McNarney, and Marshall, fully appreciating the political power of the technical services, yielded to Stimson's judgment. On October 5, Stimson officially turned down Somervell's plan.[27]

Even as Stimson was deciding against Somervell, the tremendous uproar he had feared broke out. The technical services unanimously opposed Somervell's proposal, and led by Campbell, they lobbied against it with all the force they could muster.[28]

Matters were made worse when Somervell's proposal became linked with Roosevelt's intention to appoint Marshall as supreme commander for OVERLORD, the forthcoming invasion of France. Before the president could make a final decision, however, news that Marshall was to go to Europe was leaked to the public accompanied by rumors that Somervell was going to be his replacement.

The source of these leaks is not certain, but in 1963, military commentator S. L. A. Marshall suggested that a group of young colonels in the AGF, aspiring to rapid promotion, feared their hopes might be dashed if Marshall left Washington and was succeeded by Somervell. Therefore, they leaked the story to the press along with the proposition that "Marshall in his present post is the indispensable man." Whatever the correctness of S. L. A. Marshall's contention, once the rumor appeared other interests soon became involved, turning a military squabble into a political hullabaloo.[29]

The notion of Somervell becoming chief of staff was not new to Washington gossip. As early as the summer of 1942, many of Somervell's enemies were speculating that he had his eyes on the chief of staff's post and that, through his ties with Hopkins, he would eventually be able to angle this coveted appointment.[30] Undoubtedly, Somervell hoped that one day he might be chief of staff. After all, the post was the pinnacle of his profession, and it would have been out of character for him, or any other ambitious officer, not to aspire to it.

But, there was never any possibility of Somervell replacing Marshall, as Somervell himself recognized. Roosevelt, Stimson, and Hopkins were anxious to give Marshall the oppportunity to command in the field the army that he had created and to implement OVERLORD, which bore his stamp. So, during the fall of 1943, they worked on ways to enable him to "fill one of the deepest hopes of his heart." However, Lieutenant General Dwight D. Eisenhower, commander of Allied forces in the Mediterranean, not Somervell, was their choice to replace Marshall; Somervell did not enter into their calculations. While recognizing that Somervell was a doer who had probably contributed as much as anyone to the army's effort since Pearl Harbor, they knew he did not have the stature to fill Marshall's shoes. Moreover, his aggressive style had created too many enemies for him to be effective in a larger arena. If Somervell were appointed chief of staff, the navy, the British, many figures on Capitol Hill, the press, and even elements in the army would have been sure to howl.[31]

On September 15, Stimson informed several ranking Republican members of the Senate Military Affairs Committee that the administration had no intention of having Somervell replace Marshall, whose prestige the Republican senators said was necessary to win support on the Hill for controversial measures dealing with the army. Stimson's comments apparently satisfied the senators, but they did not head off the uproar. This uproar was fueled by rumors spread by such disparate elements as army elements opposed to Somervell's reorganization plan and to his possible appointment as chief of staff, isolationists anxious to discredit the British, Republicans looking for an opportunity to attack the Roosevelt administration, and friends of Marshall who thought that the public good demanded that he remain in Washington.

Before long this uproar took on a surreal quality. In extended remarks in the *Congressional Record* for September 22, Representative Paul Shafer, Republican from Michigan, charged that a cabal in the Roosevelt administration led by Hopkins intended "to turn the War Department into a global political organization" through Somervell's reorganization plan. On September 25, the rabidly anti-administration *Washington Times-Herald, Chicago Tribune,* and *New York Daily News* reported that Shafer had informed them that five ranking army officers were to be dismissed if Somervell became chief of staff and that Hopkins's palace guard, through Somervell, intended to replace "veteran conservative generals with brains trusters."

The most stunning charges appeared in the *Washington Times-Herald* on September 25 in a front-page article by William Hutchinson of the International News Service. According to Hutchinson, a group of influential "White House advisers" was planning a "domestic coup d'etat" designed to give Somervell "personal control" of the army's procurement funds so that the army's production program could be used "as a political weapon" in the 1944 presidential race and build up Somervell "as an Army running mate for Mr. Roosevelt on a fourth-term ticket to offset the possible Republican nomination of General Douglas MacArthur." Tied into the plot, he added, was a campaign to oust Marshall from his post as chief of staff "because he was an implacable foe of politics in the army" and had to be gotten out of Washington.[32]

The orchestrated spate of editorials and columns engineered by the anti-administration groups, isolationists, and officers opposed to Somervell's reorganization plan, especially those relating to Marshall going to Europe to command OVERLORD, were partially countered by saner articles by Arthur Krock in the *New York Times*, Walter Lippmann in the *New York Herald Tribune,* Ernest

Lindley in the *Washington Post*, and David Lawrence in the *U.S. News and World Report*. Moreover, Marshall, embarrassed by the careless talk, decided to intervene. In conversations with House of Representatives leaders on the morning of September 28, he stated that he had the greatest confidence in Somervell and that the rumormongering was hurting the army.

Roosevelt similarly felt compelled to intervene, and in a news conference on September 28, he responded to the controversy by reading aloud with great mirth parts of the Hutchinson article. He then read from two articles by Walter Millis published in the *New York Herald Tribune*, which castigated the *Washington Times-Herald* and others for the "mixture of unauthenticated 'news,' rumor, guesswork and innuendo" that could only "create the maximum discussion and obstruction and baseless suspicion in the conduct of the war and our affairs." By this method of delivery, there was no doubt where Roosevelt's sentiments lay.[33]

Somervell was in the Pacific while the donnybrook over his reorganization was taking place and did not learn of the details until after it was over and letters from Styer explaining it caught up with him in China. Although stung by the unwarranted charges that had been leveled against him and the way that his name had been used in cooked-up stories regarding Marshall, he commented only briefly on the matter in a private letter to Marshall and, thereafter, remained silent. "I was much disgusted with the . . . reference to the unfavorable publicity which was given to the rumor of your appointment as supreme commander," he told Marshall. "How such swine can exist is beyond me. I am, of course, distressed that my name was mixed up in it any way, and that you had this stupid thing to contend with in addition to your other burdens."[34]

The question of Marshall possibly commanding OVERLORD continued through November 1943. However, Somervell's reorganization plan was dead even before the Hutchinson article appeared, and the uproar over it only reinforced Stimson's and Patterson's conviction that it was a "foolish proposal." There simply was not sufficient support for it to succeed. Surveying the reorganization battlefield when he returned to Washington, Somervell decided there was no hope for his plan in the foreseeable future and ordered all papers and studies on it destroyed.[35]

In hindsight, Somervell's reorganization plan was doomed from the outset. For one thing, the time was not right. Successful far-reaching reorganizations usually require a compelling reason, often a crisis, and normally must consist of "sudden, ruthless moves, carried out almost without warning" so that the opposition does not have time to mobilize. These conditions characterized Marshall's reorganization of the War Department in 1942, but they did not exist for Somervell. The system in place was working, which Somervell could not deny, and lacking a crisis, Somervell could not make a compelling argument for his plan.[36]

Somervell also displayed a lack of finesse in his handling of the proposed reorganization. The plan was developed in secrecy by the Control Division, none of whose members, except for Robinson and his deputy, were Regular Army officers with ties to the technical services. Most of Control Division came from the business world, and some had yet to don uniforms. Concentrating on his vision of an efficiently run war machine and assuming the technical services would automatically oppose him, Somervell made no attempt to sell his plan to them through a sense of participation in its inception or to make it attractive or even palatable to them.

Apparently, Somervell thought these steps were unnecessary, for he choose to rely on the command relationship that is at the heart of the military establishment. Once Stimson, Patterson, and Marshall were committed to the plan, their subordinates would have to go along with it. However, in an organization as big as the army supply system and with as many components, each having a long history of autonomous operation and leaders dreading change, command by itself, particularly in the absence of a psychological factor such as a crisis, was not sufficient to effect a far-reaching alteration.[37]

Somervell's efforts to rationalize the army's supply and administrative systems did not end with the rejection of his proposal to integrate the operations of the technical services along functional lines. Refusing to admit defeat, he continued to press for this proposal, as well as the others he had put forth, but in the face of the continued opposition of the AAF, the OPD, and the technical services they had no chance of acceptance.[38]

In fact, by the war's end, Somervell's opponents, motivated by his aggressiveness and the likely consequences of his reforms, had sufficiently mobilized to abolish his whole organization. On August 30, 1945, Handy, now deputy chief of staff, created a board of officers headed by Lieutenant General Alexander M. Patch, a veteran combat officer with no meaningful experience in organizational planning, to develop a proper organization for the postwar army. As head of the OPD, Handy had clashed with Somervell over the role of logisticians in strategic planning, and he had regularly made it clear he did not approve of Somervell's organization or policies.[39]

Consequently, he stacked the Patch Board against Somervell. None of its members came from Somervell's staff, and when Somervell requested that Clinton Robinson be appointed, Handy flatly rejected him in favor of an Ordnance Department organization and management expert who held views directly contrary to Somervell's.

The Patch Board, basing its recommendations on personal interviews with more than seventy-five civilian and military officials and numerous written communications with others, submitted its report in the middle of October 1945. In effect, it called for the elimination of Somervell's headquarters as an unnecessary echelon. The service commands were to be discontinued, and the supply and administrative services were to be continued as a separate level of the War Department organization, operating under the direction and supervision of the General Staff instead of a separate command headed by an individual like Somervell.[40]

Stung by the board's recommendations, Somervell, who was hospitalized at the time, had LeRoy Lutes prepare a strong reply. Lutes argued that the recommendations ignored the lessons of World War II and returned to the prewar organization of the War Department. The ideal arrangement, he added, was to follow Somervell's proposal that all command of supply and services should be placed in one agency headed by an individual who would act as the chief of staff's advisor on these functions.

Lutes's dissent had no effect. By the time he submitted it in November 1945, the Patch Board's recommendations had already been approved in principle, and War Department higher-ups indicated that only minor modifications would be considered. In May 1946, Eisenhower, who had replaced Marshall as chief of staff, issued a directive that abolished the ASF, vested effective control over the army's supply and service activities with the chiefs of the technical services and administrative services, and eliminated the service commands. After four years of wrangling, Somervell's opponents had triumphed. The War Department, in the words of one civilian official, again became a "loose federation of warring tribes" with "little armies within the Army."[41]

Reflecting on Somervell's efforts to reform the War Department, Marshall stated after the war that, if Somervell had not been opposed, he "would have taken the whole damn staff" and that "all the [postwar] reorganization as far as supply and the services were concerned was built on avoiding any future development of a man like General Somervell."[42] Yet, the principles that Somervell had espoused were not completely abandoned. The new conditions that accompanied the Cold War prevented a return to the relatively control-free atmosphere of a small peacetime army. Greater controls over the supply and administrative systems were required, and the new Office of the Army Comptroller picked up where the ASF had left off. Moreover, in 1962, Secretary of Defense Robert McNamara engineered a number of sweeping changes in the army organization, including the abolition of the headquarters of the technical services, except for the Surgeon General and the Chief of Engineers, and transferred their command functions to two new field commands, the Army Materiel Command and the Combat Developments Command, as well as the Defense Supply Agency.

9. CANOL

SOMERVELL WAS SINGLE-MINDED IN HIS mission of meeting the army's supply needs. Working at a nonstop pace and demanding that others do the same, insisting that military necessity must prevail, ruthlessly eliminating dead wood and cutting red tape, intolerant of indecision, and ready to run down those who got in his way, he attacked projects without rest or regard for costs. Somervell's drive got results, but it also produced mistakes. And, depending upon to whom one talked, Somervell was either a miracle man or an egotist who made colossal blunders. These aspects of Somervell can be seen in a number of his wartime endeavors, but none more starkly illustrated the strengths and weaknesses of his administrative and political styles than Canol (Canadian Oil).

Canol was born in the spring of 1942. The year before Alaska, which was accessible only be sea and air, began to take on an important role in America's strategic posture, first, as a stepping stone for ferrying airplanes to the Soviet Union for the fight against Germany and, second, as a possible base for action against Japan. Shortly after Pearl Harbor, American officials, worried about the state of the territory's defenses, concluded that a highway was needed so that Alaska could be supplied if the Japanese were able to interdict sea communications. The Canadians agreed, and in March 1942, the American and Canadian governments entered into a formal understanding that gave the Americans the right to construct a highway from Fort St. John, British Columbia, to Alaska.

Approximately 1,500 miles long and following the path of the Northwest Staging Route, a chain of airfields opened in the summer of 1941 to connect the United States and Alaska, the highway was to be completed by January 1944. The Engineers would be responsible for the construction of the pioneer road through the wilderness, and the Public Roads Administration (PRA) would be responsible for transforming it into a permanent road (see Map 1).[1]

Somervell did not actively participate in the decision to build the Alaska Highway, yet as G-4 during those months, he was vitally interested in the project since he was responsible for supplying both Alaska and military units along the highway. Consequently, in January 1942, he had James Graham, his unofficial advisor on transportation matters and a close friend since World War I, gather information about possible routes for the highway and look into the prospects for a local supply of high-octane gasoline for the highway and the airfields along the way.

In the course of his study, Graham held discussions with Dr. Vilhjalmur Stefansson, a famous Arctic explorer and a special consultant to the War and Navy Departments on Arctic problems. Since 1940, Stefansson had been calling the army's attention to the feasibility of a land route to Alaska and to the desirability of further development of the oil field at Norman Wells on the Mackenzie River in Canada's Northwest Territory, some seventy miles south of the Arctic Circle. At Norman Wells, a subsidiary of Imperial Oil, Ltd., itself a Canadian subsidiary of Standard Oil of New Jersey, had a small drilling and refining operation producing approximately 400 barrels a day, and Stefansson suggested that Imperial's operation could provide the local source of gasoline.

As the weeks passed, the deteriorating war situation added to Graham's interest in Norman Wells. Southeast Asia and its oil resources had been captured by the Japanese, oil tankers were being sunk in the Atlantic at an alarming rate, and in discussions with navy officials, he came away with the impression the navy would not or could not guarantee the security of the sea route to Alaska. All these factors convinced him that development of oil resources near Alaska was desirable.

Graham discussed the possibility of developing Norman Wells with Somervell almost nightly. The general also discussed it with Stefansson, Marshall, Roosevelt, members of the General Staff, and Brigadier General Walter B. Pyron, a special assistant to Robert Patterson on petroleum affairs and formerly a vice president of Gulf Oil Company. In their discussions, Somervell and Graham talked about the "difficulties of doing a job in a place of that kind," but the extent of these considerations in their discussions is not clear because their talks were informal and they did not prepare any written records. Apparently, most of their discussions focused on the need for a local source of gasoline, not the engineering problems, the likely cost of construction, or anything specifically involving the development of the oil field.

The project was put on a fast track when Stefansson on April 15 submitted a lengthy memorandum to Somervell summarizing the overall facts and arguments justifying the development of Norman Wells to support the Alaska Highway's and staging route's need for oil. Too busy to review the memorandum in detail, Somervell turned it over to Graham, who studied it at length with Pyron. On April 25, Pyron met with Stefansson and came away with the impression that production at Norman Wells could likely be expanded to 5,000 barrels per day, enough to satisfy the army's local requirements. By this time, Somervell and those around him were quite enthusiastic about the project, and that enthusiasm was all the general needed to make a formal decision.[2]

The catalyst for the decision was a conference held on April 29 to look at the proposal in detail and to determine whether it was worthwhile to pursue. The conferees included Major General Arthur H. Carter, chief of Somervell's fiscal office; Brigadier General St. Clair Street, an AAF officer serving with the General Staff; Pyron; Graham; two representatives from Imperial Oil and one from Standard Oil; and a representative from the Bureau of Economic Warfare. During the two-hour meeting, the Imperial representatives indicated that it might be possible to get a yield of 3,000 barrels a day from Norman Wells, although they were not optimistic. Pyron also indicated that 3,000 barrels a day was a possibility, and Street remarked that the project would be a godsend for the AAF by providing a local supply of high-octane gasoline. Few details were discussed, particularly in regard to likely problems and costs, so in the final analysis all that was really considered was the need for gasoline and a possible source of supply.

On the basis of this discussion, Graham wrote a one-page memorandum to Somervell immediately after the meeting recommending that the Engineers undertake the development of Norman Wells. Specifically, he recommended that (1) more wells should be drilled at Norman Wells to provide additional production by September 1942, (2) a four-inch pipeline should be constructed from Norman Wells to Whitehorse, Yukon Territory, and be in operation by September 15, 1942, (3) refining equipment should be transmitted to Whitehorse and erected by October 1, 1942, and (4) a transportation system from the railhead at Waterways, Alberta, to Norman Wells should be provided by June 15, 1942. That night, Somervell, without consulting anyone, approved Graham's memorandum, and on April 30, he instructed Chief of Engineers Reybold to carry out the project.

No supporting memoranda accompanied Graham's recommendation. As Somervell later explained to the Truman Committee, "there was no occasion for writing anything. . . . Everybody trusted everybody else. . . . We were doing business in a businesslike way. It culminated in a conclusion that we should drill and do this job, and that part of it was recorded."[3]

Even when viewed through the lens of wartime crisis, Graham's recommendations were cavalier. The pipeline from Norman Wells to Whitehorse, which along with the refinery eventually became known as CANOL 1, was to extend 550 miles over unsurveyed territory marked by mountainous terrain, muskeg (mossy bogs), cold weather, and heavy fogs. Yet, Graham did not consult Stefansson, the most knowledgeable individual, the Engineers, or the Interior Department about the specific geographical and climatic conditions and these conditions' probable impact upon the project. Neither he nor anyone else specifically consulted the navy about its ability to supply Alaska with oil by tankers, which could render the project unnecessary. Furthermore, Graham did not determine the amount of materials, manpower, and shipping the project required or make a systematic analysis of the time required to complete the various facets of the project. Apparently, he picked his target dates because they came at the end of the summer and much of the work had to be done seasonally. Finally, Graham did not consider the likely cost of the project, later telling the Truman Committee that "I don't regard cost in time of war."

Considering the obvious difficulties and uncertainties in the project, Graham seems either naive or foolish, but in fact, he was neither. Quite possibly, he did not pursue the many questions that should have been raised because he believed that Somervell was already sold on the concept and that an extensive examination of them would only delay the project. Any problems that developed could be dealt with as the work progressed.[4]

Somervell's casual acceptance of Graham's recommendations is even more surprising. He knew that Graham had no special background in either petroleum engineering, although the latter had been president of an oil company from 1924 to 1930, or in the conditions of the Canadian northwest, and Somervell himself knew practically nothing about oil. Nevertheless, Somervell accepted Graham's recommendations at face value and plunged ahead without consulting anyone else, later explaining that "I . . . had no reason . . . for distrusting or fearing that any of the people in my organization would tell me anything that wasn't so."

The only justification for this hasty decision was the need to utilize the summer months if the project were to be completed on schedule. However, Somervell later admitted that he knew it could not be completed by the fall of 1942 and that the fall deadline was a target that served as an incentive rather than as a realistic appraisal of the likely date, which he privately thought would be the summer of 1943. Moreover, he paid no attention to cost, stating afterward that "from an economic standpoint the whole project was cockeyed from the beginning." The military situation looked perilous in the spring of 1942, he added, and military expediency alone dictated Canol.

Somervell's personality and style also came into play. Large, difficult, unusual, and showy projects had always excited his imagination. They tested his ability and brought recognition, and he was proud of his previous success in getting things done. Somervell knew Canol would be difficult, but its very difficulty made it appealing because it would give him the opportunity to demonstrate the spirit that he wanted to guide his organization, eventually summarized with his famous slogan, "The difficult we do immediately, the impossible takes a little longer." Further, Somervell was operating in early 1942 as if the full weight of the mobilization rested on his shoulders; unless the army's needs, immediate and potential, were met as soon as possible, it would not be able to fight. Thus, he was ready to pick up and start running with any "loose ball" that happened to be "bouncing around" him.[5]

Many were not as sanguine about Canol as Somervell. On April 30, representatives of Imperial Oil and Standard Oil conferred with Thomas Robins, head of the Construction Division, about the project. Robins thought it would be much simpler and cheaper to send oil to Whitehorse by barge from Seattle, Washington, to Skagway, Alaska, and then by rail, even if it meant hazarding Japanese submarines. However, he had not been consulted beforehand, and he was not one to challenge Somervell. As a matter of fact, Robins did not even communicate his views to the general. He had a job to do, and he would carry out his orders.

Imperial Oil officials were also skeptical of the project. After consulting the Imperial representatives at the April 29 meeting, an Imperial vice president sent Carter a letter on May 2 expressing grave doubt about the feasibility of the project and recommended that the army use cargo planes instead to supply the gasoline for the highway and the air route. Carter informed Somervell of these views; however, they did not persuade the latter to rethink the project.[6]

No time was wasted in launching Canol. On May 1, the Engineers issued a letter of intent to Imperial Oil for the drilling and operation of additional wells. That same day, the Canadian government was informed of the project. It doubted the soundness of the project and was also concerned about its implications for Canadian sovereignty and the economy. However, Somervell was anxious to get it underway, and after a series of insistent inquiries from the State Department, the Canadian government gave its consent two weeks later. On May 6, the War Department added $25 million to its estimates for the fiscal year 1943 under the notation "Norman to Whitehorse Project, Canada." Outside of a general oral statement given to the Budget Bureau, there was no other description in the budget request, leaving it for all practical purposes buried in a huge authorization bill. Several days later, the Engineers negotiated a contract with several companies to construct the pipeline and refinery, with a deadline of December 31, 1942. On May 28, Standard Oil of California, brought into the project because of its technical expertise, agreed to act as consultant and operate the pipeline and refinery despite its own belief that the construction of the pipeline would take almost a year and that the ultimate yield of 100-octane gasoline from Norman Wells would not be enough to justify the effort. By this time, engineer units for the project had already been activated, and during the first weeks of June, they began to arrive in Canada.[7]

Meanwhile, opposition to Canol was emerging in the person of Harold Ickes. Secretary of the interior since 1933 and petroleum administrator for war, Ickes was a "self-described curmudgeon" who was well known for his emphasis upon frugality in government, fierce determination to protect his bureaucratic turf, and frequent forays into the territory of others. Ickes accidentally learned about Canol in early May 1942 when his deputy, Ralph K. Davis, formerly a vice-president of Standard Oil of California, heard of it from a contractor in a casual conversation in a Washington hotel lobby. From the outset, the secretary was opposed to it, partly because he had argued that all petroleum matters should be centralized in his office and Somervell had failed to consult him on such an important project. Somervell later justified his failure to consult Ickes on the grounds that his jurisdiction as petroleum administrator only extended to domestic oil considerations. Actually, Somervell knew from the Florida canal days that the combative secretary could be a problem, and he deliberately ignored him in the planning phase so as to exclude him from the project.

Moreover, Ickes opposed the project because he thought it was unsound. Before the war, Stefansson had approached him about Norman Wells, and his experts had "pronounced Stefansson's plan as utterly impractical." After confirming the existence of the project, Ickes had his experts take a second look at it, and again they pronounced it impractical.

Convinced that Canol was a gigantic waste of money, Ickes fired off a letter to Roosevelt stating that the Alaska Highway could best be supplied by tankers bringing fuel to Skagway. Later, he sent Stimson an extensive critique of the project, noting particularly the difficulties in construction and operation of the pipeline and the lack of facilities for making high-octane gasoline. "One average-size tanker could in four trips," he added, "supply as much aviation fuel as could be manufactured in this proposed 3,000-barrel refinery during the year." But Stimson, in an example of his habit of generally trusting what his generals told him, ignored Ickes and went to Roosevelt and won his complete backing for the project. Writing to Ickes on June 10, Roosevelt said,

> the Secretary of War informs me that this project is being undertaken in an effort to supply aviation and motor gasoline for use in Alaska in the event that transportation by sea should become dangerous or uncertain through enemy action. It is fully recognized that the project is not commercially feasible. The recent enemy attack on Dutch Harbor [an American base in the Aleutian Islands] discloses the possibility of great military need for this additional source of supply. . . . In view of the military needs of Alaska, the project has my full approval.[8]

Roosevelt's approval of Canol did not deter Ickes, who was confident of his assessment of Canol. Additionally, the secretary strongly disliked Somervell and resented his growing power in Washington. More than ready to chop down Somervell, he relentlessly agitated against Canol and emerged as Somervell's principal antagonist in the Canol controversy. Reflecting on the controversy after the war, Patterson opined that "the agitation against the project can be traced to the opposition of Mr. Ickes, who was tireless in stirring up protests against it."[9]

Work on Canol had no sooner started than major problems developed. Just getting men and equipment to Norman Wells was a nightmare. The route involved a 290-mile trip by railroad north from Edmonton, Alberta, to Waterways followed by a 1200-mile journey down the Athabasco and Slave Rivers, across the Great Slave Lake, and down the Mackenzie River. As the troops who were responsible for transporting men and equipment soon learned, use of the rivers and lakes this far north was possible only between early July and October 1, giving them approximately three months to bring 55,000 tons of cargo and hundreds of soldiers and civilian workers with their supporting materials to Norman Wells. Through Herculean efforts, men and supplies were pushed to Norman Wells, and before the end of July, additional wells were being drilled there and an aerial reconnaissance of the pipeline route was made.

The difficulties in moving men and supplies to Norman Wells quickly showed Canol could not be completed in 1942. In the meantime, a dependable method of getting fuel to Whitehorse had to be developed to meet more immediate needs. Thus, on June 25, Somervell approved the organization of a barge line to operate from Prince Rupert to Skagway, the laying of pipeline from Skagway to Whitehorse, and the erection of storage tanks at Whitehorse. Originally suggested by the Engineers and Ickes, this project became known as CANOL 2. Since it required diverting men and pipe from CANOL 1, completion of CANOL 1 was postponed until December 1943.[10]

Between August 17 and 22, 1942, Somervell visited Canada and Alaska to see firsthand the progress on Canol and the Alaska Highway. On August 18, he met in Edmonton with Colonel Theodore Wyman, Jr., the officer in charge of Canol, and representatives of the contractors to discuss the project's status. Encouraged by Wyman's report that 3,000-barrels-a-day production at Norman Wells would be attained, Somervell directed that Canol be expanded to include the development of a suitable method for distributing gasoline from Whitehorse to Fairbanks, Nome, and Anchorage, Alaska.[11]

From Edmonton, Somervell flew to Fort St. John, the headquarters for the construction of the southern section of the highway. He was generally pleased with the progress that he found on this section. After a slow start brought about by difficulties in pinpointing a route and bad weather, the Engineers had pushed this section along at an increasing pace during the summer, and in a brief meeting, Colonel James A. O'Connor, the officer in charge, told

Somervell that the southern section would be completed by the middle of September. Somervell then flew to Fort Nelson, British Columbia, where the northern section of the highway began. After driving "over quite a bit of the road," he flew on to Whitehorse, the focal point of much of the construction activity for both the highway and Canol.

In contrast to what he found with the southern section, Somervell was not pleased with the progress of this section. Initially, construction had proceeded fairly well, but west of Whitehorse, the Engineers ran into forbidding, heavily wooden terrain and permafrost, which defied the "heretofore tried and tested methods of road building." Once the surface of the ground was disturbed by uprooting trees, the sun brought on as much mud from the melting permafrost as heavy rains would produce. To a significant degree, this was an unexpected problem even though Stefansson had warned the army of the problem in building roads over permafrost. Prior to this time, however, no American engineer, military or civilian, had ever encountered it, and thus, no one really knew what to expect until construction was underway. For a time, the problem with permafrost practically halted progress, and only after changing their clearing methods, cordurroying their path with small trees and branches, and spreading gravel or rocks over the cordurroy, were the engineers able to push the road forward again and then only at a snail's pace of half a mile a day. At this rate, the northern section would not be finished before the arrival of the Yukon winter in October.[12]

Not fully aware of the problems created by permafrost or the difficult terrain west of Whitehorse, Somervell concluded that the slow pace resulted from the lack of drive on the part of the officer in charge of the northern section, Colonel William Hoge. In addition to the slow progress of the road, Somervell did not like other aspects of Hoge's operation. After surveying Whitehorse, he determined that things were a mess. Housing and supplies were inadequate, in part because of Hoge's decision not "to build up a big establishment" there because of the difficulty in getting supplies from Skagway, and in part because Hoge, until just recently, was under the impression that none of his troops would be wintering there. Somervell was convinced that more should have been done, especially in regard to permanent buildings and more efficient management of the narrow-gauge railroad from Skagway.

Somervell was also irked by Hoge's reaction to his scheme to extend the Alaska Highway another 800 miles to Nome, on the Bering Sea, in the belief that Nome could serve as a major naval base and logistical center on the doorstep of Asia. He had been encouraged in this belief by Frederic Delano, now chairman of the National Resources Planning Board and an advocate for some time of a railroad to Alaska that would have Nome as its last stop. Delano had also talked with Roosevelt about the potential strategic value of Nome and then intimated to Somervell that the president shared their vision. To Somervell, Delano's words were practically a presidential go-ahead, and therefore, he called for the road's extension.

Neither Hoge nor Major General Simon Bolivar Buckner, commander of army forces in Alaska, thought much of this idea. Both concluded that Anchorage could serve the same purpose as Nome and at far less cost. Hoge also argued that permafrost made the project impractical. Never one to be dissuaded by naysayers, Somervell did not react kindly to their views.

Dissatisfied with Hoge, Somervell decided to fire him, telling Wilhelm Styer that on Hoge's section "a great deal appears to be wrong and that Hoge would have to be relieved." In his defense, Hoge later said Somervell was "sore" because "I wasn't making a big enough show and spread. . . . [He] wanted to have . . . the big things and did not want to be connected with any smaller enterprise; it had to be the biggest, most expensive that anybody could have."

Hoge also felt personal factors came into play. While the two men had known each other since their cadet days at West Point and Hoge had worked under Somervell for a year in the Memphis district, they had never been close. Further, Hoge, who had succeeded Somervell as district engineer at Memphis, was a good friend of Harley Ferguson, Somervell's bitter enemy from those days. For these reasons, Hoge believed Somervell's action stemmed from vindictiveness as much as dissatisfaction with his work.

The legitimacy of Somervell's relief of Hoge is open to question. Despite many problems, Hoge was getting the job done, and Somervell was often too ready to conclude that "you were only right if you were" on his side. Still, any commander wants to have people in subordinate posts in whom he has confidence, and Somervell did not have confidence in Hoge. Somervell could also hold a grudge and at times be downright petty. Whether this side of Somervell came into play in the relief of Hoge can not be determined. However, Somervell did not consign Hoge to the boondocks. Rather, he arranged for him to have a job with Major General Jacob Devers, then commanding the armored force at Fort Knox, Kentucky. From this assignment, Hoge went on to be one of the great American tank commanders in the European war.[13]

Before returning to Washington, Somervell also visited Skagway and Fairbanks. Upon his return on August 23, he took action on two fronts to speed along the Alaska Highway. From his observations, Somervell concluded that there were not enough service troops at work on the highway to complete it before winter, nor were there enough facilities for the men working on it. Therefore, he promptly ordered that additional troops be dispatched to Canada and Alaska to assist in the project and that a hospital, rest camp, and emergency station be constructed at Whitehorse, as well as rest camps and emergency stations along the length of the highway. Somervell also concluded that everything relating to the highway, including Canol, the railroad between Skagway and Whitehorse that was now being operated by the army under a lease arranged by Somervell, and supply for the airfields in the area, should be placed under one officer to ensure the coordination of supply and administration. Accordingly, in early September, he activated the Northwest Service Command, with O'Connor in charge, an action which placed these projects under his direct control rather than Reybold's.

Backed by the men and supplies Somervell now lavished on the highway, O'Connor drove the pioneer phase of the highway through to completion, opening it to truck traffic by November 1942. Completion of the permanent phase of the highway by the PRA required another year of work.

Meanwhile, Canol expanded at a rapid rate (see Map 1). CANOL 3 provided for a two-inch pipeline to carry gasoline from the CANOL 2 pipeline to Watson Lake, Yukon Territory, along with associated storage facilities. In line with Somervell's directive for a program to distribute gasoline from Whitehorse to Alaska, CANOL 4 provided for a three-inch pipeline to carry gasoline from Whitehorse to Fairbanks. CANOL 5 provided for CANOL 4 to be extended to Tanana, Alaska; however, Somervell did not approve Wyman's plan for this project, and it was abandoned before construction was undertaken. CANOL 6 provided for a 1,000-mile overland winter supply road linking Peace River, Alberta, and Norman Wells. Wyman also expanded drilling operations at Norman Wells in the belief that the field could produce 20,000 barrels of crude oil a day. If he proved correct, this would require an even greater expansion of the project, for CANOL 1 was designed to handle about one-fourth of that amount of petroleum. Finally, in September, construction began on fourteen landing strips between Waterways and Norman Wells to facilitate the transport of supplies and equipment. Each of these enterprises spawned offshoots such as additional roads, expanded shipping facilities, and numerous camps for the workers.

After reviewing Canol in early November 1942, Somervell issued his final directive on November 16. Work on all Canol projects was to proceed as quickly as possible, with everything to be finished by December 1943.[14]

During the winter and spring of 1943, work on Canol progressed as well as possible. Temperatures that sometimes descended to -60 degrees F, transportation problems, difficulties in locating feasible pipeline routes and then laying the pipe, Ickes's ability to delay the army's acquisition and shipment of a refinery located in Texas to Whitehorse, and a host of other snags hindered progress. CANOL 2, the easiest job, was finished by the end of January 1943, and CANOL 3 was completed on May 21, 1943. Otherwise, Canol was far from finished when the Arctic summer began, by which time the strategic situation in the Pacific northwest was changing. The Japanese were being driven from the Aleutian Islands, all but eliminating the threat to Alaska and one of the basic reasons for Canol.[15]

While work on Canol went forward, opposition to the project mounted. In the summer of 1942, Stimson granted Ickes permission to send his own geologist, Glen F. Ruby, to Norman Wells to study the project. Ruby's report indicated that Norman Wells could produce 3,000 barrels of crude a day for at least two years, after which production would drop sharply. Even considering the emergency character of the "entire development," Ickes told Stimson "this is not a sufficient reserve to give proper support to the pipeline and refinery phases of the project." Consequently, he recommended that "further work on the construction of the proposed pipeline be held in abeyance and that . . . reliance be placed upon tanker shipment from California to Skagway, and transshipment from Skagway to storage at Whitehorse." The War Department rejected Ickes's recommendation, informing him that the project was fully justified since 3,000 barrels of crude were assured.[16]

Concerned about Ickes's opposition, Somervell decided to meet with him to clear the air. In their meeting, held on November 22, Ickes and Davis "told him just how" they felt about his refusal to consult them the previous spring and about the feasibility of the project. Somervell denied that he was under any obligation to consult Ickes on oil operations and indicated that he had not consulted the secretary because he was under the impression that Pyron had told Davis of the pipeline.

Despite their differences, "the interview was not strained or unpleasant." Contrary to what Ickes had expected, Somervell was conciliatory rather than "brusque or arrogant." At the end of the meeting, as Ickes recorded in his diary, Somervell "indicated that he would come to us for suggestions and advice on oil matters" and promised support for Ickes's long-standing plan to explore for oil in Alaska. Undoubtedly, Somervell was conciliatory in the belief that conciliation would lead Ickes to back away from his criticism of Canol. If this were his strategy, he totally misread Ickes.[17]

In early 1943, Ickes gained allies. Late in the fall of 1942, the WPB inadvertently heard of the project, leading Fred Searls, Jr., director of the WPB Facilities Board, to ask the War Department to provide him with information about Canol so the WPB could review the project as part of its attempt to curtail unnecessary construction. Dissatisfied with Patterson's reply that Canol was undertaken for strategic reasons, Searls fired off a letter to Patterson predicting the likely failure of the project and castigating the army for not bringing it before the WPB for an analysis of its impact upon other construction projects.[18]

Besides the WPB, Ickes found allies in the Budget Bureau. In February 1943, bureau examiners learned that the estimated cost of Canol had risen to $80 million and that Somervell was planning to spend an additional $20 million in exploratory drilling. Even though the War Department had considerable leeway in undertaking projects without prior justification to the bureau, the bureau sent two investigators to look into Canol. Their report, submitted to the War Department in June 1943, estimated that the project's cost would rise to $120 million by the end of 1944. CANOL 2, 3, and 4 were useful, the report judged, and CANOL 2 was capable of supplying all the petroleum needs of the Alaska

Highway and the staging route. However, unless absolutely vital to the war effort, the Norman Wells–Whitehorse pipeline and the refinery should be abandoned, and the JCS should review Canol in light of the fact that neither the west coast of North America nor Alaska was any longer threatened by the Japanese.

For Ickes, the examiners' findings were a boon. Frustrated by Somervell's "oil activities in the foreign field," he was determined not to permit Somervell "to set up an organization that will try to occupy the same space with us in the oil field." Now, as he wrote in his diary, "we have some facts and figures on the outrageous pipeline enterprise of Somervell's and the Army engineers in Canada and I think that we have something with which to beat the Army on the head."[19]

More immediately, Somervell had to be concerned about the reaction of some elements in the War Department to the Budget Bureau's findings. Shocked by the figures on Canol's likely cost, Stimson asked Marshall to have the project reevaluated in light of the changing strategic situation in Alaska. Marshall assigned the task to G-4 and the OPD, and both reported that the project should be dropped unless the oil that would be carried by the pipeline from Norman Wells to Whitehorse could be used "elsewhere strategically." Somervell moved quickly to "squelch the doubters" in the War Department. In a memorandum to Marshall on July 6, he wrote,

> Notwithstanding the more favorable strategic situation in the North Pacific with respect to tanker and dry cargo movements, any amount of oil that can be produced near the Alaskan Theater will relieve to a substantial extent a serious problem in addition to reducing the drain on limited production in California, and will add to the over-all supply of the United Nations.

Moreover, he added, returns from Canol would be realized "from one to two years earlier than other projects now under consideration lying outside the United States in areas which are not controlled by the United States" (i.e., Saudi Arabia, Palestine, Trans-Jordan, and the Caribbean). Considering these circumstances, he concluded, not to continue Canol "would appear inconsistent and unwise."[20]

Somervell in the summer of 1943 rested his case for Canol on the military's need for oil, the fact that construction of Canol was already underway, and the prospect that completion of Canol would "affect material savings in critical transportation facilities." In making his case to Marshall, however, he made several misleading statements. First, he stated that an intensive study of Norman Wells had been carried out before the project was undertaken. This had hardly been the case, and even the most charitable observer could at best label the study of Canol before it was initiated as superficial. Second, Somervell quoted Ickes on the necessity for the government to secure new sources of oil while falling to mention that Ickes opposed Canol. Finally, in computing the shipping savings Canol would yield, the general used the volume of crude produced at Norman Wells as a basis of comparison rather than the volume of refined products, which was one-third smaller and the correct basis of comparison for oil products brought to Alaska by tanker. Senate investigators later sharply questioned Somervell about these points, but the record does not indicate that Marshall either was aware of their misleading character or disturbed by them.[21]

Somervell's determination to push Canol through to completion reflected his belief in the project, but it also reflected his stubbornness. Supremely self-confident in his own judgment, temperamentally incapable of admitting mistakes, and regarding himself above criticism, he was ready to defend Canol against all critics. Moreover, Stimson and Patterson were willing to support him. Both had doubts about some aspects of the project, especially in regard to its long-range development, but Somervell convinced them that Canol represented money well spent, so they were ready to stand behind him. Consequently, Patterson wrote Budget Director Smith on July 27 that "we feel strongly that the Canol Project must be completed as rapidly as possible and without further interruption or delay." Estimating the total cost at $88 million, he stated that abandonment of the project would result in the loss of the $50 million already spent while spending the additional $38 million to complete it was not only financially sound but militarily necessary:

> The world-wide shortage of tankers and petroleum products is such that our offensive air operations may be limited by our capacity to produce and distribute petroleum products where needed and at the time required. The success of the Canol Project may well be the determining factor which will control the size and extent of an offensive aimed at the heart of the Japanese empire through Alaska and Siberia.

Interestingly, what had begun as a project to provide fuel for airplanes and trucks in Canada and Alaska was now being defended as potentially a major element in the overall strategy to defeat Japan. In other words, as the project's cost and critics had grown, so did Somervell's conception of the project's place in the war effort.[22]

• • •

In the summer of 1943, the Canol controversy entered a new phase after the Truman Committee decided to pursue reports of waste and mismanagement in the project. Wanting to know more about what the army was up to, a subcommittee headed by Harley Kilgore made an investigative trip to Alaska and Canada in September. Upon its return to Washington, the subcommittee prepared a critical report on Canol, prompting the Truman Committee to schedule full hearings for November 1943. Somervell was out of the country at this time, but he had anticipated that, once the Truman Committee picked up the scent of Canol, it would create trouble for him because of the hard feelings between Truman and himself. As a result, before leaving Washington, he had instructed his staff to launch a public relations offensive to build up support for the project. "It seems to me," he stated, "that our best line is that if we had the thing to do over again, we would double the size of the installation." Before long, army press offices in Washington and Edmonton were churning out stories about Canol and placing them virtually intact in newspapers and magazines in the United States and Canada.[23]

The prospect of a full Senate inquiry into Canol prompted James Byrnes, director of the OWM, to ask the JCS to reassess the strategic necessity for the project. This was the only occasion Canol officially came before them. The JCS had the Joint Production Survey Committee (JPSC) look into the project and make recommendations.

Charged with advising the JCS on the alignment of requirements with changing strategy, the JPSC studied the project in conjunction with the Army and Navy Petroleum Board. After reviewing a memorandum submitted by Somervell that retraced the ground he had covered in his July 6 memorandum to Marshall and hearing testimony from a limited number of selected witnesses, the JPSC recommended that Canol should be completed. On October 26, the JCS, without examining the evidence on which the JPSC based its recommendation, decided that completion of the project was "necessary to the war effort." When Truman later asked the reason for this decision, Admiral King, speaking for the JCS, refused the request on grounds of national security, and the JCS classified the working papers of the JPSC as secret and, thus, off limits to the Senate. Most likely, the JCS recommended Canol's completion because army specialists and Imperial Oil had estimated that Norman Wells had reserves of 35–100 million barrels of crude at a time when the military was concerned for the security of short- as well as long-term petroleum supplies.

Neither Somervell nor any of his immediate subordinates took part in the JCS's consideration of Canol, but he could not have been more pleased by their actions. Up to this time, Canol had been his project, and he had taken the heat for it. Now, the high command had associated itself with Canol. From this point on, Somervell steadfastly argued that he was merely carrying out a project directed by higher authority. Equally important, the JCS's action made it virtually impossible for civilian agencies or Congress to question Somervell about the military necessity for Canol. The JCS had ruled it necessary to the war effort, providing Somervell with a powerful weapon to counter the Truman Committee's assault against the project.[24]

The full Truman Committee began hearings on Canol on November 22,

1943. Ickes, WPB representatives, and Budget Director Smith all testified against the project. The army's defense at the outset was largely carried by Patterson, who enthusiastically praised the project. Refusing to accept Patterson's statements at face value, several senators and the committee counsel, Hugh Fulton, submitted the under secretary to a brutal cross examination, quizzing him at length about the planning for Canol and its estimated costs and alleged military necessity. In the process, Fulton signaled the likely result of the hearings when he put forward this unanswered question to Patterson: "why was it necessary to decide this in 1 day by General Somervell on a 1-page memorandum after one conference in which the only experts who had knowledge expressed considerable doubt as to whether they could get oil?" On November 23, the hearings recessed pending the testimony of Somervell, who was then attending the Cairo-Teheran Conferences.[25]

Somervell's long-awaited appearance before the committee came on December 20, 1943. Already accustomed to appearing before hostile congressional committees and well prepared for his day in court by Assistant Secretary of War Julius Amberg, he was an impressive witness. Attempting to put the committee on the defensive, he declared that Canol was a military necessity and that "it is a reckless man indeed who questions the strategy that has pulled us up and is going to lead us to victory." He added that the "whole thing was uneconomic" and that he would have been "the last man in the world" to have recommended it as a commercial undertaking. Furthermore, he reminded the committee that the project had been adopted when the Japanese were "knocking at our door," denied as "utterly without foundation" charges he undertook it without adequately consulting his superiors and associates, and affirmed that the project, while not yet finished, was entirely feasible, was being done competently, was defined by the JCS as essential to the war effort, and would require only $10 million more to complete. When Kilgore castigated him for not looking into other methods of supplying Alaska with oil and the likely cost of Canol, Somervell responded that anyone who suggested that a long investigation should have been made in 1942 "should have been courtmartialed."

However, all did not go well for Somervell. Asked to explain the details of his discussions in the spring of 1942 with Marshall about Canol, he claimed he "did not remember what was said at any of these conversations." It was a statement that spoke volumes about the haphazard manner in which he approved the project. Moreover, Somervell conceded that, if he had known that the project would not have been completed before 1944, he probably would not have approved it.

Finally, he had an embarrassing exchange with Edward H. Moore, Republican from Oklahoma and an oil man before entering the Senate. In stating that the additional wells drilled at Norman Wells indicated they had "struck a bonanza" that promised to yield 58 to 100 million barrels, Somervell characterized the Norman Wells field as the biggest oil field found in North America over the past fifteen years. Having apparently anticipated this line of defense, Moore cited twenty oil discoveries in the United States between 1930 and 1936 that were larger than Norman Wells and asserted that 100 million barrels "is no quantity of oil that would be of any emphasis whatever as to the continuation of the project."[26]

On the following day, Somervell received Roosevelt's support. Asked at a press conference if he had approved Canol as Somervell had testified, the president replied,

> I think I did, but I would have to—I would have to check it up. It was one of those projects to furnish, especially at that time, since . . . there was likelihood of a great deal of action in—in Alaska and the Aleutian Islands, I approved anything to get a new source of oil up there. It was a war measure distinctly.

Roosevelt's endorsement meant little. As Somervell expected, the committee blasted him when Kilgore submitted its findings to the Senate on January 8, 1944, in a report that had already been largely written by the time he testified. The report claimed that the project "was undertaken without adequate consideration of study," that Somervell's "continual insistence upon the project" in the face of repeated warnings about its unsoundness and excessive cost "is inexcusable," that it drained American resources instead of contributing to the war effort, that Somervell should have consulted Ickes, and that the War Department should review the project to decide whether it was worthwhile to complete it. In conjunction with his staff, Somervell prepared a reply, but his public relations people advised against responding, arguing that it would only stir up more controversy.[27]

The Truman Committee's report provided grist for newspaper and radio commentators, who citing the report's findings, concluded that Canol was untenable and branded it the war's "epic blunder" and a "fiasco." Even many in the army questioned the wisdom of ever starting the project yet alone proceeding with it once difficulties surfaced.[28]

Nevertheless, Somervell was determined to push ahead. Not to do so would be to throw away all the money that had already been poured into the project, which he was certain still had strategic merit. It could provide gasoline for ferrying aircraft to the Soviet Union by way of Alaska, and it would further build up Alaska as a base for a possible attack against Hokkaido and perhaps other Japanese territory. Even if the attack were not carried out, as long as the project was continued, the Japanese would be uncertain whether or not the United States intended to make an attack upon the Japanese homeland islands from the north. Further, Somervell believed Canol's petroleum production would provide a significant strategic reserve for the postwar years.[29]

Somervell's reasoning was strained. Gasoline for ferrying planes to the Soviet Union did not have to be provided by local sources at this point in the war. The navy had kept open the sea lanes to Alaska, and after 1943, tankers could have provided all the gasoline needed for the Alaska Highway, American forces in Alaska, and ferrying aircraft to the Soviet Union.

In addition, the continuation of Canol could hardly convince the Japanese that the United States might assault Japan by way of Alaska. For some time, Marshall had believed that the project was consuming too many engineer troops who were needed elsewhere. During the fall of 1943, he had indicated that he wanted to reduce American forces in the Northwest Service Command, and in early 1944, Somervell began the reduction, placing heavier reliance on civilian employees and even curtailing civilian employment where possible. With troops being withdrawn from Alaska and many facilities being reduced in scope and even to caretaker status, the abandonment of a petroleum project would hardly have persuaded the Japanese that an offensive through Alaska was no longer contemplated.

Lastly, Somervell was repeatedly warned by many oil experts that the reserves at Norman Wells were not as large as he hoped. They would certainly not be vital to American postwar interests.[30]

Possibly, Somervell also plunged ahead with Canol because the Truman Committee's criticism of him had been so sharp. His relations with the committee had always been prickly, and he was convinced it was using Canol to score political points and make itself look good in the public's eyes. The whole rationale of the committee, he believed, was to prove the army wrong, even if it were not. In doing so, the committee unfairly criticized hard-working military men like himself who faced mammoth responsibilities. During war, in Somervell's view, the civilian sector should operate to meet the needs of the military, and silly investigations by publicity-seeking politicians served only to take "the time of people who really didn't have the time to give" to them. Somervell was likewise convinced that the committee was out to pin something specifically on him, a belief he had harbored since his days with the Construction Division. To abandon Canol under these circumstances would be to admit the committee was right, leading only to more criticism and political obstructionism in the war effort. Instead, he would finish Canol, and subsequent events would prove his decision to undertake the project was correct.

By May 1944, the heart of Canol was officially finished. The final link in the pipeline from Norman Wells to Whitehorse was laid in February 1944, completing an incredible construction job. Two months later, after passing though ten pumping stations, the first crude reached the Whitehorse refinery, where it was converted into 100-octane aviation gasoline, motor gasoline, fuel oil, fuel gasoline, and diesel fuel.[31]

Canol was no sooner operating, however, than the army began putting in motion the machinery to shut it down. Stimson was no longer willing to defend the project, and a JCS staff report prepared in the fall of 1944 urged its abandonment because the cost of operating it exceeded the purchase price of petroleum acquired elsewhere. Somervell successfully buried the report for the time being by writing in the margin that "I approve of this but do not believe it should be submitted [to the JCS] until the war is somewhat further along." But, in early 1945, when the Senate War Investigating Committee, now headed by Senator James Mead, Democrat from New York, asserted that it wanted Canol ended and threatened another public hearing, Amberg informed Somervell it was unlikely the Congress would continue funding beyond June 30, 1945. Moreover, the JPSC and the JCS concluded that "because of their limited capacity and necessity of other sources of supply, the Norman Wells to Whitehorse crude pipeline and the refinery at Whitehorse have no permanent defense value." After a meeting of high-level officials in Somervell's office on February 15, it was decided to end the project as of June 30. Two months later, Somervell stated that Canada would be given first option to purchase the facilities. If she did not, he would charge the whole business to the waste of war.

Operations of the crude oil pipeline and the refinery ceased on April 1, and by June 30, Norman Wells was back to limited production for its ordinary regional markets. When Canada refused to exercise its option to purchase CANOL 1 (total cost $68 million), the refinery was sold in 1947 for $1 million to Imperial Oil, which dismantled it and sent it to Edmonton for use in a new oil field. The crude oil pipeline was auctioned off for junk for $700,000 by the Foreign Liquidation Commission in the same year. CANOL 3 ceased operation in August 1945, while CANOL 2 and part of CANOL 4 continued operation after the war. CANOL 6 had never proved its worth and had been abandoned after the winter of 1942–43.[32]

Canol had required the efforts of 4,000 engineer troops and 10,600 civilians working for two years. It included the oil field at Norman Wells, 1,600 miles of pipeline, a refinery, and a welter of transportation facilities, and, exclusive of the overhead of the soldiers who worked in the project, cost an estimated $134 million. From April 1944 to April 1945, 1,102,000 barrels of crude oil were sent through the pipeline from Norman Wells to Whitehorse, where they yielded 20,399 barrels of aviation fuel, 322,711 barrels of vehicle gasoline, and 276,983 barrels of diesel fuel at the astronomical cost of $3.70 a barrel. Other parts of Canol were more economical, but CANOL 1 was the core of the project, and a JCS staff report estimated that, under optimum conditions, it could produce only the equivalent of seven-tenths of one tanker load a month. Since Alaska was receiving thirteen tanker loads a month in the last year of the war, "the addition of one tanker load per month to this delivery system," the report noted, "is a minor consideration." Not surprisingly, the Mead Committee in its final report on Canol concluded that "the detriment to the war effort from the resulting waste in manpower and materials was greater than any act of sabotage by the enemy which had been disclosed."[33]

The last act of the Canol controversy was played out in the summer of 1946 when the Mead Committee submitted its final report to the Senate. Labeling Canol a "glaring . . . waste" of manpower and critical materials, it chastised Admiral King for using "the high office of the Joint Chiefs of Staff and claim of military secrecy" in 1943 "for the purpose of preventing the Congress and the people from requiring the discontinuance of a costly blunder by a fellow officer who was unwilling to admit his mistake and who was stubbornly insistent upon completing the project regardless of the cost." Canol, the committee proclaimed, was "a blot upon the records" of King and Somervell, "two otherwise capable officers."

Stung by the committee's findings, King, now retired, fired back that the report distorted the facts by not spelling out that, in sending the letter to Truman in October 1943 calling Canol essential, he was acting for the JCS and had never officially stated a position on Canol as chief of naval operations. At his request, a new hearing was held, and his concern was easily resolved.

The hearing also served another purpose, for President Truman insisted that the JCS's Canol file be turned over to the committee. The documents mentioned using Canol oil "to support a possible major air offensive against Japan" through Alaska and Siberia and in a planned attack of Paramushir Island off the Kamchatka Peninsula of the Soviet Union. Neither of these options had served as the original rationale for Canol or was seriously considered by the JCS in urging Canol's completion. King admitted as much when he told the committee that the JCS had not looked into the project but had simply affirmed the recommendations of the JPSC.[34]

Somervell, who was also retired, was likewise stung by the committee's report. Convinced that the report, which also included discussions of other examples of waste in the War Department, was an unjust attack upon his integrity designed to further the election prospects of Mead in his campaign for governor of New York, he privately called it gutter politics laced with "misconceptions, calumnies, banalities, stupidities, contradictions, ignorance and cheap sensationalism." Disdaining the opportunity to appear before the committee, he chose to fight back by asking the War Department to prepare a report on the economies he had achieved during the war and by dashing off an intemperate letter for Under Secretary of War Kenneth Royall to send to Mead if Mead used the committee's report in his campaign. Wisely, Royall chose not to use the letter or even to mount a major rebuttal to the committee. Canol had been thrashed out enough, and he did not want to call any more attention to the report.[35]

• • •

Canol provided Somervell's enemies with powerful ammunition to scar his reputation. While the initiation of the project in 1942 might plausibly be excused from "a safety-of-the-nation" angle and while the project yielded some knowledge about transportation and construction in the north and possibly hastened development there, Canol was the major blackmark on Somervell's wartime record. Cautioned repeatedly by informed people that the project was unwise, he paid no attention, and led astray by pride, he permitted it to take on a life that went far beyond its original conception and cost the government greatly in terms of critical materials and manpower. Adding to his crime, he embarrassed the Roosevelt administration and damaged the army's credibility when, on the strength of his affirmation, Stimson, Patterson, and the JCS went out on the limb and endorsed Canol. Consequently, Somervell's enemies used the hastily and ill-conceived project to demonstrate he was imperious, headstrong, and unable to consult or cooperate with others except on his own terms.

History has judged Canol as the epitome of pure folly and bad military planning, if not outright stupidity—the "quintessential white elephant of the wartime military-industrial complex." Yet, in some respects, Somervell was ahead of his time. By the middle of the 1980s, his ambitious plan to pump 20,000 barrels of crude oil a day from Norman Wells was finally realized, but now it was being done for the benefit of Imperial Oil and Exxon, not the American military, and was being carried by a twelve-inch pipeline to transfer points in Alberta.[36]

10. LOGISTICS AND STRATEGY, 1942–1943

• • • • AS ALREADY NOTED, STRATEGY AND LOgistics are interdependent, for no strategic decision can be made without reference to logistical factors. As the army's top logistician, Somervell was at the center of this interdependence since his job was to see that the army was transported and supplied. It was not an easy task, for beginning with America's entry into the war shifting strategic considerations and transportation and materiel uncertainties presented a host of perplexing problems around the globe (see Map 2).

• • •

In early 1941, American strategic planners decided, in conjunction with the British, that if the United States entered World War II, it would follow a European-first approach, even if it were also compelled to fight in the Pacific against Japan. At the ARCADIA meeting in Washington between Churchill and Roosevelt and their military staffs in late December 1941 and early January 1942, the European-first approach was reaffirmed. However, the two allies were not in agreement as to how to implement European First. For a time, the British pushed for an Anglo-American occupation of French North Africa, code named GYMNAST, but that plan was dropped early in 1942 because of British setbacks in Libya, the refusal of the French to cooperate in any African venture, and shipping shortages.

In its place, American planners proposed that American forces be concentrated in the United Kingdom for a cross-Channel invasion of Europe as soon as possible. Approved by American and British leaders in April 1942, the specific plan called for the following: (1) a buildup, code named BOLERO, of American troops and supplies in the United Kingdom; (2) preparation for launching a possible emergency landing on the continent, code named SLEDGEHAMMER, in 1942 should an imminent collapse of the Soviet Union or a possible deterioration of German strength dictate such action; and (3) a cross-Channel invasion, code named ROUNDUP, with forty-eight divisions and 5,800 aircraft, of which thirty divisions, with one million men altogether, and 3,250 aircraft would be American, and with a target date of April 1, 1943.

Following the adoption of the BOLERO-SLEDGEHAMMER-ROUNDUP plan, Allied staffs went to work on the deployment program. In this regard, Somervell's most pressing concern until the end of 1942 was the moving of cargo to the United Kingdom. Shipping was scarce, and to make matters worse, Somervell's staff determined that, if the army adhered to the normal practice of synchronizing the flow of cargo with the flow of troops, serious congestion would quickly develop in British ports. Despite the shortage of cargo ships, WSA officials assured Somervell on May 22 that they could provide enough bottoms to meet BOLERO requirements through August if he promised no ship would lack cargo when it was available. The WSA commitment gave Somervell a surplus of 70 to 100 cargo sailings for June, July, and August. However, in reality, this surplus existed only on paper, for the WSA's ability to meet the commitment was contingent upon the speedy conversion of commercial ships to war needs, the availability of escort vessels, and a decline in the rising trend of ship losses to German submarines.

Somervell fully appreciated the tenuous nature of the shipping surplus. Consequently, when he went to the United Kingdom at the end of the month to survey preparations for the buildup, he asked Lord Leathers to loan fifty cargo vessels for BOLERO shipments in July and August. Leathers, who had hoped the Americans would not make demands on British shipping until September, promised to do his best. However, he made no firm commitment, and stipulated that Somervell must make certain there was ample cargo to fill the ships.

On paper, the understandings with the WSA and Lord Leathers gave Somervell a sizable surplus of cargo shipping for the summer of 1942. Finding supplies to fill the holds was a problem. The army had to rush materiel to ports over and above the equipment and supplies that would accompany scheduled troop movements, and too often, the materiel that was the most needed in the United Kingdom was not available. As a result, Somervell earmarked whatever materiel he could for shipment, even though not all of it had been requested by the supply officers in England. Moreover, to utilize cargo shipping more efficiently, Somervell had ships loaded "full and down" (i.e., loaded with anything available on the docks rather than with items suitable for balanced loads), causing further imbalance in the flow of supplies. WSA officials, supply officers in England, and AGF officers all complained about Somervell's approach. But, his goal was to take advantage of the surplus of ships, and he argued that anything he could get to the United Kingdom now would aid the war effort in the long run.

The paper surplus in cargo shipping did not last long. Before long, many ships that had been scheduled for BOLERO were being diverted to the Middle East to rush supplies to counter the German threat in Egypt, virtually ending British participation in BOLERO. Ship sinkings further cut the BOLERO allotment, and administrative attrition (schedules going awry and loadings failing to meet expectations) eliminated others. Thus, in July, the backlog of BOLERO cargo of all kinds climbed to six times the quantity that available shipping could carry. By the end of the summer, the cargo actually shipped was only a fraction of the total that was planned, leaving a disproportionately large amount of materiel to be shipped during the winter of 1942–43.[1]

Even if the shipping problems had not been so pressing, the viability of SLEDGEHAMMER and ROUNDUP was severely handicapped by a lack of landing craft. The United States entered the war woefully unprepared for launching an amphibious invasion. The idea of using specially designed ships and small craft for directly discharging troops, vehicles, and supplies on a beach was new, and in early 1942, the United States had fewer than 1,000 landing craft on hand. In addition, the navy, which was responsible for the procurement of landing craft, showed little interest in them. It placed highest priority on the needs for fighting the Japanese in the Pacific, especially aircraft carriers and submarines, and in the Atlantic, it saw antisubmarine and escort vessels as its greatest need. While additional craft were on order, most were not scheduled for delivery until 1944, reflecting the generally low priority that the navy gave to the program.[2]

Dismayed by the landing craft situation, Roosevelt directed major increases in landing craft production on April 4 so that 2,500 craft would be ready for SLEDGEHAMMER and 8,200 for ROUNDUP. Later that month, War Department planners estimated that Roosevelt's figures were about right to carry out SLEDGEHAMMER and ROUNDUP and that all requirements could probably be met by April 1943. Actually, their estimates meant little, for they were hastily put together and impressionistic. Moreover, at a White House conference on May 5, British representatives advised that the Americans were placing too much emphasis upon smaller craft, which would be difficult to transport across the Atlantic in the limited shipping available and probably break down or swamp in the English Channel. These views surprised many of the Americans in the conference, especially Somervell who remarked that the navy had assured him the small boats were suitable. Nevertheless, the British warning made an immediate impact. On their recommendation, Roosevelt directed that a new program be drawn up that shifted emphasis to larger craft.

The shift in emphasis cast a long shadow over SLEDGEHAMMER, for it now seemed there would not be enough craft to meet the anticipated American troop contribution. Refusing to be deterred, Roosevelt ordered Somervell to submit a study showing "What we can do—not what can't we do—by September 1942 . . . in assembling landing craft to effect the BOLERO channel crossing." A week later, after studying the question with Chief of Naval Operations King, Admiral Horne, Emory Land, and Vice Admiral J. W. S. Darling of the Royal Navy, Somervell reported to Roosevelt that 1,850 landing craft would be in the United Kingdom by autumn; 1,200 of these would come from the United States, while the British would contribute the remainder. These craft would be sufficient, he added, to carry to France an expedition of about 21,000 men, 3,000 vehicles, and 300 tanks. At best, this force would constitute a large-scale raid, which was far from the original design of SLEDGEHAMMER.[3]

Lacking confidence in the navy's commitment to the landing-craft program, Somervell practically adopted it as his own and, as much as anyone, pushed it forward in the summer of 1942. One of the most notable accomplishments was the development of a new kind of vessel, called the Landing Ship Tank, or LST. Of British design, it displaced 4,000 tons and could carry more than two dozen tanks and trucks and, being flat bottomed, beach itself at low tide and float off at high tide. The navy was unimpressed with the LST. However, Somervell, recalling his days on the Mississippi, remembered that bootleggers had utilized flat-bottomed boats to land their cargoes on isolated beaches, and so, he thought that the LST design was sound and pressed hard for the program, which went far toward enabling the highly mechanized American army to land on enemy shores. Recalling Somervell's initiative, Lucius Clay later remarked that, while the landing craft program was "essentially a naval program, it was Somerville's [sic] drive and insistent [sic] that they had such a program."[4]

The same was true with the training of crews for the landing craft. In another example of the navy's small interest in landing craft, it claimed it was unable to train the large number of boat crews needed for landing operations in Europe in the fall of 1942. In May, unwilling to let the matter drop, Somervell persuaded Chief of Staff Marshall to assign to the Engineers responsibility for training army crews for some of the landing craft. Shortly afterward, Somervell reached an agreement with King that the army would train boat crews for all landing craft in the invasion force except the Landing Craft, Infantry boats and LSTs. The agreement was short-lived, however. King considered the operation of boats as the navy's proper sphere and saw Somervell's approach as only a temporary expedient. By June, King was convinced that an invasion would not take place until 1943 and that the navy could train its own crews in the additional time. As a result, he ordered the admiral responsible for training navy crews to give top priority to having the navy take over completely.

Anxious to maintain the momentum of what he had started and doubtful of the navy's commitment to the landing craft program, Somervell reached another agreement with the navy under which, for the time being, the Engineers would continue the training already started. The army would train crews for the smaller craft, the navy for the larger craft, but King would not make the agreement final until September and then only after the document formalizing it unequivocally stated that landing operations were "essentially the responsibility of the Navy." Somervell was satisfied with the agreement, which lasted until 1943 when the navy assumed complete control of landing craft training and operations. Yet, the whole affair angered him, for it had taken six months to reach an agreement that, in his view, could just as easily have been settled in the spring if the navy had accepted its responsibility.[5]

Meanwhile, the likelihood that adequate landing craft for SLEDGEHAMMER would be available was diminishing. Production and delivery schedules were lagging, while the navy's fifty-foot tank lighter, of which 415 were scheduled for delivery in June and July, was found to be unseaworthy. By the middle of July, it was obvious that Somervell's prediction that enough landing craft would be available in September to land 21,000 troops and 3,300 tanks and vehicles was off the mark. All the craft available or en route, including many too far back in the pipeline to be available in September, could land less than 16,000 troops and 1,110 tanks and vehicles. Disheartened by the numbers and certain the navy had let the army down, Somervell blasted its performance in a letter in July to Eisenhower, commander of the American troops in the United Kingdom preparing for the invasion:

> The Navy's efforts toward the completion of landing craft have been disappointing. This is just another indication of how difficult it is to force an issue when you have no control over the means of carrying it out. There is no lack of good will on their part, apparently though there was much indecision at the beginning.[6]

Somervell's involvement in BOLERO was not confined to shipping and landing craft problems. He also paid close attention to the creation of the organization in the European Theater of Operations (ETO) to handle the troops and supplies arriving in the United Kingdom. For one thing, he wanted an officer whose ability he trusted to be in charge of the supply command. Toward this end, Somervell recommended that Marshall name John Lee commander of the theater SOS. Others also passed Lee's name to Marshall. Stimson, who had known Lee for decades, thought highly of him as did Major General Mark Clark of the AGF, who later claimed he convinced Lesley McNair to suggest Lee's name to Marshall. Having come across Lee in the late 1930s while serving on the West Coast, Marshall was likewise impressed by Lee. If Marshall had any doubts about Lee's fitness, he overcame them in the light of the recommendation of Somervell, whose judgment in personnel matters carried great weight with him. In early May, Marshall selected Lee for the ETO post, and after working closely with Somervell during a two-week stint in Washington to put together a staff, Lee left for Britain on May 23.[7]

Equally important in regard to the ETO organization, Somervell told Marshall the organization of the SOS in the ETO should parallel that of the War Department ASF. Under his plan, the heads of the supply and administrative services in the ETO would be grouped in the theater SOS headquarters, leaving the theater commander's headquarters to be organized "along the general pattern of a command post with a minimum of supply and administrative services." Somervell's thinking was based on the experience of World War I when the SOS of the AEF was organized along lines that did not parallel the organization of the War Department. The lack of a parallel organization created innumerable problems in the United States and France, for there was no clearly defined command and technical channel between the two. With Somervell's plan, the theater SOS commander, while responsible to the ETO commander, would deal directly with Somervell's organization on a wide range of logistical and administrative matters, enabling Somervell to be in a position to ensure a more efficient flow of supplies to the theater.[8]

Somervell's plan for the ETO organization met strong resistance from Major General James E. Chaney, commanding general of army forces in the United Kingdom. In early May, he had presented Washington with his plans for an SOS organization in Britain and designated his choice to command it. Marshall quickly informed him that his organization, which roughly followed the World War I pattern, was unacceptable and that Lee was to organize the SOS when he arrived in Britain.

Following the instructions of Marshall and Somervell, Lee set out to place all supply and administrative functions under his command. However, to a man, Chaney and his staff criticized Somervell's plan for diminishing the authority of the theater commander. Thus, in June, Lee agreed to a compromise in which he remained in control of supply services while administrative services generally were assigned to ETO headquarters. The next month, Eisenhower, who had replaced Chaney, granted Lee broad responsibilities in supply planning and authorized direct communication between Lee's headquarters and Somervell. The arrangement was hardly the one desired by Somervell, yet he accepted it for the time being. Eisenhower, Marshall's personal choice to command the ETO, approved of the arrangement, and Somervell knew that Marshall was not inclined to interfere with Eisenhower's right to work out his own administrative arrangement.[9]

Long before the SOS arrangements in the ETO were put in final shape, Somervell made a trip to the United Kingdom. His purpose was to look into the preparations for the buildup and see at first hand the organizational problems involved in setting up Lee's supply command. Somervell left La Guardia Airport on the morning of May 25, and on May 26 he arrived in London. On May 27, Somervell met with Chaney and his staff in an unsuccessful effort to sell his plan for the theater SOS organization, and on May 28, he and Eisenhower, who had also arrived in London on May 26, met with British leaders to discuss the facilities that might be furnished to the Americans.

After an additional day of conferences and a weekend stay with some other Americans at Chequers, the prime minister's estate, Somervell undertook a whirlwind tour of ETO installations in the United Kingdom, using a special train placed at his disposal. On June 6, Somervell left Prestwick, Scotland, arriving in Washington on June 8. Later that day, Somervell met with Stimson to outline the scope of the operations needed to turn the United Kingdom into an American base.[10]

Somervell had no sooner returned home than he was bombarding Eisenhower, Lee, and the OPD with suggestions and questions on a wide range of matters in regard to BOLERO. No problem more disturbed him than the inadequate number of service troops in the United Kingdom to unload, sort, transport, and issue supplies to the combat troops. Also, construction, port, depot, and maintenance units were needed far in excess of those projected to be sent if the United Kingdom were to be turned into an effective base. Somervell's planners had estimated that the service troop component of BOLERO should be at least 35 percent, or about 350,000 men, and at the end of April, the general requested the OPD to take these figures into consideration in its troop planning for BOLERO.

However, the OPD preferred to emphasize ground and air troops and provided for a SOS component of only 277,000 men, approximately 26 percent of the total projected strength. The OPD further ruled that combat and air units would have first priority in the limited troop ship capacity available, so that by the end of September, the service troop ratio in the theater was only 21 percent. As a result, the vast quantity of supplies being sent to the United Kingdom was being managed poorly. Much of it was handled by British labor rather than by skilled service troops, was scattered throughout the countryside, and was not properly inventoried or stored.[11]

Things would not have been much different even if the OPD had been more receptive to Somervell's pleas to include more service troops in BOLERO. The Victory Program had called for service troops to constitute approximately 40 percent of the army, but as the 1942 Troop Basis took shape, service troops were downplayed out of a desire to produce fighting units as rapidly as possible. By April 1942, only 11.8 percent of the troop basis was allotted to service troops, a pitifully inadequate allowance considering that in 1918 the AEF had consisted of 34 percent service troops exclusive of those serving with combat units. During the early months of 1942, Somervell had pushed for more service troops, and in May, the OPD finally heeded his pleas and authorized an increase of 236,000 service troops as part of the overall augmentation of 750,000 troops approved by Roosevelt.

Beginning in the summer of 1942, however, demands for service troops skyrocketed to meet expanding logistical activities in Canada, Alaska, the Middle East, India, and the Pacific, and there were not enough trained units to satisfy the demand. On the assumption that a half-trained man was better than no man, Somervell sent units overseas that were not adequately trained for the jobs awaiting them, which only added to the confusion. Embittered by this reality, Somervell complained to Marshall in September that the service-troop program authorized in May had been "completely hamstrung." Eventually recognizing that a higher percentage of service troops was needed, the OPD slowed the activation of ground units and allotted Somervell more service units in the new troop basis adopted in the fall of 1942. At the year's end, service troops composed approximately 35 percent of the planned basis of 7.5 million men[12]

Despite the supplies being sent to the United Kingdom, the American establishment there depended heavily upon the British for logistical support. To the extent that the use of British support conserved valuable shipping space and took advantage of a supply system that was already operating, the arrangement made sense. However, the supplying of American forces through British channels worried Somervell. The British wanted the United States to pay for this support with reciprocal aid, which if not carefully balanced against what the American forces had received ran the risk of rendering the saving in shipping only an illusion. More importantly, Somervell feared that the reliance upon the British gave them an undue measure of control over the American supply line. Certain that the British would use their control over logistics in the United Kingdom to dictate strategy, Somervell unalterably opposed the British suggestion and "relentlessly pushed for a separate American supply system that would rely on the British only for those things they could furnish with no strings attached."[13]

The issue of providing food for American forces in the United Kingdom brought the matter to a head. In June 1942, British officials and Averell Harriman, the American lend-lease representative in London, had reached an agreement whereby American forces would rely on British sources for most of their foodstuffs, either produced locally or imported by the British in bulk. Suspecting a British plot behind the agreement, Somervell wrote Eisenhower that

> the whole scheme, in my opinion, is one on the part of the British to direct food stuffs to their control and to impose their standard of living on our troops. This was never satisfactory during the last war and I don't see why the question of what our soldiers eat should be even a matter of discussion with the British. I think that

you will be very foolish if you permit someone else to control your food. If this is done it will mean that all of your food will be moved through uncertain, uncontrolled, Lease Lend channels rather than through direct and responsible Army channels. That will be the only difference, except to introduce an additional lot of red tape at your end of the line to get the food back from the British.

Taking umbrage at Somervell's lecture, Eisenhower pointed out that he had not heard of the arrangement before Somervell's letter and "would most certainly *not* give my approval to any such idea." It was his intention, he added, only to "buy here those perishables which are plentiful at this season." Somervell was not mollified by Eisenhower's assurances, and in early August, he again challenged Eisenhower on the ration problem, telling him that he should "take the necessary steps to insure that our troops are supplied with our own food through our regular supply channels, with the exception, of *locally* grown vegetables or of British products of which there is a surplus over their own needs."[14]

The food issue was not as simple as Somervell perceived it. Diverting local surplus for consumption by American troops, despite the prevailing food shortage in the United Kingdom, was economical in the long run, and officers in Lee's command were less fearful of British control of the supply line than Somervell. Conceding these points, Somervell in September 1942 advised Lee to exploit local sources of supply for food to the maximum extent consistent with the integrity of the American supply line.[15]

Meanwhile, BOLERO had dwindled in importance after the Allied high command decided in the summer to abandon SLEDGEHAMMER and to invade French North Africa before the end of the year. Although it was not admitted at the time, these decisions also had the effect of delaying ROUNDUP, leading to the rapid deemphasis of BOLERO for the time being. No new divisions were sent to the United Kingdom for almost a year, the volume of other troop movements and cargo shipments tumbled drastically, and American forces in the United Kingdom were rapidly depleted to meet North African demands. Thus, from a peak of 228,000 troops in October 1942, American forces fell to 105,000 in March 1943. The ETO, the focal point of so much of Somervell's supply planning in 1942, had been reduced to "a stand-by theater manned by a skeleton crew."[16]

• • •

Somervell did not participate in the deliberations that led to the decision to invade French North Africa, an operation code named TORCH, yet he followed them closely. On July 19, he told Eisenhower that "we are naturally disturbed at the trend which present thought is taking" and expressed hope that, after all the conversations were over, "we will once more be moving down the groove" toward SLEDGEHAMMER. Then, on July 27, he learned that SLEDGEHAMMER was dead and received orders to "dust off" the GYMNAST plans and draw up a service troop basis for the operation. Somervell took the new strategic plans in stride. "We are busy, as you are, no doubt, in changing horses in mid-stream," he wrote Eisenhower ten days later. "We have changed the old nags so often that we are getting a little bit used to it even if their tramping around does muddy up the water a good deal."[17]

The decision to invade North Africa was followed by six weeks of tedious negotiations between American and British planners over the place, size, and timing of TORCH. Lacking definitive information on the supply requirements and time of the invasion until these negotiations were completed, Somervell had to base his initial planning on what tidbits he could glean from the ongoing negotiations, the old GYMNAST plans, and his own guesses. His principal task was to prepare the Western Task Force, which was to sail from the United States and seize Casablanca.

Unable to obtain a firm troop basis for the force, a statement of special requirements, and the sailing date and detailed composition of the first echelon, Somervell improvised. In early August, he instructed the supply services to start equipping a balanced force of 250,000 men from which the task force would be drawn, appending a long list of special equipment that would probably be needed. Little more could be accomplished, however, as uncertainty continued to cloud the operation through August.[18]

By early September, the picture began to clear considerably. After several days of intense bargaining, American and British planners on September 5 agreed on the broad outline for the operation. Simultaneous attacks were to take place: The Western Task Force, composed of troops from the United States, was to attack Casablanca; the Central Task Force, American troops from the United Kingdom, was to attack Oran, Algeria; and the Eastern Task Force, American troops from the United Kingdom to be followed by a large British force, was to attack Algiers, Algeria. The operation was tentatively scheduled for early November 1942.

The September 5 agreement enabled Somervell to move ahead with his preparations for TORCH with greater specificity. No sooner had the agreement been reached, however, than matters were complicated by the need to provide greatly increased assistance for the American forces in the United Kingdom preparing for TORCH. It had been assumed their requirements would be filled from supplies already delivered or being delivered to the United Kingdom as part of BOLERO, but the higher priority given combat troops over service troops had now caught up with Lee's SOS. Most of the equipment that was needed was available in the United Kingdom, but it had been randomly scattered among makeshift depots by British workers without records or box or crate markings. Finding the necessary equipment and delivering it to the combat troops on time was now out of the question.[19]

Somervell learned of the difficulties on September 8 when he received Message 1949 from London. Detailing at great length the essential equipment American forces in the United Kingdom required for TORCH, the message stunned him. Earlier that day, he had told Eisenhower, who was in charge of TORCH, that "this office will strain every facility to meet your requests, no matter what they may be. . . . Whatever you ask for will be produced if it is within our power to produce it." But, Message 1949 went beyond anything he had imagined and was a frank confession that things were not going well in the United Kingdom. In a letter to Lee several days later, Lutes verbalized the frustrations that all in Somervell's headquarters felt over the regrettable mess and advised him to have his staff "swarm on the British ports and depots and find out where these people have put our supplies and equipment."[20]

Lee's staff lacked the time to swarm over ports and depots. Hence, Somervell plunged into dealing with Message 1949 as best he could. It was not an easy task. Lack of time made it impossible to meet the requirements of balanced loads, especially since the first group of supplies had to be dispatched by September 12 if it were to arrive in the United Kingdom by the requested date of September 26. Under Lutes's prodding, the supply services worked around the clock to get materiel ready for shipment.

Despite these efforts, Somervell was unable to meet the requirements of Message 1949, which called for the shipment of 260,000 ship tons to the United Kingdom by October 20, but he did rush 131,000 ship tons in time to be placed on the assault convoys and also sent eight fully loaded cargo ships with special supplies to join the convoys as they left the United Kingdom for the Mediterranean.[21]

Even though Message 1949 demanded much of Somervell's attention, his principal responsibility was the equipping of the Western Task Force. It was a most exasperating task. Troop commanders ordered special equipment piecemeal, and equipment tables were slow to arrive because of the constantly changing list of units to participate in the operation. Further, commanders made matters worse by demanding plenty of the most up-to-date equipment the country could provide. Colonel Carter Magruder in Lutes's office complained that this constant stream of changes and additions was making it impossible to outfit the task force in an orderly manner, but Somervell instructed him to provide the task force with everything it asked for as long as General Patton, its commander, endorsed it. In his mind, he had no other choice. As he told Lutes on many occasions, field commanders would never accept the blame if the ASF were unable to support a campaign adequately, even if they asked for too much.

Loading was just as taxing. Basic information about the task force—convoy schedules; units assigned to specific convoys and to specific transports; items which should accompany each unit, sub-task force, and echelon; specifications of the cargo capacity of the ships—was slow in coming from the General Staff despite Somervell's incessant pleading for details. When much of it was finally received, the planning stemming from it was soon undone by the decision of Eisenhower's deputy, Mark Clark, to slash equipment by 50 percent (mostly vehicles) because of the navy's inability to provide enough escort vessels for the initial assault forces. In early October, new loading plans were worked out with the task force staff and commander, but constant changes in equipment assignments and a plethora of other nagging problems, such as inadequate marking of freight cars and a hasty final rehearsal in unloading and landing, made loading "a scrambled operation."[22]

Despite these difficulties, Somervell met the challenge of both equipping and dispatching the Western Task Force and providing additional supplies for the task forces sailing from the United Kingdom. The deadlines for sailing to make the Casablanca attack on November 8 were met when two landing forces sailed from the United States on October 23 and a third on October 24, to be joined on October 25 by a sea train with tanks and a tardy transport carrying gasoline and bombs.

The TORCH landings went off as scheduled, and by November 11, the initial objectives for all three task forces had been achieved. However, hopes for a quick conquest of Tunisia, the ultimate objective of the operation, were dashed by a poorly planned and executed offensive, stiff German resistance, and winter rain that turned the landscape into mud. As the front settled into a stalemate, Somervell faced great difficulty in shipping supplies to North Africa for the buildup there in anticipation of an offensive in the spring of 1943. Lacking sufficient escort vessels, the navy placed restrictions on the size of convoys, and constant changes in troop compositions and unexpected supply requisitions created confusion in the loading of ships in the United States and in their departure. Thus, by early 1943, cargo shipments were seriously lagging behind schedule, prompting many complaints from Eisenhower's staff.

Nevertheless, there were some notable successes in shipping supplies to North Africa. The most dramatic occurred in February 1943. As Eisenhower prepared for the spring offensive, the greatest single obstacle was the shortage of adequate rail and road transport in North Africa. The railroad from Oran eastward was in a poor state and inefficiently run, and the Algerian roads were in desperate need of repair. In addition, Eisenhower had yet to receive all the vehicles which Clark had decided to leave behind when the Western Task Force had sailed. Somervell received inklings of this situation during November and December 1942, but not until he went to North Africa in January 1943 for Roosevelt's meeting with Churchill and Free French leaders did he realize its seriousness.

At a conference on January 25 in the St. George Hotel in Algiers, Eisenhower informed Somervell and Marshall that little hope existed for a breakthrough in Tunisia until the transportation obstacle was cracked and that he desperately needed vehicles. In reality, the situation was probably not as bleak as Eisenhower painted it, for convoy UGS-3 had brought 4,500 vehicles at the end of December and UGS-4 was on the way with 5,300 more. However, Somervell, angered by the earlier complaints about delays in shipping supplies to Africa, jumped at the opportunity to get more trucks to Eisenhower to show what the ASF could accomplish. He told Eisenhower that, if the navy provided escorts, he would have a convoy ready to sail from the United States in three weeks. Admiral King, who was also in North Africa, agreed to provide escorts, and on January 26, Somervell sent a telegram to Washington ordering Styer to have a special convoy ready to sail by February 15 with a huge quantity of road and railroad equipment and other urgent items. Included were 5,400 trucks, 72 tank transporters, 2,000 trailers for the trucks, 100 locomotives, and some railroad stock.

Somervell's message startled Styer. The quantity of supplies to be sent on such short notice was unprecedented and would require an all-out effort by the ASF. Still, Styer was confident that the organization was up to the task. In contrast to previous convoys, this was a fixed entity and thus free of some of the encumbrances that had affected the earlier ones. Additionally, there was a specific order, no fluctuating troop lists of uncertain priorities, and a deadline so imminent that substantial last-minute changes were out of the question.

For the most part, things went smoothly. The WSA located twenty available cargo ships to sail from New York, Baltimore, and Hampton Roads, Virginia. Red tape was cut by having depots ship cargo to the ports without clearance, and cargo was then loaded as it arrived without priorities. Snow and rain slowed the loading, but the convoy designated UGS-5½, sailed as scheduled on February 15. It arrived in North Africa on March 6.

For Eisenhower, UGS-5½ was a godsend. The trucks greatly increased his mobility, and the locomotives prevented a complete breakdown of the North African railroads.[23] Also, by this time, the shipping bottleneck was being widened as the navy relaxed its restrictions on convoys. A number of shortages turned into surpluses, and by April, the period of emergency supply in North Africa came to an end. In May, after successful Allied offensives, German and Italian forces in Tunisia surrendered, providing the Anglo-American partners their first major victory in the war against the Axis.

• • •

TORCH presented new logistical concerns to Somervell: supplying the civilian population of North Africa and equipping the French army. It had been launched with little regard for civilian needs because Allied authorities had concluded that no shipping space could be made available for civilian imports until the military buildup in North Africa was well underway. But, within days after the invasion, it became obvious that the war had created serious economic dislocation in North Africa and that a minimum of civilian supplies must be sent to the region or else the economy would break down. Immediately, Eisenhower requested early shipment of supplies, most of them foodstuffs, through military channels, and on November 13, 1942, Roosevelt declared that every possible step would be taken to see that no inhabitant of an occupied territory went "hungry, or without the means of livelihood."

Over the next days, an organization was put together to "handle what promised to be a serious and continuing supply problem." Somervell had already recommended that lend-lease representatives in North Africa, serving as part of Eisenhower's staff, should determine civilian requirements subject to Eisenhower's approval and assignment of shipping priorities. However, Roosevelt, warned by some advisors that Somervell's plan represented a military lust for power and authority, entrusted the newly established Office of Foreign Relief and Rehabilitation Operations (OFRRO) in the State Department with responsibility for civilian relief requirements. The Office of Lend-Lease Administration was given responsibility for furnishing funds and arranging procurement, and a committee drawn from the combined boards was formed to make policy. The War Department, although it was busily procuring and shipping supplies to meet Eisenhower's initial requests, was essentially excluded from the setup.[24]

Difficulties quickly developed. Competition for shipping, port facilities, and internal transportation led to disputes between army and civilian officials over the priority to be accorded to military and civilian supplies. Eventually, limitations on shipping forced military and civilian cargoes to be loaded on the same ships, leading to complaints that army officers who were responsible for managing port operations were neglecting civilian supplies in their rush to unload military supplies. In early 1943, disgusted with the situation, Somervell wrote John McCloy, the War Department representative on the Committee of Combined Boards, that "we have had an opportunity to learn a real lesson from North Africa." That lesson, he added, "is that you cannot separate the handling of civil affairs from military operations in areas in which military operations are underway, and that an attempt to do so in an hostile country would be disastrous." Somervell's letter led to some changes in the final stages of the North African campaign when authorities agreed that all civilian supply operations in the initial occupation of Tunisia should be under military control. However, this arrangement did not serve as a precedent, for Roosevelt had already decreed that administration of civilian relief in liberated areas should be centered in the OFRRO.

Nevertheless, the trend was toward military assumption of responsibility for civil relief. Somervell, for example, emphasized that the obvious need for the military to control transportation to and from a theater, as well as security requirements, argued against allowing civilians to participate in the planning of future operations on which any intelligent program of civilian relief must depend. Over the next several months, it was agreed that the army should handle civilian supply for the first ninety days of an operation, and in July 1943, a civilian section was added to the ASP. Finally accepting Somervell's argument that the military was best equipped to handle civilian supply, Roosevelt in November 1943 reversed himself and unequivocally gave the responsibility for civilian relief to the military.[25]

The supply of civilians in North Africa coincided with the rearmament of the French army. In late 1942, American officials, wanting to add to Allied strength, decided to equip French forces in North Africa to fight alongside the Allies. At the Casablanca Conference, they gave General Henri Giraud, whom they were sponsoring as the commander of French forces, a commitment to rearm the French army. Marshall and Somervell told him that they would equip French troops with the greatest possible speed, although in their minds they had made no specific commitments as to the timing or eventual scope of the program.

Giraud came away from the conversation with a different view, stating in a memorandum that Marshall and Somervell had agreed to provide enough equipment for three armored and eight motorized divisions and an air force of 1,000 planes. Delivery of this materiel was to be accomplished by the summer of 1943. Following talks with Giraud, Roosevelt noted "Oui en principe" on a memorandum prepared by Giraud outlining his talk with Marshall and Somervell.[26]

The phrase "Oui en principe" meant a lot more to Giraud than to the Americans. He interpreted it to mean a firm commitment, whereas Roosevelt never saw it as an absolute commitment to make materiel available on any time schedule. Before long, Giraud was complaining that the current allocation of 25,000 tons per convoy for French rearmament was insufficient to meet the American commitment to him. Concerned that French dissatisfaction might create problems for the American forces in North Africa, Eisenhower asked Washington if 100,000 tons of additional cargo space might be provided as long as it was not provided at the expense of the British and American strength. Roosevelt immediately informed Eisenhower that neither he nor Marshall and Somervell had promised equipment for French units on any time schedule. However, Marshall was prepared to accede to Eisenhower's request if shipping could be found, and he had Somervell explore the matter. On February 19, Somervell asked the WSA for twenty-four ships. It was able to locate nineteen without interfering with other demands, and in mid-March, a special convoy sailed with 132,000 tons of supplies for the French.[27]

During the spring of 1943, the army accepted the eleven-division commitment as a reality, although the rate at which it was to be filled was to be governed by the shipping situation. After the special March convoy, shipments reverted to a rate of 25,000 tons a convoy, and despite pleas from the French that they were entitled to a larger allocation, Marshall and Somervell refused to budge on the grounds that the British and Americans needed all the shipping available for other operations. While unsatisfactory to the French, the 25,000-ton allocation was significant, and by the end of the North African campaign, the Americans had equipped, or were in the process of equipping, three and one-half divisions and a small air force.

In July, the French rearmament program moved into a second phase. Giraud came to the United States for a ten-day round of conferences beginning on July 7 and called for a speedy shipment of the supplies to implement the Casablanca program. Meanwhile, Eisenhower had cabled Washington that, until November 1943, port facilities in North Africa would not permit the addition of any French equipment in excess of the 25,000 tons per month already being sent. On July 8, Somervell met with Giraud to explore his needs in depth.

As Somervell expected, Giraud went beyond Eisenhower's recommendations and asked for materiel to equip four divisions and for support units to operate beside those already equipped. After discussing Giraud's request with his own staff, Somervell told Marshall that the equipment and shipping—approximately 200,000 tons requiring twenty-eight ships—could be provided if the shipping were spaced over the July, August, and September convoys. He reiterated, however, that the bottleneck was port capacity in North Africa and that "it would seem necessary . . . for any commitments to Giraud to be predicated on his having obtained a prior statement from Eisenhower to the effect that the additional shipping could be accommodated in North African ports. This is the most important element in the whole situation." On the basis of Somervell's report, Marshall promised Giraud approximately what the French had requested.[28]

Eisenhower informed Washington that the port of Casablanca could handle 200,000 tons of French rearmament materiel in August and September 1943. Thus, shipments were accelerated, and by the end of August, more than 200,000 tons had cleared American ports for North Africa. This materiel provided the French with most of the equipment needed for two armored and four infantry divisions. During the winter of 1943–44, the program was completed, although not before it was altered because the French were unable to provide the necessary supporting units to make an eleven-division force completely self-sufficient. The result was a rejuvenated eight-division French army that fought in Italy and helped to liberate France.[29]

• • •

The commitment to a European-first strategy did not mean that American leaders ignored the Pacific war. Initially, their efforts focused on efforts to send troops and supplies to island bases in the South and Southwest Pacific to guard the lifeline to Australia and New Zealand, as well as to Australia for possible transport to the Philippines, which for all practical purposes were cut off by the Japanese success at Pearl Harbor and whose beleaguered defenders could not hold out for long. To come up with shipping for this movement, the Allied chiefs in January 1942 agreed to Somervell's proposal to divert shipping for the Atlantic deployment to the Far East and to reduce lend-lease shipments to the Soviet Union. As a result of these decisions, 45,000 troops and 227,000 measurement tons of cargo were shipped to Australia during the first two months of 1942.[30]

These shipments did not go without hitches. Some scheduled departures were delayed while the navy searched for adequate shipping and, in one case, delayed twice more by the navy's decision to combine two convoys. The army was not entirely blameless, for confusion on the loading docks and inefficient labor added to the delays. But, Somervell, impatient with anything less than full speed, ignored the army's failings and frequently vented his frustration by criticizing the navy for failing to carry its weight. The army wanted to deploy men oversea as soon as possible, even if it mean running risks, while the navy, in his view, seemed more concerned with rebuilding the capital ship fleet and fighting the war on its terms.

While appreciating that Somervell was trying to shake "the cobwebs out of their pants," Marshall was not pleased with his attitude toward the navy: "I told him . . . not to insult the Navy. I said, by God, don't do it again." Somervell did not change, however, and on several further occasions, Marshall had to stroke King after Somervell ruffled the admiral's feathers with his criticism of the navy.[31]

Persuaded that the Japanese blockade of the Philippines was only paper-thin east of the islands, General Douglas MacArthur, commander of American forces in the islands, called for Washington in early 1942 to utilize the route across the central Pacific from Hawaii. Immediately, on the basis of a presidential request, Somervell swung into action. Declaring that MacArthur's proposal was "practical and desirable," he recommended that six World War I destroyers, already converted to cargo vessels with a capacity of 1,500 tons each, be assigned the mission. Roosevelt promptly approved the plan, and after delays brought about by problems in arming the vessels, providing gun crews, and working out routes, the first ship sailed from New Orleans on March 2. Two others left New Orleans later that month, while the final three sailed from the West Coast between March 16 and April 11.

None got further than Hawaii before the Philippines campaign ended in early May with the surrender of all American troops in the islands. Even if there had been more time, Somervell's scheme was likely to fail. He never submitted it to the navy for serious consideration, and after the war, a navy planner remarked that anyone familiar with the steaming characteristics of the vessels and the distances in the Pacific "would have crossed it out as a practical operation."[32]

With the Philippines lost, American plans called for commitments in the Pacific to be limited to those absolutely necessary for a defensive strategy, but this approach quickly came under question. MacArthur, now in Australia as commander of the Southwest Pacific Area (SWPA), asked for a greater concentration of resources in this area to prevent the Japanese from threatening Australia. The naval victory over the Japanese at Midway Island in early June opened up the possibility for a limited offensive to counter the Japanese threat to Australia and the line of communication from Hawaii. On July 2, Marshall and King agreed on an offensive with the ultimate objective of seizing the New Britain–New Ireland–New Guinea area.

On August 7, the South Pacific command of the Pacific Ocean Area (POA) launched the first American offensive in the Pacific with landings on the islands of Guadalcanal and Tulagi in the Solomon Islands. In addition, before the end of the month, MacArthur initiated a defensive-offensive operation in New Guinea to break the Japanese hold on the northern coast of Papua. (The American war in the Pacific was divided into two areas: the SWPA, commanded by MacArthur, and the POA, commanded by Admiral Chester Nimitz. The POA was divided into three subareas: the South Pacific, the Central Pacific, and the North Pacific.) (See Map 3.)

The Pacific operations presented logisticians with tremendous problems. Some were inherent in the Pacific war. For example, the distance from the United States to the combat zones was twice the distance from the United States to the United Kingdom, and the distances within the two Pacific areas were also imposing. Together, they created a heavy strain on the limited shipping assigned to the Pacific. This situation was further aggravated by an almost complete absence of adequate base and port facilities.

Other problems grew out of divided administrative responsibilities. There were separate supply lines for the two areas and separate supply operations for the army and the navy, creating waste and duplication in a region where facilities and resources were already in short supply. Since the European war had a higher claim on resources, the resolution of these logistical problems lay with conserving scarce shipping by better advance planning and interservice coordination, especially in the South and Central Pacific. There was less concern about these matters in the SWPA, where MacArthur had already established tight control over priorities for all forces.

Nothing demonstrated better the need for advance planning and interservice coordination than the mess at Noumea, New Caledonia, the major base supporting American operations on Guadalcanal. The invasion of Guadalcanal was undertaken with little advance planning for bases, forcing the army and navy to rely on ports like Noumea which were suitable only for leisurely peacetime commerce. Possessing few berths, Noumea was unable to keep pace with the flow of troops and supplies arriving by September 1942. On September 23, there were eighty-six ships in the harbor, either transports and cargo ships waiting to be unloaded or loaded or naval vessels waiting to be provisioned. During the next months, the congestion worsened, reaching a peak in December when there were nearly 100 ships in the harbor.

The congestion was aggravated by the lack of cooperation between the army and the navy. Acting independently on the West Coast of the United States, and with minimal coordination, each forwarded supplies to the South Pacific as soon as shipping became available. There each unloaded its ships with little reference to the discharge activities of the other or to harbor traffic. Because of a lack of storage facilities ashore, each also tended to unload supplies only as they were needed, turning the partially unloaded vessels into floating warehouses and rendering them immobile for a considerable time when they were needed elsewhere.

Unwilling to tolerate this mess, Somervell sent Lutes to the South Pacific in October to investigate the problems and recommend remedies. Lutes quickly surmised that the logistical ills there could be cured only by greater interservice cooperation. In discussions with army and navy commanders and supply officers, he called for a joint logistical staff to determine the South Pacific's requirements, assign priorities for shipping, and schedule the unloading of ships. Back in the United States in November, he urged army and navy officials in San Francisco to schedule their shipments jointly in accordance with priorities laid down by South Pacific officials and presented Somervell with a plan for the complete unification of the army and navy supply lines in the Pacific.

Lutes's trip yielded results, although not all that he had recommended. In line with his recommendations, Somervell sent more service troops to the South Pacific to unload ships and to construct storage facilities, but the joint logistical staff did not materialize. Admiral William Halsey, the South Pacific commander, preferred to leave supply administration in the hands of each service and rely on interservice boards or informal arrangements to untie the supply knots. Over the next months, these methods imposed order, and by May 1943, the congestion crisis at Noumea had abated. Yet, the basic problem of ship congestion from lack of port facilities was not solved. It was no sooner being solved at Noumea than it was reappearing elsewhere as the combat zone moved up the Solomons chain.[33]

In the meantime, Lutes's proposal for complete unification of the army and navy supply lines in the Pacific reopened a debate that had been going on intermittently since the previous spring. During the early months of the war, the services had followed a haphazard approach in establishing a system of command, administration, and flow of supplies for the Pacific islands from Hawaii to New Zealand. As a result, these functions were often divided between the two services, creating a situation that cried out for joint logistics.

Even though there was an obvious need for cooperation, Somervell was initially wary of any joint arrangement. In his opinion, the navy's logistical organization had been laggard in adjusting to wartime demands, and he feared army interests would suffer if the navy had a say-so in army supply. Moreover, Somervell feared his own organization, which was still feeling its way in developing an overseas supply mechanism, was not ready to participate in a new interservice organization in such a way to protect army interests. Writing in April to Lieutenant General Delos C. Emmons, commander of the Hawaii Department, Somervell stated that the ASF could best do its job if it controlled "both the supply facilities and the transportation necessary." He added, "We have so dominant an interest; we have so clear a responsibility in the supply of our large forces; we must definitely control the means."[34]

But after considering Lutes's proposal Somervell was now ready to back unification of transportation. He was surer of ASF's power and interests than he had been in April and confident that his headquarters could exercise effective control of the sending of supplies from depots in the United States to overseas depots because of the fully integrated ASF organization, even if the navy had responsibility for military shipping. Thus, in December 1942, Somervell proposed that the army and navy ocean transportation services be consolidated, except for the supply of the United States Fleet. The army would handle the movement of supplies to ports, storage, and loading of ships. The navy would man and repair the ships and be responsible for their routing and escort. Since in his estimate approximately 75 to 90 percent of all forces overseas would be army personnel, Somervell said the head of the consolidated service should be an army man responsible to the ASF, which in turn, would be responsible both to the chief of staff and the chief of naval operations. Overall control to assign shipping would rest with the JCS.[35]

Admiral Horne rejected Somervell's proposal, seeing it as a "thinly disguised formula" for army control of all overseas supply. Beyond this concern, though, the navy had major qualms about the organizational and procedural aspects of a unified supply line. Navy logistics were decentralized. The Naval Transportation System handled overseas supply, while the Bureau of Supplies and Accounts handled the movement of supplies to ports. Further, the navy centered its operations around task forces of fluctuating size and moving over immense distances, rendering it difficult for the navy to forecast its requirements far in advance and mandating a high degree of flexibility.

In contrast, the army's supply line was highly centralized. Somervell controlled the flow of troops and supplies from the Zone of the Interior in the United States to overseas stations and depots. Moreover, army requirements were more predictable than the navy's and thus more amenable to determination by a central headquarters. Because Somervell based his plans to centralize control of supply movements on the army's model, the navy dissented in the belief that a marriage to the army would require too drastic an adjustment in its own system.[36]

Somervell was not ready to drop the issue. Before the end of December, he sent another proposal to the navy modifying his original one. Again the navy rejected Somervell's plan, putting forth instead a proposal stressing coordination rather than unification of transportation through a system of boards operating under the JCS.

Now certain the navy would not accept a unified transportation service, Somervell fell back on a limited plan for a unified supply line overseas and cooperative arrangements at ports of embarkation. In early March 1943, the Basic Logistical Plan, which was patterned along these lines, was approved by Marshall and King. Although providing for no close-knit logistical operation in the United States, it called upon area commanders to develop unified supply staffs and joint staff planning and to submit a single consolidated priority list for men and supplies. Back on the West Coast, the existing army and navy seaboard and shipping agencies were expected to coordinate their actions in loading and scheduling ships to meet the requirements laid down by area commanders.

Intended primarily for the South and Central Pacific, the Basic Logistical Plan did not yield overly impressive results. Joint priority lists were developed slowly and uncertainly, and neither command at first created a true logistical staff. Thus, the results were hardly what Somervell had envisioned in the winter of 1942–43 when he had called for a unified logistical line stretching from the Zone of the Interior in the United States to the South and Central Pacific. However, in the face of navy opposition, there was little more that he could achieve.[37]

• • •

In 1942, China was assigned an important place in American strategy. By supplying the armies of Generalissimo Chiang Kai-shek, American planners hoped the Chinese could drive the Japanese from the Asiatic mainland or, at the least, tie down large numbers of Japanese troops. Furthermore, the AAF saw China as a giant potential base from which it could eventually bomb Japan into submission.

To carry out these plans, an effective supply link between India and China had to be established, and by the end of the year, it centered on two components: (1) the expansion of the limited airlift over the Himalayan Mountains, the Hump route, and (2) the construction of a road across northern Burma from Ledo, India, to Wanting, China, to join the Burma Road that connected Burma to China (see Map 4). In both cases the difficulties were considerable. Supplies sent to India for the airlift and the field force to recapture northern Burma from the Japanese and to construct the road had to be transported to the province of Assam, the staging area for both operations, over an inadequate river and railway system. Moreover, a shortage of supplies and shipping; the higher strategic priorities given by the CCS to BOLERO, TORCH, the Pacific campaigns, and aid to the Soviet Union; British indifference; and Chiang's reluctance to commit troops to a Burmese campaign worked against the success of either component.[38]

At the Casablanca Conference in January 1943, American and British leaders tentatively scheduled a major operation for the reconquest of Burma, code named ANAKIM, for November 1943. They also agreed to increase air operations in China. Since China was not represented at the conference, Churchill and Roosevelt dispatched General Arnold to Chungking, China, to inform Chiang of the Casablanca decisions. He was accompanied by Field Marshal Sir John Dill, the permanent representative of the Imperial General Staff in Washington, and Somervell, who was to confer with the local commanders in India about the prospects of ANAKIM and Hump operations and to ascertain what forces and supplies they needed.[39]

Somervell left Casablanca on January 24, flying to Cairo, Egypt, after stopovers at Oran and Algiers to inspect supply operations and to consult with Eisenhower on his supply and administrative organization. On January 25, Arnold and Dill left Cairo and flew directly to India, while Somervell, with General Albert Wedemeyer of the OPD at his side, toured the Middle East and Iran to investigate the prospects of opening a new supply route to the Soviet Union through the Levant and to inspect the operations of the Persian Gulf command before going to India.

On February 1, Somervell and Wedemeyer arrived in Karachi, India. There they were joined by Major General Raymond Wheeler, commander of the SOS in the China-Burma-India Theater (CBI), who briefed them on supply operations in India while they flew to New Delhi to participate in a meeting with Arnold, Dill, Lieutenant General Joseph W. Stilwell, commander of American troops in the CBI, and Field Marshall Archibald P. Wavell, the British commander in India.[40]

On February 2 and 3, the visitors from Washington engaged in intensive discussions with Wavell and Stilwell to prepare a proposal for ANAKIM that could be submitted to Chiang. They all agreed that it was essential to retake Burma in one season only, from November 1943 to May 1944, and drew up an outline plan for the campaign. It was to center around British operations along the India-Burma frontier, Chinese operations along the Burma-China frontier and the India-Burma frontier, and a direct British amphibious assault on Rangoon to open the supply route north to the Burma Road. Then, leaving the details to be worked out by the planning staffs, Arnold and Dill flew to Chungking while Somervell remained in India to look into communication and supply problems.[41]

In company with Wavell and Wheeler, Somervell flew to Assam on February 4 to inspect the Ledo Road project. The Americans had assumed that the British would bear the major responsibility for the project, but the latter dragged their feet claiming that the mountains, jungles, and swampy valleys of northern Burma made the 500-mile-long project an engineering nightmare and a waste of resources. Thus, in late October 1942, Wavell had assigned the project to the Americans, and by March 1943, the road reached the border of Burma. Somervell spent most of the day looking at the road and came away convinced that its challenging engineering aspects could be mastered if enough effort were expended.

On February 5, Somervell's party went to Imphal for a two-day visit with Brigadier General Orde Wingate's 77th Indian Brigade, which was being trained as a special force for long-range penetration into Burma behind the Japanese lines in order to disrupt communications and to create chaos. On the 7th, 8th, and 9th, they inspected other facilities in Assam and at Calcutta, where they linked up again with Arnold, Dill, and Stilwell for another conference on ANAKIM. Afterword, Somervell headed home, arriving in Washington on February 17.[42]

Somervell returned from India with two strongly held convictions that thereafter governed his thinking on the CBI. First, he rejected the claims of air power enthusiasts that the Hump airlift by itself could ferry enough supplies to China and concluded that an operation to open a land route across Burma to China was "based on common sense." Only in this way could the United States get enough supplies to China to meet Chiang's needs and for the AAF "to do a first class bombing job" against Japan. Accordingly, Somervell became a fervent champion of the Ledo Road project.

Second, Somervell concluded that the Indian Army and Indian civil servants lacked the drive necessary to turn India into an effective supply base. In his view, India could do a better job in providing sufficient tonnage to support both land and Hump operations, and to this end, he resolved to press the British to improve the situation.[43]

In contrast to most other American officers, Somervell believed some American troops should take part in the campaigns in Burma and China. Stilwell had suggested the previous summer that at least one American combat division should be committed to the Burmese operation. However, his suggestion had met with a cool reception since the competition from other theaters, with higher strategic priority, severely limited the number of American troops that could be committed to the CBI.

Nevertheless, Somervell thought it would be necessary to send a sizable American force to assist in the reconquest of northern Burma and to protect American airfields in China from Japanese attacks. While in India, he asked Wheeler to estimate the requirements needed to support 100,000 American ground forces for campaigns in Burma and China and, ultimately, 500,000 once the ground supply line into China was restored. Wheeler's plan, submitted in May, estimated that, if Burma were in Allied hands by May 1944, it would be possible to support 100,000 American troops in Yunnan, China, by the fall of 1944. As for 500,000 men, Wheeler stated that it would require an enormous expenditure of manpower and materiel and could not be accomplished before the summer of 1946.

Somervell had Lutes's office study Wheeler's plan and then expand its studies to include the whole question of the logistical feasibility of a campaign to defeat Japan by way of China. Lutes's studies were not encouraging, indicating that it would take a staggering amount of tonnage for the line of communication alone. Notwithstanding Lutes's unpromising findings, Somervell was sanguine about the possibilities of staging a major offensive in the CBI. To this end, he had plans formulated in May 1943 for moving 100,000 American troops to India for the opening of an American sector in Assam and northern Burma before the end of 1943.[44]

Before long, Somervell's optimism dimmed. Churchill feared the recapture of Burma would be costly and was not convinced that it was necessary for the defeat of Japan, and Chiang would not participate in ANAKIM if the British did not fully engage themselves. Moreover, Roosevelt had concluded ANAKIM might be too slow to aid China and that the quickest way to assist it was to concentrate most of the available resources in building up air strength in China, a view sold to him by Major General Claire Chennault, the American air commander in China. When Churchill, Roosevelt, and their staffs met at the TRIDENT Conference in Washington in May 1943, the JCS called for a concerted campaign to enlarge the capacity of the Hump airlift to 10,000 tons of supplies a month by September 1943 and for ANAKIM to begin in November 1943.

The British favored the first but not the second. During the often heated debates, Somervell contended logistical realities dictated that expanded air operations would be possible only if land communications with China were restored. Thus, he urged that construction of the Ledo Road be pushed more vigorously, which meant that the Japanese had to be expelled from northern Burma. The British countered that administrative and logistical difficulties militated against ANAKIM. Ultimately, the conferees gave priority in the CBI to expanded air operations and ruled out a full-scale ANAKIM for the time being in favor of a limited offensive to free central and northern Burma, as well as minor offensives along the coast of Burma as a prelude to an attack on Rangoon.[45]

11. LOGISTICS AND STRATEGY, 1943

• • • • FOR THE ALLIES, THE BASIC STRATEGIC decisions for 1943 were made at the Casablanca Conference. They centered on defeating the German submarine threat, increasing strategic bombing attacks against Germany, and stepping up the pressure on Axis forces in Europe and the Japanese in Asia and the Pacific. However, the specific operations to meet these objectives were matters of considerable debate and negotiation through the year's end. Within this context, there was a continued emphasis upon a European-first approach, despite substantial differences between the British and the Americans over operations in the Mediterranean and the timing of a cross-Channel invasion; expanded operations in the Pacific; and the need to resolve complex logistical problems before major operations could be launched in the CBI.[1]

• • •

At Casablanca, Allied leaders agreed that the invasion of Sicily (HUSKY) should follow the completion of the North African campaign. Logistical support of the operation was primarily a theater responsibility, yet Somervell's office had a significant role to play since the American divisions for the operation, initially the 82d Airborne and 45th Divisions and later the 36th Division, had to be sent from the United States. From the outset, Somervell's people faced difficulties in their planning for HUSKY. It was scheduled for June or July 1943, but the CCS was slow to decide on the size of the operation and its exact timing, creating confusion in the early planning for troop movements. Once the CCS settled on convoy schedules, however, the ASF swung into action with a smoothness that was a striking contrast to the confusion that had characterized the mounting of TORCH, evidence of the growing maturity that now marked the army's administrative echelons in handling the preparation and movement of troops to overseas theaters. All the convoys carrying the divisions sailed on schedule, and on July 10, 1943, HUSKY was launched. A month later Sicily was in Allied hands.[2]

Even though the focus of the Allied war effort in Europe had shifted to the Mediterranean in the fall of 1942, Somervell continued to devote considerable attention to BOLERO. At Casablanca, the CCS had approved, as part of CCS 172, Somervell's projection that 1,118,000 men could be supported in the United Kingdom by the end of 1943, approximately 1,000,000 more than were there at the beginning of the year. This was an optimistic view in light of the chronic shipping shortage, but Somervell was confident that declining losses to submarines, mounting ship construction in the United States, and savings resulting from the opening up of the Mediterranean to Allied convoys after the conquest of Sicily would make enough cargo space available in the second half of the year to support any BOLERO deployment for which troop transports and escorts could be found.

Somervell had not even returned to the United States from his post-Casablanca trip, however, than strategic planners in Washington were questioning the deployment he had outlined in CCS 172. He had called for 172,000 airmen in the United Kingdom, a figure AAF planners declared was totally inadequate for the buildup for the air bombardment of Germany (SICKLE). He also had called for four divisions to be moved to the United Kingdom by mid-August, whereas the strategic planners believed there should be six divisions there to take advantage of any sudden deterioration in German strength.

Therefore, on February 23, the OPD proposed a new deployment schedule that significantly altered CCS 172. Under it, movement of troops to the United Kingdom would be accelerated so that 600,000 would be sent by the end of September and then taper off to a strength there by the end of 1943 of 989,000 men, almost 130,000 short of Somervell's goal. The lower figure reflected the lagging numbers sent in the first quarter of 1943 because of the growing demands made upon available troop transports and escorts by the Mediterranean theater and the stepped-up American commitment in the Pacific. Of the forces to be sent to the United Kingdom, more than one half were to be air force troops.

The OPD's deployment schedule dumbfounded Somervell. "This deployment," he wrote General Handy of the OPD in early March, "was obviously made without regard to shipping." As he pointed out, OPD's call for 300,000 troops to be sent during the second quarter of 1943 was totally unrealistic because of tight shipping. He added that, if the AAF buildup projected by the

OPD were carried out, no large movement of ground troops to the United Kingdom would be possible before midyear and that the total buildup would fall short of 900,000 troops. Even that total, he stated, could be achieved only by drastically cutting the British import program.

To reconcile CCS 172 and OPD's proposal, Somervell suggested a new deployment schedule in line with shipping expectations, lowering his own sights for BOLERO in the process. To carry out HUSKY and to salvage the ground force deployment for BOLERO, he now proposed that 123,000 troops be moved to the United Kingdom in the second quarter instead of the 169,000 he had proposed in CCS 172 or the 300,000 the OPD proposed. Shipping would be obtained by diverting shipping from the import program and transferring shipping from the Pacific to the Atlantic since, in his opinion, the Pacific areas already had more than enough troops to carry out their stated objectives.

The OPD was not receptive to Somervell's suggestions. Irritated by his charge that it had overlooked the obvious shipping shortcomings and his unsolicited strategic views on the Pacific, it curtly dismissed his suggestions with the comment: "This was not provided for in the Casablanca Conference." Indicative of the hopes in Washington for BOLERO, the JCS approved the OPD deployment program despite Somervell's criticism, and it remained the official statement of American deployment objectives until some time after the TRIDENT Conference.

However, Somervell's figures could not be denied. In fact, his March projections proved overly optimistic because of HUSKY. On March 5, the CCS decided to divert British transports and a number of escort vessels from BOLERO and SICKLE to HUSKY, cutting into the flow of troops to the United Kingdom. By various means, 77,000 troops were sent in the second quarter of 1943, less than half of Somervell's original goal of 169,000 and less than his later goal of 123,000.[3]

The shipment of cargo for BOLERO was just as important to Somervell as the deployment of troops. In early 1943, prompted by the prospect that improved loading practices would significantly increase shipping space, as well as by his estimate of the likely availability of materiel and the ability of the ETO to handle this materiel, he called for the shipment of supplies and equipment to the United Kingdom at an accelerated rate, regardless of the flow of troops.

The case for preshipment, the name given to this advance shipment of supplies and equipment, seemed compelling. British ports could best handle cargo during the spring and summer when operations would be least affected by darkness and German air attacks. Since the heaviest flow of troops was not scheduled to occur until the fall and winter, it seemed only logical to make the most efficient use of port capacity and the inland transportation system by stockpiling the materiel needed to house, service, equip, and support them.

ETO headquarters in Britain agreed on the desirability of preshipment, although for a different reason. Like other theaters, the ETO was having trouble matching troops and equipment under the existing system, which often had troops arrive on fast transports days or even weeks ahead of the slow cargo ships carrying their equipment. Preshipment would reduce this problem and enable the theater to equip and train the individual soldier and troop unit in a more efficient manner.[4]

The OPD, however, initially opposed Somervell's preshipment plan. It argued that there was no assurance that enough materiel could be found for a large stockpiling program in the United Kingdom after the army's more pressing needs were met and that it was unwise to undertake preshipment when the strategic picture was still clouded. In the absence of a clear decision to carry out a cross-Channel invasion in 1944, the OPD questioned the wisdom of shipping supplies to the United Kingdom that might later have to be reloaded and shipped elsewhere. Somervell prevailed. The reduction in troop shipments that grew out of HUSKY made available 350,000 tons of surplus cargo space during the second quarter of 1943, and reluctantly, the OPD on March 16 endorsed preshipment in principle.[5]

Anticipating OPD's assent, Somervell had already initiated preparations for an early resumption of large-scale cargo shipments to the United Kingdom. On March 10, he submitted to the WSA cargo shipping requirements for forty-two sailings to the United Kingdom in April and slightly more in each of the two succeeding months, a threefold increase over the volume originally planned.

The WSA immediately looked for ways to meet Somervell's request, but it soon became apparent that Somervell was unable to provide enough cargo to fill available space. The OPD was still not totally committed to preshipment and would not permit organizational equipment for troop units to be preshipped unless the units were definitely scheduled to be deployed to the United Kingdom. Moreover, there were serious shortages of some equipment, and given the high priority of other operations and the training programs in the United States, there was little left over for BOLERO.

Hence, of Somervell's original request for forty-two sailings before the end of April, only eight actually sailed, four of them carrying cargo leftover from March. During April, Somervell struggled to arrange preshipments for May; however, his efforts fared little better than those in April. Though shipping space was available, the low strategic priority attached to BOLERO deprived him of the materiel to fill it.[6]

At TRIDENT, in May 1943, Allied leaders debated at length the future strategy for the European war. American leaders sought a firm commitment for a cross-Channel invasion in the spring of 1944, soon given the code name OVERLORD, while the British were more interested in continued operations in the Mediterranean so as to eliminate Italy from the war. Eventually, both groups decided that further action would be taken to knock out Italy as long as it did not interfere with a 1944 cross-Channel invasion, given a target date of May 1.[7]

The TRIDENT decision to continue operations in the Mediterranean significantly affected Somervell's BOLERO preshipment program, especially after the Allies followed up their success in Sicily by invading Italy in September 1943. Despite the stipulation that Mediterranean operations should be based on resources already available there, additional service troops had to be sent to the theater, cutting into the number available to be sent to the United Kingdom to construct camps and storage facilities, to unload preshipped cargo, and to develop an administrative base.

BOLERO preshipment was also hindered by difficulty in finding cargo to ship. Desperate to locate cargo, Somervell pressed theater commanders to reduce pilfering and to make more efficient use of the supplies and equipment that they had on hand to free up materiel and cargo space for preshipment. He also urged his own staff to make greater efforts. Writing to Charles Gross in June, he insisted that "we GET every ship we can and that we FILL these ships with men and their equipment. . . . I want you to scream your head off TO ME when ever this program is endangered. It is about our most important job."

Exhortations such as these were not enough to achieve the results Somervell wanted. Somervell lacked a high enough priority to get sufficient supplies and equipment to fill the allotted ships, and he was hampered by shortages of service troops and civilian labor in Britain for unloading the materiel. Thus, he was able to ship only 2.3 million tons of cargo to Britain in the May-August 1943 period, instead of the projected 3.2 million tons. Lamenting the shortfall, Somervell wrote John Lee at the end of July that "we can never recover the precious time that is now available to you during the good weather."[8]

During the summer, Somervell again had to counter the opposition of the OPD to preshipment. Suspicious that OVERLORD might be postponed or even abandoned, making preshipment a wasted effort, the OPD favored the halting of preshipment until the strategic situation was better clarified. Considering this viewpoint foolish, Somervell beseeched Marshall not to terminate preshipment unless it was certain that the cross-Channel invasion was going to be postponed.

In early August, the OPD relented and gave Somervell "a tentative go-ahead" for preshipment within the framework of the 1943 Troop Basis, and then several days later, it gave him full sanction to proceed with preshipment through the end of the year. Emboldened by the OPD's decision and expecting an extension of the program into 1944, Somervell instructed his supply service chiefs to have material ready for preshipment during the first four months of 1944 based on 1.4 million men in the United Kingdom by May 1944.[9]

Through the fall of 1943, Somervell pushed ahead with BOLERO preshipments. Backed up by the decision of the Allied high command at the Quebec

Conference in August that OVERLORD should be the major offensive for 1944, he proceeded in a more systematic fashion, but at best, preshipment was only a partial success. It was a success in the sense that the cargo shipped in advance of 1943 meant that much less had to be shipped in 1944, easing the burden of shipping and cargo distribution in the crucial months before OVERLORD. However, the lack of a higher priority for materiel to fill all available holds meant that he was unable to ship enough supplies and equipment to prevent congestion in British ports and transportation facilities as OVERLORD approached.[10]

As part of his concern with BOLERO, Somervell also closely followed the development of Lee's SOS command in the ETO. In the fall and winter of 1942–32, Somervell had emphasized to Lee the need for the control of administration and supply matters in the ETO to be concentrated in the theater SOS rather than shared with the staff in the theater headquarters. Only in this way, Somervell advised him, could operational and logistical planning be fully coordinated.

Following Somervell's advice, Lee in March 1943 proposed to Lieutenant General Frank Andrews, ETO commander, that he be named deputy theater commander for supply and administration and that the theater G-4 be placed under him. If accepted, this reorganization would give Lee a command similar to Somervell's in the sense that Somervell had gained wide authority over supply and administration of the army in the United States and had all but absorbed the War Department's G-4 functions.

Andrews rejected Lee's proposal. In his opinion, it was unsound to place the chief of a general staff division under a subordinate headquarters, and he was confident that Lee already had sufficient authority to carry out his mission without being named deputy theater commander.

Equally important, Andrews strongly disliked Lee. A bald, fussy, and "oppressively religious" man, Lee was "an able, efficient, quick thinking, aggressive operator" who projected the image of an empire builder. He had an exaggerated sense of his own importance, had eccentricities that wore badly on others, and was overly concerned with spit and polish. He also had "a supply sergeant's mentality" and doled out equipment to troops and generals alike "as if it were a personal gift" and he were rewarding friends and punishing enemies. For these reasons, using Lee's initials, J.C.H.L., enlisted men and field officers gave him such nicknames as John Court House Lee or Jesus Christ Himself Lee.

Andrews particularly disapproved of Lee's pretensions to power. Lee employed numerous secretaries to handle his correspondence and put together a special train to carry him and his staff around England, and alone among generals in the ETO, he had his stars of rank on both the front and back of his helmet.[11]

Fed up with Lee, Andrews decided in the spring of 1943 to ask Marshall to relieve Lee and send him home, but in May, Andrews was killed in an airplane crash. His replacement was Jacob Devers, Lee's classmate at West Point. More willing to tolerate Lee, Devers agreed to abolish the office of G-4 in the ETO and have its functions assumed by Lee.

At the same time, Somervell had Wilhelm Styer look into the whole dispute between Lee and ETO headquarters. Adhering to Somervell's instructions, Styer quizzed Devers about his expectations for Lee and advised the ETO commander not to let Lee's annoying quirks obscure his major qualifications. Then, in a frank discussion, Styer told Lee that he must "get in bed" with Devers and "be his right-hand man on logistic matters." Somervell's troubleshooting had the desired effect. Devers pronounced that he was perfectly satisfied with Lee and "did not want to change him."[12]

• • •

In contrast to the war against Germany, where he was concerned with specific operations, such as BOLERO, Somervell's concerns with the war against Japan in 1943 centered on organizational matters and the efficiency of the overseas supply commands. His primary concern was joint logistics in the POA, especially the Central Pacific. Somervell had been urging joint logistics since the fall of 1942, but work on joint logistics in the Central Pacific did not begin until April 1943 when Admiral Nimitz established a Joint Logistics Board and charged it with "coordinating logistical effort and procedure." (At this time, Nimitz was both commander of the POA, a joint command, and commander in chief of the Pacific Fleet, a navy command that covered all naval vessels in the Pacific except those assigned to a small fleet in the SWPA. He also exercised personal command over the Central Pacific.)

Under the principles Nimitz laid down, shipping for outlying bases would continue to follow the traditional pattern of army-navy independence, although as soon as arrangements could be perfected, the navy would take over, man, and operate all vessels engaged in this service. Somervell found little to like in Nimitz's approach, for it presaged navy control of the army's line of supply by giving the navy control of shipping to forward bases. Since the army lacked adequate representation on Nimitz's staff, Somervell considered this prospect unacceptable.

Somervell presented his case to Admirals Horne and William L. Calhoun, commander of the Pacific Fleet service force, who in April 1943 was visiting Washington. The admirals told Somervell that Nimitz intended to strengthen army representation on his staff by drawing some personnel for joint logistics from the staff of Lieutenant General Robert C. Richardson, the army commander in Hawaii. Somervell, however, argued that this step would do little good since these officers were accustomed to independent army and navy action, and so, he insisted that fresh blood from his headquarters be sent to

Hawaii for joint planning. After considerable haggling, Calhoun agreed to accept two officers from Somervell's command, the most important of whom was Edmond Leavey, Somervell's long-standing handyman from the prewar days.[13]

Leavey began his new assignment by making an extensive tour of POA supply facilities. In late July 1943, he reported his impression of the navy's supply organization to Somervell, painting a picture of a command and logistical system that was seriously deficient. "From the logistics and supply standpoint," he stated, "there seems to be no section, and not even an officer, charged with supervision of the Commander-in-Chief's staff" or "charged with supervision . . . of the overall logistics and supply situation in the Pacific."

LeRoy Lutes agreed with Leavey's findings. He had made the same observations after his trip to the Pacific in 1942, and during his second trip to the Pacific in August 1943, he found no arrangements for logistical control in the POA headquarters as provided for in the Basic Logistical Plan and almost no exchange of logistical information between the army and the navy. Like Leavey, he thought the ultimate solution was for Nimitz to exercise command of the POA through a joint theater staff, as well as through area commanders with similar joint staffs.[14]

Concluding that the navy would resist direct efforts on his part to create a joint POA staff, Somervell sent Leavey's and Lutes's findings to Marshall in hopes that the chief of staff could persuade the navy to adopt them. Spurred by Somervell's entreaties, Marshall told King that the findings of Somervell's subordinates are "a clear indication . . . of the urgent necessity of creating a Combined Theater Staff as quickly as possible." Rather than address the substance of Leavey's and Lutes's findings, King, who had never been committed to army-navy cooperation except on the navy's terms, questioned the qualifications of Somervell's subordinates to comment on the POA organization. Stung by King's reply, Marshall decided to drop the matter and let Nimitz work out his own arrangement.

Despite King's sharp response to Marshall, Nimitz on September 6 announced the formation of a joint staff in the POA. Crucial to his conversion were the recommendations of navy planners in Washington and the influence of Richardson. Under the new arrangement, there would be a joint staff organized into four sections, two commanded by naval officers and two by army officers. Leavey was designated J-4 and given responsibility for logistics.[15]

Two days after Nimitz's announcement, Somervell arrived in Hawaii during his own tour of the Pacific. He found that "the vexation shown by Admiral King" had apparently not extended to the local navy officials. Because of his outstanding capabilities, Leavey had been well received, and Somervell was confident that he would "secure the proper arrangements in the logistics field" through his "tact and downright capacity."

Nevertheless, Somervell was far from satisfied with Nimitz's actions, particularly in regard to the numerous hats Nimitz wore. In his opinion, Nimitz, as commander of the fleet, had permitted himself to become so preoccupied in details and the local situation that he had lost sight of the general picture that he had to possess to be an effective area commander. Somervell was also concerned about the lack of uniformity in the organization, command responsibilities, and methods of logistical operations in the POA subareas. Somervell's answer to these problems, as he reported to Marshall, was to separate the fleet and the Central Pacific commands, then name separate commanders for each of the subareas, and finally, create in each one an organization similar to that of the POA. Equally important, he called for "a fourth, or base, area . . . to include Hawaii and perhaps a few of the islands immediately to the south," with its commander responsible "for the operation of the supply and administrative system" for the coming offensives.

Meanwhile, army planners in the OPD, drawing upon Somervell's recommendations to Marshall and the reports prepared by Leavey and Lutes, called for a restructuring of the POA. These efforts brought few results. The navy had no intention of going beyond the creation of a joint staff at this time, and with operations in the Central Pacific pending, Somervell decided not to "rock the boat."[16]

Somervell's stop in Hawaii was part of an extended trip that he took in September and October to see firsthand the supply and organizational situation in both the Pacific areas and the CBI. After leaving Washington on September 7, he spent four days in Hawaii discussing joint supply and other problems with Richardson, Nimitz, Robert Patterson, and Lutes. From Hawaii, he went to the South Pacific and then to the SWPA, armed with information provided by Lutes.[17] In the South Pacific, Somervell visited Fiji, Noumea, Guadalcanal, and New Georgia, talking at length with combat and service commanders and touring the battlefield on New Georgia "to get first hand and fresh impressions on the subject of equipment."

Overall, Somervell was impressed with the job done by the army supply people in the South Pacific. However, two problems particularly concerned him. The first was one that he had been harping on since the outset of the war: an inadequate supply of service troops to build bases and to move supplies for current needs. Over the resistance of the AGF and the OPD, which believed rear areas were overstaffed and wanted more combat troops in the troop basis, Somervell had successfully fought to have service troops constitute 35 percent of the final 1943 Troop Basis of 7.7 million men. Even so, there were never enough service troops to do an efficient supply job, and Somervell told Marshall that the South Pacific especially "has been deficient in service troops and the lack of these troops has had a definite effect on slowing up the campaign." It was not "a case of frills," he noted, "but one of getting beans, shoes and billets to the men who are fighting and to save those fighting from being laid out with pestilence."

The second problem that bothered Somervell was an unconscionable delay in meeting requisitions, which were supposed to be processed in 90 days. However, Somervell found that it took 120 days or more to fill requisitions, partly because of the great distances involved and partly, to his chagrin, because "there had been too much disposition to get into exchanges of telegrams and not of supplies." In other words, too much red tape.

Somervell's efforts to deal with these problems brought mixed results. On his instruction, Styer reviewed all South Pacific requisitions in San Francisco and in the hands of the supply bureaus to unearth those which had been outstanding for any period of time and to speed action on them.

Somervell was less successful with service troops. The OPD regarded his recommendations for more of these troops "in general merely a repetition of known facts." After consulting the army staff in the South Pacific, it advised that, "in view of restricted lift," the command there was unwilling to sacrifice combat troops to make room for service troops, preferring to rely on the chance that sufficient numbers of them would be sent as shipping became available.[18]

From the South Pacific, Somervell went to Port Moresby, New Guinea, and then to Brisbane, Australia. He found the same problems in the SWPA that he had found in the South Pacific and proposed to deal with them by routing ships from San Francisco directly to the forward bases, accelerating the transport of service troops, and preshipping supplies "for units destined to this area." Of these approaches, only the first was put into effect. Shortages in troop transport had already created a backlog of 40,000 service troops earmarked for the SWPA, and MacArthur preferred that combat troops receive priority as long as there were enough service troops to perform minimum essential tasks. In the instance of preshipment, there was not enough equipment available to permit a BOLERO-style program without negatively affecting training at home.

While visiting MacArthur in Port Moresby, Somervell learned first hand about SWPA's shipping problems. For months, MacArthur had been complaining to Washington that lack of adequate shipping was seriously delaying his rate of advance up the coast of New Guinea, and in their discussions, MacArthur took the opportunity to educate Somervell about the situation. Impressed by MacArthur's case, Somervell arranged for seventy-one Liberty ships and five other cargo vessels to be assigned permanently to the SWPA.[19]

Following his stopover in the SWPA, Somervell went to New Delhi to begin an inspection of the CBI and to impress upon all in the theater the need to speed the flow of supplies to China. He was particularly looking forward to this stop to see if there had been significant improvement in supply operations since his previous visit earlier that year, and he was determined to knock heads if necessary to get action.

• • •

Few figures in the American high command were more enthusiastic in pressing operations in the CBI than Somervell. Ever since his visit in February 1943, he had urged greater effort to get things moving, but developments in the spring and summer of 1943 sorely disappointed him. Heavy rainfall, difficulties with native labor, and the obstacles presented by the region's climate and geography slowed the pace of airfield construction for the Hump route. Even practically halting work on the Ledo Road so that engineer units could focus on the building of airfields did not significantly speed up construction. Further, it soon became apparent that the Assam Line of Communications (LOC), a network of rail and barge lines running northeast from Calcutta into Assam, was incapable of carrying all the supplies needed for airfield construction, the airlift, the support of ground forces, and the road project. Finally, British officials in India, led by Sir Claude J. E. Auchinleck, commander in chief in India, refused to put their full weight behind a land campaign in Burma and the construction of the Ledo Road because they believed that such would place an unbearable strain on the Indian transportation system and were not necessary to Japan's defeat.

Somervell refused to accept the views of Auchinleck and his "no-can-do boys" at British General Headquarters in India. In early July, Styer visited the Ledo Road project, and he reported that some progress was being made. Joseph Stilwell said the same, emphasizing that the road was vital to his tactical operations in Burma. Several engineering and transport experts also advised Somervell that CBI's logistical problems could be solved, thus strengthening his determination to push construction of the land route to China.

Logistical factors were major points of discussion at the QUADRANT Conference, held at Quebec, Canada, in August 1943. Buoyed by the reports he had received, Somervell went to the conference convinced that improvement of the Assam LOC to acceptable standards was completely within Allied resources and that the road should be accepted as "a matter of settled policy." Unlike Auchinleck's crowd in India, the British chiefs were prepared to support land operations in Burma and to complete the land route to China if the logistical problems could be surmounted, and at their suggestion, the CCS referred these problems to a subcommittee headed by Somervell and Lieutenant General Sir Thomas Riddell-Webster, British Quartermaster General and chief supply officer.

Prodded by Somervell, the committee agreed that "if not absolutely essential to the successful conduct of the war the opening of a land route to China will greatly facilitate operations" and that the Assam LOC was the "key to the whole situation" in the CBI. Promising to speed American aid and suggesting that Americans take over operation of parts of the rail and barge lines, Somervell estimated that 102,000 tons of supplies a month could be moved over the Assam LOC by November 1943. This total, he judged, would provide the minimum necessary for building the airfields and the road and supplying the combat troops, as well as supplying 10,000 tons to move over the Hump. By January 1945, the LOC's capacity could be increased to 170,000 tons, and by January 1946, to 220,000 tons. Of this eventual capacity, 65,000 tons were to be delivered to China over the Ledo Road and 20,000 tons by the airlift.

Somervell's schedule was predicated on the completion of the Ledo Road by January 1945 and its development to full capacity as a two-way road by 1946 and the doubling of the airlift. Somervell also called for a network of pipelines, which like the Ledo Road and the airlift, would be an American operation.[20]

Owing to Somervell's forcefulness, the CCS approved the logistical plan and directed that land operations in Burma begin on February 15, 1944. Highest priority was accorded "offensive operations with the object of establishing land communications with China and improving and securing the air route," which had the effect of shifting the emphasis back from Claire Chennault's immediate air effort to the limited ground offensive. Final action on ANAKIM was deferred, although preparations for the amphibious phase, the heart of the operation, were to proceed. To carry out the QUADRANT decisions, a new combined command, the Southeast Asia Command (SEAC), was formed, with Vice Admiral Lord Louis Mountbatten of the Royal Navy as its commander and Stilwell his deputy. The British command in India under Auchinleck, considered by Somervell to be an impediment to action, was entirely separate from the SEAC and became principally an administrative headquarters.[21]

Regarding the India-China supply project as his own, Somervell plunged into it with great zeal, telling his subordinates in Washington and India that the "expansion of the capacity of the Assam L. of C. and the opening of the ground route to China are matters of paramount interest in the prosecution of the war." Because Somervell had anticipated approval of an expanded effort in the CBI, most of the material for the Ledo Road and the pipelines was already on the way to India, in port awaiting shipment, or included in the ASP for early procurement.

Not everything was going well in India, however. The Government of India readily accepted Somervell's proposal that Americans develop and operate a barge line on the Brahmaputra River as a supplement to civilian river lines, but it rejected his proposal for militarizing and placing American troops on the part of the Bengal and Assam Railway leading across Assam to Ledo. Indian officials contended that the railway was doing as well as it could and that American military operation would hurt the civil economy and lead to hostile political activity on the part of the Indian population.[22]

As these discussions were proceeding, Somervell arrived in New Delhi on October 8 to impress upon the supply organization in India the need for an all-out effort, as well as for talks with Raymond Wheeler, who had recently been named Mountbatten's principal administrative officer. Somervell's schedule also called for him to go to Chungking as Roosevelt's emissary and secure Chiang's formal approval of Mountbatten's new command.

Somervell had no sooner arrived in India, however, than he had to deal with a far more important problem: the fate of Stilwell. On his first day in New Delhi, Somervell encountered T.V. Soong, Chinese foreign minister. Soong promptly informed him that Roosevelt had agreed to a Chinese request to remove Stilwell from his command and that the formal request would be made to Somervell when he arrived in China. Somervell was completely taken back by Soong's news. Having been out of Washington since early September, he had not been privy to Soong's recent discussions with American leaders, although he was fully aware of the rancorous relationship between Stilwell and Chiang.

After his arrival in China in 1942, Stilwell had pushed Chiang to reform his army and government and to take a more active role in fighting the Japanese, but Chiang had resisted out of a desire to consolidate his own domestic strength while the Americans and the British fought the Japanese. Stilwell's "abrupt and candid manner" in dealing with Chiang further poisoned the relationship. By 1943, Chiang was looking for a way to be rid of Stilwell, and in September, while in Washington Soong presented Marshall with proposals either to eliminate Stilwell or, at least, to curb his power, especially over Chinese lend-lease. Marshall told Soong that no change was contemplated. Nevertheless, Soong did not leave Washington empty-handed. Roosevelt was wearying of the China tangle, and quite possibly, he gave Soong the impression that Stilwell would be recalled if Chiang officially requested it.[23]

Certain that Stilwell had great value to the war effort in China and that his only flaw was an inability to "make good recitations even though he knew his subject well," Somervell decided he must do what he could to keep him in his post and immediately wired Marshall that he would "of course press for status quo" in his conference with Chiang.[24] In Somervell's mind, he was more than "a mere military messenger or investigator" and, therefore, in the absence of instructions to the contrary, had a duty to do what he could to ease the strain in the Sino-American relationship because of the Chiang-Stilwell feud.

Somervell also informed Mountbatten of Soong's news and asked for his help in persuading Chiang to retain Stilwell. But if Somervell was clear on the need to keep Stilwell in China, Mountbatten was less certain. Having just assumed command of the SEAC, he did not want to get into a brawl with Chiang about Stilwell, and he told Somervell that, if he stood behind Stilwell in the face of Chiang's request for his removal, "the success of his whole command might be jeopardized." Mountbatten's message was obvious. If Stilwell were to keep his job, Somervell would have to take the lead in the fight.

On October 15, Somervell flew to Chungking, and the following day he met with Chiang, Soong serving as the interpreter. As Somervell had anticipated, the generalissimo said he wanted Stilwell recalled. Somervell said little about Chiang's demand except to ask to confer with him later about the request. Returning to his quarters in the home of General Ho Ying-chin, the Chinese war minister, Somervell contacted Stilwell and informed him of Chiang's request. He then advised Stilwell that he would request Chiang to reconsider the demand for his recall and asked Stilwell to provide "arguments with which I might arm myself." He also warned Stilwell not to make wisecracks about the Chinese leader, remarks that greatly irritated Chiang.[25]

At this point, Somervell received support from an unexpected quarter: General Ho, Madame Chiang, and Madame H.H. Kung, the wife of China's minister of finance and, like Madame Chiang, a sister of Soong. Their involvement plunged Somervell into what he described as an atmosphere of "medieval court intrigue," and an "unholy family row." Since he was new to the Byzantine world of Chinese politics, Somervell did not fully appreciate the forces at work, although he was convinced Soong had stirred up the present difficulties to expand his own power base at the expense of his brothers-in-law. In the final analysis, though, the motives of the Chinese players mattered little to him. He wanted to save Stilwell and was ready to accept help from any quarter.

In a meeting on October 17, Somervell asked Chiang to reconsider the demand for Stilwell's recall. His arguments were several: Stilwell's recall would have an unfortunate effect on American public opinion, it might lead to an American reappraisal of its China policy, and it would delay operations to open a land route to China. Somervell then broke off the meeting so that he could meet with Mountbatten, who had arrived in Chungking the previous day.

As before, Mountbatten indicated that he did not want to get into the fray, but Somervell pointed out that it would be difficult to make effective use of Chinese forces in the next months if Stilwell, the man who had organized and commanded them, were removed. Reluctantly, Mountbatten agreed to support Stilwell and told Somervell to inform Chiang that the Allies needed Stilwell's experience for the upcoming operations. With Mountbatten's backing assured, Somervell got in touch with General Ho and asked him to inform the generalissimo of Mountbatten's position.

Meanwhile, Madames Chiang and Kung were also at work. For example, Madame Chiang, at Somervell's instigation, advised Stilwell to visit Chiang and effect a rapprochement by saying that he was ready to cooperate fully and would avoid "a superiority complex." Whatever the reason—the entreaties of Somervell, the fuss made by the Soong sisters, Stilwell's willingness to be deferential toward the Chinese leader, or all of them—Chiang was ready to end the flap by permitting Stilwell to stay in China. At a party held for Mountbatten in the evening of October 17, Ho told Somervell that Chiang would meet with him the next day and "reverse his position."

In the morning of October 18 Somervell met with Chiang, Madame Chiang, General Ho, Stilwell, and Chennault. During the meeting, Chiang informed Somervell that Stilwell had completely satisfied him on their differences, which Somervell was now persuaded "apparently consisted of alleged petty slights to the Chinese and arrogance on Stilwell's part," and as the meeting progressed, Somervell became convinced that brighter days were ahead in the Sino-American relationship. Somervell's optimism proved wrong. The differences between Stilwell and Chiang involved fundamental political and military questions that transcended personality clashes and that ultimately resulted in the recall of Stilwell in the fall of 1944. For the time being, though, all was calm, and Somervell had the gratitude of both Marshall and Stimson.[26]

Unknown to Somervell, at that very time, Marshall was contemplating removing Stilwell. The chief of staff knew Stilwell did not have Roosevelt's full support, and considering all the controversy surrounding China, he concluded on October 18 that both Stilwell and American interests might best be served if Stilwell were recalled and given a new slot. Somervell would replace Stilwell, while Jacob Devers would replace Somervell.

Marshall's thinking in having Somervell replace Stilwell was apparently based on two factors. Since Somervell was a key figure in the American military machine, his appointment as Stilwell's replacement would signal the importance the United States attached to the CBI. Along the same lines, Somervell had long been a forceful advocate of an accelerated effort there, and his appointment as the top American in the CBI would go far toward making it a reality.

After discussing the situation with Stimson, Marshall radioed instructions to Somervell to remain in Chungking "until you have heard" from Washington. Somervell was surprised by Marshall's radiogram, although he discerned it was a possible precursor of another one naming him Stilwell's replacement if his intervention in Chungking failed. This prospect was disquieting to him. Though he had twice asked Marshall for an overseas command, he had no desire to relieve Stilwell, especially under the present circumstances. In his opinion, it would seem that his assumption of command was "tinged with self-interest" and potentially place him in an "extremely embarrassing" situation. Meanwhile, Marshall quickly changed his mind after Stimson convinced him that Stilwell was still the best man for the job. Four days later, after hearing from Somervell that a truce had been arranged between Chiang and Stilwell, Marshall told Somervell to "proceed on your trip."[27]

Once the Stilwell issue was behind them, the Chungking conferees addressed two other matters. During an all-day meeting on October 19, Mountbatten informed Chiang that the CCS had decided at QUADRANT to place the heaviest emphasis on ground and air operations in Burma and that these operations would temporarily reduce the airlift over the Hump. Chiang was disappointed and stated that he was most anxious that Hump tonnage not fall below 10,000 tons a month.

Somervell was also deeply disturbed by Mountbatten's presentation, which in his view "reflected . . . more the British point of view rather than that of

Combined Chiefs of Staff." In contrast to Mountbatten, he believed that the Allies could carry out the Burma operation without reducing Hump tonnage. Consequently, during a recess, he "indicated to Mountbatten that vacillation and delay with regard to supply must be replaced by determination and confidence in our ability to supply what was required for a laborious effort to clear North Burma." When the conferees reconvened, Somervell told Chiang he would see that "supply . . . [was] arranged without a serious, if any, interference with HUMP traffic."[28]

The other issue was more ticklish. At QUADRANT, Anglo-American leaders had decided that the SEAC should embrace Ceylon, Burma, Thailand, Malaya, and Sumatra. Since Thailand had been previously included in the China theater, this transfer to the SEAC was expected to cause trouble because Chiang, as Allied commander of the China theater, would undoubtedly see it as a loss of face. One of the purposes of Somervell's trip to Chungking was to secure Chiang's approval of the Thailand transfer. As anticipated, Chiang balked, telling Somervell that Thailand must be included in the Chinese theater. Any change, he emphasized, would be interpreted throughout Asia as a reassertion of British imperialism.

Acting as a mediator between Mountbatten and Chiang, Somervell worked out a solution. Under it, there was a gentlemen's agreement that Thailand would remain in the China theater. When military operations began in Thailand, the "boundaries between the two theaters are to be decided at the time in accordance with the progress of advances the respective forces made." In the end, Somervell's efforts to negotiate a firm understanding between Mountbatten and Chiang went for naught. While the arrangement was acceptable to Mountbatten and Chiang, Roosevelt, Churchill, and the CCS neither accepted nor rejected it, in effect dropping this problem for the time being.[29]

Returning to India on October 21, Somervell turned his full attention to the Assam LOC. Railway problems were particularly urgent. Since arriving in India, Somervell had suspected that neither Auchinleck nor the Government of India had any interest in increasing the capacity of the Bengal and Assam Railway, perhaps seeing this as a way to avoid a land operation in Burma. The railway had been designed by the tea industry to carry 600 tons of cargo a day, and by the summer of 1943, it was carrying 1,800 tons daily. Somervell believed it could carry much more.

Meeting in New Delhi on October 23 with Mountbatten, Stilwell, Auchinleck, and representatives of the Indian Railway Commission, Somervell stressed that a 50 percent increase in tonnage on the railway was essential by April 1944 if commitments to China were to be satisfied and offered to provide American railway battalions to operate part of the railway to insure success. When Auchinleck and the railway officials kept coming up with reasons why it could not be done, Somervell refused to take no for an answer. Mountbatten backed Somervell, telling the conferees that he could not undertake offensive operations in Burma until transportation was improved. If India could not guarantee the 50-percent increase, then, he would accept Somervell's offer of American railway men. As the conference concluded, Somervell noticed a change in Auchinleck's attitude, "from one of hostility . . . to one of cooperation and hopefulness," leaving him encouraged that the upcoming discussions between American and British officials over his proposals would yield results.[30]

On October 24, Somervell flew to the Persian Gulf. There he was impressed with the American operation of the Iranian railway to Teheran, and on October 25, he decided to send Colonel Paul Yount, head of the railway operation, to India to assist the British. As he wrote Mountbatten, "Yount has increased the monthly tonnage of this line not 50%, but 500% above the figure reached by the previous British-Iranian operation. In other words, he speaks with the voice of experience and accomplishment."

The stop in Iran also convinced Somervell that "American railway troops should be given full charge of operations of the section of the railway" in Assam. Almost lecturing Mountbatten, he insisted that "they cannot be expected to accomplish results unless they are, in fact, in power to run that section of the road. It will not do for them to work under the present management." Not wanting to antagonize Somervell because of his immense influence over American logistical commitments, Mountbatten called upon London to pressure Auchinleck and the Government of India to be more cooperative with Somervell, and, on November 14, Auchinleck and the Government of India agreed to Somervell's offer of American railway troops. These troops were to operate 804 miles of the Bengal and Assam Railway, effective March 1, 1944.[31]

Somervell's trip to the CBI resulted in other speedups in the theater buildup. With him on the spot, concrete plans for the pipelines were finalized, and in November, their construction began. After inspecting the Ledo Road project and talking with Wheeler, Somervell arranged for more heavy construction items, engineer supplies, and service troops to be sent to India to accelerate construction.[32]

Before leaving India, Somervell also dealt with a number of personnel matters to ensure the CBI had topflight people. To replace Wheeler as the top SOS man, Somervell chose William Covell. Other changes included a number of demotions. Most were carried out with little fuss. However, in the case of Brigadier General John C. Arrowsmith, Wheeler, who remained in his SOS post until the middle of November pending Covell's arrival in India, balked, causing an outburst from Somervell that starkly illuminated his cold-blooded readiness to chop off heads to get results.

Arrowsmith had been in charge of the construction of the Ledo Road, and several times in 1943, Stilwell had criticized his progress. Deciding that "Arrowsmith is a sulky, indifferent bird," Stilwell elected to "wipe the slate clean" at Ledo and, in August, ordered him to New Delhi for reassignment. Arguing that Arrowsmith was a good officer whose operation had been hindered by factors beyond his control, Wheeler chose to keep him in the CBI at the same rank so that he could save face. Somervell, though, would have none of it. Like Stilwell, he was disappointed by progress on the road and concluded that Arrowsmith had "failed to make good in position to which he had been promoted" and "should be returned to the United States and after return be demoted." No face-saving second chance should be permitted.

In a letter, Somervell took Wheeler, seven years his senior, to task for soft heartedness:

> Though I greatly respect your loyalty to people who have worked loyally for you, I feel that matters of this kind should not interfere with the proper and efficient conduct of the war, especially where there is so much to do and where no one but the best will suffice.
>
> I told you that we are willing to send you almost anyone you ask for, and we must insist that people who have failed not be shuffled around but sent home, or at least not be put in any responsible position. This completely destroyes [sic] the moral [sic] of your outfit, and from what I have heard from others about Arrowsmith, to continue him would have been hard to swallow by a considerable number of officers who have been carrying him for some time.
>
> I hope you will forgive me for writing this frankly, but the time has come where sentiment has nothing to do with the problem. Not only your reputation, but that of all America is at stake.[33]

Somervell arrived back in Washington on November 1, 1943, after having been away from the United States for two months. His accomplishments in the CBI had been impressive. They included, with the aid of Madame Chiang and others, persuading Chiang to keep Stilwell in China, dealing with Chiang over the SEAC boundary, calming Chiang over the question of supplies to China, forcing the issue about militarizing the Bengal and Assam Railway with American troops, and settling many of Wheeler's difficulties.

On November 5, Somervell reported to Roosevelt about his work in the CBI. Roosevelt, who had already been briefed by Marshall and Harry Hopkins, was delighted by the outcome of Somervell's delicate negotiations in Chungking and the steps that he had taken to provide powerful logistical support in the CBI. After more than a year of disappointments, the future of the Allied war effort in Asia "appeared to be at its brightest."[34]

• • •

In November and December 1943, Somervell attended the high-level conferences at Cairo and Teheran. These conferences grew out of Roosevelt's desire to bring together for the first time the Big Three—Churchill, Premier

Joseph Stalin of the Soviet Union, and Roosevelt—and for the first time meet Chiang face-to-face. While numerous political and military questions were scheduled for discussion, the overriding concern of American military leaders was to pin the British down to the May 1, 1944, target date for OVERLORD. Otherwise, they thought the British would continually come forth with "peripheral and indecisive ventures in the Mediterranean" that seemed to serve long-range British political purposes rather than hasten the defeat of Germany.[35]

Determined not to be outmaneuvered by the British penchant for proposing alternatives to a cross-Channel invasion as they felt had been the case in previous conferences, the American delegates brought with them sixty junior and senior specialists in strategic planning and logistics. They also summoned Eisenhower and the principal American commanders in the CBI to join them.

Further, the American delegates had planners prepare a multitude of papers on possible operations, and their logistical ramifications, that might be discussed at the conferences. Somervell's planners had prepared studies on fifteen operations so that he had at hand, as Lutes noted in his diary, "a trunk full of logistical plans to support any and every option imaginable."[36]

In discussions held in Cairo at the Mena House Hotel, almost at the base of the Pyramids, from November 22 to 26, British, American, and Chinese leaders haggled over prospective operations in the Far East and Europe. Somervell spent most of his time advising the CCS about the logistical aspects of operations to recover Burma. After lengthy discussions, the Allied leaders tentatively approved Mountbatten's plan to recapture Burma before the monsoon season in 1944 through two separate operations, code named TARZAN and BUCCANEER.

TARZAN consisted of an offensive by the American-trained Chinese soldiers stationed in India that would move from Ledo toward the important communications center of Myitkyina in northern Burma and an offensive by Chinese forces in Yunnan into northern Burma to link up with other Chinese forces at Myitkyina, as well as British land and airborne operations into central Burma. BUCCANEER, a British amphibious operation in the Bay of Bengal to recapture the Andaman Islands, would be mounted in conjunction with TARZAN to meet Chiang's long-standing demand for an amphibious operation as a condition for committing his own troops to Burma.[37]

On November 27, Churchill, Roosevelt, and their military and political advisors, minus their staffs which remained in Cairo, flew to Teheran to meet with Stalin. At this conference, the American delegates were primarily concerned with seeing that OVERLORD was carried out by the summer of 1944, although they showed a willingness to undertake additional operations in the Mediterranean if such operations did not interfere with OVERLORD.

The question of an invasion of southern France as an appendage to OVERLORD, code named ANVIL, was most important to Somervell. Considerable planning had already been done on this operation, but the only plans on hand were an out-of-date outline plan drawn up in the summer of 1943 and a logistical plan prepared earlier by Lutes and hurriedly sent from Cairo to Teheran by air courier at Somervell's request. Working feverishly into the early morning hours of November 29, American planners, with Somervell "handling the shipping support and supply factor," put together a plan for the JCS and Roosevelt. It was approved later that day by the CCS. The next day the Big Three agreed that OVERLORD would be launched in May 1944 in conjunction with a Soviet mass offensive on the Eastern Front and that along with ANVIL it would be the major Anglo-American operation in 1944.[38]

On December 1, the American and British delegates returned to Cairo to wrap up a number of outstanding questions relating to OVERLORD, ANVIL, the Mediterranean, and the war against Japan. Their most important action was to shelve BUCCANEER since its assault shipping was urgently needed for OVERLORD and ANVIL. Because Chiang, who had already returned to China, had previously stipulated that BUCCANEER was a prerequisite to Chinese participation in TARZAN, the cancellation of BUCCANEER seemed to foreclose any major campaign to recover Burma in 1944 and presaged a declining Allied belief that China was vital to victory. Somervell played a minor role in these decisions except to emphasize that the Chinese would bitterly resent a failure by the Allies to carry out the Burma campaign that Mountbatten had originally proposed.

12. LOGISTICS AND STRATEGY, 1944–1945

• • • • DURING 1944–45, THE ALLIED WAR EFFORT generally followed the strategic blueprint outlined at the Cairo and Teheran Conferences. In Europe, emphasis in the first half of 1944 was placed on the preparations for, and implementation of, OVERLORD and ANVIL, with the Italian campaign reduced to a marginal role. After Allied forces became lodged on the French coast and began pursuing retreating German forces across France to Germany's western frontier, the European war, especially from Washington's viewpoint, essentially became one of logistics.

Meanwhile, in the Pacific, the Americans drove into the western Pacific, with the CBI declining in importance. By late summer of 1945, the Americans were at the threshold of Japan and preparing final plans for the invasion of the home islands when the Japanese surrendered (see Map 5).

• • •

In 1944, offensive operations against Germany were preeminent in the Allied strategy for victory in the global war against the Axis. At Cairo and Teheran, Allied leaders had agreed that OVERLORD and ANVIL would be launched in May 1944. Later, OVERLORD was postponed to June 1944 to wait for another month's production of landing craft, and ANVIL was placed in limbo.

Given the top priority assigned to OVERLORD, shipping for carrying troops and cargo to the United Kingdom was abundant. In fact, the major tangle with shipping now grew out of the limited capacity of ports, railways, and depots in the United Kingdom to handle the flow of troops and supplies. Eventually, this tangle was unraveled by loading vessels in the United States and sending them to the United Kingdom, where they would remain in harbor until called forward for discharge directly on the continent.[1]

The materiel picture was generally encouraging. Huge tonnages of supplies were sent to the United Kingdom in the five months preceding OVERLORD as a result of the productivity of American industry, the availability of shipping, and the greater efficiency that now marked the ASF. Even so, Somervell faced numerous challenges, many of which grew out of the practice of Dwight Eisenhower, commander of Supreme Headquarters, Allied Expeditionary Force (SHAEF), the headquarters of the invasion force, to make special requests for equipment with little advance notice to Washington. Often Somervell's subordinates challenged these requests because they simply could not provide the requested equipment in the short time remaining. However, Somervell took the position that

> The best course of action . . . would be to accept . . . [Eisenhower's] requests unless they are obviously out of line and to act on them promptly and then do our utmost to fill them. This has been our philosophy since the beginning of the war. If there is to be a change to the old method of requiring lengthy explanations for every request that stultifies all supply requirements, I hope the Army will not be a party to it.

Somervell was as good as his word. When Eisenhower notified him that there was a shortage of spare parts and equipment for tanks and vehicles issued to the British under lend-lease, Somervell put his "expediting forces to work at full speed to make up the shortages" and quickly eased "the situation considerably." In another instance, when he was called upon to reequip two airborne divisions, Somervell had all the equipment shipped from New York within a week.[2]

Despite all the attention he devoted to the shipping and supplies aspects of BOLERO and OVERLORD, no problem was more exasperating to Somervell than the ongoing turmoil with Lee's organization. Shortly after assuming command of SHAEF in early 1944, Eisenhower, who served both as commander of SHAEF and commanding general of the ETO, United States Army, had upgraded Lee's status. Realizing there was a shortage of qualified staff officers and anxious to avoid establishing an additional staff, he consolidated ETO Headquarters with Lee's headquarters and placed both under Lee's command. He also named Lee deputy ETO commander in line with Somervell's long-standing argument that a rear area should be under a top-flight man with wide responsibility for administration and supply.

Before long, however, Eisenhower had second thoughts about Lee. Finding many faults in Lee's organization and angry because Lee had a habit of issuing orders without consulting him, he advised his intimates that "he did not fully trust General Lee and his organization to do the job" and referred to Lee in "less than glowing terms."[3]

Many of the shortcomings in Lee's organization related to such vital matters as supply records and administrative procedures, stock control systems, and overlapping and ambiguous responsibilities of the base commanders, port commanders, and the chief of transportation. These were compounded by weaknesses in Lee's staff. His chief of staff, Brigadier General Roy Lord, did not have wide experience in logistics, and a number of the officers holding key posts during the final planning phase for OVERLORD were new to their positions and only beginning to get hold of the details of the operation's logistical problems.

The situation was exacerbated by Eisenhower's bitterness over having Lee's promotion to lieutenant general forced on him. In January 1944, Somervell had suggested to Eisenhower that Lee should be promoted to lieutenant general. Eisenhower, seeing no justification for the promotion, inferred that Somervell wanted it so the ASF chief could argue for his own promotion to full general since he held a more important post than Lee. Therefore, Eisenhower refused to recommend Lee's promotion to Marshall.

Several weeks later, however, Marshall promoted Lee to three stars without consulting Eisenhower, prompting Eisenhower to conclude that Somervell had pulled strings behind his back to get what he wanted. Actually, it was somewhat less conspiratorial.

Eisenhower's chief of staff, Walter Bedell Smith, had been promoted to lieutenant general, and MacArthur had then insisted that his chief of staff, Richard K. Sutherland, should also be promoted. Not wanting to submit one name, Marshall had decided to promote others to the same rank at the same time. Seeing Lee's name on a recent list of officers to be considered for promotion and assuming that Lee had Eisenhower's recommendation, he had placed Lee's name and Raymond Wheeler's name on the promotion list along with Sutherland's. Eisenhower swallowed Lee's promotion after Marshall explained the circumstances to him, but he resented that Lee had been the beneficiary of army politics to get a promotion Eisenhower thought was not warranted.[4]

The difficulties engulfing Lee also generated discord in his relationship with other commands and for a time caused Eisenhower to consider asking for his replacement. As commander of the theater's SOS, Lee headed one of the three major coordinate commands for American forces in Europe, and as deputy theater commander, he spoke for Eisenhower on such matters as supply allocations. This arrangement was resented by Lieutenant General Carl Spaatz, commander of the AAF in Europe, and Lieutenant General Omar Bradley, commander of the American First Army. They argued that, by wearing two hats, Lee could hardly act as a disinterested party when there might be conflict between the AAF and the SOS or between ground forces and the SOS.

Whatever the merits of their suspicions and objections, there was a noticeable tension between Lee's staff and other headquarters that reached down to lower echelons. Combat commands complained that Lee's SOS felt no sense of urgency about filling their requests. Poor liaison and coordination between Lee's SOS and other commands added to the friction.[5]

In April, Somervell sent LeRoy Lutes to the United Kingdom to check up on last minute needs of OVERLORD and to evaluate the efficiency of Lee's operation. Lutes spent more than a month on this assignment, visiting the various headquarters and inspecting as many facilities as possible. While there, he sent Somervell a steady stream of letters and memoranda detailing his findings, as well as recommendations to Lee and Eisenhower to improve conditions.

Overall, he found that the supply situation was satisfactory and that Lee was doing "a fine job." However, Lutes also noted there were grave weaknesses that "boded ill for the future," especially for the all-important buildup in France following the invasion. Consequently, he advised Lee to make a number of organizational and procedural changes and, most importantly, to develop better relationships with Eisenhower's headquarters. Lutes was careful, though, not to excite Eisenhower about the deficiencies he unearthed out of fear Eisenhower might request Lee's relief. As Lutes informed Somervell, "I have kept in mind that General Lee is your appointee and that MY LOYALTY TO YOU MUST BE FIRST."[6]

On Lutes's advice, Somervell did not directly involve himself in the ETO logistical organization out of concern that both Lee and Eisenhower would regard his involvement as unwanted interference. Yet, he followed the situation closely and counseled Lutes on the proper way to "make all these fellows lie in the same bed and like it." Beyond specific recommendations on personnel, Somervell suggested that the situation would improve dramatically if Lee did "a good deal of missionary work in instilling in his staff's mind the idea that they are over there to supply our customers and not to tell their customers what they want. . . . As long as one maintains that attitude and if the supplies are delivered promptly I can not see how any friction could result." He also suggested that Eisenhower might well "knock some heads together and straighten them out," especially in regard to Bradley and Spaatz.

Following through at least partly on Somervell's suggestions, Lutes lectured Lee on the need for missionary work. However, he refrained from advising Eisenhower to "wield a club" on his people in the belief that the latter might resent Washington telling him how to handle his subordinates and instead advised "him to put his faith in Lee."

Not fully appreciating his uncertain standing in Eisenhower's eyes or that, through Lutes, his old friend Somervell was trying to save his job, Lee viewed

Lutes's visit and Somervell's apparent overseeing of his operation as demeaning, and he indicated that he preferred no more checks be made on his operations. Eisenhower, in contrast, was most pleased with Lutes's visit and asked Somervell to leave him in Europe for another two to three months to act as a logistical troubleshooter, a request Somervell refused since he relied so heavily upon the cool and efficient Lutes for supply planning in Washington. Before leaving, Lutes informed Eisenhower that the assault forces for OVERLORD were sufficiently equipped and that Lee's staff, while "not the tops," was "learning" and would improve "as the attack progresses." Eisenhower, in turn, stated he was now satisfied with Lee and abandoned, at least temporarily, any thought of replacing him.[7]

On June 6, 1944, OVERLORD was launched, causing the logistical problems of the war in Europe to change quickly. Now the major problem was not so much to see how many men and how much materiel could be sent to the United Kingdom but how effectively Eisenhower's armies could be supplied as they broke out of the Normandy bridgehead and advanced across France. The critical factor was the capacity of ports, followed by the capacity of roads, rail lines, airfields, and storage facilities, all of which were outside Somervell's direct responsibility. Eisenhower was also plagued with critical shortages of many major items after attrition and expenditure proved to be higher than expected. Somervell usually did what he could to see that Eisenhower received the materiel he needed, even if it exceeded the quantities originally earmarked for the theater.

In August 1944, Somervell and Robert Patterson traveled to Europe to see how well the troops were being supplied. Leaving Washington late in the evening of August 8, the Somervell-Patterson party flew to Naples, Italy. There, they devoted four days to touring facilities and visiting the fighting front.

They then joined Winston Churchill on the destroyer HMS *Kimberly* on August 15 to observe the Allied invasion of southern France at the Bay of St. Tropez, now under the code name of DRAGOON. Churchill and his two American guests saw little of the landings because the captain of the *Kimberly*, worried about the safety of his high-ranking passengers, refused to approach the beach any closer than 7,000 yards. Two days later, the Somervell-Patterson party went ashore to visit the headquarters of the American Seventh Army and the American 3d Division.[8]

The Somervell-Patterson party next flew to England, where on August 20, they met with Lee and toured a number of facilities. They then visited American forces in France, which were now racing for the German border after the St. Lo breakout. Somervell also toured the port of Cherbourg and OMAHA Beach, one of the major landing points for American troops on June 6. After spending three more days in England for conferences and dinner parties, the Somervell-Patterson party returned to the United States on August 27.

Somervell was generally encouraged about what he saw and heard in Europe. "The commanders are first rate—Eisenhower, Bradley [commander of the American Twelfth Army Group], [Lieutenant General Courtney] Hodges [commander of the American First Army], and Patton [commander of the American Third Army]," he concluded. "Eisenhower [was] very sanguine," while Patton was "full of life, banging away." Patton, Somervell observed, "wants to go straight through to Germany without stopping . . . and wants to push as fast as he can, before they can organize in front of him. Has no worry about supply. Certain that he will go fast unless higher command stops him. No worry about flanks. Has Germans on the run." With bold action, Somervell was optimistic that the Allies could finish the war in Europe, perhaps before the end of the year. "The job now," Somervell said, "is swift pursuit. Patton has the right idea—straight ahead, and let the air forces take care of the flanks."[9]

However, all was not perfect in Somervell's view. The original plans had called for troops and supplies to be sent from the United States directly to France as soon as Cherbourg and additional ports were captured, but these plans were hampered by the delay in the Allied taking of Cherbourg, the extensive damage done to its facilities by the Germans, the slowness in restoring the port to operation, and the failure to capture any other major port on the Atlantic coast of France before September. As a result, in September, with Allied armies already on the German border, there was not enough deep-water berthing capacity for the vessels bringing supplies for Eisenhower, and more than half of his supplies were still being discharged over the Normandy beaches.[10]

The failure to secure adequate berthing capacity in northwestern Europe soon caused ships to pile up off the coast of France. Lacking capacity, Lee's command was unable to discharge ships at the rate originally scheduled, forcing many ships to remain tied up in Channel waters still fully or partially loaded. In effect, they had become floating warehouses. During September, only 95 ships out of a scheduled 175 were discharged on the continent, leaving 80 ships sitting idle in the area. In early October, more than 200 ships were awaiting unloading. Even so, ETO officials claimed that new arrivals should continue at a rate of 265 per month through the end of 1944, a calculation based on the supply requirements of the ETO rather than its ability to unload ships.[11]

This immobilization of shipping coincided with a loss of momentum all along the front. As Allied armies raced across France, they outran their supplies, which in some places were stored in depots hundreds of miles behind them. Extraordinary steps were taken to get supplies to the fighting men, but adequate supplies for continued offensives by all Allied troops could not be moved on the spur of the moment. Tragically for those who hoped for an early end to the war, Allied offensives in the fall achieved little in the face of stout German resistance and bad weather. By December, it was obvious that the war in Europe would last at least another winter.

• • •

During the fall of 1944, Allied leaders faced a shipping crisis that threatened to stall the global war effort. In Europe, the lack of adequate port facilities had produced a shipping congestion that turned cargo vessels into floating warehouses and dangerously affected the availability of shipping for the movement of men and supplies from the United States to the fighting fronts.

The same was true in the Pacific. Although the acute shortage of the fall of 1942 had eased, shipping remained a pressing problem because of long distances, greater requirements growing out of the accelerated operations, congestion at New Guinea ports that delayed the unloading of ships, and MacArthur's tendency to retain ships in the SWPA to transport men and supplies between Australian ports and from Australia to New Guinea.

By the early fall of 1944, demands for more shipping for the invasions of Leyte and Luzon in the Philippines were causing the situation in the SWPA to reach crisis proportions. The area ports and the landing sites on Leyte were not able to handle all the ships arriving from the United States, and thus, scores were sitting idly at Hollandia in New Guinea and Leyte for want of facilities ashore. So great was the shipping problem that, unless additional shipping was transferred to the Pacific from the Atlantic or unless the idle pools of shipping in the SWPA were broken up, there was little possibility that the Luzon operation could go forward as scheduled. If that were not enough, there were growing demands for shipping to meet civilian requirements for liberated Europe and to transport lend-lease supplies to the Soviet Union in anticipation of its entry into the war against Japan.[12]

As the crisis emerged, WSA officials and the army and navy moved aggressively to solve it. Warned by his shipping people about the growing mess in the ETO, Somervell directed Lee to release ships as soon as possible and request sailings only when he was certain that the ships could be unloaded expeditiously. Lee's shipping officials responded by reducing their requests, but they still asked for far more than they could really expect to unload. In defense of his staff, Lee argued it was "the theater's responsibility to provide a flow of supplies" to the combat troops, even if it meant using ships as floating warehouses when they were needed elsewhere.

Unwilling to accept Lee's position, Somervell informed him in October that the sailings for the remainder of the year would be scheduled only in accordance with the demonstrated ability of the ETO to reduce substantially the bank of unloaded ships. Lee protested, insisting that the large backlog of ships had been the major factor making it possible for him to meet Eisenhower's high priority demands for rations, gasoline, and ammunition. The cuts, in other words, would result in serious overall shortages. He further insisted that ship unloading would soon improve with the expected performance of LeHavre and

Rouen in France and of Antwerp in Belgium and with the transfer of one of the artificial harbors used in OVERLORD from British to American hands. Eisenhower joined Lee in objecting to the cuts, advising Somervell that "so far as I am able to pierce through the maze of conflicting considerations, you may be sure I will NOT demand of you anything that appears unwarranted or unusable."[13]

Somervell was not moved by their objections. In his view, the worldwide shipping situation was too serious to permit Lee to use nearly 200 ships as warehouses. Certainly, he agreed that the ETO should have a safe working margin of ships on hand—perhaps 75 to 85—but any more could not be tolerated. Somervell also refused to accept Lee's optimistic predictions about future unloading capabilities, for the ETO had yet to live up to anything approaching its predictions. Writing to Lee in November 1944, Somervell made his position clear, stating,

> Owing to our previous disappointments with the results attained, it is necessary for us to gauge the rate by the results rather than by the estimates. Had we followed your request for shipping there would now be over 500 ships standing by in England and adjacent waters and our ability to supply you would have been seriously curtailed. It is necessary therefore that your headquarters cease repeating by rote figures previously arrived at and take a realistic view of the situation. To do otherwise destroys confidence in the estimates and delays our supply of the equipment which you can actually handle. You may be sure that our response will be immediate as soon as your ability to handle more is demonstrated.[14]

Besides reducing sailings, Somervell dispatched troubleshooters to the ETO to look into its vexing shipping problems. In October, he sent Lucius Clay to do something about the delay in unloading ships. Clay gave special attention to the problems at Cherbourg, and by recommending a number of organizational changes, he significantly improved the port's performance.

More importantly, Somervell sent Brigadier General John Franklin, director of water transportation in the Transportation Corps, to the ETO to aid Lee in improving the turnaround of shipping and to gather more realistic estimates of its future discharge capabilities. In a series of conferences with high-level theater officials, Franklin gained their acceptance of Somervell's right to review and revise their estimates, and then, he closely surveyed port operations to get a sound basis for estimating ETO's discharge capabilities. His findings reinforced Somervell's conviction that the theater's estimates had little value.[15]

Somervell's concern over shipping was not confined to the ETO. As the number of unloaded ships in Hollandia and off Leyte mounted, it became obvious that they could not be unloaded for some time. Therefore, he urged MacArthur to tailor his shipping requests to a realistic discharge capability and pressed him to release ships for return to the west coast. If these steps were not taken, he warned, there would have to be a sharp reduction in sailings from the United States. Irked by Somervell's warning and not wanting "to get another one," MacArthur told his shipping people to get the ships unloaded. Over a period of time they reduced the backlog, but they were not able to eliminate it.[16]

As the shipping crisis worsened, Somervell decided that drastic steps had to be taken to ensure "sailings sufficient to support the military effort during coming months." At his instigation, the JCS on November 18 urged Roosevelt to solve the crisis by eliminating all American assistance to the British import program, by reducing assistance to British and Soviet lend-lease and civilian relief in the Mediterranean and Northwestern Europe, and by securing more shipping from British sources.

The WSA strongly opposed Somervell's proposals. Unwilling to upset "long-standing arrangements on American aid to British shipping programs," it asserted that idle pools of shipping in overseas theaters were the crux of the crisis. These pools could best be solved by developing an effective system to reduce military sailings to theaters where ports were already clogged, not by reducing sailings for other programs. Emory Land of the Maritime Commission also took up the fight against Somervell's proposals, lecturing the JCS on the military's misuse of shipping and demanding "that theater commanders be held accountable for making realistic appraisals of reception capacity and reducing their requirements if congestion develops."[17]

Roosevelt decided to accept neither the JCS's nor the WSA's positions in toto. On the one hand, he asked that the WSA negotiate with the British for a reduction in the British import program during December 1944 and January and February 1945, instructed that use of American shipping for civilian purposes "be cut to the bone," and suggested that the navy readjust its Mediterranean convoy cycle to reduce shipping from the United States. On the other hand, he told the JCS to make the "most urgent representation" to theater commanders to eliminate the idle shipping pools and not to seek any additional transfer of British-controlled shipping until he was satisfied that the military had done everything possible to coordinate the number of sailings from the United States with the reception capacity of the respective theaters. Given the burden of proving it was efficiently utilizing shipping, the JCS on December 9 prohibited theater commanders from using ocean-going ships as warehouses and directed that theater shipping needs must be based on a realistic assessment of the ability to unload them.[18]

Somervell did not wait for the JCS's decision before taking additional steps to untangle the worldwide shipping knot. On November 23, he informed MacArthur that he must cut his retentions by twenty ships and that some sailings for December would be postponed. MacArthur, who never showed any awareness of the seriousness of the worldwide shipping situation or the fact that the congestion might be relieved without jeopardy to his plans, immediately protested, saying that any curtailment of shipping should be postponed for two months so that he could complete the Leyte operation and launch the Luzon invasion. Somervell refused to budge, and in early December, he pressed the SWPA to reduce its retentions to 100 ships by January 15, 1945, and informed MacArthur that ten sailings from the United States in December would be deferred. Again, MacArthur protested, and again, Somervell held his ground, insisting that he had made generous provision for MacArthur's requirements. Somervell reinforced this reply with a plea for MacArthur to look at the shipping situation through Washington's eyes and "find a moment to give direction towards a vigorous effort to improve the turn around situation."[19] Responding to Somervell's plea, MacArthur further cut retentions in the SWPA, and Washington continued to pare sailings. Along with the stabilization that came with the winding down of the fighting on Leyte and administrative reforms within the area, these actions helped end the worst of the shipping tangle in the SWPA.

The shipping tie-up in the ETO also gradually improved. The opening of Antwerp to Allied traffic at the end of November 1944 eased the situation, but equally important, was the steady pressure Somervell maintained on ETO shipping authorities. In December, he sent Charles Gross to Europe to see how better use could be made of port facilities. He also insisted that twenty-five out of thirty-five Liberty ships that the ETO had retained to carry supplies from the United Kingdom to the continent must be returned to the United States, as well as twenty-one other Libertys that were partially loaded with nonessential supplies. Appreciating that Somervell meant business, ETO officials implemented additional measures to regulate shipping, including the establishment of a committee to insure that ETO's requirements for supplies corresponded to the quantities that could be unloaded.[20]

In the final analysis, the impact of the fall 1944 shipping crisis on military operations is difficult to assess because too many other factors came into play to permit definite conclusions. Nevertheless, shipping was a critical resource in the fall of 1944, and Somervell, before and after the JCS's directive, helped eliminate the congestion in overseas theaters that was at the core of the crisis. By insisting on proper logistical management in European and Pacific ports and curtailing sailings from the United States when necessary, he minimized the wasteful military shipping practices that had helped spawn the congestion and ameliorated the crisis.

• • •

Throughout the winter of 1944–45, Somervell was preoccupied with the logistics of the ETO. The port problem was on the road to solution. However, other logistical problems gripped the theater and made this winter one of the most crisis-ridden periods of the war for him.

For one thing, the tension between Lee's command and Eisenhower's field commanders had not abated. At the request of the field commanders, Eisenhower had stripped Lee of his post as deputy ETO commander, but the bad feelings remained. The field commanders repeatedly complained that the Communications Zone (COMZ), the name given to Lee's command after the invasion and its move to France, did not sufficiently appreciate the urgency of the needs of the front line troops or show "the proper zeal in meeting them." They were especially infuriated by Lee's handling of his own headquarters.

Ignoring Eisenhower's frequently expressed view that all major headquarters should stay clear of large cities, Lee in September transferred his forward headquarters of 8,000 officers and 21,000 enlisted men from their tent camp near Cherbourg to Paris. This move took two weeks and diverted motor and air transportation at the very time that supply shortages were seriously affecting the field armies. By mid-October, Lee's staff had occupied 167 hotels in Paris and another 129 in the Seine Base Section. Meanwhile, Eisenhower's staff and other organizations were using twenty-five hotels. Lee justified the move on the grounds that it was only logical to have his headquarters at Paris because it was the transportation hub of France, a point Eisenhower later conceded, and that for health reasons his doctors had advised him to get his men out of tents. However, the image of Lee's men living snugly in Paris while fighting men suffered in the wet and cold enraged Eisenhower and prompted several of Eisenhower's key people, badly needing the gasoline and trucks that Lee had preempted for his move to Paris, to yell for Lee's scalp.[21]

Somervell was also concerned about the inadequacy of the distribution system in Europe. As Allied armies roared across France, there had been little time to develop intermediate depots, properly echeloned in depth, for storing supplies so as to alleviate the pressure at the ports and to maintain close support of the troops at the front. Moreover, inventory and supply control were often haphazard. Supplies were unloaded at the ports and stored so hastily that supply officers lost track of them. Thus, when units requisitioned items, it was often easier to place a new order in the United States than search warehouses in Europe. Somervell had early urged Lee to develop adequate depots and a more effective control system, but the COMZ was slow to remedy these shortcomings because of the optimism of the late summer that the war might soon be over and because the needs of the buildup for the fall offensives absorbed most of its energy.

A final problem in the ETO that concerned Somervell was the shortage of specific supplies, most notably artillery ammunition. When the tempo of fighting increased in 1944 and the expenditure of artillery ammunition exceeded the anticipated rate, Lutes predicted a critical shortage of shells by November. Somervell reacted by allocating ammunition to each theater on the basis of its number of active weapons and ordered the construction of additional facilities to increase production. It took time, however, for the new facilities to come on line, and in the meantime, Somervell had to press for maximum production by existing facilities through manpower deferments and even the furloughing of men from uniform to work in munitions plants. These measures were having an impact by the fall, but in early November, Somervell warned Eisenhower that production increases would be matched by rising troop strength and that the demands from all theaters were so great that he would have trouble meeting his requests for the next three to six months.

Somervell's reply angered Eisenhower, who predicted his reserves would be practically exhausted by the middle of December and that the present supply rate for heavy artillery would limit him to static operations. Convinced the supply of ammunition was crucial to his operations, Eisenhower had Major General Harold R. Bull, SHAEF G-3, and Clay, still in France, thoroughly study ETO's assets and estimated expenditures and their tactical implications. After completing their study, Bull and Clay flew to Washington to impress upon Somervell that the theater's stated requirements must be met or else offensive operations would be seriously hampered or even halted.[22]

The Bull-Clay findings unsettled Somervell, and he quickly moved to do what he could to meet ETO's needs. He ransacked military posts to find stray shells and, through special handling, tried to reduce the delivery time for shipping shells. More importantly, he "pulled out all stops" in trying to increase production by resisting early reconversion and by imploring management and workers in shell plants to spare no effort on the shop floor. Reporting on his actions, Somervell wrote Lee on December 1 that "this is the last rabbit we can pull out of the hat and I believe that we have thrown in the hat too. So what we are doing represents an all-out effort." It would be weeks, though, before these emergency steps would have an effect on the availability of ammunition at the front. So, for the time being, Eisenhower's troops had to depend on their reserves and the existing rate of supply.[23]

As reports of supply problems in Europe became regular fare, some pointed the finger of blame at Somervell. Infuriated by these charges, he sent Henry Aurand to France to determine the true story about the ammunition shortages and to remain there as a troubleshooter. However, Aurand's mission was a bust. Eisenhower's staff regarded him as an unwanted interloper and treated him cooly, and Aurand further irritated them by preparing a highly critical report that recommended the sacking of a number of top SHAEF officers. Making short work of Aurand, they ignored his findings and arranged for him to be given an insignificant assignment—commanding general of the Normandy Base Section.[24]

Faced with the failure of Aurand's mission, Somervell tried a slightly different approach in early December by sending Lutes to France to make an on-the-ground survey of the ETO's supply situation for Eisenhower. At Somervell's insistence, he was also to determine if any of the supply deficiencies in Europe could be laid at ASF's feet and to ensure that Eisenhower's field commanders did not blame Somervell for deficiencies for which the ETO was responsible. In contrast to Aurand, Lutes was well received by Eisenhower's staff because most liked him.

As he made his rounds of the front and rear areas, Lutes found that the supply machine was not running smoothly. It "does run," he told Somervell, and "no one can say supply here has failed." However, he added "that many procedures are not as we would like to see them." Lacking confidence in Lee's organization, field commanders padded their requisitions to build up their reserves as a cushion against unpredictable deliveries and employed hundreds of "bloodhounds" to range over the COMZ to follow through on their requisitions and to ensure the proper delivery of supplies. Moreover, Lutes found many shortcomings in COMZ's management practices and recommended specific improvements to Eisenhower and Lee. Eisenhower responded by stating that he was not happy with Lee, but in the absence of a specific failure, he would not fire him.[25]

While in France, Lutes sent Somervell a steady stream of reports confirming that the ETO was suffering from genuine supply problems. As Lutes uncovered much that was wrong, Somervell grew quite angry. He appreciated that the rapid growth of the COMZ brought about by the quick advance across France in the summer had created disruptions. However, Lutes's reports convinced him that Lee's staff had not worked hard enough to overcome them. Somervell was particularly incensed that field commanders were sending expediters to the rear. In his opinion, it represented an appalling lack of confidence in the COMZ that had to be reversed if Lee were to keep his job. Resolved to see that Lee got his house in order, Somervell wrote Lutes,

> I regard it as essential that you inform Lee of the antagonism which exists toward him in the minds of Patton, Bradley, Hodges, et al. . . . It is essential that it be closed off if the Services of Supply over there is to function properly. A lack of confidence or antagonism has no place in a situation of that kind. I do not care who is right and who is wrong, the point is that we have to satisfy our customers and do so in a way which pleases them.[26]

In January 1945, Somervell made his own trip to France to check into complaints about Lee's COMZ. On his arrival on January 9, he spent several days in Paris discussing the supply situation with Eisenhower and his staff, Lee and his staff, and Lutes, who then returned to Washington. Thereafter, Somervell visited the combat headquarters and inspected numerous supply facilities before spending a few days in England and then touring the port facilities at Antwerp and LeHavre. Everywhere he asked detailed questions about the supply picture, leading one of Lee's supply chiefs to comment that he "demonstrated a wider knowledge of supply problems than any individual who had visited this Theater during the past two and a half years."²⁷

As a result of his visit, Somervell became convinced that ETO's need for artillery ammunition, tanks, general purpose weapons, and tires was so critical that no effort should be spared at home in meeting those needs. Elaborating on this requirement in a letter to Wilhelm Styer, he said, "Insofar as we back home are concerned the problem is distinctly clear. IT IS PRODUCTION, PRODUCTION, AND MORE PRODUCTION, WITH THE GREATEST EMPHASIS ON THE ITEMS WHICH WE ALL KNOW TO BE SO CRITICAL." Somervell, likewise, found that, in too many cases, units had been in France for several months before they were completely equipped. "This is lousy and I want to send somebody to jail for it," he told Styer. "The whole outfit has been cautioned about this time and time again. We have sent inspectors to ports to be sure that these things do not occur and nevertheless they continue to occur. Drastic action must be taken to stop this in its tracks."²⁸

The visit also confirmed for Somervell the shortcomings that Lutes had identified in Lee's organization. Using Lutes's findings and recommendations as a starting point, he suggested a number of ways to improve the COMZ organization in a scathing memorandum he submitted to Lee before leaving France. While granting that Lee had a tough job and had accomplished much, Somervell criticized him for not demanding more from his men, insisting that more could be accomplished if there were higher performance standards. Somervell's specific recommendations covered the gamut of Lee's operations, but most centered on better planning, the development of a depot system in depth with proper stock control so that supplies could be quickly sorted out and delivered, the organization of an effective transportation system, and the formation of a control section in COMZ's headquarters to keep Lee informed of the progress made toward specific goals. To see that this was done, Somervell temporarily assigned Clinton Robinson to Lee to organize the section and to design the reporting procedures. Warned by Eisenhower to implement Somervell's recommendations, Lee carried them out, although progress was often slow.²⁹

Somervell also took the opportunity of his visit to look closely into the shipping situation in the ETO. While the backlog of unloaded ships had been significantly reduced by the end of 1944, the number of ships waiting to be unloaded continued to exceed those being worked in the ports. Nevertheless, Somervell was ready to increase sailings to meet Eisenhower's most critical needs. Lee's staff told Somervell that the ETO was short 33,000 vehicles and that with currently scheduled shipments it would be short 30,000 on February 1 and 35,000 on March 1. After reviewing ETO's future requirements, Somervell increased its request for February sailings of ships carrying vehicles from twenty-five to thirty and directed Gross in Washington to dispatch an additional fifty ships with vehicles in March. By the time Allied armies crossed the Rhine River in March, these shipments were relieving the vehicle deficit.[30]

Despite his willingness to increase sailings to meet ETO's specific needs, Somervell was still concerned about the large number of ships sitting idle in ports. To alleviate the backlog, he advised Lee to shift as many ships as possible from the severely crowded port of Antwerp to Marseilles, which up to this time had been used primarily for supplying troops in southern France, and not to let "anything interfere with your cutting down on movements to your theater." As a result of this recommendation, the backlog declined rapidly. In early February 1945, the number of ships being unloaded exceeded those sitting idle for the first time, and at the end of the month, the backlog totaled less than 100 ships. A month later, it was reduced to fifty-seven ships. Gratified by these results and confident that Lee's staff was now providing him with accurate estimates of its shipping requirements, Somervell agreed to cease reviewing them and to schedule sailings as requested.[31]

Somervell was generally satisfied with the results of his visit to France. He had personally seen the supply situation and had arranged for a major overhaul of Lee's organization and procedures. In one respect, however, his visit had been a disappointment. By the time of the Battle of the Bulge in December 1944, the American army in Europe was seriously short of riflemen. The JCS reacted by rushing more troops to Europe, while Eisenhower ordered his rear area be combed to locate men suitable for combat. Both the COMZ and the AAF were reluctant to release men, so Marshall decided in early January 1945 that there must be a drastic effort to find additional troops in the ETO.

Among several steps he took, Marshall asked Somervell to look into the matter with the expectation that by straightening out Lee's setup he could free up large numbers of men for the front line. Under Somervell's pressure to cut the fat in his command, Lee assigned 21,000 men for infantry retraining during the first weeks of 1945, and under later pressure from Washington, he released more men. However, his subordinates resisted turning over large numbers of men for combat duty, and it took months for Somervell's organizational reforms to yield even a small percentage of the number of riflemen Marshall had in mind. Apparently unaware of the difficulties Somervell had faced, Marshall later commented that this was one of the few troubleshooting jobs Somervell had failed to handle satisfactorily.[32]

At the end of January 1945, Somervell went to Marseilles to join Marshall, who was making his way to the Soviet Union for a conference of Allied leaders at Yalta in the Crimea. From Marseilles, Somervell accompanied the chief of staff to Malta for a meeting of the CCS. On February 3, Roosevelt, Churchill, the CCS, and their advisors flew 1,500 miles from Malta to Yalta for their second wartime meeting with Soviet leaders. Unlike the previous high-level conferences that he had attended, Somervell took a backseat at Yalta. Postwar political problems were of paramount importance, and outside of incidental matters relating to supplies and cargo shipping, few discussions directly involved him.[33] Following the end of the conference on February 11, Somervell returned to the United States.

By the end of March 1945, victory over Germany was clearly in sight. Nevertheless, Somervell resisted any letup in these final days, insisting that military necessity must prevail in all supply matters until Germany surrendered.

Somervell's major concern now was the question of civilian supply. In 1943, the military had taken over responsibility for civilian relief in liberated areas, and not surprisingly, it had subordinated it to military necessity by limiting relief to the minimum necessary to curb disease and unrest.

By the fall of 1944, however, there was widespread malnutrition in France and Belgium, and their economies were in disarray. French and Belgian officials called for increased imports for civilian relief and the rehabilitation of the economy, and the British, the WSA, and the State Department agreed with them. The British and the State Department argued that military success in Europe depended on political stability and that it could be ensured only if living standards in the liberated areas were quickly raised. The WSA, meanwhile, saw the civilian program as a way to weaken the military's hold over shipping and recommended that "some civilian body or individual" be authorized to decide how much shipping should be allocated to civilian programs.

Not unexpectedly, Somervell opposed the French-Belgian program. Certain it would hinder the military effort, he said that shipments should be limited to items of military necessity and remain under military control. The British, however, insisted that the CCS conduct an overall survey of the shipping situation with a view toward increasing civilian imports.

Worried that the British and French would turn civilian imports into a major political issue, Harry Hopkins on January 14, 1945, reached an agreement with British Minister of State Sir Richard Law to commence national import programs on a limited scale and to establish shipping allocations for them for the first quarter of 1945. Somervell opposed the agreement, for shipping studies revealed that there would be a shortage of cargo shipping for military purposes during the first six months of 1945 if Germany continued to fight. He was also convinced that, once Germany was defeated, the expanded civilian program would utilize shipping that should be used for the redeployment of troops from Europe to the Pacific to defeat Japan.

Following his recommendation, the JCS at a meeting at Malta on January 30 presented Roosevelt a strongly worded memorandum expressing grave concerns "over the present determined effort to divert resources to non-military uses" and "over the implied willingness of the British to consider qualifying our objective of ending the war at the earliest possible date." Warning Roosevelt that an accelerated civilian import program could delay the end of the war and lead to the "unnecessary loss of lives," they requested an absolute first priority on all shipping, as well as civilian requirements being limited to essential needs. Shipping for postwar rehabilitation, they added, should be allocated only after all military needs in Europe and the Pacific had been filled. Whether justified by the circumstances, the military, with Somervell in the vanguard, intended to keep hogging the shipping.

Roosevelt agreed to the JCS's request, and at Yalta, he resisted British efforts to secure a larger place for civilian rehabilitation in shipping allocations before the end of the war in both Europe and the Pacific. Yet, the Hopkins-Law Agreement was essentially confirmed, for its allocations were included in the shipping budget agreed to at the conference. No decision was made on the question of final authority in allocations, so in effect the deliberations at Malta and Yalta provided that the civilian import programs would go ahead with the understanding that military needs would have priority.[34]

As Allied armies thrust into Germany, making final victory in Europe within weeks a foregone conclusion, the question of terminating military control of civilian relief and rehabilitation in liberated areas came to the forefront. The State Department and representatives of the liberated nations wanted the military out of civilian affairs as quickly as possible, arguing that the military naturally concentrated on mere relief and eschewed a balanced economic program that would enable an early start on rehabilitation. In the matter of turning over control of French railways to the French government, Somervell quickly emerged as the principal advocate of continued military control, succinctly putting forth the military's position in a message to Patterson at the end of January. "Since the transportation system of France involves complex relationships between railways, port facilities, and highway transport," he stated, "the further complications introduced by the independent handling and movement of supplies inland by the French might well produce disastrous consequences to logistical arrangements of our Army and delay the termination of the war."

Somervell's objection to civilian control was sound, for there was obvious danger in dividing control of the supply line between the military and the provisional national governments in liberated countries that had little experience in handling the transportation and supply problems of modern war. Still, it was obvious that the long-term national interest of the United States would best be served by putting the liberated countries on the path to full rehabilitation as quickly as possible, a goal that could not be achieved as long as the military was in control. Hence, in April 1945, the military began to relent in the case of France, and by the fall, termination had been completely effected.[35]

• • •

During the last two years of the war, Somervell maintained a close interest in the CBI. By the end of 1943, Allied operations there included the Hump airlift, the development of a land route to connect India and China, and an AAF assault against Japan, code named MATTERHORN. Under the latter, B-29s, operating from bases in the Cheng-tu area west of Chungking and supplied by their own airlift from Calcutta, would strike at Japan's steel industry. MATTERHORN imposed a severe drain on the already overburdened logistical operation in the CBI. Airfields had to be built in the vicinity of Calcutta, additional items had to be supplied to India and China, gasoline and supplies had to be flown over the Hump to Cheng-tu until MATTERHORN became self-supporting, and the construction of airfields at Cheng-tu by the Chinese government had to be arranged and supervised. Somervell had been skeptical about the air assault when it was originally proposed since it would place a severe strain on CBI's logistical capacity, but once it was approved by the CCS in November, he put the full weight of the ASF behind it.[36]

Matters were complicated by the souring of American relations with Chiang. Much of this centered around money matters.[37] In 1941, a 20 to 1 exchange rate had been established as the official rate between the yuan and the dollar. However, that rate soon had no realistic relationship to the actual purhasing power of the dollar on the black market because of the spiraling inflation in China, and by the time Somervell visited Chungking in October 1943, the black market rate had reached 120 to 1. Advised by Stilwell that the refusal of the Chinese to alter the exchange rate was causing exorbitant costs for American projects in China, Somervell proposed to T. V. Soong and Finance Minister Kung that the Chinese government make available the yuan to support American troops in China and pay for military construction. One-fifth of the yuan would be purchased by the United States at the official rate of 20 to 1, and the balance would be considered as China's contribution to the war effort. In this way, American costs in China would more accurately reflect comparable costs in the United States. The Chinese showed little interest in Somervell's proposal and indicated they would give "a cold reception" to other American proposals in regard to exchange rates.[38]

At the Cairo Conference, Chiang asked Roosevelt for a billion-dollar loan in gold to ease China's financial plight. Roosevelt refused to commit himself, but to assuage Chiang, he said that the United States would "bear the full cost of its military effort in China." Roosevelt's commitment did not satisfy Chiang, however, and the subsequent cancellation of BUCCANEER stung him because it had been the major concession that he had gained from his meeting with Churchill and Roosevelt. In retaliation, Chiang informed Roosevelt on December 9, 1943, that he was going to delay Chinese participation in TARZAN, the land operation in Burma. He further stated that, if China were to stay in the war, it had to have a billion-dollar loan in gold to maintain its economy, as well as more aid from the United States. Also, he told Stilwell that the United States would have to pay the entire cost of constructing the Cheng-tu airfields at the rate of 20 to 1 even though the black market rate was now 240 to 1.

Chiang's demands infuriated American officials. They were not alarmed by his veiled threat to withdraw from the war. As Somervell remarked to the JCS in a meeting on December 15, "he is now associated with the eventual winner of the war," and it was unlikely that he would "withdraw from this association despite the disappointment at the loss of the Burma campaign." But, the Americans thought Chiang's financial demands were not warranted on any grounds and were nothing more than a blatant attempt by Chiang to maximize his possible take from the United States. Equally important, they had expended considerable effort to aid China and expected their money's worth. After pleas from Roosevelt, Chiang in January 1944 permitted the American-trained Chinese forces in India to be employed in the drive toward Myitkyina in northern Burma, which Stilwell had recently launched, but he refused to budge on the use of Chinese troops who were to push into Burma from China or on his aid and monetary demands. To Americans, the conclusion was inescapable: Chiang was linking aid and money with operations in Burma.[39]

When Chiang sent the United States a virtual ultimatum on the exchange rate issue in January 1944, Somervell was outraged, for he calculated that the airfields would cost $800 million if Chiang held to the 20 to 1 rate instead of the $20 million that the United States estimated they should cost. The army could not possibly defend $800 million before Congress, so Somervell told Secretary of the Treasury Morgenthau, Stimson, and Marshall that it was time to get tough with Chiang. He proposed that the army might crack down on the Chinese by denying them gasoline or shipping space, it might withdraw American support from Chiang and spend as much as $100 million to buy one of his rivals, or it might even "stop building airports in China and . . . approach Japan from another direction."

Entrusted with the job of coordinating all policy statements on the exchange issue among the interested government agencies, Somervell prepared a hard-hitting response to Chiang's ultimatum. He stated that the United States must have a suitable arrangement for paying for its military program in China, either by a realistic exchange rate, outright donations from the Chinese, or some form of reverse lend-lease. Roosevelt approved Somervell's draft. However, he then decided not to send it unless the State Department approved. Fearful that Somervell's draft was "much too strong" and might lead to an irrevocable break between the United States and China, State withheld its assent and convinced Roosevelt to send a softer reply that proposed an interim rate more favorable to the United States, as well as negotiations for a permanent solution.[40]

The Chinese reply to Roosevelt's message was not acceptable, but the AAF had to have the airfields for MATTERHORN completed as soon as possible, even if the costs were excessive. Although still feeling imposed upon by Chiang, Somervell and his colleagues now took a softer line so that the airfields would get built. As a quick fix, the United States in effect agreed to a temporary exchange rate of 100 to 1. During the spring of 1944, American and Chinese officials negotiated at a desultory pace for a permanent understanding while construction on the airfields went ahead at a satisfactory rate. By June 1944, the Cheng-tu airfields were practically completed, and in November, Somervell's office finalized their cost by settling the account for the year at $185 million. The whole affair soured Somervell on the Chinese leadership and persuaded him that they were extortionists and scarcely worthy of American support.[41]

While American and Chinese officials haggled over exchange rates, American strategic planners were rethinking the place of China in the war. Doubtful that the Chinese had the stomach for any real fighting and that the overland route to China would be secured and readied in time for Chinese troops to undertake major offensives against the Japanese before 1946 or 1947, the OPD in early 1944 recommended that the United States limit its role in China to air operations and concentrate on the drive against Japan across the Pacific. Under their plan, Stilwell would seize Myitkyina in order to shorten the air route to China by building airfields in the surrounding area, but there would be no advance or development of the Ledo Road beyond Myitkyina, except possibly for a one-way gravel road.

The British, thinking along the same lines, suggested that the Ledo Road was now "out of step with global strategy" and should be halted at Myitkyina. The AAF, which chose to bet all its money on air supply of China, agreed, as did the navy, which questioned any operation that might detract from its amphibious operations in the Pacific. Somervell was wary of any strategy that downgraded the land route to China. Unlike many American planners, Somervell doubted that Japan could be defeated without a major campaign on the Asian mainland. As long as there was even a possibility that the United States might require a port in China to play a role in the invasion of Japan, then, completion of the land route was desirable so that tactical air units and Chinese troops could assist in its capture.[42]

Despite the imposing coalition opposing him, Somervell prevailed. By the middle of May, Stilwell's troops were approaching Myitkyina. Since the advance was going well, Somervell, arguing that it would now be foolish to abandon the road or the pipeline, advised Thomas Handy that Stilwell and Mountbatten should be instructed "to construct and maintain the maximum ground line communications to CHINA, particularly the LEDO-KUNMING Road and the pipelines paralleling that road."

The OPD vetoed Somervell's proposal on the grounds that "it would simply mean no agreement by the British Chiefs of Staff unless we also agreed to furnish additional forces which we cannot spare from our major effort in the Pacific." Moreover, the JCS and the CCS were determined that the emphasis in the CBI must be placed on the air route. Therefore, on May 27 and June 8 respectively, they directed Stilwell and Mountbatten to gave priority to the buildup of the air link to China in order to assist future operations in the Pacific. However, Somervell persuaded the high command to advise the Allied commanders that they were also "to be prepared to exploit the development of overland communications to China" within the constraints "dictated by the forces at present available or firmly allocated" to them. While vague, these instructions kept the Ledo Road and the pipeline projects alive as part of the CBI logistical plan.[43]

As the future of American operations in the CBI were being debated, work went ahead on the most pressing projects. In William Covell, the SOS commander in the CBI, Somervell had a leader who understood what Somervell expected of him. When Covell had been named to the post, Somervell had told him not to tolerate any slack performance. After being on the job a few days, Covell wrote Somervell that "we will make every effort to adjust men to jobs they CAN fill but we will be ruthless in getting rid of the hopeless ones." Covell was true to his word. He sent the weak links home, and where possible, Somervell sent him the replacements he needed. Before long, there was an energy in the command that had been previously lacking.[44]

Covell's most important task at first was to improve the Calcutta-Assam LOC supply line. The docks at Calcutta were clogged with supplies, and it required more than sixty days to ship supplies from Calcutta to Assam because of the inefficient operation of the rail and barge lines. To Somervell, the problem was simple: there was no military director for either and, thus, it seemed, no priority for military supplies. At his request, Marshall wrote Roosevelt at the end of January 1944 urging him to ask Churchill to place Calcutta and more of the Assam LOC under military control. British civilian authorities in India opposed military control, but whether by Churchill's intervention or not, Viceroy Wavell instituted changes in early February. Although Calcutta was not placed under military control, a civilian controller was given full power over the port's operations, and the United States was given complete use of the King George V Docks. A month later, Covell negotiated a system of partial military control for the Assam LOC that included turning over more of the railway to American troops.[45]

By the middle of March, American port companies had the King George V Docks completely cleared, and in April, Covell wrote Somervell that "no special concern need be given to the capacity of the port of Calcutta." At the same time, with American railway troops on the job, rail traffic on the Bengal and Assam Railway jumped significantly, and in May, Covell told Somervell that "the problem of the Assam LOC is licked and should remain so except for acts of God and of the public enemy." By July 1944, the Assam LOC was handling as much monthly tonnage as had been established as the target for January 1946, with the prospect of further increases.[46]

Somervell was pleased by these developments, yet he had no sooner ensured at the end of May 1944 that the Ledo Road would continue as part of the CBI logistical plan than he had to fight a new battle to keep it from being downgraded. With an American landing in the Philippines apparently close at hand, the OPD in July 1944 proposed that road work beyond Myitkyina should be limited to an expeditious improvement of old trails so as to accommodate the movement of trucks and artillery. OPD's proposal angered Somervell. Arguing that too much effort had gone into the project to see it downgraded, Somervell told Handy that a two-way road could be completed before the 1945 monsoons and that it could yet play a significant role in the war if the American drive in the Pacific were seriously delayed.

The OPD was not moved by Somervell's argument. In August it advised Marshall that, if the Ledo Road were reduced to one-way traffic, it could still meet the minimum needs of the Chinese divisions that had been trained and equipped by the United States. Looking to conserve men for Pacific operations, Marshall agreed with the OPD and ordered that construction between Myitkyina, which was finally captured in August, should be limited to a one-lane, all-weather road with a minimum of permanent bridges and one six-inch and two four-inch pipelines to China.[47]

Through the fall of 1944, work went ahead on the Ledo Road at a rapid rate (see Map 4). By October, construction had reached the vicinity of Myitkyina. Thereafter, progress was swift. On January 27, 1945, Chinese troops advancing from India made contact with those who had advanced into Burma from Yunnan. The linkup with the Burma Road had been achieved, finally opening the land route to China. Six months later, a four-inch pipeline to Kunming, China, was completed. In the meantime, at the suggestion of Chiang, the Ledo Road-Burma Road was renamed the Stilwell Road. However, to many who were aware of Somervell's unbending support of the project, it should have been renamed Somervell's Road.[48]

Meanwhile, the place of China in the war effort further declined. Chennault's air operations in China proved disappointing, and in the summer and fall of 1944, Japanese advances forced him to devote most of his forces to the defense of his bases. MATTERHORN also proved disappointing, and in early 1945, logistical considerations and a Japanese threat to its bases led to its abandonment. Furthermore, in the fall of 1944, the long-standing feud between Chiang and Stilwell finally caused Roosevelt to recall Stilwell. Under these circumstances, there was no inclination to increase any investment in the CBI. Where once Americans had entertained high hopes about China in the war effort, they now saw it as little more than a backwater.

Even so, Somervell stubbornly refused to accept as final Marshall's decision that the Ledo Road beyond Myitkyina should be one-way. He contended that continuous traffic could not be maintained during the monsoon season unless it was widened to two lanes and that a one-way road along with the airlift could not provide enough supplies for the projected operations in China in 1945, but the decision went against him. Since the airlift was to be enlarged by the assignment of more transports to the theater and the use of airfields in Bengal freed by the ending of MATTERHORN, the Air Transport Command (ATC) argued that it could meet all the demands placed upon it. For a time, it seemed Somervell's concerns were justified, for the ATC had trouble living up to its projections. In May, however, the ATC was able to improve its performance, ending any question of further development of the Ledo Road as far as the high command was concerned.[49]

Despite Somervell's failure to get formal approval for expanding the Ledo Road project, work proceeded along the lines he advocated. Certain a one-lane road would be too difficult to maintain during the monsoon, the Engineers, with Somervell's consent, widened the road beyond Myitkyina to two lanes after all, and Somervell laid on procurement of enough bridging to complete the task. By April 1945, the road was two-lanes wide from Myitkyina to Bhamo, and by June, it was two lanes as far as the Burma Road. In addition, a six-inch pipeline was completed to Myitkyina, one four-inch to Kunming, and another four-inch to Bhamo.[50]

Although it was a great engineering feat, the Ledo Road, like so much of what the United States attempted in the CBI, was largely a futile enterprise. Built at an estimated cost of $148 million, it was never able to deliver the supplies originally projected. At most, it played a role in supplying Stilwell's drive to eliminate the Japanese from northern Burma, assisted the Hump airlift, and provided the Chinese with vehicles and gasoline in the summer of 1945. Moreover, maintenance consumed a prohibitive amount of resources, and the ATC delivered in several days what the road and pipeline could in a month.

Somervell, however, never doubted the wisdom of the project. His only regret was that it was "never carried through as planned and was never used as planned because of vacillation in the top command." Had there been better management in the earlier stages of the construction and had the "original decision been followed through vigorously," he later lamented, "the results in CBI could have been obtained a year sooner."[51]

• • •

As the war against Germany approached its end, Somervell increasingly turned his attention to the logistics of a one-front war against Japan. His primary concern was the planning for redeployment, which he dubbed the "biggest moving job in history." Redeployment entailed the reversing of the whole logistical processes of the European and Mediterranean theaters and the shifting of the center of gravity of the logistical processes in the United States from the east to the west coast so that the United States could concentrate the brunt of its military power in the Western Pacific against Japan. Precise planning for the efficient use of shipping, inland transportation in the United States, and staging areas and ports was required since redeployment would involve troop and supply movements of unprecedented size over longer distances and in a shorter time period than in any previous operation.[52]

Somervell had his staff first look at the redeployment issue in the spring of 1943, but lacking any indication from the JCS about the size of the forces to be utilized in the invasion of Japan, his efforts had an air of unreality about them. In August 1944, as Germany appeared on its last legs, redeployment planning took on a sense of urgency. The OPD established a committee to lay down policies for the redeployment of the army, and in early September, it submitted specific recommendations. Redeployment was still divorced from a definite strategy, though, and leery of what demands redeployment would place upon him, Somervell steadily bombarded the OPD and Marshall with memoranda demanding a firm redeployment troop basis on which he could base planning for procurement and the movement of troops and supplies.[53] They, however, could provide him with little immediate help until Allied planners hashed out the final plans for the defeat of Japan.

In April 1945, the JCS finally approved a redeployment plan based on the assumption that it would take eighteen months to defeat Japan after the surrender of Germany, which was expected to be accomplished by July 1945. Even so, the plan was not final in regard to many crucial elements and, in all probability, was adopted because Somervell's pleas convinced Marshall that some planning decision had to be made. Not surprisingly, therefore, Somervell was still complaining about the lack of strategic guidance when the European war ended in May and the JCS were preparing to issue their final directive for the invasion of Kyushu, Operation OLYMPIC. Originally scheduled for December 1, 1945, the target date was later moved up to November 1 because the weather conditions were more suitable in November than December. The main island of Honshu was to be attacked in 1946.[54]

Development of the redeployment plan was complicated by the issue of command in the Pacific. Until this issue was resolved, many of the logistical details could not be settled. A unified joint command was the ideal situation; however, everyone knew it would be practically impossible to achieve. Facing large-scale land operations in the proposed invasion of Japan, the army would not consider entrusting the command of its divisions to a naval officer. And the navy would not consider turning over the direction of its vast fleets to an army officer. Therefore, from the army point of view, its interests would best be protected by having separate army and navy commands, each controlling its own resources and coordinating its operations in line with the strategy laid down by the JCS. In effect, the joint logistical system that had been developed in POA had to be unscrambled.

After much resistance from the navy, the army finally achieved its objective. On April 3, 1945, the JCS designated MacArthur as commander in chief of all army forces in the Pacific and placed almost all army resources there under his command and similarly placed all naval forces in the Pacific under Nimitz's command. However, progress in developing a new logistical system in the POA was slow. The JCS's directive had essentially left this task to mutual agreement between MacArthur and Nimitz, but little was initially accomplished, for Nimitz resisted turning over army forces and resources in the POA to MacArthur until the operation to seize Okinawa, which started on April 1, was completed. Moreover, he indicated that he would not turn over resources until a possible landing on the China coast that he had been advocating as a preliminary step to the invasion of Japan was completed. Nimitz's obstinacy made it difficult for MacArthur to make a firm estimate of the forces and resources that would be available for OLYMPIC and consequently compounded Somervell's planning.

Infuriated by Nimitz's stalling, Somervell bitterly complained to Marshall on May 21 that the navy's failure to comply with the spirit of the JCS directive threatened the army's ability to assemble troops and supplies for OLYMPIC. A new JCS directive on May 25 authorizing OLYMPIC went far toward addressing Somervell's concerns because it led Nimitz to cancel both operations in the Ryukyus beyond Okinawa and preparations for an invasion of China, but it did not make any definite provision as to the time Nimitz should release army resources. A month later, service representatives worked out some limited arrangements for the Kyushu operation. However, they made no mention of the release of army garrisons or shipping in the POA. Hence, Somervell continued to complain that the existing system created needless uncertainty in requirements for the Pacific war.[55]

Redeployment officially began on May 12, 1945. Despite some problems in obtaining sufficient shipping because of competing demands, the army began the move of 1.2 Million men from Europe (800,000 by way of the United States and 400,000 directly) to the Pacific, the transfer of 5 million tons of supplies and equipment from Europe to the Pacific, and the return of another 5 million tons of materiel to the United States. At the same time, Somervell was rushing supplies to the Pacific for the final assault against Japan. Lacking hard data from MacArthur's headquarters on the reception capacity in the Pacific, he shipped supplies on the basis of the gross capacity of the Pacific areas to receive them, not a careful matching of cargoes and specific destinations. Then, as MacArthur finalized his plans, Somervell had to make a flurry of changes, a process that was not completed when the war ended.[56]

During July, Somervell escaped some of his problems by going to Europe for the Potsdam Conference. Since most matters on the agenda were essentially political in character, Somervell spent his days looking into the disposition of

American supplies and captured or surrendered German equipment, as well as fighting bed bugs and mosquitoes. Following the conference, he toured American facilities in Germany, the Low Countries, Italy, and France and then returned to Washington in early August. As soon as the atomic bombs were dropped on the Japanese cities of Hiroshima and Nagasaki, he began completing plans for the demobilization of the army. Meeting with his staff on August 10, he emphasized that he wanted the same sense of urgency that had prevailed in the mobilization of the army to prevail in its demobilization. Five days later, Japan sued for peace, effectively ending World War II.[57]

• • •

By the summer of 1945, Somervell had decided to leave the army as soon as circumstances permitted. In March 1945, he had been promoted to the temporary rank of full general, making him one of eleven four-star generals on active duty. (In 1948, Somervell was promoted to the permanent rank of four-star general on the retired list.) But, as he examined his prospects in the postwar army, he found little that was appealing.

It was already known that the post of chief of staff would probably be filled by Eisenhower because of the stature he had achieved as the victor over Hitler. Other than that post, Somervell could not see any challenge or degree of responsibility in the peacetime army comparable to what he had experienced as the army's chief logistician. Somervell was also anxious to try something else and, at the same time, improve his personal finances. Both considerations prompted him to look at private business because it would give him a new field to conquer and the opportunity to improve his financial picture.[58]

Three days after V-J Day, Somervell told Marshall that he wanted to leave the army on the day that Marshall, who would soon be stepping down from his post, retired. Meanwhile, Somervell was busy overseeing many aspects of the army's demobilization and working behind the scenes to see that members of his first team were promoted on the permanent list and received appropriate postwar assignments. On October 14, he went to the Ashford General Hospital in White Sulphur Springs, West Virginia, for a complete physical examination and "a repair job on a hernia" that he had "nursed thru the war." The repair job took two operations and kept Somervell out of Washington for more than a month.[59]

On November 20, 1945, Marshall retired from the army, but Somervell's departure was postponed by his recovery from the operations. On December 17, 1945, he performed his last major duty in uniform by testifying before the Senate Military Affairs Committee in support of the War Department's proposal for unification of the armed services. Citing numerous examples of army-navy competition in procurement, he urged the creation of a director of common supply in a unified military establishment who would be responsible for such noncombat units as the medical and quartermaster corps, nursing, and procurement services. Somervell would not be around for the real fight over unification, which was not accepted then and not completely now. Several days later, his retirement set for April 30, 1946, he began a 120-day terminal leave.[60]

• • •

Somervell's work as the army's chief logistician during World War II was marked by a consistent ability to get things done. Drawing upon the managerial skills that he had developed before the war, surrounding himself with skilled subordinates, infusing his organization with his own driving personality, and recognizing that logistics was a major key to victory, he spared no effort to ensure that the American fighting man had everything he needed to win the war. In carrying out his mission, Somervell was not without his faults. Having little use for opposing authority, he too readily feuded with other agencies in and outside the army. Impatient with delay, he sometimes too readily sacked officers without taking into full account the difficulties that they faced. And, always anxious to tackle a challenge, he too readily pushed extravagant projects with little regard for their costs and ultimate value to the war effort.

These faults pale in the light of his contributions to victory. Speaking years later, Marshall left no doubt about the value of Somervell's work. "He was one of the most efficient officers I have ever seen." He "got things done in Calcutta as fast as he did in the meadows around the Pentagon. Whenever I asked him for something he did it and got it." Marshall went on to say, "if I went into control in another war, I would start looking for another General Somervell the very first thing I did and so would anybody else who went through that struggle on this side."[61]

13. INDUSTRIAL MANAGER

• • • • SOMERVELL BEGAN HIS RETIREMENT BY moving to Ocala, Florida, where he sifted through a number of business opportunities. The most intriguing was an offer from Koppers Company. Only days after Somervell had arrived in Florida, Frank R. Denton, vice president and chief executive of the Mellon National Bank and Trust Company of Pittsburgh, Pennsylvania, had visited him to discuss the presidency of Koppers. Denton, who had served under Somervell in the ASF as deputy director of the Production Division, was sent to Florida by Richard K. Mellon, the overseer of the vast Mellon holdings and another ASF veteran. From their wartime contacts with him, both Denton and Mellon believed that Somervell was a "scorcher" as a manager and just the man to take over from the caretaker management that had been running Koppers since 1944. Denton brought with him a 147-page prospectus outlining the direction they wanted the company to take, and after reviewing it thoroughly and traveling to Pittsburgh to discuss the position with Mellon, Somervell in March 1946 accepted their offer to become the company's president at an annual salary of $75,000.[1]

Koppers was the dog of the Mellon holdings. It had come into existence in the early years of the century to manufacture a by-product coke oven that made it possible to recover the chemicals which previously had been lost up the chimney of the old-fashioned beehive coke oven. Under the leadership of Henry B. Rust, president from 1915 until 1933, it experienced spectacular growth. Afflicted with conglomeritis, Rust expanded in many directions—soft-coal mining, construction and operation of artificial gas and by-product coke plants, ownership of a steel company and blast furnaces, refining of crude tar, wood preserving, the manufacture of piston rings, and effective control of the Virginian Railroad and Eastern Gas and Fuel Associates, a public-utility holding company. During World War II, the company got into still another field when it built and operated a plant at Kobuta, Pennsylvania, for the government to manufacture styrene and butadiene for the synthetic rubber program.

While spectacular, the growth had brought problems. There were more than 150 companies in the Koppers empire, and each operated, for all practical purposes, as an autonomous enterprise. No "two ever pulled together," even though most were in one way or another related to a lump of coal. Koppers always made money. However, it required most of its earnings and large amounts of Mellon credit to keep it going in the never-ending task of rounding-out its empire.[2]

During World War II, Richard Mellon decided to clean up the Koppers mishmash. Spurred by poor earnings from the public utilities and the obvious need to bring order to the corporate structure, he had the company reorganized in 1944. Plans were developed to sell Eastern Gas and Fuel, which had the effect of taking Koppers out of the utility business and almost everything that went with it, such as the coal mining and railroad operations. Other elements were consolidated into one company, but the reorganization did not deal with one overriding problem—the need for fresh leadership.

J.P. Tierney, who had been running the company since Rust's retirement, died in 1944, and Mellon saw no effective replacement among the existing executives. Most seemed to be too much a part of the Rust tradition of operations, and Mellon concluded that Koppers needed a new executive outside of the Rust past to pull it together. After a thorough search, he judged that Somervell had the planning, organizing, and administrative expertise to do the job.[3]

Although he had not previously been in business, Somervell was not concerned about the demands of his new job. Koppers had only 14,000 employees and approximately 60 facilities, and running it could hardly be any more difficult than supplying an army fighting a global war. To his way of thinking, the army and business were very much alike except that the test in business was more immediate, namely how much money the company made the last year. Somervell was also certain that he would succeed. His army experience had exposed him to many business and financial problems. Moreover, as Denton and Mellon made clear, Koppers needed centralized direction above all else, and Somervell was confident that the control system he had developed and implemented while in the army would bring order out of the chaos at Koppers.

Finally, Mellon had promised practically a free hand to Somervell to do what had to be done with Koppers.

• • •

Somervell took over at Koppers on May 1, 1946, and spent the next two months sizing up the company's operations. Despite the 1944 restructuring, little had changed. The operating divisions were functioning as feudal kingdoms in the same manner as they had when they were separate companies. Each had its own sales offices, production department, and research facilities (if any), and they were only loosely tied together by central staff departments. There was no across-the-board company policy, and vice presidents often did not talk to each other. Even within a division, there was no unity, and thus several sales offices would sometimes compete with each other by submitting bids to provide materials for the same contract. At the company's headquarters in Pittsburgh, the president's office had so little staff that Somervell "had to do his own figuring with his own pencil."[4]

In July 1946, Somervell moved to change all that. Building on the start already taken in 1944, he proposed that Koppers be restructured around eight operating divisions and eight staff departments that would impose functional authority on the divisions. He also drew up a statement of objectives along with a program for accomplishing them. Several directors opposed Somervell's proposals on the grounds that he wanted to make too many changes too quickly, but Somervell had anticipated this opposition and had prepared for it by having Mellon, who was not present at the July 29 board meeting when Somervell's proposals were discussed, provide him with a letter of endorsement. After Somervell read Mellon's letter, the board granted its approval, and there was no longer any doubt that Somervell was in charge.[5]

The most notable aspect of the Somervell organization was the creation of the Control Section in his office. It would be his eyes and ears, furthering the unity and centralized control that Somervell believed was essential to the company's long-term success. To head the Control Section, Somervell chose George M. Walker, a civil engineer who had worked with the construction division, the gas and coke division, and the finance department, as well as at Kobuta. Walker's first assignment was to develop and implement a reporting mechanism so that Somervell could have continual supervision of the company's entire organization. Modeling it after Somervell's wartime system, Walker had the reporting system operating within months, and by 1948, it was completely in place.

Somervell would state the overall direction that he wanted the company to take, and then, the Control Section negotiated an annual program for each division against which monthly, quarterly, and yearly progress could be measured. The program spelled out, among other things, targets for sales and profits, inventory forecasts, and raw material and capital requirements. The staff departments also drew up programs covering their projected activities and expenses. Taken together, these programs constituted the Koppers corporate program.[6]

The development of the program involved considerable tug and pull between Walker and the division heads. Somervell insisted upon demanding goals, while the division heads were wary of specific goals against which their performance could be measured, especially profits. As Somervell later remarked about the "innate conservatism of the average businessman," he will "hit his sales estimates . . . within 10 percent but on profits the tendency is for a man to discount his own estimates by anything from 10 to 25 percent, depending on his nature. After all, nobody likes to be asked why he didn't make his goal." Once Walker had negotiated a program with a division head, it went to Somervell for his review, and he either approved it or kicked it back for renegotiation.

The monthly progress report was the measuring stick for the program. About the fourth day of each month the divisions and departments started sending detailed reports on sales, profits, investments, inventories, unfilled orders, and other matters for the previous month to the Control Section. Control analyzed them, looking particularly to see where a division had fallen short of its goals or greatly exceeded them and, then, determining what accounted for the performance. It put all pertinent information into a 100-to 150-page report replete with tables, graphs, and charts. The core of the report was the detailed data for every division and, within each division, for every plant and product for the month and the year to date. Goal figures for comparison and each manager's thoughts on the outlook for the future were also included. On the third Thursday of the month, the report was sent to Somervell and about 130 company executives. Over the next several days, Somervell studied it thoroughly, generously dotting his copy with questions written in red ink based on a briefing given him by Walker.

On the following Tuesday, the company's operating committee—Somervell and the division and department heads—met to discuss the report. The meeting began early, and it could last well into the evening. At all times, Somervell was in charge. He went over the report in great detail, praising good results and asking questions about below par performances. Possessing the ability, as one manager recalled, "to make you squirm by looking right through you" and ready "to rip you up one side and down the other" if displeased, Somervell could be quite severe in his questioning. By the end of the meeting, Somervell had "an accurate, complete, up-to-date picture" of practically every company activity, while every manager had been compelled to "face up squarely to every detail" in his operations and every problem he confronted.

Somervell gave the Control Section other jobs as well. Shortly after the section was created, Somervell told Walker to prepare an organization manual. Koppers never had such a manual previously, and Somervell believed that clear-cut lines of authority and areas of responsibility, such as he had known in the military, were essential if the company were to operate efficiently. Only if jobs and functions were nailed down, could the reporting system work.

Walker completed the manual by the end of 1946 and revised it in 1949. It spelled out job descriptions for every manager in the company, as well as limits of authority and responsibility. Walker's Control Section also drew up a procedural manual detailing how transactions should be handled and developed standard forms for the company.

The Koppers managers greeted the Control Section "with a great deal of anxiety and trepidation" and "a certain amount of resentment." They complained that Walker wanted too much information from them, that it took too much time to prepare the reports, and that Control would try to tell them what to do, and certainly, many did not like the Control Section because "it had the facts by which performance could be judged." Gradually, Koppers's managers adapted to Somervell's notion of control. In his seventeen years at Koppers, Walker had come to know many of the managers, making it easier to sell the new system to them than if he had been an outsider. Moreover, the managers realized that they had no choice. Walker had the backing of Somervell in everything he did, and Somervell had the backing of Mellon.

Finally, it soon became apparent that the Control Section had achieved its purpose. Through the reporting mechanism and the organization and procedures manuals, Somervell was pulling the company together. What previously had been separate operations were now being unified and coordinated to provide a solid foundation for directed growth and improved profit performance. Koppers, as one executive later commented, was becoming capable of doing things it could not previously have done.[7]

Somervell's control methods were at the cutting edge of management principles in the late 1940s. Many had been long taught in business schools and practiced in numerous firms, but Somervell's system stood out because of the emphasis he placed upon detail and, most importantly, upon the role of the Control Section. Other firms usually spread the responsibilities for programming, planning, coordinating, reporting, and so forth among several departments or assigned them as secondary duties to a unit like the finance department. In both cases, these responsibilities were often performed less vigorously, if at all. At Koppers, Somervell concentrated them in one section and placed that section in his office so that he could personally direct the business. Before long, many firms were sending requests to Koppers to learn more about his methods, and in 1949, they received extensive attention in national and trade publications.[8]

The introduction of his management methods was the most important change that Somervell brought to Koppers in his first years, but his presence was soon felt in other areas as well. Where previously Koppers's management had pretty much been an old boys club, Somervell began to bring in new blood, often recruiting former ASF people for key posts.

In addition to changes in personnel, he instituted an incentive payment plan for key individuals that provided substantial salary increments for those whose divisions earned more money than "what might reasonably be expected under existing market conditions." Later, Somervell added stock options and phantom stock (an executive was assigned stock, but not ownership of it, and received dividends and the increased value of the stock when he retired) to round out the plan.

Somervell also did not lose sight of the importance of getting the most from the hundreds of salaried employees who made the company run on a day-to-day basis. It was not uncommon for a salaried employee in one division to receive considerably more pay than one in another division even though both had the same job. This type of incongruity grated on Somervell's sense of order because he was convinced inequities like these impeded performance by sapping morale. Thus, he had every salaried position in the company evaluated to determine an appropriate classification and then implemented a companywide pay program based on a specified salary range for each classification.

Other changes were no less significant. Consolidated sales officers were set up in a number of cities, and an annual sales meeting was instituted so that Somervell could inspire the troops "on the battlefront" and have them work in step.[9]

Not surprisingly, considering his wartime role, Somervell readied Koppers for mobilization in case war came again. Wanting to avoid the delays in industrial mobilization experienced in the early days of World War II, he had a company mobilization plan prepared. Under it, the complete production capacity of each Koppers plant was inventoried, estimates were made of the raw materials that would be required for maximum production, and a survey was conducted to determine if there were additional products that the company could manufacture for the government if an emergency arose. On the basis of these findings, company planners drew up a list of plant allocations, tentative production schedules, and additional equipment that might be needed for war output. Koppers was one of the first large corporations to draw up a complete mobilization plan, and in speeches and articles, Somervell urged other companies to emulate Koppers.[10]

As the operating head of Koppers, Somervell pushed an aggressive program of diversification and expansion. He particularly emphasized the chemical operations, regarding them as his pet project. During the war, the company's success in producing butadiene and styrene at Kobuta had convinced company officials that Koppers could have a good future in organics after the war. By the time Somervell joined the company, the decision had been made to move into chemicals on a large scale, and Walker had already negotiated the purchase of the styrene side of the plant from the War Assets Administration, as well as the lease of the other portions of the plant. Later, Koppers bought the butadiene side and acquired facilities to produce chemicals used in the manufacture of resins, adhesives, and pharmaceuticals; chemicals used in the rubber industry and in lubricating oils, synthetic resins, and disinfectants; hydrogen cyanide and sulfuric acid; ethylbenzene; and polythylene.[11]

Over the next few years, Somervell plowed much of the company's capital funds into the chemical operations. Initially, the Chemical Division lost its shirt. But through stepped-up marketing and the development of an expanding product line, its sales skyrocketed, and within five years, it was in second place among the company's divisions in net profits. It produced nearly 20 percent of the nation's styrene and 15 percent of the nation's polystrene, an important ingredient in plastics, and it was the nation's leading producer of resorcinol. Somervell was careful, however, not to bite off more than the company could handle. As a result, he passed up a lot of products like phenol plastics "in which the weight of volume or of competition" had beaten down the profit margin. While never a chemical company in terms of Dow, DuPont, or Monsanto, Koppers, under Somervell, carved out a profitable niche for itself and became "a tidy little chemical company."[12]

The success of other divisions was mixed. The wood preserving division had always emphasized the sale of treated railroad ties and utility poles, but Somervell pushed it to go after the agricultural and industrial market for wood products, such as fence posts, and throughout his tenure it held a steady course in sales and profits. The gas and coke, metal products, and tar products divisions, meanwhile, accounted for considerable sales volume, but were unspectacular in terms of profits.

Finally, the Engineering and Construction Division, the direct descendant of the original coke oven business and the most mercurial division because of its dependence on industrial construction and heavy industry activity, emerged as the company leader in sales and profits. By acquiring in 1949 the Freyn Engineering Corporation and the Open Hearth Combustion Company, leaders in the design and engineering of blast furnaces, open hearth furnaces, and their auxiliaries, Koppers could now engineer and build whole steel mills instead of just coke ovens. The division also built plants for the production of chemicals and gas utilities and other industrial structures.[13]

Somervell closely followed developments with the divisions, not only through the progress reports but also through frequent visits to company facilities. Already well briefed about a facility's function by the Control Section, he would arrive exactly on time. Meticulously dressed and all-business, Somervell always made "a hell of an impression" upon the employees in the facility and automatically commanded respect. He would be armed with specific questions, see everything, and never wander off the subject. If employees were not telling him something he wanted to know, he was telling them something he wanted them to know.

On several occasions, Somervell went abroad to look into the company's foreign operations, traveling to Britain, France, and Turkey in the spring of 1950 and to Chile in the fall of 1950 to participate in the ceremonies for opening a steel plant that Koppers had built. He returned to South America in the fall of 1952. In general, however, Somervell was not especially interested in overseas ventures. While appreciating the need to get business where it was available, he was concerned about "the difficult national and racial relationships which we have to maintain, and also with the difficulty of handling Americans so far away from home."[14]

By the early 1950s, Koppers was a new company. As Mellon had anticipated, Somervell had brought order out of chaos. What previously had been a host of different operations was now a company working toward a common goal. Clear-cut lines of authority and responsibility had been established, and a definite program of growth had been instituted, with a comprehensive system for checking progress. According to one account, Mellon never attended a stockholders' meeting of one of his companies unless he was dissatisfied with the management. After 1946, he had no need to attend a stockholders' meeting at Koppers. Recognizing Somervell's accomplishment, Mellon had him named chairman of the board in March 1950, as well as president, and raised his salary to $125,000.[15]

During Somervell's tenure, Koppers's sales and profits rose dramatically. From $112 million in 1946, sales climbed to $285 million by 1951, and profits climbed from $3 million to $10 million. Book value per share of common stock, $26 in 1946, was nearly $50 in 1951. After 1951, sales and profits leveled off somewhat, and in 1954, they sagged considerably, largely because of a drop in defense orders following the end of the Korean War and a decline in orders for plants that accompanied reduced operations in the steel industry.

Part of Koppers's surge could be attributed to the favorable economic climate of the post-1945 boom, but equally important were the greater efficiency and the controlled expansion that Somervell brought to the company. Never again would Koppers be called a dog. Under Somervell, it had experienced a remarkable comeback.[16]

• • •

Outside of his work with Koppers, Somervell's life after his years in uniform was routine and rather uneventful. Now that he was no longer in Washington, Somervell largely dropped out of the public limelight. In general, he refused to lend his name in support of specific national policies, and for the most part, he refused to take an active part in matters involving the army on the grounds that he did not want it to appear "that I am still trying to run these officers after having gone on the retired list." As he told Ferdinand Eberstadt, "I used to object strenuously to retired officers telling us on the active list how we should conduct our business." Behind the scenes, though, Somervell put in his views against the emasculation of his wartime centralization of service and supply activities but with no result.[17]

Somervell had no direct involvement with the Korean War, although privately he was quite critical of President Truman's leadership. Stunned by the administration's apparent floundering after Douglas MacArthur's defeat at the hands of the Chinese at the end of 1950, he wrote Levin Campbell "that given proper leadership we could do a great job of it. With the gent we have in Washington, however, I am afraid that this is a forlorn hope."

In the spring of 1951, Charles Wilson, who had recently been named head of the Office of Defense Mobilization, asked Somervell to return to government service as director of the Defense Procurement Administration. Wilson's request appealed to Somervell's sense of duty, and for two days, he wrestled with the matter. However, doubting that Truman was willing to go all out to win the war and suspecting that the president was setting him up as a possible scapegoat if trouble developed in the mobilization, Somervell turned down Wilson's request. Truman then personally asked Somervell to reconsider but to no avail. Somervell did not want to be part of a Truman operation.[18]

Increasingly, Somervell was bothered by health problems. Except for the hernia operations at the end of World War II, he had always been in good health and had rarely missed a day's work, but in the fall of 1953, he had an appendectomy, and in the spring of 1954, he had another operation to repair the old hernia that had popped out again. Then, in September 1954, he suffered a severe heart attack, and following his release from the hospital, he went to Ocala for an extended period of recuperation. Slowly he regained his strength, and many at Koppers headquarters expected him to return to the job as the old Somervell. However, he decided in early 1955 to relinquish his position as president and drop out of the company's day-to-day operations. Shortly thereafter, on February 13, Somervell suffered a fatal heart attack while sitting with his wife at their home in Ocala. He was 62 years of age.[19]

APPENDIX

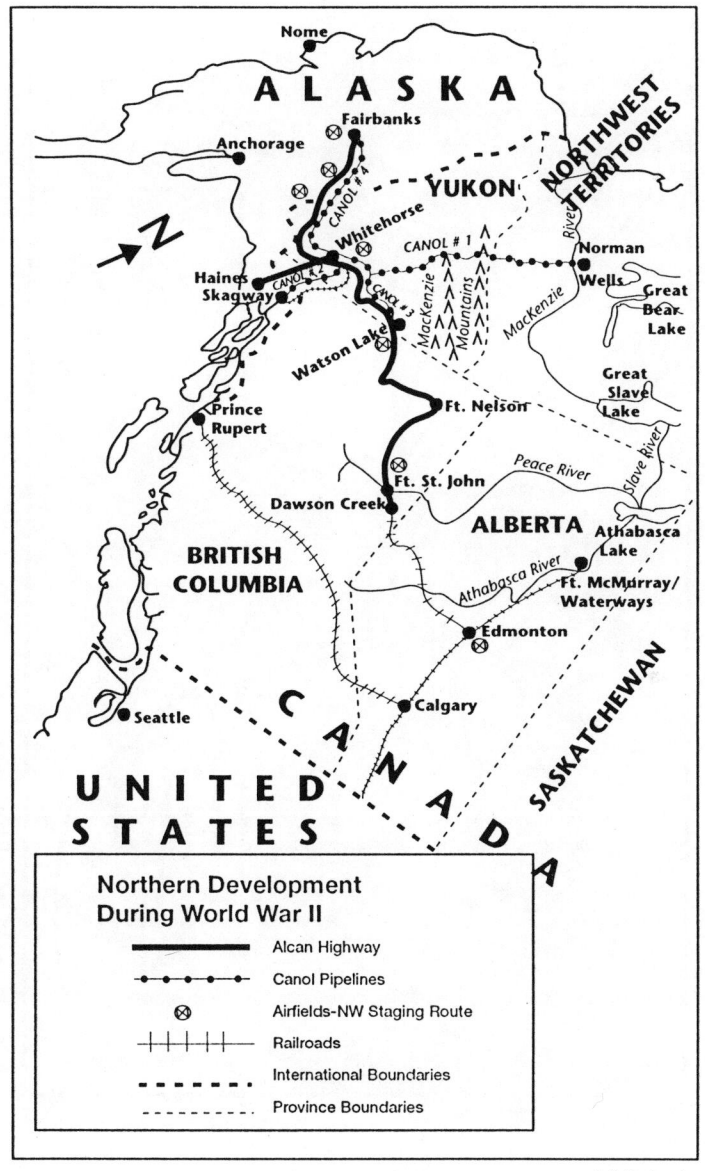

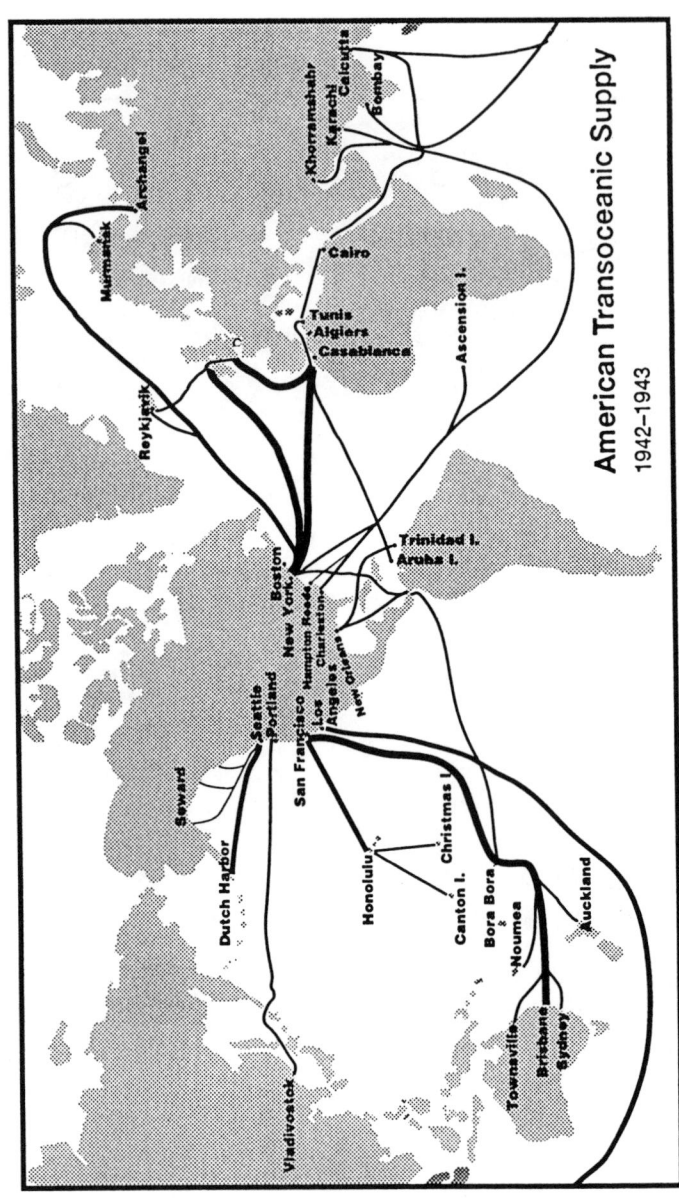

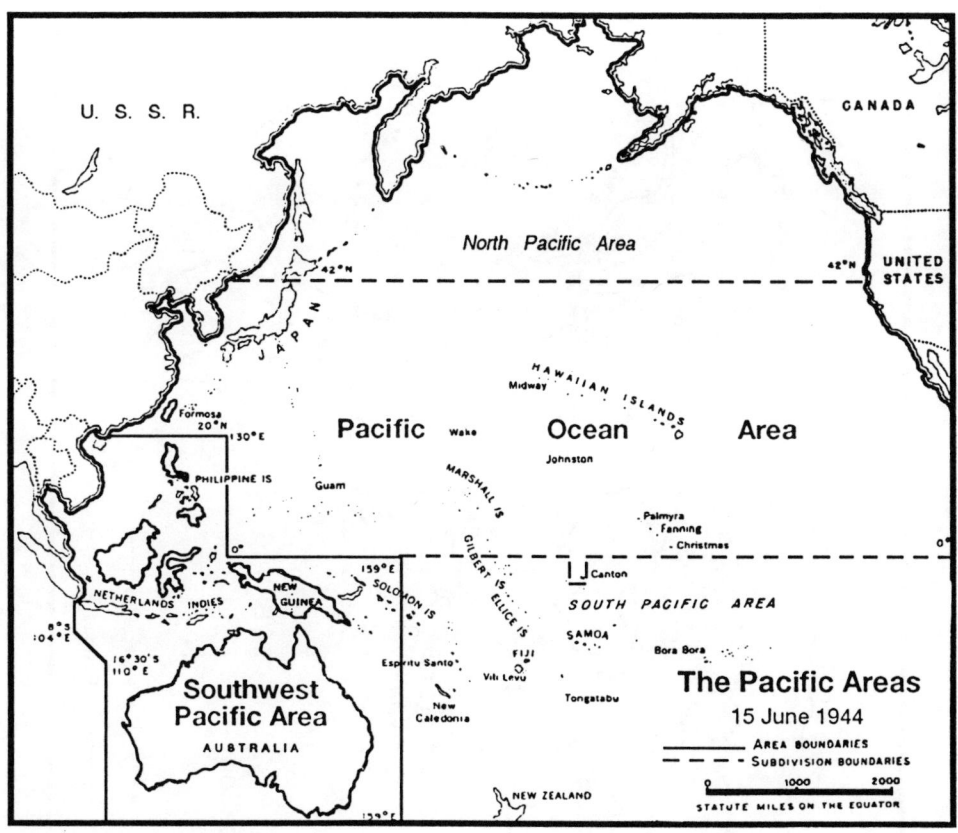

Courtesy of the U.S. Army Center of Military History

R. Johnstone

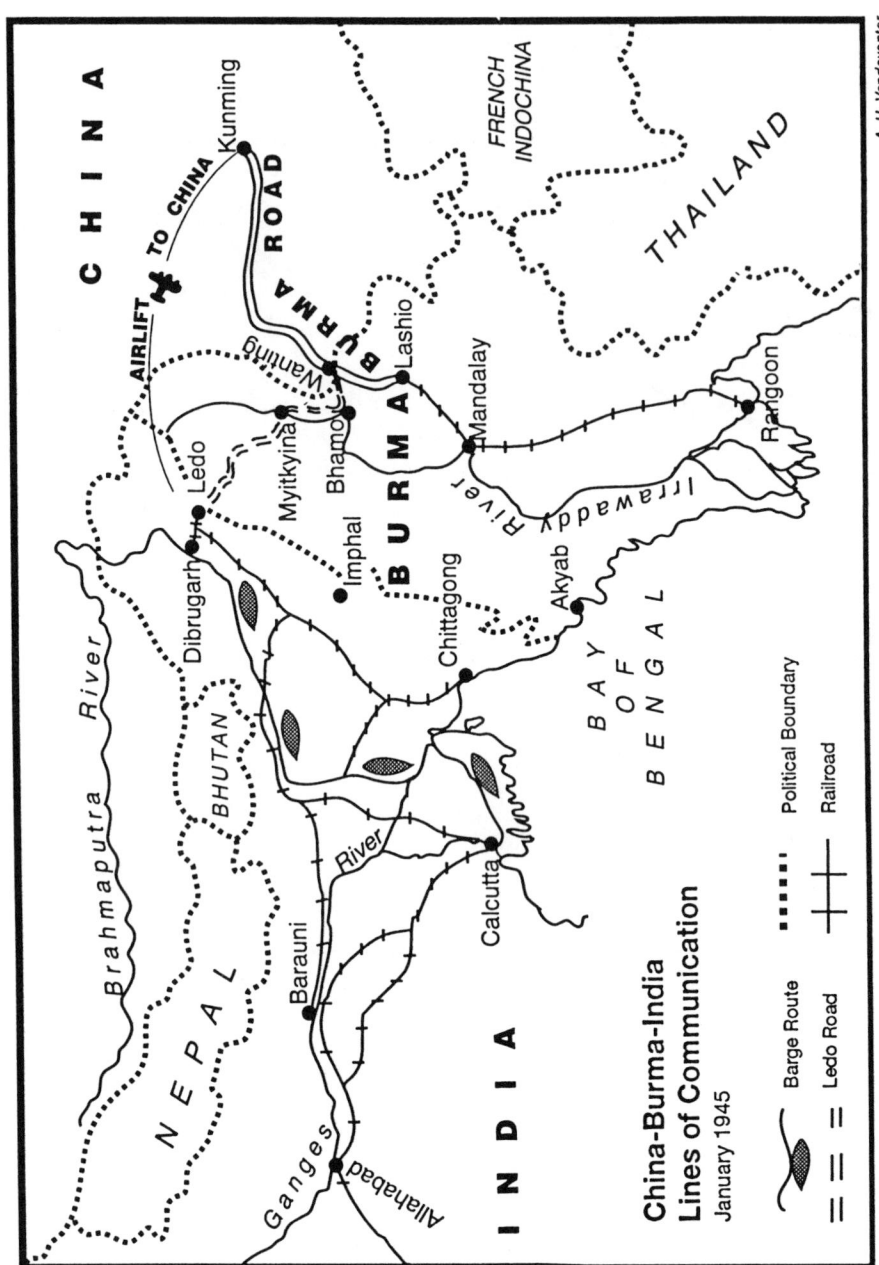

Appendix **265**

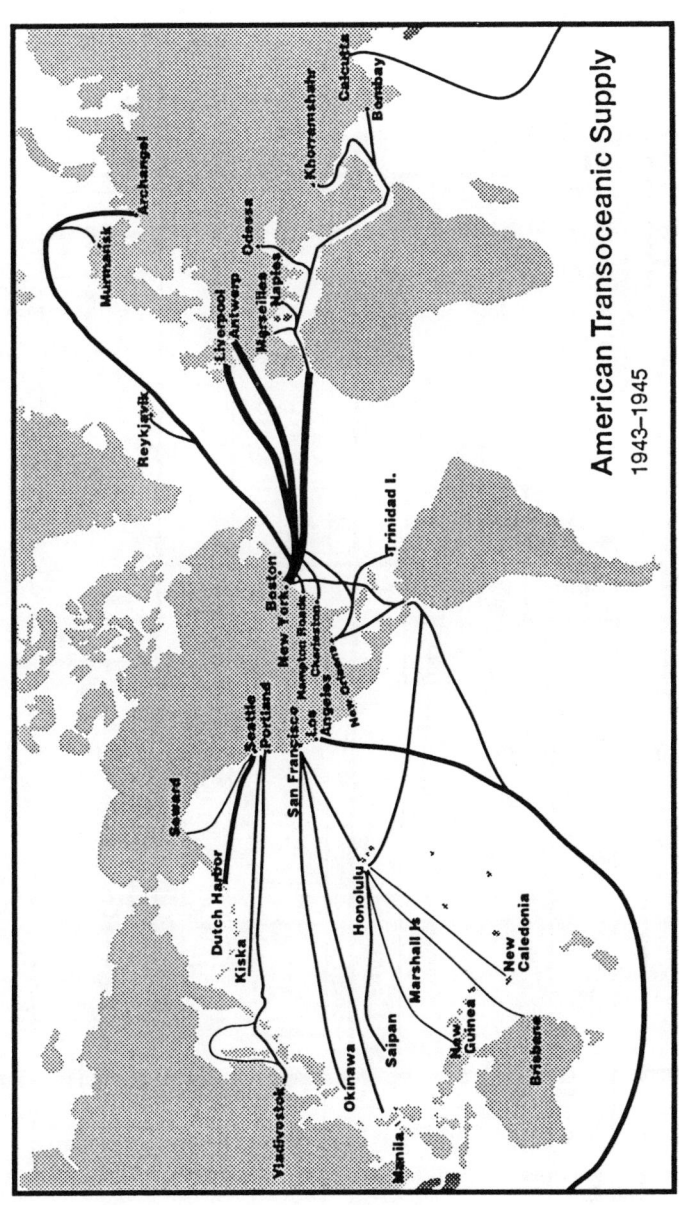

Courtesy of the U.S. Army Center of Military History

Organization of the Army   9 March 1942 (The Marshall Reorganization)

SECRETARY OF WAR
- Under Secretary of War
- Assistant Secretary of War for Air
- Public Relations
- Administrative Assistant and Chief Clerk
- Administrative Assistant and Chief Clerk

CHIEF OF STAFF

DEPUTY CHIEF OF STAFF
- Secretariat

GENERAL STAFF
- WPD
- G-1
- G-2
- G-3
- G-4
- Military Intelligence Service

SPECIAL STAFF
- INSPECTOR GENERAL
- LEGISLATIVE & LIAISON DIVISION

- Commanding General Army Ground Forces
  - Task Force
  - Defense Command
  - Theater
- Commanding General Army Air Forces
- Commanding General Services of Supply

Courtesy of the U.S. Army Center of Military History

Appendix 267

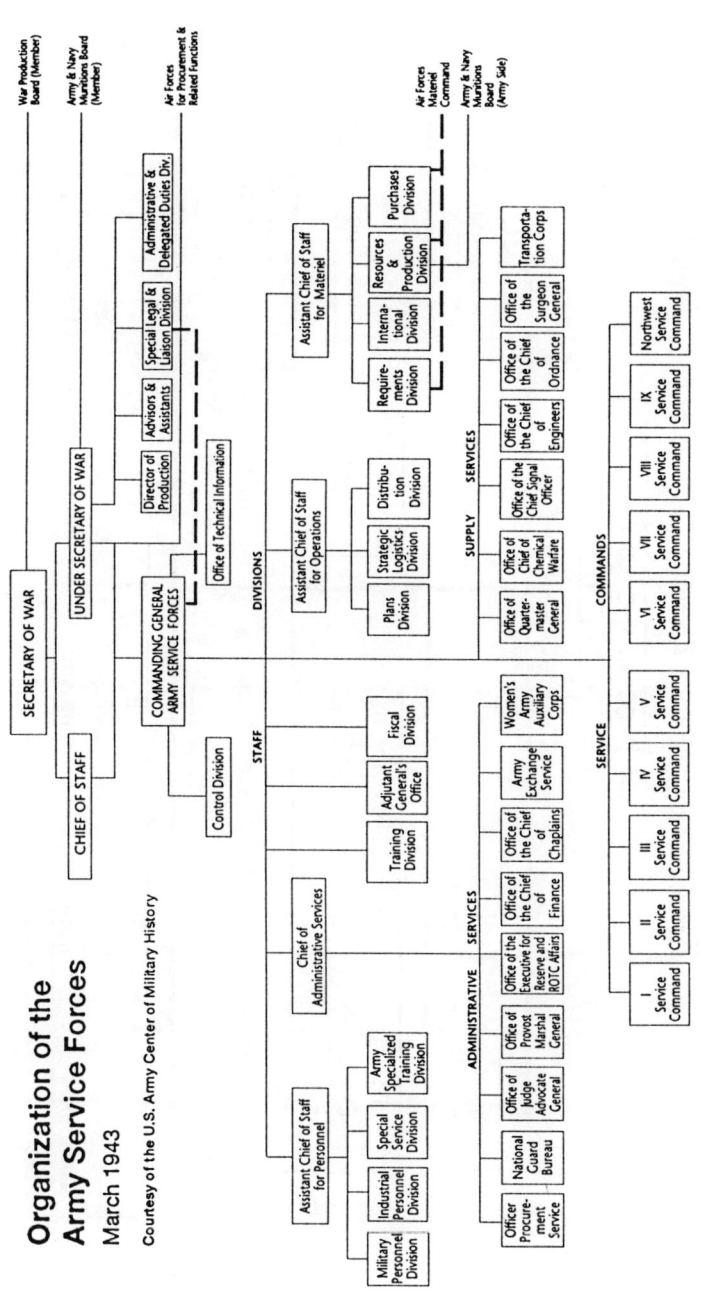

268 Appendix

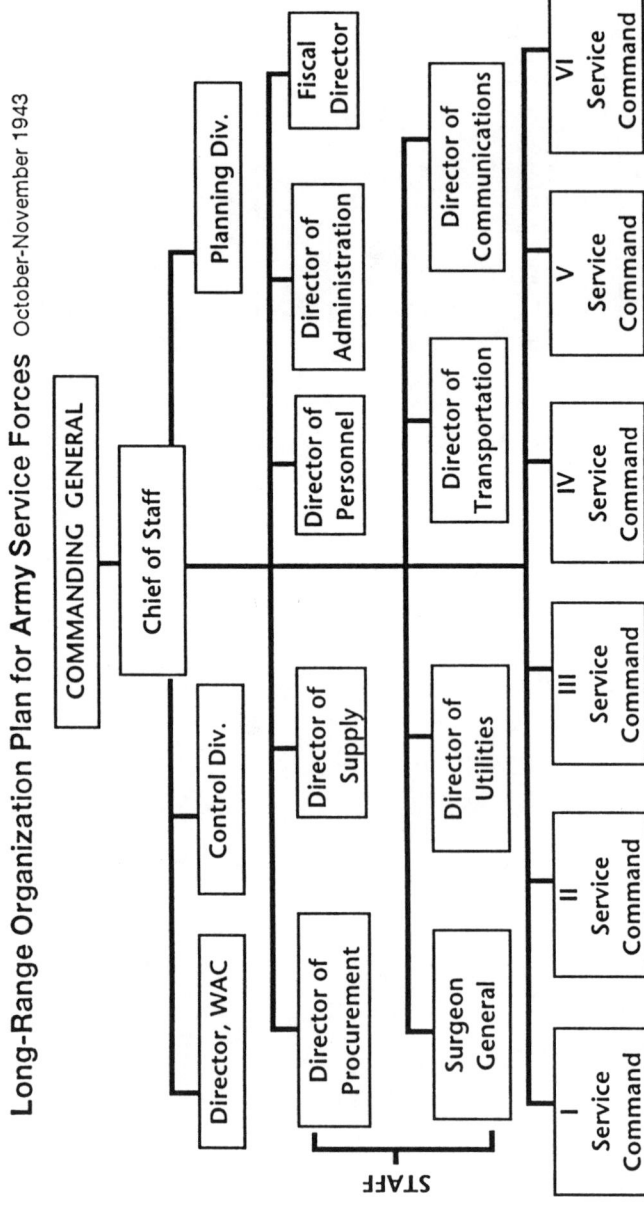

Long-Range Organization Plan for Army Service Forces October–November 1943

Courtesy of the U.S. Army Center of Military History

GLOSSARY

Acronyms

AAF	Army Air Forces
AEF	American Expeditionary Forces
AFG	American Forces in Germany
AGF	Army Ground Forces
ANMB	Army and Navy Munitions Board
ASF	Army Service Forces
ASP	Army Supply Program
ATC	Air Transport Command
CBI	China-Burma-India Theater
CCS	Combined Chiefs of Staff
CMP	Controlled Materials Plan
COMZ	Communications Zone
CPRB	Combined Production and Resources Board
CPS	Combined Staff Planners
ETO	European Theater of Operations
JAdC	Joint Administrative Committee
JCS	Joint Chiefs of Staff
JLC	Joint Logistics Committee
JPS	Joint Staff Planners
JPSC	Joint Production Survey Committee
LOC	Line of Communications
MAB	Munitions Assignments Board, Washington

OFRRO	Office of Foreign Relief and Rehabilitation Operations
OPD	War Department General Staff, Operations Divisions
OPM	Office of Production Management
OWM	Office of War Mobilization
OWMR	Office of War Mobilization and Reconversion
PEC	Production Executive Committee
POA	Pacific Ocean Area
PRA	Public Roads Administration
PRP	Production Requirements Plan
SEAC	Southeast Asia Command
SHAEF	Supreme Headquarters, Allied Expeditionary Force
SOS	Services of Supply
SWPA	Southwest Pacific Area
WMC	War Manpower Commission
WPA	Works Progress Administration
WPB	War Production Board
WPD	War Plans Division
WSA	War Shipping Administration

Code Names

ARCADIA	U.S.-British conference held at Washington, December 1941–January 1942.
ANAKIM	Plan for recapture of Burma.
ANVIL	Early plan for invasion of southern France.
BOLERO	Buildup of U.S. forces and supplies in the United Kingdom for cross-Channel invasion.
BUCCANEER	Plan for an amphibious operation in Andaman Islands.
DRAGOON	Invasion of southern France, August 1944.
GYMNAST	Early plan for invasion of North Africa.
HUSKY	Invasion of Sicily, July 1943.
MATTERHORN	Plan for bombing Japan from bases in Cheng-tu, China.
OCTAGON	U.S.-British conference held at Quebec, September 1944.
OLYMPIC	Plans for the invasion of Kyushu.
OVERLORD	Invasion of Normandy, June 1944.
QUADRANT	U.S.-British conference held at Quebec, August 1943.
ROUNDUP	Plan for a cross-Channel invasion in 1943.
SICKLE	Buildup of U.S. Eighth Air Force in the United Kingdom.
SLEDGEHAMMER	Plan for a limited cross-Channel invasion in 1942.
TARZAN	India-based portion of a general offensive in Burma.
TORCH	Invasion of North Africa, November 1942.

TRIDENT	U.S.-British conference held at Washington, May 1943.

Wartime Positions of Major Figures

Auckinleck, Sir Claude J.E.	British commander in chief in India, 1943–1947.
Aurand, Henry S.	Defense aid director of the War Department, 1941–1942; chief of the International Division, ASF, 1942; secretary of the CPRB, 1942; commander of the Sixth Service Command, 1942–1944.
Byrnes, James F.	Head of the OWM, 1943–1944; head of the OWMR, 1944–1945.
Carter, Arthur H.	Fiscal director, ASF.
Chennault, Claire L.	Commander of the China Air Task Force, 1942–1943; commander of the Fourteenth Air Force, 1943–1945.
Clay, Lucius D.	Assistant chief of staff for materiel, ASF, 1942–1943; director of materiel, ASF, 1943–1944.
Connolly, Donald H.	Commander of the Persian Gulf Service Command.
Covell, William E. R.	Member of the Engineering Branch, Construction Division, 1941; commander of the SOS, CBI, 1943–1945.
Devers, Jacob	Chief of Armored Force, Fort Knox, Ky., 1941–1943; commander of the ETO, 1943; commander of the North African Theater of Operations, 1943; deputy supreme Allied commander, Mediterranean Theater, 1944; commander of the Sixth Army Group, 1944–1945.
Douglas, Lewis W	Deputy administrator, WSA.

Eberstadt, Ferdinand	Chairman of the ANMB, 1941–1942; vice chairman of the WPB in charge of program determination, 1942–1943.
Eisenhower, Dwight D.	Chief of the OPD, 1942; commander of the ETO, 1942; commander of Allied forces in North Africa, 1942–1943; commander of Allied forces in the Mediterranean, 1943; commander, SHAEF, 1943–1945.
Forrestal, James F.	Under secretary of the navy, 1940–1944; secretary of the navy, 1944–1947.
Gregory, Edmund B.	Quartermaster general of the army.
Gross, Charles P.	Chief of the Transportation Corps.
Halsey, William F., Jr.	Commander of the South Pacific, POA.
Handy, Thomas T.	Chief of the OPD, 1942–1944; deputy War Department chief of staff, 1944–1946.
Harriman, W. Averell	President Roosevelt's lend-lease representative in England, 1941–1943.
Hartman, Charles B.	Chief of the Construction Division, 1940.
Ho Ying-chin	Chinese war minister.
Hopkins, Harry L.	Unofficial advisor to President Roosevelt.
Horne, Frederick J.	Vice chief of naval operations and the senior naval supply officer.
Ickes, Harold L.	Secretary of the interior and petroleum administrator for war.
King, Ernest J.	Chief of naval operations.
Kung, H. H.	Chinese finance minister.
Land, Emory S.	Chairman of the United States Maritime Commission and war shipping administrator.

Leahy, William D.	President Roosevelt's personal chief of staff and chairman of the JCS.
Lear, Ben	Commander of the AGF, 1944–1945.
Leathers, Lord Frederick	Head of the British Ministry of War Transport.
Leavey, Edmond H.	Head of the Engineering Branch, Construction Division, 1940–1941; member of the headquarters staff, POA, 1943–1945.
Lee, John C. H.	Commander of the SOS, ETO, 1942–1944; commander of the COMZ, ETO, 1944–1945.
Lutes, LeRoy	Assistant chief of staff for operations, ASF, 1942–1943; director of plans and operations, ASF, 1943–1945.
Lyttelton, Sir Oliver	British minister of production.
MacArthur, Douglas	Commander of the SWPA.
Marshall, George C.	War Department chief of staff.
McCloy, John J.	Assistant secretary of war.
McNair, Lesley J.	Commander of the AGF, 1942–1944.
McNarney, Joseph T.	Deputy War Department chief of staff, 1942–1944.
Moore, Richard C.	War Department G-4, 1940; deputy War Department chief of staff, 1940–1942.
Mountbatten, Lord Louis	Supreme Allied commander, SEAC.
Nathan, Robert R.	Chairman of the Planning Committee, WPB.
Nelson, Donald M.	Chairman of the WPB.

Nimitz, Chester W.	Commander of the POA.
Olmstead, Dawson	Chief signal officer, 1941–1943.
Patterson, Robert P.	Under secretary of war.
Reybold, Eugene B.	Acting War Department G-4, 1940–1941; chief of engineers, 1941–1945.
Robinson, Clinton F.	Head of the Control Section, Construction Division, 1940–1941; head of the Control Division, ASF, 1942–1945.
Salter, Sir Arthur	Head of the British Merchant Shipping Mission in Washington, D.C.
Smith, Harold D.	Director of the Budget Bureau.
Soong, T. V.	Chinese foreign minister.
Stilwell, Joseph W.	Commander of the CBI, 1942–1944.
Stimson, Henry L.	Secretary of war.
Styer, Wilhelm D.	Chief of staff, Construction Division, 1940–1941; chief of staff, ASF, 1942–1945.
Truman, Harry S.	Chairman of the Senate Special Committee Investigating the National Defense Program, 1941–1944; president of the United States, 1945–1953.
Venning, Walter	Director general of the British Ministry of Supply Mission in Washington, D.C.
Wavell, Archibald P.	British commander in chief in India, 1942–1943; viceroy of India, 1943–1947.
Wedemeyer, Albert C.	Member of the OPD, 1942–1944.
Weeks, Sir Ronald M.	Deputy chief of the Imperial General Staff.

Wheeler, Raymond A.	Commander of the SOS, CBI, 1942–1943; principal administrative officer of the SEAC, 1943–1945.
Wilson, Charles E.	Vice chairman of the WPB in charge of production and chairman of the PEC.

NOTES

Abbreviations used in Notes and Bibliography

AP	Aurand Papers
CD	Clay Diary
CF	Clay File
COHC	Columbia Oral History Collection, Columbia University
CP	Campbell Papers
DP	Douglas Papers
EHF	Engineers Historical File, U.S. Army Corps of Engineers Historical Office, Ft. Belvoir, Virginia
EL	Eisenhower Library, Abeliene, Kansas
EP	Eisenhower Papers
GCF	General Correspondence File
HF	Historical File
HP	Hopkins Papers
ID	International Division
IP	Ickes Papers
KP	Kemmerer Papers
LF	Lutes File
LP	Lutes Papers
MLF	George C. Marshall Library, Lexington, Virginia
NA	National Archives, Washington, D.C.
NYT	*New York Times*
PP	Patterson Papers
RG	Record Group
RP	Roosevelt Papers
SF	Somervell File
SP	Somervell Papers
USAMHI	U.S. Army Military History Institute, Carlisle Barracks, Pennsylvania
USBOB	United States Bureau of the Budget

USCPA	United States Civilian Production Administration
WNRC	Washington National Records Center, Suitland, Maryland
WP	Williams Papers

On Citation of Sources: In order to avoid an excessively large number of notes, I have sometimes collected the references for one or more paragraphs into a single note. Sources in each note are generally given in the order in which the information or quotation under citation appears.

Introduction

1. Huston, 1966, vii–viii; Leighton, 1990, 678–686.
2. Doig and Hargrove, 1987, 1–23.
3. Reese, 1984, 189.
4. Hewes, 1975, 1–76, 299–365.
5. Cuff, 1973; Ohl, 1975, 35–47.
6. Gough, 1991, 259–75.
7. Huston, 1966, 420.
8. Reese, 1984, iv–v.
9. Armitstead, 1967, 271–73.

Chapter 1. Soldier and Manager

1. B. B. Somervell to Miss Daisy, February 4, 1951, copy in author's possession; S. S. Griswold to J. K. Ohl, May 11, 1987; manuscript history of the Somervell family, 68–93, in possession of Mrs. Susan S. Griswold; "Tribute to Dr. Somervell," December 2, 1920, copy in author's possession.

2. B. B. Somervell to Miss Daisy, February 4, 1951, copy in author's possession.

3. S. S. Griswold to J. K. Ohl, May 11, 1987.

4. Murphy, 1943, 88; *The Brecky, 1909,* 66.

5. Dunbar, 1940a, 22; Janney, 1944, 87; Murphy, 1943, 88.

6. C. C. Reid to J. M. Dickinson, March 27, 1909, GCF #1431290, RG #94, NA.

7. General Merit Roll of the Graduating Class of 1914, United States Military Academy Library and Archives; *Howitzer, 1914,* 83; Efficiency Report of Brehon B. Somervell, June 15, 1914, GCF #1431290, RG #94, NA.

8. Interview with Lucius D. Clay, USAMHI.

9. Ambrose, 1983, 52–53.

10. B. B. Somervell to The Adjutant General, September 27, 1914, GCF #1431290, RG #94, NA; B. B. Somervell to S. Cosby, March 9, 1927, SP; Dunbar, 1940a, 21.

11. Proceedings of a Board of Officers to Determine Fitness for Promotion, November 16–19, 1914, and Somervell Efficiency Report, December 13, 1914, GCF #1431290, RG #94, NA.

12. Somervell Efficiency Reports, 1914, 1915, 1916, GCF #1431290, RG #94, NA; reminiscences of Lucius D. Clay, 406–407, COHC; interviews with Hugh Casey and with John Hardin, EHF.

13. Interview with John Hardin, EHF.

14. Proceedings of a Board of Officers to Determine Fitness for Promotion, April 27, 1917, GCF #1431290, RG #94, NA.

15. Reminiscences of Norman F. McDonald, 15th Engineers, World War I Survey, USAMHI.

16. *Historical Report of the Chief Engineer,* 1919, 292–293; Parsons, 1920, 13–17, 94–95.

17. Janney, 1944, 87.

18. *Historical Report of the Chief Engineer,* 1919, 299–302.

19. Murphy, 1943, 91; reminiscences of John C. H. Lee, 38, 84, USAMHI; telephone conservation with Mrs. Susan Griswold, February 8, 1992.

20. *89th Division: A Summary of Operations in the World War,* 1944, 36.

21. Report on Meuse-Argonne Offensive, 89th Division, October 19th to November 11th, 1918, extract from personal diary of Major General W. M. Wright, commanding 89th Division, November 5, 1918, Records of the 89th Division, RG #120, NA; English, 1920, 204–206 and 389.

22. Reminiscences of John C. H. Lee, 38, USAMHI.

23. Allen, 1923, 27–28.

24. Allen, 1923, 24, 116, 120; Twichell, 1974, 226–227; Coffman, 1966, 212.

25. W. D. Hines to F. D. Roosevelt, March 14, 1933, RP, OF 51-A.

26. "New G-4," 69.

27. Coffman and Herrly, 1977, 55–73; Blumenson, 1989, 2–13; reminiscences of Lucius D. Clay, 273–274, COHC.

28. *The General Service Schools Annual Report, 1923,* 39.

29. NYT, April 8, 22, 1925.

30. A copy of the report, *Report on Danube Navigation . . . ,* is located in SP; also see Somervell, 1926, 301–310.

31. Pappas, 1967, 100–38; Ball, 1983, 145–255; Anders, 1985, 140–145; Ambrose, 1983, 85.

32. "The Use of Negro Manpower in War," War College Archives, USAMHI.

33. "Possible Blue Wars, Their Causes and Purposes," February 6, 1926, War College Archives, USAMHI.

34. Maass, 1951, 20–36; reminiscences of Lucius D. Clay, 135, COHC; B. B. Somervell to S. D. Sturgis, Jr., March 12, 1953, SP.

35. Cowdrey, 1978, 43, 52.

36. Interview with Hugh Casey, EHF.

37. Somervell, *Report to the Chief of Engineers, United States Army, on Application for Preliminary Permit from Federal Power Commission by the Potomac River Corporation for Power Development of the Potomac River,* 1929.

38. Green, 1962, vol. 2, 286–290; "The Potomac and Power," 357; E. Jadwin to E. E. Bonner, August 2, 1929, Senate Committee on District of Columbia, *George Washington Memorial Parkway: Hearings,* 82–86 (hereinafter, as *George Washington Memorial Parkway*).

39. Reminiscences of Gilmore D. Clark, 156–160, and of Horace M. Albright, 492–496, COHC.

40. *George Washington Memorial Parkway*, 57–77.

41. U. S. Grant 3d to A. Capper, March 24, 1930, *George Washington Memorial Parkway*, 95–96; NYT, April 13, 1930; "Congress Gives Great Aid to Park Development in Federal City Region," 152.

42. *Chief of Engineers Annual Report, 1932,* 1964–1967; *Chief of Engineers Annual Report, 1933,* 1271–1273; F. Clay, 1976, 118–119, 121, 123, 128.

43. F. Clay, 1976, 119–120, 130–131; reminiscences of Lucius D. Clay, 133, COHC; "Scientific Taming of the Father of Rivers Begins," 15–16; "Progress of the Mississippi's 'New Deal,' " 17.

44. Interview with William M. Hoge, USAMHI; F. Clay, 1976, 128–131.

45. NYT, May 5, 1933.

46. W. D. Hines to B. B. Somervell, April 28, 1933, SP.

47. Somervell speech, November 1, 1934, SP; S. S. Griswold to J. K. Ohl, August 30, 1987.

48. B. B. Somervell to E. W. Kemmerer, January 16, 1934, KP.

49. Kemmerer Turkish diary, November 10, 1933, to January 11, 1934, G. H. Dorr to W. W. Kemmerer, January 10, 1934, KP.

50. B. B. Somervell to G. H. Dorr, March 12, 1934, H. A. Smith to E. W. Kemmerer, March 10, 1934, KP.

51. Kemmerer Turkish diary, April 16 to 30, 1934, KP.

52. NYT, July 15, 1934; reminiscences of James M. Barker, 319–320, COHC. A copy of the report, *A General Economic Survey of Turkey, 1933–1934,* is located in SP.

53. E. M. Markham to D. MacArthur, April 2, 1934, G. H. Dern to F. D. Roosevelt, July 2, 1934, RP, OF 51-A.

54. F. A. Delano to M. H. McIntyre, February 24, March 27, 1934, RP, OF 51-A.

55. Reminiscences of Lucius D. Clay, 408–409, COHC; J. Smith, 1990, 112–113.

56. Anders, 1985, 160.

57. Buker, 1975, 164–165; G. H. Dern to H. C. Ickes, May 3, 1934, Rivers and Harbors File, RG #77, WNRC.

58. Somervell, Digest of Reports on the Atlantic-Gulf Ship Canal, SP.

59. NYT, September 14, 1935; Davenport, 1935, 7–9, 48–50.

60. Somervell, 1936, 170–174.

61. NYT, September 16, 19, October 2, 4, 1935; "Florida Canal, Oliver Twists, and Uncle Sam," 601–602; Davenport, 1935, 9.

62. NYT, October 20, November 24, December 8, 27, 1935, January 6, 1936; Davenport, 1935, 9; for Ickes's opposition to the canal, see Ickes, 1953, 488–489, 502, 513–514, and 541–542.

63. "Sore Thumb," 11–12; "Exit White House Pet: Senate Makes Short Shrift of Florida Ship Canal," 6–7; *Chief of Engineers Annual Report, 1936,* 602; NYT, July 12, 1936.

64. NYT, November 18, 1936; House Committee on Rivers and Harbors, *Atlantic-Gulf Ship Canal, Fla.: Hearings,* 385–437, 496–509; House Committee on Rivers

and Harbors, *Atlantic-Gulf Ship Canal Across Florida: Hearings,* 90–110; Senate Committee on Commerce, *Florida Ship Canal: Hearings,* 261–269; Tebeau, 1971, 405–406.

Chapter 2. A One-Man Show

1. Ohl, 1985, 268–279.
2. Blumberg, 1979, 70–95.
3. Blumberg, 1979, 100, 119 n. 1, 300–301; reminiscences of John Carmody, 332, and of Lucius D. Clay, 141–142, COHC; J. Smith, 1990, 61–64.
4. NYT, July 4, 1936.
5. Dunbar, 1940b, 27.
6. NYT, July 4, August 4, 5, 8, 13, September 7, October 23, 1936.
7. Flanagan, 1940, 181–182, 188–189; Mathews, 1967, 102–103; NYT, December 1, 2, 1936; Bentley, 1988, 246–247.
8. Mangione, 1972, 89; Penkower, 1977, 50; McMahon, 1972, 56; McKinzie, 1973, 98.
9. Heckscher, 1978, 142; Blumberg, 1979, 103; NYT, December 7, 8, 9, 10, 12, 1936; telephone conversation between Harry Hopkins and Brehon Somervell, December 11, 1936, HP.
10. NYT, December 23, 1936, January 23, 1937; Flanagan, 1940, 189–190.
11. Blumberg, 1974, 197–198; Dunbar, 1940b, 17.
12. NYT, June 23, 26, August 22, 30, September 16, October 12, 1937.
13. Blumberg, 1979, 108–109; NYT, September 14, November 30, December 24, 1938.
14. Blumberg, 1979, 109; B. B. Somervell to F. C. Harrington, March 19, 1937, State Series File, New York City, RG #69, NA; Dunbar, 1940b, 26–27; NYT, August 4, 1936.
15. Millett, 1938, 68–73; NYT, August 22, October 3, 1936.
16. NYT, August 4, 19, 20, September 16, November 7, 1936, May 18, 31, September 23, 1937; Blumberg, 1979, 110–115; " 'Career-Men,' WPA Frankenstein?" 10–11.
17. Telephone conversation between Aubrey Williams and Brehon Somervell, September 29, 1936, WP.
18. Telephone conversations between Aubrey Williams and Brehon Somervell, October 16, November 27, 1936, and between Fiorello La Guardia and Aubrey Williams, November 27, 1936, WP; F. La Guardia to B. B. Somervell, January 4, 1937, B. B. Somervell to H. L. Hopkins, January 6, 1937, telephone conversation between Harry Hopkins and Brehon Somervell, March 10, 1937, HP; NYT, February 7, 1937; B. B. Somervell to H. L. Hopkins, July 27, 1937, State Series File, New York City, RG #69, NA.
19. Telephone conversation between Harry Hopkins and Brehon Somervell, November 9, 1937, HP; B. B. Somervell to F. LaGuardia, November 10, 1937, State Series File, New York City, RG #69, NA.
20. Dunbar, 1940b, 29.
21. B. B. Somervell to J. McKenzie, July 9, 1937, and B. B. Somervell to F. La Guardia, November 11, 1937, State Series File, New York City, RG #69, NA.;

telephone conversation between Aubrey Williams and Brehon Somervell, August 26, 1937, WP; NYT, September 10, 1937.

22. Reminiscences of William Delano, 83–85, COHC; Somervell, 1940, 62–72; Blumberg, 1979, 133.

23. "La Guardia's Coup," 48; NYT, September 29, 1938, October 16, 1939; "New York Marks Airport Victory," 18, 20; G. C. Marshall to B. B. Somervell, October 25, 1939, MLF; Payne, 1951, 112; Sherwood, 1950, 76; Perret, 1991, 26–27.

24. NYT, May 4, June 8, 1939; House Subcommittee on Appropriations, *Investigation and Study of the Works Progress Administration: Hearings,* 1298.

25. NYT, July 16, 18, 28, August 1, 7, 8, 18, 21, September 1, 9, October 21, 1939; B. B. Somervell to F. C. Harrington, February 14, 1940, State Series File, New York City, RG #69, NA.

26. "Mutiny on the Bounty," 13–14; "War on Congress," 10–12; "The WPA Strike," 43–44; B. B. Somervell to F. C. Harrington, February 10, 1940, State Series File, New York City, RG #69, NA; Blumberg, 1979, 246–249; NYT, July 6, 7, 8, 9, 10, 11, 13, 16, 18, 21, 22, 26, 27, 28, 30, August 1, 5, 7, 8, 17, 19, 21, September 1, 9, 21, 1939; Goulden, 1972, 67–68.

27. Contreras, 1983, 155; reminiscences of Holger Cahill, 295, COHC; McMahon, 1972, 74; Monroe, 1975, 64–67; McDonald, 1969, 407.

28. NYT, November 5, 1939; McKinzie, 1973, 165.

29. Monroe, 1976, 8–11; McKinzie, 1973, 165–166, 171 n. 48; NYT, July 7, 9, 10, 12, September 8, 1940; reminiscences of Holger Cahill, 293–295, COHC.

30. Blumberg, 1979, 262–264; NYT, June 23, 24, 25, 28, and 29, July 1, 2, August 29, 1940.

31. F. D. Roosevelt to H. B. Woodring, May 22, 1940, RP, OF 444-C; R. C. Moore to D. M. Matheson, January 3, 1956, EHF; B. B. Somervell to F. D. Roosevelt, October 19, 1940, RP, OF 25; G. C. Marshall to Major Smith, October 25, 1940, MLF; interview with Julian L. Schley, EHF.

32. NYT, November 8, 9, 16, 1940; Blumberg, 1979, 265–266.

Chapter 3. Construction Division

1. G. C. Marshall to W. Bryden, November 8, 1940, MLF.

2. Fine and Remington, 1972, 152–243; Pogue, 1966, 106–107; R. Smith, 1959, 444–447; *Richmond Times-Dispatch,* June 11, 1989.

3. Fine and Remington, 1972, 256–259; J. J. McCloy to J. A. Remington, August 13, 1957, EHF; Stimson diary, December 11, 19, 1940, Stimson Papers; NYT, December 14, 20, 1940.

4. Interviews with Elmer G. Thomas, and Edmund B. Gregory, and Malcolm Pirnie and Stephen F. Voorhees; E. B. Gregory to A. C. Smith, March 25, 1955, EHF.

5. Fine and Remington, 1972, 258–267; Somervell, 1941a, 51–53.

6. Fine and Remington, 1972, 273–279; Stimson diary, December 31, 1940, January 2, 1941, Stimson Papers.

7. House Subcommittee on Appropriations, *Fourth Supplemental National Defense Appropriations Bill for 1941: Hearings,* 13–114; Fine and Remington, 1972, 279–280; NYT, February 26, March 2, 1941.

8. Fine and Remington, 1972, 280–308; J. J. McCloy to J. A. Remington, August 13, 1957, EHF; NYT, April 23, 1941.

9. Fine and Remington, 1972, 309–341; report, "Activities of the Construction Division, July 1940–November 1941," EHF; Campbell, 1946, 101–116.

10. Fine and Remington, 1972, 342–348; NYT, March 31, 1941.

11. Fine and Remington, 1972, 348–354; NYT, April 17, 1941; Somervell, 1941b, 116.

12. R. P. Patterson to Chiefs of Supply and Services and War Department Facilities Board, April 5, 1941, GCF, RG #77, WNRC.

13. Interview with Richard H. Tatlow, III, comments by Leslie Groves on Fine and Remington manuscript, EHF; L. H. Campbell to A. C. Smith, March 10, 1955, CP.

14. R. P. Patterson to The Chief of Ordinance and The Quartermaster General, April 5, 1941, B. B. Somervell to L. H. Campbell, April 12, 1941, L. H. Campbell to B. B. Somervell, April 17, 1941, GCF, RG #77, WNRC; Fine and Remington, 1972, 357–363.

15. Fine and Remington, 1972, 377–378; interviews with Elmer E. Kirkpatrick, and Gavin Hadden, and Clarence Renshaw, EHF.

16. House Committee on Military Affairs, *Inquiry As To National Defense Construction: Hearings,* 145–161, 177–186, 308–319; interviews with Clarence Renshaw, EHF.

17. Fine and Remington, 1972, 388–390; Senate Special Committee Investigating the National Defense Program, *Investigation of the National Defense Program, Progress of National Defense Program: Hearings,* 264–302, 308–353.

18. Riddle, 1964, 76, 172; B. B. Somervell to W. Styer, July 26, 1952, SP; NYT, August 15, 1941; "Brass Hats in a Blitzkrieg," 153–154; Toulmin, 1947, 51–62; "Congress Criticizes Army Construction Costs," 26–28.

19. "Billion Dollar Watchdog," 13–15; Truman, 1973, 140; Ferrell, 1983, 32; McCullough, 1992, 262; Daniels, 1971, 278; Ferrell, ed., 1983, 479.

20. Fine and Remington, 1972, 411–417; House Committee on Appropriations, *Military Establishment Appropriation Bill for 1942: Hearings,* 393–444, 680–688; Stimson diary, September 25, 26, 27, October 2, 7, 1941, Stimson Papers.

21. Perret, 1991, 77; Bland, Ritenour, and Wunderlin, 1986, 531–532; B. B. Somervell to O. Campbell, August 27, 1954, SP.

22. Interviews with Hugh Casey, EHF, and Robert W. Colglazier, USAMHI.

23. Fine and Remington, 1972, 431; Stimson diary, July 22, 24, 1941, Stimson Papers.

24. NYT, July 25, 1941; interviews with Ferdinand J. C. Dresser and with Leslie R. Groves, EHF; B. B. Somervell to R.P. Patterson, July 25, 1941, B. B. Somervell to D. M. Nelson, August 2, 19, 1941, GCF, RG #92, WNRC; interview with Paul Caraway, USAMHI; Goldberg, 1992, 29.

25. NYT, August 6, 1941; "The Army Raises a Ghost," 58–59; reminiscences of Gilmore D. Clarke, 147, COHC; Fine and Remington, 1972, 434.

26. NYT, August 8, 1941; reminiscences of Horace M. Albright, 502–504, COHC; Senate Subcommittee on Appropriations, *First National Defense Appropriation Bill for 1942: Hearings,* 171–183; R. P. Patterson to A. B. Adams, August 8, 1941, PP; Ickes diary, August 27, 1941, IP.

27. *Complete Presidential Press Conferences,* 1972, vol. 9, 94–97; B. B. Somervell to H. L. Stimson, August 20, 1941, PP; NYT, August 20, 21, 22, 26, 1941.

28. *Complete Presidential Press Conferences,* 1972, vol. 9, 112–118, 126–129, 135; NYT, August 27, 30, September 3, 1941; B. B. Somervell to H. L. Stimson, August 30, 1941, RP, President's Secretary's File, War Department; reminiscences of Gilmore D. Clarke, 149–155, COHC.

29. Fine and Remington, 1972, 437; Goldberg, 1992, 38–46.

30. Brinkley, 1988, 74–75; Pogue, 1973, 40; interview with Luther M. Leisenring, EHF; J. J. O'Brien to R. P. Patterson, September 16, 1944, PP; NYT, August 26, 1941; Perret, 1991, 79; Goldberg, 1992, 59–91.

31. Fine and Remington, 1972, 440, 460–462; interview with Michael Madigan, comments by Leslie Groves on Fine and Remington manuscript, EHF.

32. Interviews with Edmund B. Gregory, and Michael Madigan, and Julian L. Schley, and Leslie R. Groves EHF; Stimson diary, June 13, 1941, Stimson Papers.

33. B. B. Somervell to E. Reybold, September 8, 1941, EHF.

34. Interviews with Eugene Reybold and with James H. Burns, EHF.

35. Comments by Samuel D. Sturgis, Jr., on Fine and Remington manuscript, EHF; E. B. Gregory to B. B. Somervell, December 8, 1941, SP; NYT, February 1, 1942; Stimson diary, February 7, 1942, Stimson Papers; Murphy, 1943, 92.

Chapter 4. Organizing for War

1. Interview with Mary B. Pagan, EHF.

2. Hughes diary, December 15, 1941, Hughes Papers; Leighton and Coakley, 1955, 129–132, 195–198; Lieutenant Colonel Simon M. Franks, "The Determination of Army Supply Requirements," prepared in 1945, 17–19, Center of Military History Research Files; Sherwood, 1950, 137–141; telephone conversation, February 25, 1992, and interview with Robert Nathan, June 14, 1992.

3. Leighton and Coakley, 1955, 199; J. Smith, 1990, 119.

4. Brigante, 1950, 9–44; Polenberg, 1972, 221.

5. B. B. Somervell to L. D. Clay, March 8, 1942, D. M. Nelson to F. D. Roosevelt, March 31, 1942, G. C. Marshall to F. D. Roosevelt, April 1, 1942, CF, RG #160, NA; interview with Lucius D. Clay, USAMHI; B. B. Somervell to A. R. Glancy, September 1, 1948, B. B. Somervell to L. W. Koenig, July 7, 1954, SP; USCPA, 1947, 281–282; Thomson and Mayo, 1960, 233–239; J. Smith, 1990, 121–126; Hooks, 1991, 115; Leighton and Coakley, 1955, 198–201, 603; Tenney diary, March 21, 1942, Tenney Papers.

6. B. B. Somervell to E. S. Land, January 31, 1942, G-4/29717–116, RG #165, NA.

7. B. B. Somervell to G. C. Marshall, December 11, 1941, MLF; B. B. Somervell to C. P. Gross, January 13, 1942, HF, RG #336, WNRC.

8. Draft, G. C. Marshall to F. D. Roosevelt, no date, SF, RG #160, NA.

9. Leighton and Coakley, 1955, 210–211.

10. G. C. Marshall to H. A. Stark, December 31, 1941, G-4/33920, RG #165, NA; B. B. Somervell to H. L. Hopkins, December 31, 1941, SF, RG #160, NA; Wardlow, 1951, 188; Millett, 1954, 255.

11. Stimson diary, February 2, 1942, Stimson Papers; Leighton and Coakley, 1955, 217.

12. Interview with LeRoy Lutes, 77–78, EL; Stimson diary, January 5, 1942, Stimson Papers; reminiscences of Goldthwaite H. Dorr, 73–74, COHC; G. H. Dorr, memorandum, "Notes on the Activities of an Informal Group in Connection with Supply Organization in the War Department—January–May, 1942," 1–13, SP (hereinafter, as Dorr memorandum).

13. Millett, 1954, 34–35; reminiscences of Bernard L. Gladieux, 323–325, COHC.

14. Interview with Sidney P. Spalding, USAMHI; Stimson diary, February 18, 1942, Stimson Papers.

15. Morison, 1960, 407.

16. Reminiscences of Edward Greenbaum, 31–34, of H. Friedlich, 23–24, of William C. Marbury, 12–13, 36–37, and of Bayard Schieffelin, 12–13, COHC.

17. F. C. Foy to J. E. Hewes, July 11, 1975, SP; reminiscences of Howard Petersen, 20–21, COHC.

18. Reminiscences of Edward Greenbaum, 35–38, COHC; Millett, 1954, 173–177; L. Lutes to P. Y. Hammond, February 2, 1954, SP.

19. Millett, 1954, 36 n. 51.

20. Reminiscences of Harvey H. Bundy, 183–184, COHC; Pogue, 1966, 297–298; Bland, 1991, 626.

21. Interview with Lucius D. Clay, USAMHI, and reminiscences of Lucius D. Clay, 262, 266–268, 294–295, 311, 334, 342, 426, COHC; J. Smith, 1990, 98–99, 111, 113–114.

22. Interviews with LeRoy Lutes, 80–88, EL, and Henry Aurand, USAMHI; L. Lutes to B. B. Somervell, January 15, 1942, LP, RG #200, NA; L. Lutes to B. B. Somervell, January 14, 1947, SP; Lutes, 1952a, 2–6; L. Lutes to B. B. Somervell, March 7, 1944, AP.

23. B. B. Somervell to G. C. Marshall, March 15, 1942, SF, RG #160, NA.

24. Green, Thomson, and Roots, 1955, 95; Sherwood, 1950, 160–161; Hughes diary, May 6, 1942, Hughes Papers; Stimson diary, May 14, 1942, Stimson Papers; interviews with Sidney P. Spalding, USAMHI, and James H. Burns, EHF; reminiscences of Isador Lubin, 98, COHC; L. H. Campbell to W. D. Styer, August 24, 1942, CP.

25. C. Smith, 1956, 55; Coll, Keith, and Rosenthal, 1958, 135; Thompson, Raynor, Harris, Oakes, and Terrett, 1957, 59; Brophy and Fisher, 1959, 93–96.

26. Millett, 1954, 312–321; Hewes, 1975, 101–103.

27. Somervell, 1944a, 257.

28. Minutes of Conference of Commanding Generals of Service Commands, Chicago, Illinois, July 30–August 1, 1942, 206, 211, 213–214, Styer File, RG #160, NA.

29. Robinson, 1944, 260–267; Hewes, 1975, 94–96.

30. Richard M. Leighton, "History of the Control Division, ASF, 1942–1945," Styer File, RG #160, NA; Tenney diary, December 23, 1941, March 30, April 17, 1942, Tenney Papers.

31. Minutes of Conference of Commanding Generals of Service Commands, Chicago, Illinois, July 30–August 1, 1942, 209, Styer File, RG #160, NA; Millett, 1954, 377.

32. Minutes of Conference of Commanding Generals of Service Commands, Chicago, Illinois, July 30–August 1, 1942, 205, Styer File, RG #160, NA; Hewes, 1975, 96.

33. Millett, 1954, 378.

34. B. B. Somervell to R. Moore, January 22, 1942, SF, RG #160, NA; Leighton and Coakley, 1955, 200, 295–296; R. Smith, 1959, 144–146.

35. B. B. Somervell to L. Lutes, May 15, 1942, LF, RG #160, NA; B. B. Somervell to J. H. Burns, August 15, 1942, SF, RG, #160, NA; L. Lutes to B. B. Somervell, September 30, 1942, LP, RG #200, NA; Leighton and Coakley, 1955, 296–298.

36. "Procedure for the Determination and Administration of the Army Supply Program," sent by B. B. Somervell to G. C. Marshall, September 21, 1942, MLF; L. Clay, 1943, 96–97, 225–230, 232; Leighton and Coakley, 1955, 298–301; R. Smith, 1959, 147–154; reminiscences of Lucius D. Clay, 295–297, 514, COHC; Perret, 1991, 74–75.

Chapter 5. Industrial Mobilization

1. Koistinen, 1984, 96.

2. Dorr memorandum, 62–67, SP; USCPA, 1947, 212–213; Millett, 1954, 442–445.

3. USCPA, 1947, 521; Hooks, 1991, 105, 145; Nelson 1946, 198–201; Millett, 1954, 190; Warth, 1984, 313; Fischer, 1945, 486; Catton, 1948, 115; Christman, 1971, 85 n. 49; Koistinen, 1964, 639–646.

4. Nelson, 1946, 358–359; Christman, 1973, 81–83; *The Journals of David E. Lilienthal,* 1964, 304.

5. B. B. Somervell to J. L. Weiner, April 11, 1943, CF, RG #160, NA; telephone conversation, February 27, 1992, and interview with Robert Nathan, June 14, 1992.

6. Dorr memorandum, 74, SP; Millett, 1954, 446–451; USBOB, 1946, 129; USCPA, 1947, 258; reminiscences of John Lord O'Brien, 545–547, COHC; "The S.O.S.," 70; Clay desk diary, May 21, 1942, CD, RG #160, NA.

7. USBOB, 1946, 129; NYT, June 24, 1942; "Here Comes the Army," 16; reminiscences of John Lord O'Brien, 570, COHC; Christman, 1973, 83.

8. Reminiscences of Henry A. Wallace, 1658, COHC; Blum, 1973, 94; Ickes diary, June 14, July 5, 26, 1942, IP.

9. Telephone conversation, February 27, 1992, and interview with Robert Nathan, June 14, 1992.

10. Nelson, 1946, 380; Brigante, 1950, 45, 56; Murphy 1943, 94.

11. Brigante, 1950, 65–71; USCPA, 1947, 283–287; Douglas diary, September 4, 1942, DP.

12. Brigante, 1950, 71–75.

13. B. B. Somervell to R. R. Nathan, September 12, 1942, SF, RG #160, NA.

14. B. B. Somervell to D. M. Nelson, September 12, 1942, SF, RG #160, NA; B. B. Somervell to G. C. Marshall, no date, MLF; reminiscences of Lucius D. Clay, 470, COHC; J. Smith, 1990, 148.

15. Polenberg, 1972, 222–223; B. B. Somervell to R. P. Patterson, September 16, 1946, B. B. Somervell to J. E. Brigante, February 1, 1950, SP; Hooks, 1991, 97; Brigante, 1950, 76–81.

16. R. R. Nathan to B. B. Somervell, September 17, 1942, SF, RG #160, NA.

17. Telephone conversation, February 27, 1992, and interview with Robert Nathan, June 14, 1992.

18. Brigante, 1950, 91–92.

19. USCPA, *Minutes of the War Production Board, Jan. 20, 1942–Oct. 9, 1945*, 139–142 (hereinafter, as *Minutes of the WPB*); Brigante, 1950, 90–96; Blum, 1973, 119; reminiscences of Morris Rosenthal, 195, COHC.

20. R. P. Patterson to B. B. Somervell, October 7, 1942, SF, RG #160, NA.

21. Reminiscences of Lucius D. Clay, 317, 324, 365–366, 469–470, COHC; R. Smith, 1959, 156–158; Feagin and Riddell, 1990, 67.

22. Blum, 1973, 120–121; USCPA, 1947, 288–289; *Minutes of the WPB*, 142–145.

23. R. Smith, 1959, 156; Polenberg, 1972, 244; reminiscences of Henry A. Wallace, 1895, COHC; Brigante, 1950, 101–104; Catton, 1948, 43; Koistinen, 1964, 653; *Minutes of the WPB*, 145–146.

24. D. M. Nelson to Joint Chiefs of Staff, October 19, 1942, SF, RG #160, NA; Nelson, 1946, 380–381; Leighton and Coakley, 1955, 604–608; Leighton, 1969, 244–245.

25. R. Smith, 1959, 555–564; Christman, 1971, 181–182; Millett, 1954, 210.

26. Hooks, 1991, 169–170; USCPA, 1947, 221, 293–297, 462; Connery, 1951, 171; Koistinen, 1964, 641–644.

27. Nichols, 1981, 74; Warth, 1984, 160; Christman, 1971, 76–78, 94–95.

28. R. Smith, 1959, 567–573; USCPA, 1947, 474–485; Christman, 1971, 180–201; Hooks, 1991, 172.

29. Nelson, 1946, 383–384; USCPA, 1947, 506–507; USBOB, 1946, 301–302.

30. Koistinen, 1964, 657; NYT, September 18, 1942.

31. USCPA, 1947, 509–513.

32. B. B. Somervell, O. P. Nichols, S. M. Robinson, and R. E. Davison to C. E. Wilson, November 16, 1942, SF, RG #160, NA; Clay desk diary, November 16, 1942, CD, RG #160, NA.

33. Millett, 1954, 221–222; L. D. Clay to C. E. Wilson, November 24, 1942, CF, RG #160, NA.

34. Leahy, 1950, 130–131.

35. Nelson, 1946, 384–387; NYT, November 25, 1942; D. M. Nelson to H. L. Stimson, November 26, 1942 (two letters), SF, RG #160, NA; Millett, 1954, 222–224, 457; USCPA, 1947, 514–516; Koistinen, 1964, 659.

36. Koistinen, 1984, 100; Pepper, 1942, 702–704.

37. B. B. Somervell to C. Pepper, December 5, 1942, SP.

38. Robey, 1942, 66; USBOB, 1946, 280–281; Lash, 1975, 143–144, 166–167; Koistinen, 1964, 695; Millett, 1954, 282–294; R. Smith, 1959, 238–242; Stimson and Bundy, 1948, 491–496; R. P. Patterson to B. B. Somervell, September 11, 1946, October 24, 27, 1947, SP.

39. Cuff, 1984, 114–115; Hooks, 1991, 145–146.

40. Peltason, 1950, 30–33; Catton, 1948, 207–209; Schwarz, 1981, 453–457; Polenberg, 1972, 228; Bernstein, 1967, 161–162.

41. Peltason, 1950, 20–24.

42. Catton, 1948, 242–244; Koistinen, 1964, 662, 700–703; Hooks, 1991, 171–172.

43. "Good News is Bad News," 19; B. B. Somervell to G. C. Marshall, June 30, 1943, SF, RG #160, NA; B. B. Somervell to J. W. Peltason, January 17, 1950, SP; Peltason, 1950, 24–27; Nelson, 1946, 403–409.

44. Reminiscences of Lucius D. Clay, 505, COHC; Millett, 1954, 227–228; Catton, 1948, 232–234; Hooks, 1991, 174.

45. Millett, 1954, 212; Fischer, 1945, 487; B. B. Somervell to F. Eberstadt, October 9, 1945, C. E. Wilson to B. B. Somervell, April 5, 1948, B. B. Somervell to W. L. Chenery, April 5, 1948, B. B. Somervell to J. D. Millett, September 2, 1949, SP.

46. Peltason, 1950, 34–38; Sitterson, 1945, 37–39; Bernstein, 1967, 162–163; USCPA, 1947, 731–735; Koistinen, 1964, 508.

47. USCPA, 1947, 801–802; Sitterson, 1945, 89–92; Peltason, 1950, 60–64; Bernstein, 1967, 166; Hooks, 1991, 174–175.

48. Peltason, 1950, 67–83; Sitterson, 1945, 92–102.

49. NYT, July 4, 5, 9, August 2, 1944; Peltason, 1950, 84–86.

50. Somers, 1950, 189–91; Sitterson, 1945, 110–118; Koistinen, 1964, 719–721; NYT, August 6, 7, 11, September 1, 3, 1944; Peltason, 1950, 87–89.

51. B. B. Somervell to J. D. Millett, September 2, 1949, SP.

52. Peltason, 1950, 114–119; Sitterson, 1945, 155.

53. Peltason, 1950, 117–124; Byrnes, 1958, 246; NYT, November 21, 22, 29, December 2, 3, 5, 1944; Memorandum of Agreement, November 23, 1944, SF, RG #160, NA; USCPA, 1947, 812; Sitterson, 1945, 163–164; Fischer, 1945, 488–489.

54. Senate Special Committee to Investigate the National Defense Program, *Investigation of the National Defense Program: Hearings*, 11989–12016; NYT, December 7, 1944; Nichols, 1981, 480; Peltason, 1950, 127–129; Somers, 1950, 193–194.

55. Koistinen, 1964, 737–740; Sitterson, 1945, 165–167; *Minutes of the WPB*, 382–383; Polenberg, 1972, 235–236; Bernstein, 1967, 243–260.

Chapter 6. Shipping

1. Browder and Smith, 1986, 166–172.

2. Browder and Smith, 1986, 176; Wardlow, 1951, 188; "The S.O.S.," 164–165.

3. Ballantine, 1949, 88–89; Leighton and Coakley, 1955, 218.

4. B. B. Somervell to L. W. Douglas, June 10, 1942, L. W. Douglas to B. B. Somervell, June 10, 1942, MLF; Memorandum Covering the Inter-Departmental Relationship between the Army and the War Shipping Administration, June 13, 1942, SF, RG #160, NA.

5. L. W. Douglas to B. B. Somervell, June 13, 1942, HF, RG #336, WNRC; B. B. Somervell to H. L. Hopkins, June 14, 1942, J. H. Graham to B. B. Somervell, ca. June 30, 1942, SF, RG #160, NA; Millett, 1954, 257–258.

6. L. W. Douglas to B. B. Somervell, October 9, 1942, SF, RG #160, NA.

7. Leighton and Coakley, 1955, 616–617.

8. Douglas diary, October 12, 1942, DP.
9. Douglas diary, September 4, October 12, 19, 1942, DP; Browder and Smith, 1986, 181, 185.
10. B. B. Somervell to L. W. Douglas, October 19, 1942, SF, RG #160, NA.
11. Douglas diary, October 23, 1942, DP; Clay desk diary, October 24, 1942, CD, RG #160, NA.
12. Douglas diary, October 27, 1942, DP; Millett, 1954, 267.
13. Browder and Smith, 1986, 185–187; Douglas diary, December 18, 1942, DP; Leighton and Coakley, 1955, 618–619.
14. H. L. Stimson to E. S. Land, December 23, 1942, SF, RG #160, NA; W. D. Leahy to F. D. Roosevelt, December 26, 1942, MLF.
15. Minutes of meeting at Admiral Leahy's office, December 28, 1942, MLF; Douglas diary, December 28, 1942, DP.
16. Douglas diary, December 28, 31, 1942, January 4, 1943, DP; G. C. Marshall to L. W. Douglas, December 31, 1942, W. D. Leahy to G. C. Marshall and E. King, December 31, 1942, MLF; B. B. Somervell to W. D. Leahy, January 2, 1943, SF, RG #160, NA; Leighton and Coakley, 1955, 621–622; Browder and Smith, 1986, 188–189.
17. L. W. Douglas to F. D. Roosevelt, January 18, 1943, DP; W. D. Styer to J. McCloy, February 5, 1943, MLF; Browder and Smith, 1986, 189–190; Millett, 1954, 259; Wardlow, 1951, 190–200; Leighton and Coakley, 1955, 622–623.
18. Leighton, 1960, 199–207; Browder and Smith, 1986, 191–193.
19. Wedemeyer, 1958, 171–174; Pogue, 1973, 17–18; McJimsey, 1987, 269–270; Leighton and Coakley, 1955, 671 n. 30; B. B. Somervell to W. D. Styer, January 19, 23, 1943, Styer File, RG #160, NA.
20. Leighton and Coakley, 1955, 681.
21. Behrens, 1955, 336–339; Browder and Smith, 1986, 193–194; Harriman, 1975, 184.
22. Leighton and Coakley, 1955, 681–682.
23. Howard, 1972, 272.
24. Leighton and Coakley, 1955, 682.
25. Douglas diary, February 19, 1943, DP.
26. Browder and Smith, 1986, 195; Leighton and Coakley, 1955, 691.
27. Douglas diary, March 1, 12, 1943, DP; Leighton and Coakley, 1955, 691–692; Browder and Smith, 1986, 195–196.
28. Howard, 1972, 294–295; Leighton and Coakley, 1955, 692–693.
29. C. P. Gross to G. C. Marshall, March 17, 1943, MLF.
30. McJimsey, 1987, 285; L. D. Clay to W. D. Styer, March 20, 1943, MLF.
31. G. C. Marshall to H. L. Hopkins, March 22, 1943 DP, B. B. Somervell to G. C. Marshall, March 25, 1943, MLF; Leighton and Coakley, 1955, 697–698.
32. Douglas diary, March 19, 1943, DP.
33. Douglas diary, March 29, 30, 1943, DP; Leighton and Coakley, 1955, 699–701; Browder and Smith, 1986, 197–198; McJimsey, 1987, 285.
34. Douglas diary, April 7, 1943, DP; draft memorandum for Roosevelt's signature, B. B. Somervell to H. L. Hopkins, April 12, 1943, HP; Leighton and Coakley, 1955, 701–702.

35. Douglas diary, May 7, 1943, DP; Coakley and Leighton, 1968, 82–83.

36. Douglas diary, May 22, 23, 1943, DP; Browder and Smith, 1986, 199–200; Meetings of American and British Shipping Experts, May 22, 1943, Department of State, *Foreign Relations of the United States: The Conferences at Washington and Quebec,* 175–177.

37. Leighton, 1960, 222–223; Coakley and Leighton, 1968, 18, 84–86; Huston, 1966, 431.

38. Millett, 1954, 259–260; Browder and Smith, 1986, 202.

Chapter 7. The Allied Supply Orbit

1. Leighton and Coakley, 1955, 247–257; Coakley and Leighton, 1968, 628–629.

2. B. B. Somervell to G. C. Marshall, August 2, 1942, MLF; reminiscences of Henry A. Wallace, 1881–1882, COHC; Stone, 1988, 130; Stoler, 1989, 80.

3. B. B. Somervell to L. D. Clay, July 27, 1942, ID, RG #160, NA; reminiscences of Lucius D. Clay, 300, 382, 428–429, COHC; Reese, 1984, 51; J. Smith, 1990, 132.

4. H. S. Aurand to B. B. Somervell, July 18, 1942, ID, RG #160, NA; Reese, 1984, 52–53; H. S. Aurand to B. B. Somervell, March 7, 1944, AP; Leighton and Coakley, 1955, 262; Danchev, 1990, 186.

5. Leighton and Coakley, 1955, 262–264, 266–267; Hall and Wrigley, 1956, 153.

6. Hall and Wrigley, 1956, 155–156; Gwyer and Butler, 1964, 558; McJimsey, 1987, 227; Fennelly, 1965, 115.

7. Reese, 1984, 53; B. B. Somervell, to J. H. Burns, August 14, 1942, SF, RG #160, NA; Hall and Wrigley, 1956, 157; B. B. Somervell to G. C. Marshall, October 14, 1942, B. B. Somervell to Executive, Munitions Assignments Board, no date and October 5, 1942, CF, RG #160, NA; Leighton and Coakley, 1955, 281–282; Gwyer and Butler, 1964, 559–560; Rosen, 1951, 149–150; J. Smith, 1990, 134; Danchev, 1990, 208, 213.

8. Clay desk diary, August 27, 1942, CD, RG #160, NA; Reese, 1984, 146–147; reminiscences of Henry A. Wallace, 2117, COHC; Stacy, 1970, 175–176; Fennelly, 1965, 115–118; J. Smith, 1990, 133–134; Danchev, 1990, 196.

9. Weigley, 1967, 448.

10. Leighton and Coakley, 1955, 282–290; Hall and Wrigley, 1956, 190; B. B. Somervell to W. Venning, February 26, 1943, SF, RG #160, NA.

11. Hall and Wrigley, 1956, 191; Leighton and Coakley, 1955, 284–285; Weigley, 1967, 448.

12. Coakley and Leighton, 1968, 630–642, 648–649.

13. Hall and Wrigley, 1956, 159, 197; Danchev, 1986, 84.

14. B. B. Somervell to G. C. Marshall, April 18, 1944, JSC 77$\frac{1}{3}$, "Policy Concerning Assignment of Lend-Lease Munitions Following the Defeat of Germany," May 5, 1944, HP.

15. B. B. Somervell to G. N. Macready, May 18, 1944, G. N. Macready and W. Venning to B. B. Somervell, June 16, 1944, W. Venning to B. B. Somervell, July 18, 1944, G. Edgerton to B. B. Somervell, August 7, 1944, ID, RG #160, NA; Coakley and Leighton, 1968, 658–661.

16. Dobson, 1986, 180; Herring, 1971, 263.
17. Dobson, 1986, 186–190; Thorne, 1978, 384–390; NYT, August 23, 1944.
18. "Lend-Lease Policy After the Defeat of Germany," September 7, 1944, HP.
19. Thorne, 1978, 390; Dobson, 1986, 192; Coakley and Leighton, 1968, 661; F. D. Roosevelt to G. C. Marshall, September 9, 1944, Department of State, *Foreign Relations of the United States, 1944,* Vol. 3, *The British Commonwealth and Europe,* 57; B. B. Somervell to G. C. Marshall, September 11, 1944, SF, RG #160, NA.
20. Coakley and Leighton, 1968, 662; Blum, 1967, 317–319; Dobson, 1986, 210–211; Hathaway, 1981, 72–88.
21. Coakley and Leighton, 1968, 662–670; Herring, 1971, 274–277.
22. Coakley, 1959, 166–173.
23. Motter, 1952, 192–204; Leighton and Coakley, 1955, 577–583.
24. C. Gross to B. B. Somervell, December 31, 1942, HF, RG #336, WNRC.
25. Leighton and Coakley, 1955, 587–589; Howard, 1972, 260–261.
26. B. B. Somervell to W. D. Styer, January 20, 1943, resume of matters presented at staff conference, February 23, 1943, Styer File, RG #160, NA; log of General Somervell's Party, January 29–31, 1943, B. B. Somervell to L. Lutes, February 22, 1943, B. B. Somervell to L. D. Clay, February 22, 1943, SF, RG #160, NA.
27. Leighton and Coakley, 1955, 589.
28. B. B. Somervell to F. D. Roosevelt, February 21, 1943, RP, PSF War Department.
29. Leighton and Coakley, 1955, 590–592.
30. B. B. Somervell to D. Connolly, July 10, 1943, SF, RG #160 NA; Motter, 1952, 400–407.

Chapter 8. War Department Battles

1. B. B. Somervell to S. D. Sturgis, Jr., March 12, 1953, SP; "Engineering Influence," Hughes diary, January 9, 1942, Hughes Papers.
2. Reminiscences of F. T. Davison, 253–4, COHC; interview with Theron D. Weaver, EHF; Millett, 1954, 125, 136–137.
3. B. B. Somervell to H. H. Arnold, April 21, 1943, CF, RG #160, NA; F. C. Foy to J. E. Hewes, July 11, 1975, SP; Millett, 1954, 125–127; reminiscences of William Marbury, 10–11, COHC.
4. B. B. Somervell to G. C. Marshall, April 30, June 30, 1943, SF, RG #160, NA; Millett, 1954, 129–130, 134–136, 163; B. B. Somervell to G. C. Marshall, September 27, 1944, G. C. Marshall to H. H. Arnold, B. Lear, and B. B. Somervell, October 26, 1944, MLF.
5. H. H. Arnold, B. Lear, and B. B. Somervell to G. C. Marshall, November 27, 1944, T. T. Handy to B. B. Somervell, December 28, 1944, SF, RG #160, NA.
6. B. B. Somervell to G. C. Marshall, August 6, 1945, SF, RG #160, NA.
7. L. J. McNair to B. B. Somervell, June 24, 1943, SF, RG #160, NA; Hewes, 1975, 138.
8. B. B. Somervell to T. T. Handy, September 4, 1942, SF, RG #160, NA; Millett, 1954, 112–115, 118; Lutes speech, January 29, 1951, AP; Lutes, 1952b, 11–12; interviews with Carter Magruder and with Paul Caraway, USAMHI; B. B. Somervell

to International Secretariat of the Joint Chiefs of Staff, December 24, 1942, LP, RG #200, NA; Perret, 1991, 76.

9. B. B. Somervell to G. C. Marshall, September 9, 1942, Chief of Staff File, RG #165, NA; B. B. Somervell to G. C. Marshall, September 21, 1942, MLF.

10. Cline, 1951, 259–260; Leighton and Coakley, 1955, 651–652; Millett, 1954, 119.

11. W. D. Styer to J. T. McNarney, no date, B. B. Somervell to G. C. Marshall, March 27, 1943, SF, RG #160, NA.

12. B. B. Somervell to S. D. Embick, April 7, 1943, SF, RG #160, NA; S. D. Embick to G. C. Marshall, April 23, 1943, MLF; Leighton and Coakley, 1955, 653–655; Millett, 1954, 121–122; Cline, 1951, 261; Coakley and Leighton, 1968, 94.

13. B. B. Somervell to G. C. Marshall, March 27, April 3, 1943, SF, RG #160, NA; Hewes, 1975, 138.

14. Cline, 1951, 270–271.

15. T. T. Handy to G. C. Marshall, April 6, 1943, MLF; Millett, 1954, 147.

16. B. B. Somervell to G. C. Marshall, June 1, 1943, R. G. Moses to B. B. Somervell, June 3, 1943, LP, RG #200, NA; L. J. McNair to B. B. Somervell, June 24, 1943, SF, RG #160, NA; Cline, 1951, 273.

17. Coakley and Leighton, 1968, 101–104; Millett, 1954, 143–145.

18. Hewes, 1975, 97–98.

19. L. H. Campbell to H. C. Thomson, July 15, September 7, 1949, CP.

20. Green, Thomson, and Roots, 1955, 93–95, 103–105.

21. Thompson et al., 1957, 536–561; B. B. Somervell to D. Olmstead, February 26, 1943, SF, RG #160, NA.

22. B. B. Somervell to D. Olmstead, March 13, 1943, SF, RG #160, NA.

23. Thompson et al., 1957, 560–562.

24. Thompson et al., 1957, 562–563; G. C. Marshall to B. B. Somervell, June 11, 1943, B. B. Somervell to G. C. Marshall, June 13, 1943, MLF.

25. Stimson diary, September 6, 1943, Stimson Papers.

26. B. B. Somervell to G. C. Marshall, September 12, 1943, SF, RG #160, NA.

27. Stimson and Bundy, 1948, 451–452; Stimson diary, September 16–18, 21, 24, 1943, Stimson Papers; W. D. Styer to B. B. Somervell, October 2, 3, 14, 1943, SF, RG #160, NA.

28. Reminiscences of Lucius D. Clay, 341, COHC; J. Smith, 1990, 161; L. H. Campbell to H. C. Thomson, September 7, 1949, CP; Green, Thomson, and Roots, 1955, 119–120.

29. Pogue, 1973, 266–267.

30. Ickes diary, June 14, October 10, 1942, January 2, 1943, IP; Douglas diary, October 12, 1942, DP; comments by Leslie Groves on Fine and Remington manuscript, EHF.

31. Reminiscences of Lucius D. Clay, 304–305, COHC; interview with Lucius D. Clay, USAMHI; J. Smith, 1990, 267; Pogue, 1973, 267; Sherwood, 1950, 759–761.

32. Pogue, 1973, 267–268; Millett, 1954, 408–409; Sherwood, 1950, 760.

33. Pogue, 1973, 270–271; *Complete Presidential Press Conferences,* 1972, vol. 11, 106–111.

34. B. B. Somervell to G. C. Marshall, October 24, 1943, SF, RG #160, NA.
35. Hewes, 1975, 141–142.
36. Pogue, 1973, 266.
37. Millett, 1954, 414–416.
38. C. F. Robinson to B. B. Somervell, July 15, 1944, Control Division File, RG #160, NA; Hewes, 1975, 142–145; Millett, 1954, 422.
39. L. Lutes to B. B. Somervell, July 7, 1947, LP, RG #200, NA.
40. Transcript and summaries of the Patch Board interviews are located in the files of the U.S. Army Center of Military History.
41. Hewes, 1975, 146–162; Huston, 1966, 420, 683; Millett, 1954, 422–427; Lutes memorandum, LP, RG #200, NA.
42. Bland, 1991, 445, 626.

Chapter 9. Canol

1. Twichell, 1992, 12–69; Coates and Morrison, 1992, 23–35; Dziuban, 1959, 217–222.
2. Twichell, 1992, 148–54. The best source for the role of Somervell and Graham in the birth of Canol is Senate Special Committee Investigating the National Defense Program, *Investigation of the National Defense Program: The Canol Project: Hearings*, 9381–9406, 9573–9595, 9655–9717 (hereinafter, as *The Canol Project*); also see Vilhjalmur Stefansson, "Local Oil Supply," April 15, 1942, *The Canol Project*, 9846–9849. For Stefansson's account of his involvement in the inception of Canol, see Stefansson, 1958, 330–332, and Stefansson, 1964, 327–329.
3. J. H. Graham to B. B. Somervell, April 29, 1942, *The Canol Project*, 9842–9843; *The Canol Project*, 9676; memorandum re conference, April 29, 1942, B. B. Somervell to E. Reybold, April 30, 1942, *The Canol Project*, 9842–9844.
4. Riddle, 1964, 104–105; Toulmin, 1947, 65–68; Twichell, 1992, 256–257.
5. *The Canol Project*, 9677–9680; Riddle, 1964, 105; Leahy, 1950, 127; reminiscences of Anthony McAuliffe, 64–65, COHC.
6. Riddle, 1964, 106; Toulmin, 1947, 73–74; memorandum re conference, April 30, 1942, R. V. LeSueur to A. H. Carter, May 2, 1942, J. H. Graham to A. H. Carter, May 5, 1942, *The Canol Project*, 9845, 9855–9858.
7. Stacy, 1970, 384–385; Dziuban, 1959, 229–230; O'Brien, 1970, 102; McCartney, 1988, 61–62; Dod, 1966, 320–322; Toulmin, 1947, 74; J. L. Hanna to H. L. Stimson, June 4, 1942, J. L. Hanna to R. W. Coghill, April 1, 1943, *The Canol Project*, 9889–9892.
8. H. L. Ickes to F. A. Delano, December 20, 1943, January 1, 1944, SF, RG #160, NA; H. L. Ickes to H. L. Stimson, no date, *The Canol Project*, 9528.
9. *New York Post*, July 29, 1946; Fradkin, 1977, 63.
10. Barry, 1976, 252–267; Woodman, 1977, 18–22; Dod, 1966, 320–324; Coates and Morrison, 1992, 63–66.
11. B. B. Somervell, Memo for Record, August 18, 1942, Styer File, RG #160, NA.
12. Resume of matters presented at staff conference, August 25, 1942, Styer File, RG #160, NA; Dod, 1966, 299–313; interview with William M. Hoge, USAMHI.

13. Twichell, 1992, 203–205; resume of remarks made by General Somervell as a result of his inspection trip to Alaska, August 24, 1942, Styer File, RG #160, NA; interview with William M. Hoge, USAMHI; Greenwood, 1985, 49–51.

14. J. H. Graham to B. B. Somervell, October 12, 1942, B. B. Somervell to W. D. Styer, October 2, 1942, Styer File, RG #160, NA; Dod, 1966, 325–326; Barry, 1976, 254–266; O'Brien, 1970, 103–104.

15. Woodman, 1977, 23–26.

16. H. L. Ickes to H. L. Stimson, October 29, 1942, Ickes diary, November 8, 1942, IP; also see Glen W. Ruby, "Report on Petroleum Production and Future Possibilities of the Mackenzie River District, N.W.T. Canada," October 31, 1942, *The Canol Project,* 9849–9855.

17. Ickes diary, November 15, 22, 1942, IP.

18. Riddle, 1964, 109–111; F. Searls, Jr., to R. P. Patterson et al., December 16, 1942, January 3, 15, 1943, R. P. Patterson to F. Searls, Jr., December 19, 1942, January 14, 1943, H. L. Whitney to D. M. Nelson, March 29, 1943, *The Canol Project,* 9873–9879.

19. H. D. Smith to H. L. Stimson, March 24, April 9, 1943, W. Coy to H. L. Stimson, June 2, 1943, H. L. Ickes to W. Coy, June 19, 1943, *The Canol Project,* 9861–9865; Ickes diary, March 14, June 13, 1943, IP.

20. R. G. Moses to B. B. Somervell, June 30, 1943, B. B. Somervell to G. C. Marshall, July 6, 1943, *The Canol Project,* 9900–9902; B. B. Somervell to T. T. Handy, July 20, 1943, SF, RG #160, NA.

21. Riddle, 1964, 112.

22. R. P. Patterson to H. D. Smith, July 27, 1943, SF, RG #160, NA; Fradkin, 1977, 69.

23. Fradkin, 1977, 73–74.

24. Millett, 1954, 393–394; Riddle, 1964, 112–113; Randall, 1985, 161–162.

25. *The Canol Project,* 9596–9597, 9605–9606, 9623; "The Price of Unpreparedness," 17–18; Fradkin, 1977, 75.

26. *The Canol Project,* 9655–9717; NYT, December 21, 1943.

27. *Complete Presidential Press Conferences,* 1972, vol. 11, 234; B. B. Somervell to F. D. Roosevelt, January 1, 1944, RP, PPF 8354; F. A. Delano to H. L. Ickes, December 21, 27, 1943, F. A. Delano to B. B. Somervell, January 4, 1944, SF, RG #160, NA; Neuberger, 1948, 421; Senate Special Committee Investigating the National Defense Program, *Additional Report of the Special Committee Investigating the National Defense Program;* NYT, January 9, 1944; Maddox, 1981, 126; Fradkin, 1977, 75–76; "A Report on the Summary and Conclusions of the Truman Committee's Canol Report," SP.

28. Harris, 1945, 513–514; Neuberger, 1948, 415–421; reminiscences of Leslie R. Groves, 11–12, COHC.

29. L. Lutes to B. B. Somervell, July 27, 1944, MLF; B. B. Somervell to L. Lutes, August 22, 1946, LP, RG #200, NA; Millett, 1954, 394.

30. B. B. Somervell to G. C. Marshall, January 21, 1944, Styer File, RG #160, NA; Riddle, 1964, 119–120; Fradkin, 1977, 75.

31. Woodman, 1977, 26.

32. Fradkin, 1977, 77–78; *The Canol Project,* 23010; Woodman, 1977, 27.

33. Senate Special Committee Investigating the National Defense Program, *Fifth Annual Report of the Special Committee Investigating the National Defense Program*, 23–25; Dod, 1966, 338–339; Fradkin, 1977, 78; Chester, 1983, 104.

34. Senate Special Committee Investigating the National Defense Program, *Fifth Annual Report of the Special Committee Investigating the National Defense Program*, 23–25; Fradkin, 1977, 78–79; Riddle, 1964, 117–118.

35. L. Lutes to B. B. Somervell, August 31, September 23, 1946, SP; draft of letter prepared by B. B. Somervell, B. B. Somervell to K. C. Royall, September 21, 1946, K. Detzer to L. Lutes, September 27, 1946, LP, RG #200, NA.

36. J. K. Lippert to R. C. Kyser, no date, SP; Dod, 1966, 339; Woodman, 1977, 28; Millett, 1954, 394–395; Coates and Morrison, 1992, 36, 40, 66–67; Twichell, 1992, 273, 313.

Chapter 10. Logistics and Strategy, 1942–1943

1. Leighton and Coakley, 1955, 368–373; interview with Carter Magruder, USAMHI; C. B. Magruder to R. Arnebeck, October 23, 1971, Magruder Papers; Everett Hughes, "Supply from the Rear," Hughes Papers.

2. Matloff and Snell, 1953, 186, 192; Perret, 1991, 134, 181–182.

3. Leighton and Coakley, 1955, 378–381; Steele, 1973, 132.

4. Reminiscences of Lucius D. Clay, 349–350, COHC; J. Smith, 1990, 116; Perret, 1991, 134.

5. Coll, Keith, and Rosenthal, 1958, 367–379; Pogue, 1966, 331; B. B. Somervell to G. C. Marshall, June 15, 1942, MLF; Dunn, 1980, 67–69.

6. B. B. Somervell to D. D. Eisenhower, July 19, 1942, D. D. Eisenhower to B. B. Somervell, July 27, 1942, EP.

7. Perret, 1991, 303; telephone conversation with Forrest C. Pogue, October 26, 1991; reminiscences of John C. H. Lee, 81, USAMHI; Beck, Bortz, Lynch, Mayo, and Weld, 1985, 24; Bykofsky and Larson, 1957, 75.

8. Ruppenthal, 1953, 36; B. B. Somervell to J. E. Chaney, May 14, 1942, B. B. Somervell to D. D. Eisenhower, June 22, 1942, MLF; European Theater of Operations Organization, Moses Papers.

9. Reminiscences of John C. H. Lee, 82–83, USAMHI; Ruppenthal, 1953, 36–44; Leighton and Coakley, 1955, 243.

10. L. Lutes, diary of trip to England, L. Lutes to E. Reybold, June 18, 1942, LP, RG #200, NA; NYT, May 28, 1942; Lutes, 1952b, 6–9; interview with LeRoy Lutes, 114–122, EL; Ferrell, 1981, 56–61; Sherwood, 1950, 581–582; Stimson diary, June 8, 1942, Stimson Papers; Ickes diary, June 14, 1942, IP.

11. Ruppenthal, 1953, 56–57; Leighton and Coakley, 1955, 366–367; interview with Carter B. Magruder, USAMHI; Lutes speech, January 29, 1951, AP; Lutes, 1952b, 10–11.

12. Leighton and Coakley, 1955, 347–349.

13. Leighton and Coakley, 1955, 494; B. B. Somervell to J. C. H. Lee, March 10, 1943, CF, RG #160, NA.

14. B. B. Somervell to D. D. Eisenhower, July 19, August 6, 1942, D. D. Eisenhower to B. B. Somervell, July 27, 1942, EP.

15. B. B. Somervell to J. C. H. Lee, October 30, 1942, CF, RG #160, NA; Leighton and Coakley, 1955, 495–496.

16. Leighton and Coakley, 1955, 482–487.

17. B. B. Somervell to D. D. Eisenhower, July 19, August 6, 1942, EP.

18. Leighton and Coakley, 1955, 424–426; W. D. Styer to G. C. Marshall, August 21, 1942, SF, RG #160, NA.

19. Leighton and Coakley, 1955, 429.

20. Leighton and Coakley, 1955, 429–430; B. B. Somervell to D. D. Eisenhower, September 8, 1942, EP; L. Lutes to J. C. H. Lee, September 12, 1942, LP, RG #200, NA.

21. Lutes speech, January 29, 1951, AP.

22. Interview with Carter Magruder, USAMHI; Lutes, 1952b, 11; Leighton and Coakley, 1955, 439–445; Bykofsky and Larson, 1957, 143; Wharton, 1943, 95–100.

23. Leighton and Coakley, 1955, 474–477; Bykofsky and Larson, 1957, 165–166; D. D. Eisenhower to G. C. Marshall, February 4, 1943, in Hobbs, 1971, 98–99; minutes of conference at Hotel St. George, Algiers, January 25, 1943, D. D. Eisenhower to B. B. Somervell, January 27, May 28, 1943, W. D. Styer to B. B. Somervell, June 13, 1943, SF, RG #160, NA; Eisenhower, 1948, 148–149.

24. B. B. Somervell to G. C. Marshall, November 11, 1942, SF, RG #160, NA.

25. B. B. Somervell to G. C. Marshall, March 25, 1943, CF, RG #160, NA; Coakley and Leighton, 1968, 737–747.

26. Leighton and Coakley, 1955, 511–514.

27. Leighton and Coakley, 1955, 514–515; B. B. Somervell to J. R. Deane, March 3, 1943, CF, RG #160, NA; Matloff, 1959, 56–57.

28. B. B. Somervell, memorandum, July 6, 1943, B. B. Somervell to G. C. Marshall, July 10, 1943, H. Giraud to L. D. Clay, July 10, 1943, G. C. Marshall to Generals Arnold, Somervell, McNarney, Handy, and Moses, July 12, 1943, SF, RG #160, NA; Pogue, 1973, 239–240.

29. B. B. Somervell to G. C. Marshall, August 16, 1943, MLF; Coakley and Leighton, 1968, 703–709.

30. Hughes diary, December 15, 1941, Hughes Papers; Eisenhower, 1948, 22–24; Ferrell, 1981, 42–43; B. B. Somervell to G. C. Marshall, January 12, 1942, G-4/29717–115, RG #165, NA; Leighton and Coakley, 1955, 154–158; Matloff and Snell, 1953, 114–119.

31. B. B. Somervell to G. C. Marshall, January 24, 1942, G-4/29717–114, RG #165, NA.

32. B. B. Somervell to G. C. Marshall, February 9, 1942, E. J. King to G. C. Marshall, May 27, 1943, T. T. Handy to G. C. Marshall, June 24, 1943, MLF; Wardlow, 1951, 213; Bland, 1991, 297.

33. L. Lutes to B. B. Somervell, October 17, 1942, LP, RG #200, NA; Lutes 1952c, 2-7; interview with LeRoy Lutes, 131–148, EL; Leighton and Coakley, 1955, 398–404.

34. B. B. Somervell to D. C. Emmons, April 28, 1942, HF, RG #336, WNRC.

35. B. B. Somervell to F. J. Horne, December 13, 1942, SF, RG #160, NA.

36. Bykofsky and Larson, 1957, 205; Ballantine, 1949, 126–128.

37. Leighton and Coakley, 1955, 658–659.
38. Leighton and Coakley, 1955, 532–541; Hayes, 1982, 242.
39. Matloff, 1959, 33–36; B. B. Somervell to W. D. Styer, January 20, 1943, Styer File, RG #160, NA.
40. Log of General Somervell's party, January 24–February 1, 1943, SF, RG #160, NA; Wedemeyer, 1958, 193–197.
41. Romanus and Sunderland, 1953, 272–277; Hayes, 1982, 336–342; Matloff, 1959, 78–80.
42. B. B. Somervell to A. P. Wavell, August 16, 1943, SP; log of General Somervell's party, February 4–12, 1943, SF, RG #160, NA; O. F. Bryan to H. K. Hastings, February 25, 1943, MLF; resume of staff conference, February 24, 1943, Styer File, RG #160, NA; NYT, February 12, 16, 21, 1943.
43. Reminiscences of Henry A. Wallace, 1895, COHC; B. B. Somervell to O. Ward, May 1, 1950, SP; Millett, 1954, 65.
44. Romanus and Sunderland, 1953, 289–290; B. B. Somervell to T. T. Handy (March 3, 1943), SF, RG #160, NA; B. B. Somervell to R. A. Wheeler, March 13, 1943, LP, RG #200, NA; Leighton and Coakley, 1955, 545–546.
45. Howard, 1972, 445–446; Coakley and Leighton, 1968, 79–81, 504–506; B. B. Somervell to O. Ward, May 1, 1950, SP.

Chapter 11. Logistics and Strategy, 1943

1. Wilt, 1991, 517–529.
2. Coakley and Leighton, 1968, 44–48.
3. B. B. Somervell to T. T. Handy, March 3, 1943, SF, RG #160, NA; Leighton and Coakley, 1955, 687–690; Coakley and Leighton, 1968, 48–51.
4. B. B. Somervell to C. P. Gross, February 9, 1943, SF, RG #160, NA. For a detailed look at the flow of troops and cargo to Britain before D-Day, see Leighton, 1946, 3–39.
5. Coakley and Leighton, 1968, 51–52; Bykofsky and Larson, 1957, 98–99; Millett, 1954, 69.
6. Coakley and Leighton, 1968, 53–55; Bykofsky and Larson, 1957, 100–102.
7. B. B. Somervell to G. C. Marshall, May 14, 1943, SF, RG #160, NA; A. G. Trudeau to B. B. Somervell, May 15, 19, 1943, Trudeau Papers; Matloff, 1959, 126–135; Coakley and Leighton, 1968, 58–76; Pogue, 1973, 198–208.
8. B. B. Somervell to D. D. Eisenhower, March 23, 1943, EP; B. B. Somervell to G. C. Marshall, May 7, 1943, MLF; B. B. Somervell to C. P. Gross, June 27, 1943, HF, RG #336, WNRC; B. B. Somervell to J. C. H. Lee, July 30, 1943, SF, RG #160, NA.
9. Stoler, 1977, 97–102; B. B. Somervell to G. C. Marshall, July 20, 1943, SF, RG #160, NA; T. T. Handy to B. B. Somervell, August 4, 1943, MLF; Coakley and Leighton, 1968, 195–197.
10. G. C. Marshall to W. S. Churchill, September 4, 1943, MLF; W. D. Styer to B. B. Somervell (June 8, 1943), SF, RG #160, NA; Bykofsky and Larson, 1957, 101–107; Coakley and Leighton, 1968, 240–245.
11. Irving, 1981, 88–89; Ambrose, 1969, 346; telephone conversations with John

Griswold, December 14, 1991, and with Mrs. Susan S. Griswold, February 8, 1992. For a contemporary characterization of Lee, see "The Miracle of Supply," 20–22.

12. European Theater of Operations Organization, Moses Papers; W. D. Styer to B. B. Somervell (June 8), June 13, 1943, SF, RG #160, NA; Ruppenthal, 1953, 159–163.

13. Coakley and Leighton, 1968, 445–446; F. J. Horne to B. B. Somervell, April 22, 1943, B. B. Somervell to F. J. Horne, April 22, 1943, SF, RG #160, NA; J. A. Ulio to E. H. Leavey, June 12, 1943, Styer File, RG #160, NA; L. Lutes to E. H. Leavey, June 11, 1943, LP, RG #200, NA.

14. E. H. Leavey to B. B. Somervell, July 29, 1943, SF, RG #160; L. Lutes to B. B. Somervell, August 11, 1943, G. C. Marshall to E. J. King, August 26, 1943, MLF.

15. G. C. Marshall to E. J. King, August 26, 1943, E. J. King to G. C. Marshall, August 30, 1943, MLF; Coakley and Leighton, 1968, 447; Morton, 1962, 495–496.

16. B. B. Somervell to G. C. Marshall, September 12, 1943, B. B. Somervell to C. W. Nimitz, September 22, 1943, SF, RG #160, NA; C. W. Nimitz to B. B. Somervell, October 22, 1943, B. B. Somervell to C. W. Nimitz, November 4, 1943, MLF; Coakley and Leighton, 1968, 447–454; Morton, 1962, 496–501.

17. L. Lutes to B. B. Somervell, September 9, 1943, MLF; log of Pacific trip, September 9, 1943, "One Ocean," PP; diary of trip to the South Pacific, September 9, 1943, LP, RG #200, NA.

18. B. B. Somervell to G. C. Marshall, September 19, 1943, C. D. Silverthorne to T. T. Handy, October 30, 1943, MLF; B. B. Somervell to G. C. Marshall, September 22, 27, 1943, SF, RG #160, NA. For a general look at the service troop issue in 1943, see Millett, 1954, 59, 160; L. J. McNair to B. B. Somervell, June 24, 1943, Styer File, RG #160, NA; interview with Thomas Handy, 292–293, EL; B. B. Somervell to G. C. Marshall, July 15, 1943, SF, RG #160, NA; B. B. Somervell to G. C. Marshall, April 15, 19, 1943, MLF; Coakley and Leighton, 1968, 395, 410–414, 494–498, 570–573.

19. B. B. Somervell to G. C. Marshall, October 3, 1943, B. B. Somervell to W. D. Styer, October 3, 1943, SF, RG #160, NA; B. B. Somervell to D. MacArthur, October 3, 1943, MLF; James, 1975, 352–353.

20. B. B. Somervell to O. Ward, May 1, 1950, SP; Coakley and Leighton, 1968, 502–508; Anders, 1965, 77–81; Meeting of the Combined Chiefs of Staff, August 14, 1943, Department of State, *Foreign Relations of the United States: The Conferences at Washington and Quebec,* 860–861; B. B. Somervell to Joint Chiefs of Staff, August 19, 1943, B. B. Somervell et al. to Combined Chiefs of Staff, August 23, 1943, Styer File, RG #160, NA; Dod, 1966, 426–427.

21. Coakley and Leighton, 1968, 508–9.

22. B. B. Somervell to W. D. Styer, August 22, 1943, Styer File, RG #160, NA; B. B. Somervell to R. A. Wheeler, August 24, 1943, SF, RG #160, NA; Dod, 1966, 429–430; Coakley and Leighton, 1968, 509–510; Bykofsky and Larson, 1957, 552.

23. The works discussing Stilwell's relationship with Chiang are legion. Stilwell's position is best presented in Tuchman, 1970. Chiang's position is best presented in Liang, 1972.

24. B. B. Somervell to G. C. Marshall, October 10, 1943, MLF. Somervell's account of his involvement in the Stilwell-Chiang episode of October 1943 is found in

B. B. Somervell to G. C. Marshall, October 20, 24, 1943 (two messages), SF, RG #160, NA; B. B. Somervell to O. Ward, May 1, 1950, SP.

25. Tuchman, 1970, 497; Romanus and Sunderland, 1953, 378; B. B. Somervell to J. W. Stilwell, November 9, 1943, SF, RG #160, NA. Stilwell, known as Vinegar Joe for his acid tongue, freely used nicknames, many of them derogatory, for almost everybody. Chiang was Peanut or Chinese Jack; Mountbatten was Looie, and Lieutenant General Carten DeWiart, the British liaison officer in China, was the Wart. Many people, including Somervell, liked Stilwell, but many in the British and Chinese armies disliked him for his grating manner, and several of his chief subordinates despised him. In the latters' eyes, he was a poor strategist, failed to look after the welfare of his men, and was too stingy in praising or decorating them. See Perret, 1991, 294–295.

26. Schaller 1979, 143–144; Ziegler, 1988, 8–13; Ziegler, 1985, 244; Bond, 1974, 113; Feis, 1953, 78–79; Stilwell, 1948, 232, 235; Stimson and Bundy, 1948, 536; Stimson diary, November 1, 4, 1943, Stimson Papers.

27. W. D. Styer to B. B. Somervell, October 18, 22, 1943, MLF.

28. Minutes of Conference Held at the Generalissimo's Residence on 19th October 1943, MLF; Romanus and Sunderland, 1953, 380. Somervell's account of the Hump issue can be found in B. B. Somervell to G. C. Marshall, October 20, 25, 1943, SF, RG #160, NA.

29. Matloff, 1959, 239–325; Romanus and Sunderland, 1953, 380–381; B. B. Somervell to G. C. Marshall, October 20, 21, 25, 1943, SF, RG #160, NA; B. B. Somervell to J. Dill, November 3, 1943, telephone conversations between T. T. Handy and B. B. Somervell, November 5, 1943, and between T. T. Handy and G. N. Macready, November 5, 1943, MLF.

30. Ziegler, 1988, 20; Ziegler, 1985, 258; Bond, 1974, 114; B. B. Somervell to G. C. Marshall, October 25, 1943, SF, RG #160, NA.

31. B. B. Somervell to L. Mountbatten, October 25, 1943, MLF; B. B. Somervell to R. A. Wheeler, October 25, 1943, SF, RG #160, NA; Romanus and Sunderland, 1956, 13; Kirby, 1961, 32; Ziegler, 1985, 258; Coakley and Leighton, 1968, 512.

32. B. B. Somervell to W. D. Styer, October 23, 1943, MLF; B. B. Somervell to W. D. Styer, October 21, 22, 1943, SF, RG #160, NA; Dod, 1966, 436–437; Romanus and Sunderland, 1956, 14.

33. Interview with Frederick S. Strong, EHF; Anders, 1965, 80–85; Stilwell, 1948, 218; B. B. Somervell to G. C. Marshall, October 18, 24, 25, 1943, R. A. Wheeler to B. B. Somervell, October 26, 1943, MLF; B. B. Somervell to R. A. Wheeler, October 27, 1943, SF, RG #160, NA.

34. NYT, November 5, 1943; Romanus and Sunderland, 1953, 384–389.

35. For discussion of the strategic decisions at Cairo-Teheran, see Matloff, 1959, 334–387; Pogue, 1973, 297–325; Leighton, 1959, 182–209; Leighton, 1963, 919–937; Eubank, 1985; and Sainsbury, 1986.

36. C. B. Magruder to B. B. Somervell, November 1, 1943, Director of Plans and Operations Subject File, RG #160, NA; diary of trip to the Middle East . . . 1943, November 22, 1943, LP, RG #200, NA; interview with LeRoy Lutes, 162–163, 169, EL.

37. Sainsbury, 1986, 170; Hayes, 1982, 525; Coakley and Leighton, 1968, 278.

38. Meeting of the President With the Joint Chiefs of Staff, November 28, 1943,

Department of State, *Foreign Relations of the United States: The Conferences at Cairo and Teheran,* 477; Matloff, 1959, 356–369; diary of trip to the Middle East . . . 1943, November 27, 1943, LP, RG #200, NA; Coakley and Leighton, 1968, 284–290; also see interviews with LeRoy Lutes, 166–170, and with Thomas Handy, 185–188, 235–238, EL.

Chapter 12. Logistics and Strategy, 1944–1945

1. B. B. Somervell to G. C. Marshall, March 7, 1944, MLF; Coakley and Leighton, 1968, 353–355, 365–368; Bykofsky and Larson, 1957, 107–109.

2. Somervell, 1944b, 86–96; B. B. Somervell to G. C. Marshall, February 7, 1944, MLF; D. D. Eisenhower to B. B. Somervell, March 16, April 4, 12, 1944, B. B. Somervell to D. D. Eisenhower, May 12, 1944, Styer File, RG #160, NA.

3. D. D. Eisenhower to B. B. Somervell, January 27, March 19, 1943, B. B. Somervell to D. D. Eisenhower, March 1, 1943, EP; Pogue, 1954, 267; Irving, 1981, 88; L. Lutes to B. B. Somervell, May 22, 1944, LP, RG #200, NA.

4. Telephone conversations with John Griswold, December 14, 1991, and with Mrs. Susan S. Griswold, February 8, 1992; Ambrose, 1969, 346–347; Pogue, 1973, 362–363.

5. Ruppenthal, 1953, 262–268; Pogue, 1954, 267.

6. B. B. Somervell to D. D. Eisenhower, March 17, 1944, L. Lutes to B. B. Somervell, April 12, 15, 26, 29, May 6, 8, 11, 12, 1944, LP, RG #200, NA; Lutes, 1952d, 4–8, 96, Lutes, 1953, 2–9; Perret, 1991, 305.

7. B. B. Somervell to L. Lutes, April 18, May 1, 4, 1944, SF, RG #160, NA; L. Lutes to B. B. Somervell, May 9, 22, 1944, D. D. Eisenhower to B. B. Somervell, May 10, 1944, B. B. Somervell to D. D. Eisenhower, May 11, 1944, LP, RG #200, NA.

8. NYT, August 13, 14, 16, 17, 1944. For the itinerary of the Somervell-Patterson party, see Edward Martin, Jr., Informal Record of Trip, 8–27 August 1944, SF, RG #160, NA; Churchill, 1953, 94–95; B. B. Somervell to G. C. Marshall, August 18, 1944, MLF.

9. Irving, 1981, 249.

10. Millett, 1954, 82.

11. Coakley and Leighton, 1968, 372–374, 385–387; Ruppenthal, 1959, 126–128.

12. Coakley and Leighton, 1968, 455–470; Matloff, 1959, 463–464; Wardlow, 1951, 291–292.

13. D. D. Eisenhower to B. B. Somervell, November 5, 1944, EP.

14. B. B. Somervell to J. C. H. Lee, November 18, 1944, SF, RG #160, NA; Coakley and Leighton, 1968, 386–387; Ruppenthal, 1959, 126–130.

15. B. B. Somervell to L. D. Clay, October 21, 1944, B. B. Somervell to J. C. H. Lee, October 24, 1944, SF, RG #160, NA; reminiscences of Lucius D. Clay, 436, COHC; J. Smith, 1990, 182–185; Bykofsky and Larson, 1957, 309–311; Wardlow, 1951, 287–289.

16. B. B. Somervell to D. MacArthur, November 5, 1944, LP, RG #200, NA; James, 1975, 501–502.

17. G. C. Marshall to The Joint Chiefs of Staff, November 17, 1944, MLF; Coak-

ley and Leighton, 1968, 555–556.

18. Coakley and Leighton, 1968, 556; Wardlow, 1951, 295–297.

19. B. B. Somervell to D. MacArthur, December 27, 1944, MLF.

20. B. B. Somervell to J. C. H. Lee, December 1, 1944, SF, RG #160, NA; Ruppenthal, 1959, 131–133; Wardlow, 1951, 289–291.

21. Telephone conversation with John Griswold, December 14, 1991; L. Lutes to B. B. Somervell, December 17, 1944, LP, RG #200, NA; Huston, 1966, 531; Ambrose, 1969, 487–488; Pogue, 1954, 321–323; Irving, 1981, 288; J. Smith, 1990, 181; Perret, 1991, 372–373.

22. Weigley, 1981, 375–377; Ruppenthal, 1959, 263–269; J. Smith, 1990, 185–187.

23. B. B. Somervell to J. C. H. Lee, December 1, 1944, B. B. Somervell to L. Lutes, December 12, 27, 1944, SF, RG #160, NA; B. B. Somervell to D. D. Eisenhower, December 12, 1944, EP; Weigley, 1981, 665–666.

24. Irving, 1981, 309–310; Reese, 1984, 83–107.

25. Irving, 1981, 329–343; L. Lutes to B. B. Somervell, December 7, 8, 17, 20, 22, 31, 1944, LP, RG #200, NA; Ruppenthal, 1959, 348–363.

26. B. B. Somervell to L. Lutes, December 27, 1944, SF, RG #160, NA.

27. B. B. Somervell to G. C. Marshall, January 11, 1945, MLF; B. B. Somervell to W. D. Styer, January 11, 1945, SF, RG #160, NA; B. B. Somervell to W. D. Styer, January 19, 1945, LP, RG #200, NA; R. J. Littlejohn to B. B. Somervell, January 18, 1945, Littlejohn Papers.

28. B. B. Somervell to W. D. Styer, January 11, 25, 1945, SF, RG #160, NA.

29. B. B. Somervell to J. C. H. Lee, January 24, 1945, SF, RG #160, NA; B. B. Somervell to D. D. Eisenhower, January 26, 1945, EP; Ruppenthal, 1959, 362–363; Weigley, 1981, 667.

30. B. B. Somervell to W. D. Styer, February 12, 1945, SF, RG #160, NA; Ruppenthal, 1959, 243.

31. B. B. Somervell to J. C. H. Lee, January 30, 1945, SF, RG #160, NA; Ruppenthal, 1959, 399.

32. Pogue, 1954, 391–393; Pogue, 1973, 497–498; Bland, 1991, 390–391, 523, 578, 626; Weigley, 1981, 662–665.

33. Millett, 1954, 86.

34. Coakley and Leighton, 1968, 773–784; B. B. Somervell to W. D. Styer, January 5, 1945, SF, RG #160, NA; McJimsey, 1987, 349–353; B. B. Somervell to J. McCloy, February 18, 1945, CF, RG #160, NA.

35. Coakley and Leighton, 1968, 784–789.

36. Romanus and Sunderland, 1956, 114–115.

37. For an overview of the exchange problem, see "Resume of Chinese Exchange Situation," 19 May 1944, prepared by Lucius D. Clay, Department of State, *United States Relations with China,* vol. 1, 497–502.

38. Blum, 1967, 108–110; B. B. Somervell to T. V. Soong, October 17, 1943, MLF; American Embassy, Chungking, to Secretary of State, December 19, 1943, conference in secretary's office, December 23, 1943, Senate Subcommittee to Investigate the Administration of the Internal Security Act and Other Internal Security Laws of the Committee on the Judiciary, *Morgenthau Diary (China),* vol. 1, 922–923, 968–969 (here-

inafter, as *Morgenthau Diary*); B. B. Somervell to H. M. Morgenthau, Jr., January 3, 1944, CF, RG #160, NA.

39. Romanus and Sunderland, 1956, 71–82, 297–299, 302; Matloff, 1959, 434–435.

40. Blum, 1967, 114–117; "China Loans," January 18, 1944, conference in secretary's office, January 19, 1944, *Morgenthau Diary,* vol. 1, 1022–1024, 1027–1030; Stimson diary, January 19, 1944, Stimson Papers; Romanus and Sunderland, 1956, 299–300; J. Smith, 1990, 176.

41. Stimson diary, February 19, 1944, Stimson Papers; A. H. Carter to B. B. Somervell, February 18, 1944, SF, RG #160, NA; B. B. Somervell to J. Stilwell, February 29, March 3, 1944, B. B. Somervell to H. L. Stimson, June 25, 1944, L. D. Clay to B. B. Somervell, July 17, 1944, CF, RG #160, NA; Clay desk diary, October 9, 1944, CD, RG #160, NA; B. B. Somervell to D. W Bell (October 6, 1944), MLF; conference with Doctor Kung, November 25, 1944, *Morgenthau Diary,* vol. 1, 1360–1389; Denning, 1986, 150–151; J. Smith, 1990, 178–179.

42. Coakley and Leighton, 1968, 516–518; Matloff, 1959, 435–440; Wedemeyer, 1958, 261.

43. B. B. Somervell to T. T. Handy, May 22, 1944, T. T. Handy to B. B. Somervell, May 24, 1944, B. B. Somervell to G. C. Marshall, May 31, 1944, MLF; Coakley and Leighton, 1968, 511–519; Hayes, 1982, 580–582; Anders, 1965, 143–146.

44. W. E. R. Covell to B. B. Somervell, November 16, 1943, B. B. Somervell to W. E. R. Covell, December 31, 1943, SF, RG #160, NA.

45. Romanus and Sunderland, 1956, 259–267.

46. Romanus and Sunderland, 1956, 269–270; H. H. Arnold to B. B. Somervell, March 17, 1944, W. E. R. Covell to B. B. Somervell, April 20, 1944, SF, RG #160, NA; Coakley and Leighton, 1968, 522–524; Bykofsky and Larson, 1957, 563–574.

47. Romanus and Sunderland, 1956, 387–389; Dod, 1966, 463–464; Anders, 1965, 146–149.

48. Romanus and Sunderland, 1959, 136–141.

49. Romanus and Sunderland, 1959, 318–321; Coakley and Leighton, 1968, 622–624.

50. Anders, 1965, 213; Dod, 1966, 663; H. S. Aurand to B. B. Somervell, June 24, August 27, 1945, AP.

51. Wedemeyer, 1958, 293–294; Chennault, 1949, 273; B. B. Somervell to J. P. McWorter, June 9, 1953, B. B. Somervell to O. Ward, May 1, 1950, SP.

52. Coakley and Leighton, 1968, 539; also see Somervell, 1945, 24–25, 94, 96, 98.

53. For an example, see B. B. Somervell to G. C. Marshall, March 5, 1945, MLF.

54. B. B. Somervell to W. D. Styer, March 29, 1945, SF, RG #160, NA; *Minutes of the WPB,* 399; Coakley and Leighton, 1968, 584–593.

55. Coakley and Leighton, 1968, 579–583, 608–612; B. B. Somervell to J. E. Hull, November 7, 1944, B. B. Somervell to G. C. Marshall, February 23, August 15, 1945, B. B. Somervell to T. T. Handy, February 27, 1945, MLF; L. Lutes to B. B. Somervell, July 28, 1945, LP, RG #200, NA.

56. Coakley and Leighton, 1968, 610–619.

57. B. B. Somervell to L. Lutes, July 21, 1945, LP, RG #200, NA; B. B.

Somervell to M. L. Somervell, July 23, 1945, SF, RG #160, NA; NYT, July 30, 1945; B. B. Somervell to D. D. Eisenhower, August 2, 28, 1945, D. D. Eisenhower to B. B. Somervell, August 21, 1945, EP; minutes of staff conference, August 10, 1945, SP.

58. Interview with Mr. and Mrs. E. Macdonald Matter, December 28, 1987.

59. B. B. Somervell to G. C. Marshall, August 18, 1945, SP; NYT, August 19, September 21, October 10, November 21, 22, 1945; Ickes diary, August 26, 1945, IP; "General Supply," 54, 56; H. M. Pasco to G. C. Marshall, October 26, 1945, MLF; B. B. Somervell to D. D. Eisenhower, November 8, 1945, EP; L. Lutes to B. B. Somervell, October 20, 27, 30, November 2, 3, 6, 14, 1945, L. Lutes to W. D. Styer, October 27, 1945, LP, RG #200, NA.

60. G. C. Marshall to B. B. Somervell, October 26, 1945, MLF; NYT, December 18, 20, 27, 1945.

61. NYT, February 14, 1955; Bland, 1991, 445.

Chapter 13. Industrial Manager

1. NYT, March 18, 1946; interview with Mr. and Mrs. E. Macdonald Matter, August 15, 1988; minutes of board of directors meeting of Koppers Company, Inc., March 25, 1946, Beazer East, Inc., Records; *Pittsburgh Post-Gazette,* March 26, 1946.

2. "Koppers," 67–74, 132, 143, 136, 139; Foy, 1958, 10–24; Hersh, 1978, 308–310; Koskoff, 1978, 120–122, 300–301; Windisch, 1955, 17, 19, 21–22; "Comeback at Koppers," 67–69.

3. *Koppers News,* March–April 1945; *Moody's Manual of Investments, 1946,* 2147–2154; *Commercial and Financial Chronicle,* May 26, 1947; "Comeback at Koppers," 69–70.

4. "Comeback at Koppers," 70; interviews with Fletcher Byrom, July 12, 1989; with Douglas Grymes, July 22, 1989; and with George M. Walker, July 26, 1989; "The Cover," 8; B. B. Somervell to D. D. Eisenhower, May 9, 1946, EP.

5. Minutes of board of directors meeting of Koppers Company, Inc., July 16, 29, 1946, Beazer East, Inc., Records; *Koppers News,* August–September 1946; NYT, September 26, 1946.

6. Interview with George M. Walker, July 26, 1989.

7. Interviews with George M. Walker, July 26, 1989; with Fletcher Byrom, July 12, 1989; and with Douglas Grymes, July 22, 1989; minutes of board of directors meeting of Koppers Company, Inc., January 27, 1947, Beazer East, Inc., Records; Somervell, 1948; "Somervell Uses a Military Idea to Run Koppers Co.," 70–75; "How Gen. Somervell Runs Koppers," 67–72; "The Control Section: A New Aid to Management," 4–9.

8. B. B. Somervell to G. C. Marshall, May 31, 1949; MLF; interviews with Fletcher Byrom, July 12, 1989; with Douglas Grymes, July 22, 1989; with Walter McCutcheon, August 9, 1988; and with George M. Walker, July 26, 1989; F. Davis to J. Hewes, June 27, 1975, SP.

9. Minutes of board of directors meeting of Koppers Company, Inc., January 27, February 24, 1947, Beazer East, Inc., Records; B. B. Somervell to A. M. Scaife, November 26, 1947, SP; interviews with Fletcher Byrom, July 12, 1989, and with Douglas Grymes, July 22, 1989; Somervell, "Leadership," address given at executive

orientation of Koppers Company, Inc., April 20, 1948, Beazer East, Inc., Records; *Koppers News,* March 1947, May 1948, May 1949; B. B. Somervell to D. D. Eisenhower, January 27, 1947, EP; address by General Somervell, January 23, 1947, Beazer East, Inc., Records.

10. NYT, May 29, June 1, October 26, 1947; "General Somervell Says: Industry must Act Now to Stop World War III," 66–71; "Actual Plan for Defense," 128–129; "Industry Makes Its War Plans," 26; *Koppers News,* July 12, 1954.

11. Interview with George M. Walker, July 26, 1989; *Pittsburgh Press,* June 14, 1946; NYT, August 28, December 31, 1946; minutes of board of directors meeting of Koppers, Inc., August 26, September 30, December 30, 1946, Beazer East, Inc., Records; *Koppers Company Annual Report for 1946.*

12. NYT, July 1, 1947, January 1, 1949, January 2, 1952, September 9, 1953; Crain, 1949, 65; "Comeback at Koppers," 140, 142; *Koppers Company Annual Report for 1952, 1953, 1954, 1955*; "Koppers' Step to Profits," 80.

13. "Comeback at Koppers," 68, 72, 138, 140; NYT, December 5, 1947, May 2, 1949; *Koppers News,* February 1948; "Koppers Geared to High Production Levels as 1951 Opens," 108; "Koppers Plans more Expansion in 1952," 230–231.

14. Interviews with Douglas Grymes, July 22, 1989; with Walter McCutcheon, August 9, 1988; with B. T. Larkin, August 2, 1989; and with Mrs. Fred C. Foy, August 7, 1989; B. T. Larkin to the Commanding Officer, Fort Lee, Virginia, May 4, 1989, copy in author's possession; interview with George M. Walker, July 26, 1989; B. B. Somervell to W. Chandler, December 5, 1950, SP.

15. Minutes of board of directors meeting of Koppers Company, Inc., March 27, 1950, Beazer East, Inc., Records; Foy, 1958, 31–32; Hersh, 1978, 383.

16. B. B. Somervell to W. de Krafft, July 23, 1951, SP; "Comeback at Koppers," 67–68, 142; *Koppers Company Annual Report for 1954; Commercial and Financial Chronicle,* May 26, 1955.

17. B. B. Somervell to R. P. Patterson, November 14, 1947, B. B. Somervell to F. E. Eberstadt, August 13, 1947, SP; B. B. Somervell to L. Lutes, November 10, 1948, January 16, 1950, LP, RG #200, NA.

18. B. B. Somervell to L. H. Campbell, January 3, 1951, B. B. Somervell to C. E. Wilson, April 4, 1951, H. S. Truman to B. B. Somervell, April 23, 1951, B. B. Somervell to H. S. Truman, April 25, 1951, SP.

19. B. B. Somervell to D. D. Eisenhower, April 21, 1954, SP; *Pittsburgh Post-Gazette,* September 28, 1954; B. B. Somervell to W. E. Covell, January 2, 26, 1955, Covell Papers; interview with Mr. and Mrs. E. Macdonald Matter, August 15, 1988; *Pittsburgh Sun-Telegraph,* February 14, 1955.

BIBLIOGRAPHY

Archival Sources

National Archives. RG #69. Records of the Works Progress Administration.
——— . RG #94. Records of the Office of the Adjutant General.
——— . RG #120. Records of the American Expeditionary Forces.
——— . RG #160. Records of the Army Service Forces.
——— . RG #165. Records of the Office of the Chief of Staff.
——— . RG #200. Collection of Personal Papers.
Washington National Records Center. RG #77. Records of the Office of the Chief of Engineers.
——— . RG #92. Records of the Office of the Quartermaster General.
——— . RG #336. Records of the Office of the Chief of Transportation.

Miscellaneous Records

Beazer East, Inc. Records. Pittsburgh, Pennsylvania.
George C. Marshall Research Library. Library Files.
United States Army Center of Military History. Research Files.
United States Army Corps of Engineers. Engineers Historical File.
United States Army Military History Institute. War College Archives.
United States Military Academy Library and Archives. Library Files.

Papers of Public Persons

Aurand, Henry S. EL.
Campbell, Levin H. USAMHI.
Covell, William E. Hoover Institution on War, Revolution and Peace.
Douglas, Lewis W. University of Arizona Library.
Eisenhower, Dwight D. EL.
Hopkins, Harry L. Franklin D. Roosevelt Library.
Hughes, Everett. Library of Congress.
Ickes, Harold L. Library of Congress.
Kemmerer, Edward W. Princeton University Library.
Littlejohn, Robert J. USAMHI.

Magruder, Carter B. USAMHI.
Moses, Raymond G. USAMHI.
Patterson, Robert P. Library of Congress.
Roosevelt, Franklin D. Franklin D. Roosevelt Library.
Somervell, Brehon B. USAMHI.
Stimson, Henry L. Yale University Library.
Tenney, Clesen H. USAMHI.
Trudeau, Arthur G. USAMHI.
Williams, Aubrey. Franklin D. Roosevelt Library.

Interviews and Reminiscences

Albright, Horace M. Reminiscences. COHC.
Aurand, Henry S. Interview. USAMHI.
Barker, James M. Reminiscences. COHC.
Bundy, Harvey H. Reminiscences. COHC.
Burns, James H. Interview. EHF.
Byrom, Fletcher. Interview with the author, July 12, 1989, Carefree, Arizona.
Cahill, Holger. Reminiscences. COHC.
Caraway, Paul. Interview. USAMHI.
Carmody, John. Reminiscences. COHC.
Casey, Hugh. Interview. EHF.
Clark, Gilmore D. Reminiscences. COHC.
Clay, Lucius D. Interview. USAMHI, and Reminiscences. COHC.
Colglazier, Robert W. Interview. USAMHI.
Davison, F. T. Reminiscences. COHC.
Delano, William A. Reminiscences. COHC.
Dorr, Goldthwaite H. Reminiscences. COHC.
Dresser, Ferdinand J. C. Interview. EHF.
Foy, Mrs. Fred C. Interview with the author, August 7, 1989, Ligonier, Pennsylvania.
Friedlich, H. Reminiscences. COHC.
Gladieux, Bernard L. Reminiscences. COHC.
Greenbaum, Edward. Reminiscences. COHC.
Gregory, Edmund B. Interview. EHF.
Griswold, John. Telephone conversation with the author, December 14, 1991.
Griswold, Mrs. Susan S. Telephone conversation with the author, February 8, 1992, and correspondence.
Groves, Leslie R. Interview. EHF, and Reminiscences. COHC.
Grymes, Douglas. Interview with the author, July 22, 1989, Pittsburgh, Pennsylvania.
Hadden, Gavin. Interview. EHF.
Handy, Thomas T. Interview. EL.
Hardin, John. Interview. EHF.
Hoge, William M. Interview. USAMHI.
Kirkpatrick, Elmer E. Interview. USAMHI.
Larkin, B. T. Interview with the author, August 2, 1989, Valencia, Pennsylvania.
Lee, John C. H. Reminiscences. USAMHI.

Leisenring, Luther M. Interview. EHF.
Lubin, Isador. Reminiscences. COHC.
Lutes, LeRoy. Interview. EL.
Madigan, Michael. Reminiscences. EHF.
Magruder, Carter B. Interview. USAMHI.
Marbury, William C. Reminiscences. COHC.
Matter, Mr. and Mrs. E. Macdonald. Interviews with the author, December 28, 1987, and August 15, 1988, Pittsburgh, Pennsylvania.
McAuliffe, Anthony. Reminiscences. COHC.
McCutcheon, Walter. Interview with the author, August 9, 1988, Pittsburgh, Pennsylvania.
McDonald, Norman F. World War I Survey. USAMHI.
Nathan, Robert. Telephone conversation with the author, February 25, 1992, and interview with the author, June 14, 1992, Bethesda, Maryland.
O'Brien, John Lord. Reminiscences. COHC.
Pagan, Mary B. Interview. EHF.
Petersen, Howard. Reminiscences. COHC.
Pirnie, Malcolm, and Voorhees, Stephen F. Interview. EHF.
Pogue, Forrest C. Telephone conversation with the author, October 26, 1991.
Renshaw, Clarence. Interviews. EHF.
Reybold, Eugene. Interview. EHF.
Rosenthal, Morris. Reminiscences. COHC.
Schieffelin, Bayard. Reminiscences. COHC.
Schley, Julian L. Interview. EHF.
Spalding, Sidney P. Interview. USAMHI.
Strong, Frederick S. Interview. EHF.
Tatlow, Richard H., III. Interview. EHF.
Thomas, Elmer G. Interview. EHF.
Walker, George M. Interview with the author, July 26, 1989, White Stone, Virginia.
Wallace, Henry A. Reminiscences. COHC.
Weaver, Theron D. Interview. EHF.

Public Documents

Chief of Engineers Annual Report, 1932, 1933, 1936.
The General Service Schools Annual Report, 1923.
Historical Report of the Chief Engineer, American Expeditionary Forces, 1917–1919. Washington, D.C.: Department of War, 1919.
Somervell, Brehon. B. *Report to the Chief of Engineers, United States Army, on Application for Preliminary Permit from Federal Power Commission by the Potomac River Corporation for Power Development of the Potomac River.* Washington, D.C.: U. S. Engineer Office, 1929.
U. S. Bureau of the Budget. *The United States at War: Development and Administration of the War Production Program by the Federal Government.* Washington, D.C.: Bureau of the Budget, 1946.
U.S. Civilian Production Administration. *Industrial Mobilization for War.* Washington,

D.C.: Government Printing Office, 1947.
——— . *Minutes of the War Production Board, Jan. 20, 1942–Oct. 9, 1945.* Washington, D.C.: Civilian Production Administration, 1946.
U. S. Congress. House. Committee on Appropriations. *Military Establishment Appropriation Bill for 1942: Hearings.* 77th Cong., 1st sess., 1941.
——— . Committee on Military Affairs. *Inquiry As to National Defense Construction: Hearings.* 77th Cong., 1st sess., 1941.
——— . Committee on Rivers and Harbors. *Atlantic-Gulf Ship Canal Across Florida: Hearings.* 76th Cong., 1st sess., 1939.
——— . Committee on Rivers and Harbors. *Atlantic-Gulf Ship Canal, Fla.: Hearings.* 75th Cong., 1st sess., 1937.
——— . Subcommittee of the Committee on Appropriations. *Fourth Supplemental National Defense Appropriation Bill for 1941: Hearings.* 77th Cong., 1st sess., 1941.
——— . Subcommittee of the Committee on Appropriations. *Investigation and Study of the Works Progress Administration: Hearings.* 76th Cong., 1st sess., 1939.
U. S. Congress. Senate. Committee on Commerce. *Florida Ship Canal: Hearings.* 76th Cong., 1st sess., 1939.
——— . Committee on District of Columbia. *George Washington Memorial Parkway: Hearings.* 71st Cong., 2d sess., 1930.
——— . Special Committee Investigating the National Defense Program. *Additional Report of the Special Committee Investigating the National Defense Program.* 78th Cong., 1st sess., 1944.
——— . Special Committee Investigating the National Defense Program. *Fifth Annual Report of the Special Committee Investigating the National Defense Program.* 79th Cong., 2d sess., 1946.
——— . Special Committee Investigating the National Defense Program. *Investigation of the National Defense Program: Progress of National Defense Program: Hearings.* 77th Cong., 1st sess., 1941.
——— . Special Committee Investigating the National Defense Program. *Investigation of the National Defense Program: The Canol Project: Hearings.* 78th Cong., 1st sess., 1944.
——— . Special Committee Investigating the National Defense Program. *Investigation of the National Defense Program: Hearings.* 78th Cong., 2d sess., 1944.
——— . Subcommittee of the Committee on Appropriations. *First National Defense Appropriation Bill for 1942: Hearings.* 77th Cong., 1st sess., 1941.
——— . Subcommittee to Investigate the Administration of the Internal Security Act and Other Internal Security Laws of the Committee on the Judiciary. *Morgenthau Diary (China).* 89th Cong., 1st sess., 1965. 2 vols.
U. S. Department of State. *Foreign Relations of the United States: The Conferences at Cairo and Teheran, 1943.* Washington, D.C.: Government Printing Office, 1961.
——— . *Foreign Relations of the United States: The Conferences at Washington and Quebec, 1943.* Washington, D.C.: Government Printing Office, 1970.
——— . *Foreign Relations of the United States: 1944.* Vol. 3, *The British Commonwealth and Europe.* Washington, D.C.: Government Printing Office, 1965.
——— . *United States Relations With China, With Special Reference to the Period, 1944–1949.* Washington, D.C.: Government Printing Office, 1949. 2 vols.

Newspapers

Commercial and Financial Chronicle, 1947-1955.
Koppers News, 1945-1955.
New York Post, 1946.
New York Times, 1925-1953.
Pittsburgh Post-Gazette, 1946-1954.
Pittsburgh Press, 1948.
Pittsburgh Sun-Telegraph, 1955.
Richmond Times-Dispatch, 1989.

Articles, Books, and Dissertations

"Actual Plan for Defense." 1948. *Mill and Factory* (June): 128-129.
Allen, Henry T. 1923. *My Rhineland Journal.* Boston: Houghton Mifflin Company.
Ambrose, Stephen E. 1969. *The Supreme Commander: The War Years of General Dwight D. Eisenhower.* Garden City, New York: Doubleday and Company.
———. 1983. *Eisenhower.* Vol. 1, *Soldier, General of the Army, President Elect, 1890–1952.* New York: Simon and Schuster.
Anders, Leslie. 1965. *The Ledo Road: General Joseph W. Stilwell's Highway to China.* Norman, Oklahoma: University of Oklahoma Press.
———. 1985. *Gentle Knight: The Life and Times of Major General Edwin Forrest Harding.* Kent, Ohio: Kent State University Press.
Armitstead, Paul Thompson. 1967. "Retired Military Leaders in American Business." Ph.D. diss., University of Texas.
"The Army Raises a Ghost." 1941. *Time* (August 18): 58-59.
Ball, Harry, P. 1983. *Of Responsible Command: A History of the U.S. Army War College.* Carlisle Barracks, Pennsylvania: Alumni Association of the U.S. Army War College.
Ballantine, Duncan S. 1949. *U.S. Naval Logistics in the Second World War.* Princeton, New Jersey: Princeton University Press.
Barry, P. S. 1976. "The Prolific Pipeline: Getting Canol Under Way." *Dalhousie Review* 56 (Summer): 252-267.
Beck, Alfred, Abe Bortz, Charles W. Lynch, Linda Mayo, and Ralph F. Weld. 1985. *The Corps of Engineers: The War Against Germany.* In *U.S. Army in World War II.* Washington, D.C.: Center of Military History.
Behrens, C. B. A. 1955. *Merchant Shipping and the Demands of War.* London: Her Majesty's Stationary Office.
Bentley, Joanne. 1988. *Hallie Flanagan: A Life in the American Theatre.* New York: Alfred A. Knopf.
Bernstein, Barton J. 1967. "The Debate on Industrial Reconversion: The Protection of Oligopoly and Military Control of the Economy." *American Journal of Economics and Sociology* 26 (April): 159-172.
"Billion Dollar Watchdog." 1943. *Time* (March 8): 13-15.
Bland, Larry, ed. 1991. *George C. Marshall: Interviews and Reminiscences for Forrest Pogue.* Lexington, Virginia: George C. Marshall Research Foundation.
Bland, Larry, Sharone Ritenour, and Clarence E. Wunderlin, eds. 1986. *The Papers of*

George Catlett Marshall. Vol. 2, *"We Cannot Delay," July 1939–December 6, 1941*. Baltimore: Johns Hopkins University Press.

Blum, John Morgan. 1967. *From the Morgenthau Diaries: Years of War, 1941–1945*. Boston: Houghton Mifflin Company.

———, ed. 1973. *The Price of Vision: The Diary of Henry A. Wallace, 1942–1946*. Boston: Houghton Mifflin Company.

Blumberg, Barbara Marilyn. 1974. "The Works Progress Administration in New York City: A Case Study of the New Deal in Action." Ph.D. diss., Columbia University.

———. 1979. *The New Deal and the Unemployed: The View from New York City*. Lewisburg, Pennsylvania: Bucknell University Press.

Blumenson, Martin. 1989. "America's World War II Leaders in Europe: Some Thoughts." *Parameters* 19 (December): 2-13.

Bond, Brian, ed. 1974. *Chief of Staff: The Diaries of Lieutenant-General Sir Henry Pownall*. Vol. 2, *1940–1944*. Hamden, Connecticut: Archon Books.

"Brass Hats in Blitzkrieg." 1941. *Nation* (August 23): 153-154.

The Brecky, 1909.

Brigante, John E. 1950. *The Feasibility Dispute: Determination of War Production Objectives for 1942 and 1943*. Washington, D.C.: Committee on Public Administration Cases.

Brinkley, David. 1988. *Washington Goes to War: The Extraordinary Story of the Transformation of a City*. New York: Alfred A. Knopf.

Brophy, Leo P., and George F. B. Fisher. 1959. *The Chemical Warfare Service: Organizing for War*. In *U.S. Army in World War II*. Washington, D.C.: Office of the Chief of Military History.

Browder, Robert Paul, and Thomas G. Smith. 1986. *Independent: A Biography of Lewis W. Douglas*. New York: Alfred A. Knopf.

Buker, George E. 1975. *Sun, Sand and Water: A History of the Jacksonville District U.S. Army Corps of Engineers, 1821–1975*. Jacksonville, Florida: U.S. Army Corps of Engineers.

Bykofsky, Joseph, and Harold Larson. 1957. *The Transportation Corps: Operations Overseas*. In *U.S. Army in World War II*. Washington, D.C.: Office of the Chief of Military History.

Byrnes, James F. 1958. *All in One Lifetime*. New York: Harper and Brothers.

Campbell, Levin H., Jr. 1946. *The Industry-Ordnance Team*. New York: Whittlesey House.

"'Career-Men,' WPA Frankenstein?" 1937. *Literary Digest* (June 12): 10-11.

Catton, Bruce. 1948. *The War Lords of Washington*. New York: Harcourt, Brace and Company.

Chennault, Claire. 1949. *Way of a Fighter*. New York: G. P. Putnam's Sons.

Chester, Edward W. 1983. *United States Oil Policy and Diplomacy: A Twentieth-Century Overview*. Westport, Connecticut: Greenwood Press.

Christman, Calvin L. 1971. "Ferdinand Eberstadt and Economic Mobilization for War, 1941-1943." Ph.D. diss., Ohio State University.

———. 1973. "Donald Nelson and the Army: Personality as a Factor in Civil-Military Relations During World War II." *Military Affairs* 37 (February): 81-83.

Churchill, Winston S. 1953. *The Second World War*. Vol. 6, *Triumph and Tragedy*.

Boston: Houghton Mifflin Company.
Clay, Floyd D. 1976. *A Century on the Mississippi: A History of the Memphis District, U.S. Army Corps of Engineers, 1876–1976*. Memphis, Tennessee: U.S. Army Corps of Engineers.
Clay, Lucius D. 1943. "The Army Supply Program." *Fortune* (February): 96-97, 225-230, 232.
Cline, Ray S. 1951. *Washington Command Post: The Operations Division*. In *U.S. Army in World War II*. Washington, D.C.: Office of the Chief of Military History.
Coakley, Robert W. 1959. "The Persian Corridor as a Route for Aid to the U.S.S.R. (1942)." In *Command Decisions*, ed. Kent Roberts Greenfield. New York: Harcourt, Brace and Company.
Coakley, Robert W., and Richard M. Leighton. 1968. *Global Logistics and Strategy, 1943–1945*. In *U.S. Army in World War II*. Washington, D.C.: Office of the Chief of Military History.
Coates, K. S., and W. R. Morrison. 1992. *The Alaska Highway in World War II: The U.S. Army of Occupation in Canada's Northwest*. Norman, Oklahoma: University of Oklahoma Press.
Coffman, Edward M. 1966. *The Hilt of the Sword: The Career of Peyton C. March*. Madison, Wisconsin: University of Wisconsin Press.
Coffman, Edward M., and Peter F. Herrly. 1977. "The American Regular Army Office Corps Between the World Wars: A Collective Biography." *Armed Forces and Society* 4 (November): 55-73.
Coll, Blanche D., Jean E. Keith, and Herbert H. Rosenthal. 1958. *The Corps of Engineers: Troops and Equipment*. In *U.S. Army in World In World War II*. Washington, D.C.: Office of the Chief of Military History.
"Comeback at Koppers." 1952. *Fortune* (January): 67-71, 137-38, 140, 142.
Complete Presidential Press Conferences of Franklin D. Roosevelt. 1972. 12 vols. New York: DaCapo Press.
"Congress Criticizes Army Construction Costs." 1941. *Constructor* (September): 26-28.
"Congress Gives Great Aid to Park Development in Federal City Region." 1930. *American City* (July): 152.
Connery, Robert H. 1951. *The Navy and the Industrial Mobilization in World War II*. Princeton, New Jersey: Princeton University Press.
Contreras, Belisario R. 1983. *Tradition and Innovation in New Deal Art*. Lewisburg, Pennsylvania: Bucknell University Press.
"The Control Section: A New Aid to Management." 1949. *Modern Management* (October): 4-9.
"The Cover." 1946. *Business Week* (May 11): 8.
Cowdrey, Albert E. 1978. *A City for the Nation: The Army Engineers and the Building of Washington, D.C., 1790–1967*. Washington, D.C.: Office of the Chief of Engineers.
Crain, Murray E. 1949. "How Koppers Launched a New Product for 53% Gain." *Industrial Marketing* (November): 65.
Cuff, Robert D. 1973. *The War Industries Board: Business-Government Relations during World War I*. Baltimore: Johns Hopkins University Press.
———. 1984. "Commentary." In *The Home Front and War in the Twentieth Century:*

Proceedings of the Tenth Military History Symposium, USAF Academy, 1982. Washington, D.C.: Office of Air Force History.
Danchev, Alex. 1986. *Very Special Relationship: Field-Marshall Sir John Dill and the Anglo-American Alliance, 1941–44.* London: Brassey's Defence Publishers.
———. 1990. *Establishing the Anglo-American Alliance: The Second World War Diaries of Brigadier Vivian Dykes.* London: Brassey's Defence Publishers.
Daniels, Jonathan. 1971. *The Man of Independence.* Port Washington, New York: Kennikat Press.
Davenport, Walter. 1935. "Splitting Florida." *Collier's* (December 14): 7-9, 48-50.
Denning, Margaret B. 1986. *The Sino-American Alliance in World War II. Cooperation and Dispute Among Nationalists, Communists, and Americans.* Berne: Peter Lang.
Dobson, Alan P. 1986. *U.S. Wartime Aid to Britain, 1940–1946.* New York: St. Martin's Press.
Dod, Karl C. 1966. *The Corps of Engineers: The War Against Japan.* In *U.S. Army in World War II.* Washington, D.C.: Office of the Chief of Military History.
Doig, Jameson W., and Erwin C. Hargrove. 1987. "Leadership and Political Analysis." In *Leadership and Innovation: A Biographical Perspective on Entrepreneurs in Government,* ed. Jameson W. Doig and Erwin C. Hargrove. Baltimore: Johns Hopkins University Press.
Dunbar, L. D. 1940a. "Army Man at Work." *New Yorker* (February 10): 22-27.
———. 1940b. "Army Man at Work." *New Yorker* (February 17): 27-30.
Dunn, Walter Scott, Jr. 1980. *Second Front Now—1943.* Tuscaloosa, Alabama: University of Alabama Press.
Dziuban, Stanley W. 1959. *Military Relations Between the United States and Canada, 1939–1945.* In *U.S. Army in World War II.* Washington, D.C.: Office of the Chief of Military History.
89th Division: A Summary of Operations in the World War. 1944. Washington, D.C.: American Battle Monuments Commission.
Eisenhower, Dwight D. 1948. *Crusade in Europe.* Garden City, New York: Doubleday and Company.
English, George H., Jr. 1920. *History of the 89th Division, U.S.A.* Denver: The War Society of the 89th Division.
Eubank, Keith. 1985. *Summit at Teheran.* New York: William Morrow and Company.
"Exit White House Pet: Senate Makes Short Shrift of Florida Ship Canal." 1936. *Literary Digest* (March 28): 6-7.
Feagin, Joe R., and Kelly Riddell. 1990. "The State, Capitalism, and World War II." *Armed Forces and Society* 17 (Fall): 53-79.
Feis, Herbert. 1953. *The China Tangle.* Princeton, New Jersey: Princeton University Press.
Fennelly, John F. 1965. *Memoirs of a Bureaucrat: A Personal Story of the War Production Board.* Chicago: October House.
Ferrell, Robert H. 1983. *Harry S. Truman and the Modern American Presidency.* Boston: Little, Brown and Company.
———, ed. 1981. *The Eisenhower Diaries.* New York: W. W. Norton and Company.
———, ed. 1983. *Dear Bess: The Letters from Harry to Bess Truman, 1910–1959.* New York: W. W. Norton and Company.
Fine, Lenore, and Jesse Remington. 1972. *The Corps of Engineers: Construction in the*

United States. In *U.S. Army in World War II*. Washington, D.C.: Office of the Chief of Military History.
Fischer, John. 1945. "The Army Takes Over." *Harper's Magazine* (May): 481-491.
Flanagan, Hallie. 1940. *Arena: The History of the Federal Theatre*. New York: Benjamin Blom.
"Florida Canal, Oliver Twists, and Uncle Sam." 1935. *Literary Digest* (October 12): 34.
Foy, Fred C. 1958. *Ovens, Chemicals and Men! Koppers Company, Inc.* New York: The Newcomen Society.
Fradkin, Philip L. 1977. "The First and Forgotten Pipeline." *Audubon* (November): 58-79.
"General Somervell Says: Industry Must Act Now to Stop World War III." 1947. *Factory Management and Maintenance* (August): 66-71.
"General Supply." 1945. *Newsweek* (October 1): 54, 56.
Goldberg, Alfred. 1992. *The Pentagon: The First Fifty Years*. Washington, D.C.: Office of the Secretary of Defense.
"Good News is Bad News." 1943. *Time* (July 12): 19.
Gough, Terrence J. 1991. "Origins of the Army Industrial College: Military-Business Tensions After World War I." *Armed Forces and Society* 17 (Winter): 259-275.
Goulden, Joseph C. 1972. *Meany*. New York: Atheneum.
Green, Constance McLaughlin. 1962. *Washington: A History of the Nation's Capital, 1800-1950*. 2 vols. Princeton, New Jersey: Princeton University Press.
Green, Constance McLaughlin, Harry C. Thomson, and Peter C. Roots. 1955. *The Ordnance Department: Planning Munitions for War*. In *U.S. Army in World War II*. Washington, D.C.: Office of the Chief of Military History.
Greenwood, John T. 1985. "General Bill Hoge and the Alaska Highway." In *The Alaska Highway: Papers of the 40th Anniversary Symposium*, ed. Kenneth Coates. Vancouver: University of British Columbia Press.
Gwyer, J. M. A, and J. R. M. Butler. 1964. *Grand Strategy*. Vol. 3, *June 1941–August 1942*. London: Her Majesty's Stationary Office.
Hall, H. Duncan, and C. C. Wrigley. 1956. *Studies of Overseas Supply*. London: Her Majesty's Stationary Office.
Harriman, Averell, with Elie Abel. 1975. *Special Envoy to Churchill and Stalin, 1941–1946*. New York: Random House.
Harris, Edward A. 1945. "Canol, the War's Epic Blunder." *Nation* (May 5): 513–514.
Hathaway, Robert M. 1981. *Ambiguous Partnership: Britain and America, 1944–1947*. New York: Columbia University Press.
Hayes, Grace Person. 1982. *The History of the Joint Chiefs of Staff in World War II: The War Against Japan*. Annapolis, Maryland: United States Naval Institute Press.
Heckscher, August, with Phyllis Robinson. 1978. *When La Guardia Was Mayor: New York's Legendary Years*. New York: W. W. Norton.
"Here Comes the Army." 1942. *Time* (August 3): 16-17.
Herring, George C., Jr. 1971. "The United States And British Bankruptcy, 1944-1945: Responsibilities Deferred." *Political Science Quarterly* 86 (June): 260-280.
Hersh, Burton. 1978. *The Mellon Family: A Fortune in History*. New York: William Morrow and Company.
Hewes, James E., Jr. 1975. *From Root to McNamara: Army Organization and Administra-*

tion, *1900–1963*. Washington, D.C.: Center of Military History.
Hobbs, Joseph Patrick, ed. 1971. *Dear General: Eisenhower's Wartime Letters to Marshall*. Baltimore: Johns Hopkins Press.
Hooks, Gregory. 1991. *Forging the Military-Industrial Complex: World War II's Battle of the Potomac*. Urbana, Illinois: University of Illinois Press.
"How Gen. Somervell Runs Koppers." 1949. *Modern Industry* (May 15): 67-72.
Howard, Michael. 1972. *Grand Strategy*. Vol. 4, *August 1942–September 1943*. London: Her Majesty's Stationary Office.
Howitzer, 1914.
Huston, James A. 1966. *The Sinews of War: Army Logistics, 1775–1953*. Washington, D.C.: Office of the Chief of Military History.
Ickes, Harold L. 1953. *The Secret Diary of Harold L. Ickes*. Vol 1, *The First Thousand Days, 1933–1936*. New York: Simon and Schuster.
"Industry Makes Its War Plans." 1950. *Business Week* (August 19): 26.
Irving, David. 1981. *The War Between the Generals: Inside the Allied High Command*. New York: Congdon and Weed.
James, D. Clayton. 1975. *Years of MacArthur*. Vol. 2, *1941–1945*. Boston: Houghton Mifflin and Company.
Janney, John. 1944. "The Man Behind the Invasion." *American Magazine* (June): 24-25, 87, 89.
The Journals of David E. Lilienthal. Vol. 1, *The TVA Years, 1939–1945*. 1964. New York: Harper and Row.
Kirby, Woodburn S. 1961. *The War Against Japan*. Vol. 3, *The Decisive Battles*. London: Her Majesty's Stationary Office.
Koistinen, Paul A. C. 1964. "The Hammer and the Sword: Labor, the Military, and Industrial Mobilization, 1920-1945." Ph.D. diss., University of California, Berkeley.
———. 1984. "Warfare and Power Relations in America: Mobilizing the World II Economy." In *The Homefront and War in the Twentieth Century: Proceedings of the Tenth Military History Symposisum, USAF Academy, 1982*. Washington, D.C.: Office of Air Force History.
"Koppers." 1937. *Fortune* (April): 67-74, 132, 134, 136, 139.
Koppers Company Annual Report, 1946–1955.
"Koppers Geared to High Production Levels as 1951 Opens." 1951. *Blast Furnace and Steel Plant* (January): 108.
"Koppers Plans More Expansion in 1952," 1952. *Blast Furnace and Steel Plant* (February): 230-231.
"Koppers' Step to Profits." 1955. *Chemical Week* (January): 80.
Koskoff, David E. 1978. *The Mellons: The Chronicle of America's Richest Family*. New York: Thomas Y. Crowell Company.
"La Guardia's Coup." 1938. *Time* (September 12): 48.
Lash, Joseph P., ed. 1975. *From the Diaries of Felix Frankfurter*. New York: W. W. Norton and Company.
Leahy, William D. 1950. *I Was There*. New York: McGraw-Hill.
Leighton, Richard M. 1946. "Preparation for Invasion: The Problem of Troop and Cargo Flow Before D-Day." *Military Affairs* 10 (Spring): 3-39.

―――. 1959. "OVERLORD versus the Mediterranean at the Cairo-Tehran Conference (1943)." In *Command Decisions*, ed. Kent Roberts Greenfield. New York: Harcourt, Brace and Company.

―――. 1960. "U.S. Merchant Shipping and the British Import Crisis." In *Command Decisions*, ed. Kent Roberts Greenfield, 2d ed. Washington, D.C.: Office of the Chief of Military History.

―――. 1963. "OVERLORD Revisited: An Interpretation of American Strategy in the European War, 1942–1944." *American Historical Review* 68 (July): 919–937.

―――. 1969. "The American Arsenal Policy in World War II: A Retrospective View." In *Some Pathways in Twentieth-Century History: Essays in Honor of Reginald Charles McGrane*, ed. Daniel R. Beaver. Detroit: Wayne State University Press.

―――. 1990. "Logistics." *Encyclopedia Britannica*. vol. 29, 15th ed.: 678-686.

Leighton, Richard M., and Robert W. Coakley. 1955. *Global Logistics and Strategy, 1940-1943*. In *U.S. Army in World War II*. Washington, D.C.: Office of the Chief of Military History.

Liang, Chin-Tung. 1972. *General Stilwell in China, 1942–1944: The Full Story*. New York: St. John's University Press.

Lutes, LeRoy. 1952a. "Supply Reorganization for World War II—I." *Antiaircraft Journal* 95 (March-April): 2-6.

―――. 1952b. "Supply: World War II; The Flight to Europe in 1942." *Antiaircraft Journal* 95 (May-June): 6-9.

―――. 1952c. "Supply: World War II; To the South Pacific—Fall 1942." *Antiaircraft Journal* 95 (July-August): 2-7.

―――. 1952d. "Supply: World War II; For Eisenhower's First Crusade." *Antiaircraft Journal* 95 (November–December): 4–8, 96

―――. 1953. "Supply: World War II; For Eisenhower's First Crusade." *Antiaircraft Journal* 96 (January-February): 2–9.

Maass, Arthur. 1951. *Muddy Waters: The Army Engineers and the Nation's Rivers*. Cambridge, Massachusetts: Harvard University Press.

Maddox, Robert Franklin. 1981. *The Senatorial Career of Harley Martin Kilgore*. New York: Garland Publishing, Inc.

Mangione, Jerre. 1972. *The Dream and the Deal: The Federal Writers' Project, 1935–1943*. Boston: Little, Brown and Company.

Mathews, Joan De Hart. 1967. *The Federal Theatre, 1935–1939: Plays, Relief, and Politics*. Princeton, New Jersey: Princeton University Press.

Matloff, Maurice. 1959. *Strategic Planning for Coalition Warfare, 1943-1944*. In *U.S. Army in World War II*. Washington, D.C.: Office of the Chief of Military History.

Matloff, Maurice, and Edwin M. Snell. 1953. *Strategic Planning for Coalition Warfare, 1941–1942*. In *U.S. Army in World War II*. Washington, D.C.: Office of the Chief of Military History.

McCartney, Laton. 1988. *Friends in High Places. The Bechtel Story, The Most Secret Corporation and How It Engineered the World*. New York: Simon and Schuster.

McCullough, David. 1992. *Truman*. New York: Simon and Schuster.

McDonald, William F. 1969. *Federal Relief Administration and the Arts*. Columbus, Ohio: Ohio State University Press.

McJimsey, George. 1987. *Harry Hopkins: Ally of the Poor and Defender of Democracy*. Cam-

bridge, Massachusetts: Harvard University Press.
McKinzie, Richard D. 1973. *The New Deal for Artists.* Princeton, New Jersey: Princeton University Press.
McMahon, Audrey. 1972. "A General View of the WPA Federal Art Project in New York City and State." In *The New Deal Art Projects: An Anthology of Memoirs,* ed. Francis V. O'Connor. Washington, D.C.: Smithsonian Institution Press.
Millett, John D. 1938. *The Works Progress Administration in New York City.* Chicago: Public Administration Service.
——— . 1954. *The Organization and Role of the Army Service Forces.* In *U.S. Army in World War II.* Washington, D.C.: Office of the Chief of Military History.
"The Miracle of Supply." 1944. *Time* (September 25): 20-22.
Monroe, Gerald M. 1975. "The '30s: Art, Ideology and the WPA." *Art in America* 63 (November-December): 64-67.
——— . 1976. "Mural Burning By the New York City WPA." *Archives of American Art Journal* (16): 64-67.
Moody's Manual of Investments, 1946. 1946. New York: Moody's Investment Service.
Morison, Elting E. 1960. *Turmoil and Tradition: A Study of the Life and Times of Henry L. Stimson.* Boston: Houghton Mifflin and Company.
Morton, Louis. 1962. *Strategy and Command: The First Two Years.* In *U.S. Army in World War II.* Washington, D.C.: Office of the Chief of Military History.
Motter, T. H. Vail. 1952. *The Persian Corridor and Aid to Russia.* In *U.S. Army in World War II.* Washington, D.C.: Office of the Chief of Military History.
Murphy, Charles J. V. 1943. "Somervell of the S.O.S." *Life* (March 8): 82-84, 86, 88, 94.
"Mutiny on the Bounty." 1939. *Time* (July 17): 13–14.
Nelson, Donald. 1946. *Arsenal of Democracy: The Story of America's War Production.* New York: Harcourt, Brace and Company.
Neuberger, Richard L. 1948. "The Great Canol Fiasco." *American Mercury* (April): 415–421.
"New G-4." 1941. *Time* (December 8): 69.
"New York Marks Airport Victory." 1939. *Business Week* (October 7): 18, 20.
Nichols, H. G., ed. 1981. *Washington Dispatches 1941–1945: Weekly Political Reports from the British Embassy.* Chicago: University of Chicago Press.
O'Brien, Charles F. 1970. "The Canol Project: A Study in Emergency Military Planning." *Pacific Northwest Quarterly* 61 (April): 101-108.
Ohl, John Kennedy. 1975. "General Hugh S. Johnson and the War Industries Board." *Military Review* 55 (May): 35-47.
——— . 1985. *Hugh S. Johnson and the New Deal.* DeKalb, Illinois: Northern Illinois University Press.
Pappas, George S. 1967. *Prudens Futuri: The U.S. Army War College, 1901–1967.* Carlisle Barracks, Pennsylvania: Alumni Association of the U.S. Army War College.
Parsons, William Barclay. 1920. *The American Engineers in France.* New York: D. Appleton and Company.
Payne, Robert. 1951. *The Marshall Story: A Biography of George C. Marshall.* New York: Prentice Hall.
Peltason, Jack. 1950. *The Reconversion Controversy.* Washington, D.C.: Committee on

Public Administration Cases.
Penkower, Monty Noam. 1977. *The Federal Writers' Project: A Study in Government Patronage of the Arts*. Urbana, Illinois: University of Illinois Press.
Pepper, Claude. 1942. "To Smash the Final Bottleneck." *New Republic* (November 30): 702-704.
Perret, Geoffrey. 1991. *There's A War To Be Won: The United States Army in World War II*. New York: Random House.
Pogue, Forrest C. 1954. *The Supreme Command*. In *U.S. Army in World War II*. Washington, D.C.: Office of the Chief of Military History.
———. 1966. *George C. Marshall*. Vol. 2, *Ordeal and Hope*. New York: Viking Press.
———. 1973. *George C. Marshall*. Vol. 3, *Organizer of Victory*. New York: Viking Press.
Polenberg, Richard. 1972. *War and Society: The United States, 1941–1945*. Philadelphia: J. B. Lippincott.
"The Potomac and Power." 1930. *Nature Magazine* (June): 35.
"The Price of Unpreparedness." 1943. *Time* (December 6): 17-18.
"Progress of the Mississippi's 'New Deal.'" 1934. *Literary Digest* (September 22): 17.
Randall, Stephen J. 1985. *United States Foreign Oil Policy, 1919–1948: For Profits and Security*. Kingston: McGill-Queen's University.
Reese, John Russell. 1984. "Supply Man: The Army Life of Lieutenant General Henry S. Aurand, 1915-1952." Ph.D. diss., Kansas State University.
Riddle, Donald H. 1964. *The Truman Committee*. New Brunswick, New Jersey: Rutgers University Press.
Robey, Ralph. 1942. "Civilian vs. Military Control of Production." *Newsweek* (December 7): 66.
Robinson, C. F. 1944. "Management Control in the Army Service Forces." *Public Administration Review* 4 (Autumn): 260-267.
Romanus, Charles F., and Riley Sunderland. 1953. *Stilwell's Mission to China*. In *U.S. Army in World War II*. Washington, D.C.: Office of the Chief of Military History.
———. 1956. *Stilwell's Command Problems*. In *U.S. Army in World War II*. Washington, D.C.: Office of the Chief of Military History.
———. 1959. *Time Runs Out in CBI*. In *U.S. Army in World War II*. Washington, D.C.: Office of the Chief of Military History.
Rosen, S. McKee. 1951. *The Combined Boards of the Second World War: An Experiment in International Administration*. New York: Columbia University Press.
Ruppenthal, Roland G. 1953. *Logistical Support of the Armies*. Vol. 1, *May 1941–September 1944*. In *U.S. Army in World War II*. Washington, D.C.: Office of the Chief of Military History.
———. 1959. *Logistical Support of the Armies*. Vol. 2, *September 1944–May 1945*. In *U.S. Army in World War II*. Washington, D.C.: Office of the Chief of Military History.
Sainsbury, Keith. 1986. *The Turning Point*. New York: Oxford University Press.
Schaller, Michael. 1979. *The U.S. Crusade in China, 1938–1945*. New York: Columbia University Press.
Schwarz, Jordan A. 1981. *The Speculator: Bernard M. Baruch in Washington, 1917–1965*. Chapel Hill, North Carolina: University of North Carolina Press.
"Scientific Taming of the Father of Rivers Begins." 1933. *Literary Digest* (July 29): 15-16.

Sherwood, Robert E. 1950. *Roosevelt and Hopkins: An Intimate History*. rev. ed. New York: Harper and Brothers.
Sitterson, J. Carlyle. 1945. *Development of the Reconversion Policies of of the War Production Board, April 1943 to January 1945*. Washington, D.C.: War Production Board.
Smith, Clarence McKittrick. 1956. *The Medical Department: Hospitalization and Evacuation, Zone of the Interior*. In *U.S. Army in World War II*. Washington, D.C.: Office of the Chief of Military History.
Smith, Jean Edward. 1990. *Lucius D. Clay: An American Life*. New York: Henry Holt and Company.
Smith, R. Elberton. 1959. *The Army and Economic Mobilization*. In *U.S. Army in World War II*. Washington, D.C.: Office of the Chief of Military History.
Somers, Herman Miles. 1950. *Presidential Agency: The Office of War Mobilization and Reconversion*. Cambridge, Massachusetts: Harvard University Press.
Somervell, Brehon. 1926. "Navigation Problems on the Danube." *Military Engineer* 18 (July-August): 301-310.
———. 1936. "Atlantic-Gulf Ship Canal." *Military Engineer* 28 (May-June): 170-174.
———. 1940. "Planning North Beach Airport." *Engineering News-Record* (March 28): 62-72.
———. 1941a. "The Man With the Contract." *Constructor* (March): 51-53.
———. 1941b. "The Temporary Emergency Construction Program." *Constructor* (July): 71–74, 107-108, 112–113, 116.
———. 1944a. "Management." *Public Administration Review* 4 (Autumn): 257-259.
———. 1944b. "The Men Behind the Invasion." *Reader's Digest* (May): 86-96.
———. 1945. "The Biggest Moving Job in History." *American Magazine* (July): 24-25, 94, 96, 98.
———. 1948. *Organization Controls in Industry*. New York: American Management Association.
"Somervell Uses a Military Idea to Run Koppers Co." 1949. *Business Week* (May 14): 70-75.
"Sore Thumb." 1936. *Time* (February 17): 11-12.
"The S.O.S." 1942. *Fortune* (September): 66-71, 164, 166.
Stacy, C. P. 1970. *Arms, Men and Governments: The War Policies of Canada, 1941–1945*. Ottawa: Queen's Printer.
Steele, Richard W. 1973. *The First Offensive 1942: Roosevelt, Marshall and the Making of American Strategy*. Bloomington, Indiana: Indiana University Press.
Stefansson, Vilhjalmur. 1958. *Northwest to Passage: The Search of Western Man for a Commercially Practical Route to the Far East*. New York: Duell, Sloan and Pearce.
———. 1964. *Discovery: The Autobiography of Vilhjalmur Stefansson*. New York: McGraw-Hill.
Stilwell, Joseph W. 1948. *The Stilwell Papers*. New York: William Sloane.
Stimson, Henry L., and McGeorge Bundy. 1948. *On Active Service in Peace and War*. New York: Harper and Brothers.
Stoler, Mark A. 1977. *The Politics of the Second Front: American Military Planning and Diplomacy in Coalition Warfare, 1941–1943*. Westport, Connecticut: Greenwood Press.
———. 1989. *George C. Marshall: Soldier-Statesman of the American Century*. Boston: Twayne Publishers.

Stone, I. F. 1988. *A Nonconformist History of the War Years, 1939–1945*. Boston: Little, Brown and Company.
Tebeau, Charton W. 1971. *A History of Florida*. Coral Gables, Florida: University of Miami Press.
Thompson, George Raynor, Dixie R. Harris, Pauline M. Oakes, and Dulany Terrett. 1957. *The Signal Corps: The Test*. In *U.S. Army in World War II*. Washington, D.C.: Office of the Chief of Military History.
Thomson, Harry C., and Linda Mayo. 1960. *The Ordnance Department: Procurement and Supply*. In *U.S. Army in World War II*. Washington, D.C.: Office of the Chief of Military History.
Thorne, Christopher. 1978. *Allies of a Kind: The United States, Britain, and the War Against Japan, 1941-1945*. New York: Oxford University Press.
Toulmin, Harry Aubrey, Jr. 1947. *Diary of Democracy: The Senate War Investigating Committee*. New York: Richard A. Smith.
Truman, Margaret. 1973. *Harry S. Truman*. New York: William Morrow.
Tuchman, Barbara W. 1970. *Stilwell and the American Experience in China, 1911-1945*. New York: Macmillan Company.
Twichell, Heath, Jr. 1974. *Allen: The Biography of An Army Officer, 1859-1930*. New Brunswick, New Jersey: Rutgers University Press.
―――. 1992. *Northwest Epic: The Building of the Alaska Highway*. New York: St. Martin's Press.
"War on Congress." 1939. *Time* (July 24): 10-12.
Wardlow, Chester. 1951. *The Transportation Corps: Responsibilities, Organization, and Operations*. In *U.S. Army in World War II*. Washington, D.C.: Office of the Chief of Military History.
Warth, Terry Riordin. 1984. "Donald Marr Nelson: Archetypical Businessman-Bureaucrat: A Study of the Growing Interdependency Between Private Enterprise and American Government." Ph.D. diss., University of Southern California.
Wedemeyer, Albert C. 1958. *Wedemeyer Reports!* New York: Henry Holt.
Weigley, Russell F. 1967. *History of the United States Army*. New York: Macmillan Company.
―――. 1981. *Eisenhower's Lieutenants: The Campaign of France and Germany, 1944–1945*. Bloomington, Indiana: Indiana University Press.
Wharton, Don. 1943. "How the North African Campaign was Organized." *Reader's Digest* (February): 95-100.
Wilt, Alan F. 1991. "The Significance of the Casablanca Decisions, January 1943." *Journal of Military History* 55 (October): 517-529.
Windisch, Richard P. 1955. "Koppers Co." *Barron's* (September 12): 17, 19, 21-22.
Woodman, Lyman L. 1977. "Canol: Pipeline of Brief Glory." *The Northern Engineer* 9 (Summer): 14-28.
"The WPA Strike." 1939. *Newsweek* (July 17): 43-44.
Ziegler, Philip. 1985. *Mountbatten: The Official Biography*. London: Collins.
―――, ed. 1988. *Personal Diary of Admiral the Lord Mountbatten: Supreme Allied Commander South-East Asia, 1943–1946*. London: Collins.

INDEX

Air Transport Command (ATC), 247
Alaska Highway, 161–162, 166–171
Allen, Henry T., 14
Alsberg, Henry G., 28
Amberg, Julius, 175, 178
American Expeditionary Forces (AEF), 13, 15, 186, 187
American Federation of Labor's Building and Construction Trades Council in New York City, 34
American Forces in Germany (AFG), 14, 15
ANAKIM, 108, 112, 114–115, 202–204, 216
Andrews, Frank, 210
ANVIL, 223–224, 225
ARCADIA, 127, 181
Army Air Forces (AAF), 62, 70, 90, 134, 163, 206, 228, 239; and the ASF, 143–145, 148, 149, 153, 159; and the CBI, 201, 203, 242–244
Army Ground Forces (AGF), 62, 67, 153, 156, 183, 213
Army Industrial College, 6

Army Materiel Command, 160
Army and Navy Munitions Board (ANMB), 39, 57, 83–84
Army and Navy Petroleum Board, 174
Army Service Forces, 138, 139, 186, 191, 193, 200, 206, 237, 242; and the AAF, 143–145; creation of, 61–62; and the General Staff, 146–151; organization of, 64–67; and the supply bureaus, 66–67, 151–160 and the WPB, 72–97; and the WSA, 98–116
Army Supply Program (ASP), 70–71, 94, 127, 129, 132–133, 144, 150, 195, 216
Army War College, 16–17
Arnold, Henry, 62, 104, 137, 145, 202–203
Arrowsmith, John C., 221–222
Assam Line of Communications, 215–216, 220–222, 245
Auchinleck, Claude, J.E., 215–216, 220–221
Aurand, Henry S., 60, 65, 128–131, 236–237

322   INDEX

Baruch, Bernard, 87
Basic Logistical Plan, 201, 212
Batcheller, Hiland, 96
Batt, W.L., 81
Bengal and Assam Railway, 216, 220–222
Bergstrom, George E., 47, 49, 51
BOLERO, 107–111, 182–189, 190, 206–211, 225–229
Bradley, Omar, 227, 230
Brewster Corporation, 93
British import crisis, 106–116
British Ministry of War Transport, 59, 99, 100
BUCCANEER, 223–224, 242
Buckner, Simon Bolivar, 169
Budget Bureau, 47, 165, 171, 172
Bulge, Battle of the, 97, 137, 239
Bull, Harold R., 236
Bureau of Economic Warfare, 163
Bureau of Supplies and Accounts, 200
Burns, James H., 66
Byrnes, James, 89–90, 174; and reconversion, 94–97

Cairo Conference, 222, 224, 225, 242
Cahill, Holger, 35
Calhoun, William L., 211–212
Campbell, Levin, 44, 66, 152, 156, 260
Canol: construction of, 167–170, 177; evaluation of, 180; inception of, 161–165; liquidation of, 178; opposition to, 170–173; and the Truman Committee, 173–177, 178–179
Canol 1, 164, 167, 170, 178
Canol 2, 167, 170, 171, 178
Canol 3, 170, 171, 178
Canol 4, 170, 171, 178
Canol 5, 170
Canol 6, 170, 178
Carter, Arthur H., 163, 165
Casablanca Conference, 107–109, 140, 195, 202, 205–206
Casey, Hugh, 17
CCS 172, 109–110, 206–207

Central Pacific area, 198, 201, 211, 213
Chaney, James E., 186–187
Chemical Division (Koppers), 257–258
Chemical Warfare Service, 42
Chennault, Claire, 204, 218
Chiang Kai-shek, 201–204, 216–224, 242–243, 246
Chiang, Madame, 218, 222
Chicago Tribune, 157
China-Burma-India Theater (CBI), 201–204, 214–224, 241–247
Churchill, Winston D., 50, 100, 106–107, 109, 131, 135–136, 138–139, 181, 192, 202, 204, 220, 222–223, 229, 239, 242, 245
Clark, Mark, 185, 192
Clarke, Gilmore D., 49–51
Clay, Lucius D., 64, 103, 112, 129, 184, 232, 236; and industrial mobilization, 86, 92–93, 97; and Brehon B. Somervell, 22, 65
Combat Developments Command, 160
Combined Chiefs of Staff (CCS), 75, 107, 111–112, 115, 128, 130–131, 133, 139–140, 147, 202, 205–207, 215–216, 219–220, 223–224, 239–240, 242, 244–245
Combined Production and Resources Board (CPRB), 130–131
Combined Staff Planners (CPS), 147
Command and General Staff College, 15–16
Commission on Fine Arts, 49–51
Committee of Combined Boards, 194
Communications Zone (COMZ), 235, 239; Somervell's inspection of 237–238
Congressional Record, 157
Connolly, Donald H., 139, 141
Construction Division, 38–54
Control Division (ASF), 64, 68–70, 151–152, 154, 159
Control Section (Koppers), 254–256, 258
Controlled Materials Plan (CMP), 84–85

Conway, Granville, 103
Covell, William E.R., 45, 221, 245
Cramton-Capper George Washington Memorial Parkway Bill, 18–19
Crowell, Benedict, 39–40

Danube River report, 16
Darling, J.W.S., 184
Davis, Ralph K., 166, 171
Defense Procurement Administration, 260
Defense Supply Agency, 160
Delano, Frederic A., 49, 168
Delano, William A., 32
Denton, Frank R., 252–253
Dern, George, 21
Devers, Jacob, 169, 211, 219
Dill, John, 202–203
Dorr, Goldthwaite, 21, 60, 73
Douglas, Lewis: and the British import crisis, 106–116; as deputy WSA administrator, 98–99; and loading and unloading of cargo vessels, control of, 99–106; and shipping, allocation of, 99–100; and Somervell, 99–100, 102–103, 116
DRAGOON, 229

Eastern Gas and Fuel Associates, 253
Eberstadt, Ferdinand, 84–85, 91, 259
Eden, Anthony, 111, 113
Edgerton, Glen, 22
89th Division (U.S. Army), 13, 14
82d Airborne Division (U.S. Army), 205
Eisenhower, Dwight D., 156, 160, 223, 250; as ETO commander, 185–190; and North African operations, 191–196; as SHAEF commander, 226–232, 235–239
Emergency Relief Act of 1935, 23
Emergency Relief Act of 1939, 34
Emergency Relief Act of 1940, 36
Emergency Relief Bureau, 28
Emmons, Delos C., 200
Engineer School, 12

Engineering and Construction Division (Koppers), 258
Engineers, Corps of, 17, 26, 53–54, 160, 247; and Canol, 162–164, 165, 167, 168; and landing craft crews, 184–185; and Somervell's assignments with, 10–12, 15, 16, 17–20, 22–24, 38
European Theater of Operations (ETO), 181–189, 206–211, 223–230, 231–232, 234–239
Executive Order 9082, 61

Feasibility Dispute, 56–58, 76–83, 101, 114, 131
Federal Art Project, 35–36
Federal Power Commission, 18
Federal Theatre Project, 34
Federal Writers' Project, 28
Ferguson, Harley B., 19–20, 169
15th Engineer Regiment (U.S. Army), 12
Florida Canal Project, 22–24
Foreign Liquidation Commission, 178
Forrestal, James, 93, 136
45th Division (U.S. Army), 205
Franklin, John, 232
Freyn Engineering Corporation, 258
Fulton, Hugh, 175

G-1 (War Department), 149
G-2 (War Department), 149
G-3 (War Department), 149
G-4 (War Department), 5, 55, 60, 64, 149, 150–151, 172, 210
Gardner, O.F., 20
General Staff (War Department), 4–5, 145–151
Giraud, Henri, 195–196
Goethals, George W., 5
Graham, James, 162–164
Graves, Ernest, 12–13
Gregory, Edmund B., 40, 53, 54
Gross, Charles, 64, 103, 110–115, 209, 234, 238
Groves, Leslie, 47

324 INDEX

Guide to North Little Rock: Industrial Center of Arkansas, 28
GYMNAST, 181, 190

Halsey, William, 189
Handy, Thomas, 147, 150, 159, 206, 244, 246
Hanson, Elisha, 18
Hardin, John, 12
Harriman, Averell, 110, 188
Harrington, Francis, 26
Hartman, Charles D., 38–42, 45
Henderson, Leon, 79–82
Henkel, August, 35
Hines, Walker D., 14, 16, 19, 20
Ho Ying-chin, 218
Hodges, Courtney, 230
Hogan, John P., 39
Hoge, William, 168–169
Hoover, Herbert C., 19
Hopkins, Harry L., 39, 40, 58, 59, 66, 156–157, 222; and industrial mobilization, 77–79, 86–87; and lend-lease, 130, 133, 136; and shipping, 99, 103–105, 106, 110, 112–114, 240; and the WPA, 25–32, 37
Hopkins-Law Agreement, 240–241
Horne, Frederick J., 147, 184, 200, 211
House Appropriations Committee, 33–34, 48
House Military Affairs Committee, 45–46
House Public Buildings and Grounds Committee, 48
House Subcommittee on Deficiency Appropriations, 42
Hull, Cordell, 135, 136
HUSKY, 205–208
Hutchinson, William, 157–158

Ickes, Harold L., 24, 49, 76; and Canol, 166–167, 170–172, 175–176
Imperial Oil, Ltd., 162–163, 165, 174, 178, 180
Indian Railway Commission, 220

Ingles, Harry C., 154
Interdepartmental Board of Review, 22–23
Interior, Department of, 164
International Division, 129
Industrial mobilization, 5–6; and army-WPB relations, 6, 72–76, 88–90; and military requirements, determination of, 56–58, 76–83; and production scheduling, control of, 85–88; and raw materials, control of, 74–75, 83–85; and reconversion, 90–97
Iranian Mission, 138
Iranian State Railway, 138, 139

Jadwin, Edgar, 12, 19–20
John McShain, Inc., 48
Johnson, Hugh S., 25
Joint Administrative Committee (JAdC), 148–149
Joint Chiefs of Staff (JCS), 58, 82, 97, 104, 107, 112, 115, 147, 148, 207, 224, 233–234, 239–241, 248–249; and Canol, 170, 174–175, 178–180; and the CBI, 201, 204, 243–245; and lend-lease, 131, 134, 136, 137
Joint logistics, 199, 201, 211–213, 248–249
Joint Logistics Board, 211
Joint Logistics Committee (JLC), 134, 137
Joint Military Transportation Committee, 149
Joint Production Survey Committee (JPSC), 174, 178
Joint Staff Planners (JPS), 147–149

Kemal, Mustafa, 21
Kemmerer, Edward C., 20, 21
Kilgore, Harley M., 88, 173, 175–176
Kimberly, HMS, 229
King, Ernest J., 104, 174, 179, 184–185, 193, 201, 212
Knox, Frank, 87

Koppers Company, 252–259
Krock, Arthur, 157
Krug, Julius A., 95, 96
Kung, H.H., 242
Kung, Madame H.H., 218
Kuznets, Simon, 76–80

La Guardia, Fiorello, 26, 29, 31, 37
La Guardia Airport, 32–33, 34
Land, Emory S., 58, 59–60, 98–99, 104, 106, 184, 233
Landing craft, 183–185
Law, Richard, 240
Lawrence, David, 158
League of Nations, 16
Leahy, William, 82, 87, 104–105, 136, 137
Lear, Ben, 145
Leathers, Frederick, 107–109, 110, 115–116, 182
Leavey, Edmond, 41, 43, 47, 212–213
Ledo Road, 201, 203–204, 215–216, 221–222, 244–247
Lee, John C.H., 54; as chief of SOS, ETO, 185–187, 189, 209, 226–228, 231–231, 235–239; and Somervell, 13, 14, 52, 210–211, 226–228, 231–232, 235–239
Lend-lease, 7; administration of, 127–129; and aid for Britain, 127–137; and aid for the Free French, 193–196; and aid for the Soviet Union, 137–142; the common pool for, 127–134; consignment of, 101–103; and Stage II aid for Britain, 134–137
Lindley, Ernest, 157–158
Lippmann, Walter, 157
Logistical operations: in the CBI, 201–204, 214–224, 241–247; in the ETO, 182–189, 206–211, 223–224, 225–230, 231–232, 234–239; in North Africa, 189–196; in the Pacific, 196–201, 211–214, 231–234, 247–249

Logistical planning, 6–7, 145–151
Logistics, 3
Logistics Group, 146, 148–149
Lord, Roy, 227
Lutes, LeRoy, 139, 160, 191, 204, 223–224, 235; and the ETO, 228–229, 236–237; and joint logistics, 199–200, 212–213; and Somervell, 65
Lyttelton, Oliver, 106–107, 130, 142

MacArthur, Douglas, 197, 198, 214, 227, 232–234, 249, 260
McCloy, John, 50, 56, 103, 194
McMahon, Audrey, 35
McNair, Lesley J., 62, 145, 150, 185
McNamara, Robert, 160
McNarney, Joseph T., 60–61, 147, 150, 154–156
McNutt, Paul, 93
Macready, George N., 134
Madigan, Michael J., 39, 52–53
Magruder, Carter, 191
March, Peyton C., 5
Maritime Commission, 58, 86
Markham, Edward M., 21, 23, 26
Marshall, George C., 39, 42, 47–48, 52–53, 55–59, 79–80, 136, 139, 160, 192, 195–196, 250; and Canol, 162, 172, 174–175, 177; and the CBI, 217, 219, 222, 243, 245–246; and the ETO, 184–186, 188, 209, 227, 239; and Pacific operations, 197–198, 201, 212–213, 248; and shipping, 104–105, 107, 109, 111; and Somervell, 3, 33, 36–37, 40, 41, 54, 63–64, 160, 239, 250, 251; and the War Department, reorganization of, 5, 60–62, 145, 147–148, 150, 154–159
Marshall, S. L. A., 156
MATTERHORN, 242–243, 246–247
Maxwell, Russell L., 150
May, Stacy, 76, 86
Mead, James, 178–179

Mellon, Richard K., 252–254, 256, 259
Meuse-Argonne Offensive, 13–14
Millett, John, 73
Millis, Walter, 158
Mississippi River Commission, 19
Mitchell, James P., 45
Moore, Edward H., 175–176
Moore, Richard C., 36, 39, 41, 53–54, 56, 65, 67, 71
Morgenthau, Henry Jr., 135, 137, 243
Morgenthau Plan, 136
Moses, Raymond, 150
Mountbatten, Louis, 216–221, 223–224, 244–245
Munitions Assignments Board, Washington (MAB), 127–128, 131, 132–133
Munitions Assignments Board, London, 128

Nathan, Robert, 76, 78–80, 82–83
National Association of Manufacturers, 96
National Capital Park and Planning Commission, 18, 49
National Defense Act of 1920, 5, 15, 61
National Defense Advisory Commission, 43
National Emergency Council, 22
Naval Transportation System, 200
Navy, U.S., 99, 134, 148, 162, 177, 231, 244; and industrial mobilization, 77–78, 86, 90, 93, 96; and landing craft, 184–185; and Pacific operations, 197–201, 211–213, 248–249
Nelson, Donald, 72, 89–90, 130; and military procurement, responsibility for, 73–74; and military requirements, determination of, 56–58, 76–83; and production scheduling, control of, 85–88; and raw materials, control of, 74–75, 83–85; and reconversion, 90–95; and Somervell, 74–76
Nelson-Patterson agreement, 73–74, 86–87
New York Daily News, 157

New York Herald Tribune, 157, 158
New York Times, 96, 157
New Yorker, 26
Nimitz, Chester, 198, 211–213, 249
Northwest Service Command, 170, 177
Northwest Staging Route, 162

O'Connor, James A., 167, 170
OCTAGON, 135–137
Office of the Army Comptroller, 160
Office of Defense Mobilization, 260
Office of Defense Transportation, 99
Office of Foreign Relief and Rehabilitation Operations (OFRRO), 194
Office of Lend-Lease Administration, 194
Office of Production Management (OPM), 43
Office of War Mobilization (OWM), 89–90
Office of War Mobilization and Reconversion (OWMR), 94, 97
Olmstead, Dawson, 67, 152–154
OLYMPIC, 248–249
Open Hearth Combustion Company, 258
Operations Division (OPD), 145–150, 159, 172, 187–188, 206–209, 213–214, 244, 246, 248
Ordnance Department, 42–43, 44, 66, 151–152
OVERLORD, 156–158, 208–210, 223–224, 225–229, 232

Pacific Ocean Area (POA), 198, 211–213, 249
Pacific operations, 198–201, 211–214, 247–249
Panuch, J. A., 92–93
Patch, Alexander, 159
Patch Board, 159–160
Patterson, Robert P., 61, 100, 144, 213, 229, 241; and the army construction program, 39, 44, 48, 49, 53, 54; and Canol, 162, 167, 171, 173, 175, 180; and industrial mobilization, 79,

81, 86, 93; and Somervell, 62–63;
  and the War Department, reorganization of, 151, 155, 158, 159
Patton, George S., 153, 191, 230
Pentagon, 47–52
Pepper, Claude, 88
Pershing Punitive Expedition, 11
Persian Gulf Service Command,
  139–142
Peterson, Virgil, 38, 39, 43
Planning Committee (WPB), 57, 85, 92;
  and the Feasibility Dispute, 76–83
Potomac River power controversy,
  18–19
Preshipment (ETO), 207–210
Priority Regulation 25, 94–97
Production Executive Committee
  (PEC): and production scheduling,
  85–87; and reconversion, 91–94
Production Requirements Plan (PRP),
  84–85
Production scheduling, 85–88
Public Buildings Association, 47
Public Roads Administration (PRA),
  162, 170
Purchase, Storage and Traffic Division, 5
Pyron, Walter B., 162–163, 171

QUADRANT, 116, 209, 215–216,
  219–220
Quartermaster Corps, 38–39, 52–53, 64

Raw materials, 74–75, 83–85
Reconversion, 90–97
Redeployment, 247–249
Reid, Charles C., 10
Renshaw, Clarence D., 51
Reybold, Eugene, 48, 53, 54, 163, 170
Rhine River report, 14
Richardson, Robert C., 211, 213
Riddell-Webster, Thomas, 215
Ridder, Victor F., 25–26, 27, 29
Robins, Thomas M., 53–54, 165
Robinson, Clinton, 41, 60, 64, 67,
  69–70, 159, 238

Robinson, S. M., 79
Roosevelt, Franklin D., 23, 24, 29, 31,
  32, 42, 43, 50, 53, 58, 59, 60, 66,
  156, 158, 188, 192, 239; and Canol,
  162, 166, 168, 176; and the CBI,
  202, 204, 217, 219–220, 222–223,
  242–243, 245; and the ETO, 181,
  183, 222–224; and the French,
  aid for, 194–195; and industrial
  mobilization, 6, 56–58, 72–73, 75,
  83, 87, 89, 95; and lend-lease aid,
  131, 133, 134, 136, 138–139,
  140–141; and the Pentagon, 3,
  49–51; and shipping, 98–99, 104,
  106–108, 112–113, 116, 233,
  240–241; and Somervell, 22, 29, 36,
  37, 40
Rootes, William, 131
ROUNDUP, 182–183, 189
Royall, Kenneth, 179
Ruby, Glen F., 170
Rust, Henry B., 252–253

Salter, Arthur, 103, 110, 114
Schley, Julian L., 38, 52–53
Searls, Fred J., 171
Senate Appropriations Committee, 49
Senate Committee on the District of
  Columbia, 18–19
Senate Military Affairs Committee,
  250–251
Senate Special Committee Investigating
  the National Defense Program
  (Truman Committee/Mead Committee), 46; and Canol, 163, 164,
  173–177, 178–179
Service commands, 65–66, 67, 154, 159
Service troops, 187–188, 213–214
Services of Supply (ETO), 186–186,
  190–191, 210–211, 226–229, 230
Services of Supply (War Department), 61
Shafer, Paul, 157
Shingler, Don G., 138
Shipping, 6; allocation of, 99–100,
  240–241; and the British import

crisis, 106–116; the crisis of 1944, 230–234, 238–239; for the ETO, 182–183, 206–207; the loading and unloading of cargo vessels, control of, 99–106; and Persian Gulf operations, 138–142; and the WSA, creation of, 58–60
SICKLE, 206, 207
Signal Corps, 67, 152–154
SLEDGEHAMMER, 182–185, 189–190
Smith, Harold D., 41, 49–50, 105, 173, 175
Smith, Walter Bedell, 227
Somervell, Anna Purnell (wife), 14, 55
Somervell, Brehon B.: personal: ancestry and parents of, 9–10; appearance of, 11; birth and childhood of, 9–10; death of, 260; education of, 10; health of 250, 260; as a manager, 4, 8; marriages of, 14; personality of, 4, 8, 9, 11–12, 164–165; work habits of, 11, 12, 17, 30, 32, 161
—career to 1942: at the Army War College, 16–17; and Clay, 22; at the Command and General Staff College, 15–16; and the Construction Division, completion of first-wave training camps and munitions plants, 41–43; and the Construction Division, congressional investigation of, 45–47; and the Construction Division, reorganization of, 40–41, 45; and the Construction Division, the second-wave training camps and munitions plants, 43–45; and the Construction Division, transfer of the division to the Corps of Engineers, 53–54; as Construction Division head, appointment of, 38–40; as Construction Division head, evaluation of, 54; and construction work in France during World War I, 12–13; and the Danube River report, 16; and decorations, 14, 15; as district engineer for Memphis, 19–20; as district engineer for Ocala, 22–24; as district engineer for Washington, D.C., 17–19; and the Engineers, Corps of, 10–12, 15, 16, 17–20, 22–24, 38, 53–54; as G-4, appointment of, 54; and Hopkins, 26, 28, 29, 37, 39, 40; and La Guardia Airport, 32–33; and Lee, 13–14, 52; and Marshall, 33, 36–37, 40, 41, 54; and the National Emergency Council, 22; and the Ordnance Department, 44; and the Pentagon, 47–52; and the Potomac River power project, 18–19; promotions of, 11, 12, 13, 14, 22; and relations with fellow officers, 12, 13–14, 19–20, 22, 42; Rhine River report, 14; and Roosevelt, 22, 29, 36, 37, 40; as a staff officer during World War I, 13–14; and the Turkish economic survey, 20–21; at West Point, 10; and the WPA in New York City, arts projects of, 27–28, 34–36; and the WPA in New York City, budget of, 28–29, 30, 31–32; and the WPA in New York City, Communists in, 27, 35–36; and the WPA in New York City, congressional investigation of, 24, 27. 35–36; and the WPA in New York City, departure from, 36–37; and the WPA in New York City, employment quotas of, 27–29, 32, 34; and the WPA in New York City, labor policy of, 25–26, 27–28, 34–36; and the WPA in New York City, organization of, 29–30; as WPA administrator in New York City, appointment of, 26; as WPA administrator in New York City, evaluation of, 37
—the ASF: and the ammunition crisis of 1944, 115–236; and the AAF, 143–145; the organization of, 64–67; appointment as chief of,

61–62; and the armed services, unification of, 250–251; and the Assam LOC, 215–216, 220–222, 245; and BOLERO, 182–189, 206–211, 226–229; and the British import crisis, 106–116; at the Cairo Conference, 222, 224; and Canol, construction of, 167–170; and Canol, inception of, 162–165; and Canol, liquidation of, 178; and Canol, opposition to, 170–173; and Canol, evaluation of role in, 180; and Canal, and the Truman Committee's investigation of, 173–177, 178–179; at the Casablanca Conference, 107–109, 140, 195; and China, financial arrangements with, 242–244; and the CBI, 201–204, 214–224, 241–247; and civilian aid, 194–195, 240–241; and Lucius D. Clay, 64–65; and the common pool, 127–137; and the COMZ, 235–239; and Lewis Douglas, 98–99, 102–103, 116; and the ETO, 181–189, 206–211, 223–224, 225–230, 231–232, 234, 234–239; and the Feasibility Dispute, 56–58, 76–83; as G-4, 55, 129, 143, 146; and the General Staff, 145–151; and joint logistics, 199–201, 211–213, 248–249; and landing craft, 183–185; and the Ledo Road, 202–204, 215–216, 221–222, 244–245, 246–247; and Lee, 185–186, 210–211, 226–228, 231–232, 235–239; and lend-lease, 7; and lend-lease aid for Britain, 127–137; and lend-lease aid for the French, 193–196; and lend-lease aid for the Soviet Union, 137–142; and the loading and unloading of cargo vessels, control of, 99–106; and logistical planning, 7, 70–71, 145–151; and Lutes, 65; at the Malta and Yalta Conferences, 239–240; management philosophy of, 67–71; and the manpower crisis of 1945, 239; and military requirements, determination of 56–58, 70–71, 76–83; and Marshall, 63–64, 250–251; and military procurement, responsibility for, 72–76, 88–90; and the navy, 183–185, 197–201, 211–213, 248–249; and Nelson, 74–76; and North African operations, 189–193; and the Ordnance Department, 151–152; and Pacific operations, 196–201, 211–214, 231–234, 247–249; and Patterson, 62–63; and Persian Gulf operations, 139–142; at the Potsdam Conference, 249–250; and preshipment, 207–210; and production scheduling, control of, 85–88; and promotions of, 62, 250; and raw materials, control of 83–85; and reconversion, 90–97; and redeployment, 247–249; retirement from the army, 250; and service troops, 187–188; and shipping, 206–207; and shipping, allocation of, 99–100, 240–241; and shipping crisis of 1944, 230–234, 238–239; and the Signal Corps, 152–154; and the SOS, ETO, 186–187, 226–230; and Soviet aid, shipping for, 140–142; and Stage II aid for Britain, 134–137; and Stilwell, 217–219; and the supply bureaus, 5, 8, 66–67, 70, 143, 151–160; at the Teheran Conference, 223–224; and the War Department, reorganization of, 60–62, 143–160; and the WPB, 5, 72–97; and the WSA, 6, 58–60, 98–116

—Koppers: diversification of, 257–258; leadership of, 259; management practices at, 254–257, 258; reorganization of, 254–257; selection as president of, 252

Somervell, Louise Hampton Wartmann (second wife), 14
Somervell, Mary S. Burke (mother), 9, 10
Somervell, Richard Bullock (grandfather), 9
Somervell, William Taylor (father), 9, 10
Soong, T. V., 217–218, 242
South Pacific area, 198–199, 201, 213–214
Southeast Asia Command (SEAC), 216–217, 220, 222
Southwest Pacific Area (SWPA), 198, 214, 231–234
Spaatz, Carl, 227
Spot authorization. *See* Priority Regulation 25
Stage II aid, 134–137
Stalin, Joseph, 223
Standard Oil of California, 165
Standard Oil of New Jersey, 162–164, 165, 180
State, Department of, 165, 240–241, 243
Stefansson, Vilhjalmur, 162–163, 166, 168
Stilwell, Joseph W., 202–203, 215, 217–222, 242–246
Stimson, Henry L., 66, 104, 136, 139, 185, 187, 219, 243; and the army construction program, 38, 40, 42, 48, 50, 52–54; and Canol, 166, 170–173, 178, 180; and industrial mobilization, 87–88; and the War Department, reorganization of, 61, 155–159
Street, St. Clair, 163
Styer, Wilhelm B., 41, 64, 140, 158, 169, 193, 211, 214–215, 238
Sultan, Dan, 22
Supply bureaus, 4–5, 64, 66–67, 151–160
Supply Priorities and Allocation Board, 56
Supreme Headquarters, Allied Expeditionary Force (SHAEF), 226, 236
Surgeon general, 160
Sutherland, Richard K., 227

Taft, William Howard, 155
TARZAN, 223–224, 242
Teheran Conference, 223–224, 225
Theater Group, 146
36th Division (U.S. Army), 205
Thomason, R. Ewing, 45
Tierney, J.P., 253
"To Smash the Final Bottleneck" (Pepper), 88
Tolan, John H., 88
TORCH, 140, 147, 153, 189–192, 206
Transportation Corps, 64, 136, 141
TRIDENT, 114–116, 204, 207–209
Truman, Harry S., 46–47, 137, 174, 179, 260
Turkish economic survey, 20–21, 60

Under Secretary of War, Office of, 5, 55, 60, 62–63, 64
United Kingdom Commercial Company, 139
U.S. News and World Report, 158

Variety, 28
Venning, Walter, 134–135
Victory Program, 56, 58, 70, 187
Villa, Pancho, 11
Virginian Railroad, 253

Walker, George M., 254–256
Wallace, Henry A., 75, 80
War Assets Administration, 257
War, Department of, 4–6, 26, 56, 128–129, 194, 250; and the army construction program, 40, 41, 42, 43, 47–48; and Canol, 165, 171–172, 176; and industrial mobilization, 89, 90, 94; and reorganization of, 60–62, 144–160
War Industries Board, 5–6
War Manpower Commission (WMC), 93–96
War Munitions Program, 57, 71, 76
War Plans Division (WPD), 56

War Powers Act, 61
War Production Board (WPB), 144, 171, 175; and the ASF, 6, 72–97; and military requirements, determination of, 57–58, 76–83; and production scheduling, control of, 85–87; and raw materials, control of, 83–85; and reconversion, 90–97
War Shipping Administration (WSA), 182–183, 193, 195, 208, 231, 233; and aid for the Soviet Union, 138, 140–142; and the ASF, 6, 99–116; and the British import crisis, 106–116; and creation of, 59–60; and Lewis Douglas as deputy administrator of, 98–99; and loading and unloading of cargo vessels, control of, 99–106; and shipping, allocation of, 99–103, 240
Washington Post, 158
Washington Times-Herald, 157–158
Wavell, Archibald P. 202–203

Wedemeyer, Albert, 147, 202
Weeks, Ronald M., 132
Weeks-Somervell agreement, 132–133
Wesson, Charles, 66, 152
West Point, 10
Wheeler, Raymond, 202–204, 216, 221–222, 227
Williams, Aubrey, 30
Wilson, Charles E., 260; and production scheduling, control of, 85–86, 88; and reconversion, 91–95
Wingate, Orde, 203
Wood, Leonard, 155
Woodrum, Clifton, 33, 47, 48
Works Progress Administration (WPA), 24; in New York City, 25–37, 45; and use of army engineers, 26, 32
Wyman, Theodore Jr., 167, 170

Yount, Paul, 221

Zone of the Interior, 200–201